Good Finance Guide for Small Businesses

GOOD
FINANCE
GUIDE
for Small Businesses

How to raise, manage and grow
your company's cash

A & C Black • London

First published in Great Britain 2007
A & C Black Publishers Ltd
38 Soho Square, London W1D 3HB

Actionlists © Cobweb Information Ltd 2007
Directory © TMRM Ltd 2007

British Library Cataloguing in Publication Data
A CIP record for this book is available from the British Library.

ISBN-13: 978-0-7136-8209-0

This book is produced using paper that is made from wood grown in managed, sustainable forests. It is natural, renewable and recyclable. The logging and manufacturing processes conform to the environmental regulations of the country of origin.

Design by Fiona Pike, Pike Design, Winchester
Typeset by RefineCatch Limited, Bungay, Suffolk
Printed in the United Kingdom by Caligraving

Contents

Company admin, tax and payroll

Coping in a cash-flow crisis

A note to the user

Welcome to the *Good Finance Guide for Small Businesses*, the sister publication to the *Good Small Business Guide*. Raising and managing money is one of the biggest headaches entrepreneurs and business managers have to face, and in this book you'll find jargon-free, practical strategies to cope with a wide range of financial conundrums.

We've only included a very small amount of material from the *Good Small Business Guide* where absolutely necessary, so that you can see the whole picture about a particular topic or process. We hope that you find all the other new, targeted material makes your life easier. Good luck!

Finance Glossary

Finance and accounting terminology can be complicated and confusing, especially if you have just started your business or are dealing with this type of language for the first time.

This glossary defines and explains the key terms that are regularly used when running a business, especially when you are dealing with finance professionals such as accountants. It will prove particularly useful if you are looking through business accounts or preparing financial information for your own business. It will also explain many of the terms you'll be coming across again and again as you work through this book.

A

Accounting code: Numbers or letters assigned to budget or cost centres within an organisation to simplify allocation of income, expenditure and balance sheet captions.

Accounting period: The regular period (normally a year) for which a business accounts for its income, expenditure, assets and liabilities.

Accounts: The financial records of a business. These show an analysis of the profit and loss account and the balance sheet.

Accounts payable: Money that a business owes to suppliers for products and services purchased on credit (also known as creditors).

Accruals: A term used in accounts to describe income that is due, or costs that are incurred, during an accounting period but not received or paid during that accounting period.

Acid test ratio: The current assets of a business, minus stocks and divided by current liabilities. The ratio shows whether a business would be able to pay its debts (if it needed to pay creditors) with no time to sell any of its assets. The business passes the test if the result is one or higher, though for most businesses an acid test of better than 0.7 is adequate.

Added value: This is the value of improvement made to goods or services at any particular stage in their production.

Amortisation: An annual charge made in a business' profit and loss account to reduce the value of an intangible asset as shown in the business balance sheet.

Annual Percentage Rate (APR): Where interest on loans is expressed as something other than a yearly rate (1.5% per month, for example), APR is the equivalent rate over a year.

Appropriation account: The part of the profit and loss account that shows how the profit has been divided (or appropriated) into dividends and reserves.

Assets: A business' goods, resources and property that have a monetary value.

Audit: An examination and verification of a business' financial and accounting records and supporting documents by a professional accountant. A legal requirement for limited companies over a certain size or turnover, audits must be undertaken and signed by an accountant who is a registered auditor.

Authorised capital: The maximum share capital a company is allowed to issue under its memorandum of association. An increase in authorised capital can only take place in accordance with procedures laid down in the Companies Act 1985.

B

BACS: a scheme used to process financial transactions electronically. Most employees are paid by BACS these days, and it can also be used to pay VAT and other taxes. Now a standalone term, it was originally an acronym for 'Bankers Automated Clearing Services'. Payments transferred by BACS normally take three days to clear.

Bad debts: Debts owed to a business that are unlikely to be received and should be written off.

Balance sheet: A statement providing a snapshot of everything a business owes and owns at a particular moment in time.

Bankruptcy: A situation where an individual is incapable of settling their debts and has been served with a bankruptcy order by a court.

Base rate: The rate of interest, set by the Bank of England, on which financial institutions base their lending rates. Their lending rates will be a certain percentage above the base rate, and their savings rates below. When the base rate changes, this generally affects all their other rates (though it is sometimes possible to negotiate fixed rates on loans).

Bookkeeping: Recording the financial transactions of a business in its books and keeping those accounts in order, either for a review or an external inspection.

Book value: Value of an asset as shown in the accounting records. Book value usually means original value less accumulated depreciation, though in the case of premises it may mean the latest valuation.

Books: A business' financial records; for example, its cash book, sales ledger, purchase ledger and payroll.

Break-even point: Point at which income from sales exactly equals the total of a business' costs.

Budget: A plan for the allocation and use of resources, often involving the production of an itemised list of expected income and expenditure for a given future period.

Business angel: A private equity investor, usually with a business background, who is able to make a small-scale equity investment in a young business to help it grow. Business angels sometimes also supply hands-on expertise to assist in the running of the business.

Business plan: A document detailing the future direction of a business, setting out its objectives and how they are to be achieved.

C

Capital: Money brought into a business by way of share capital and loan capital, as well as retained earnings.

Capital employed: Capital introduced plus retained profit plus long-term loans. Some definitions exclude long-term loans while others include short-term loans. Capital employed is equal to the net worth of a business.

Capital Gains Tax: A tax payable by individuals based on the chargeable gains made from selling or disposing of assets. This is likely to be an important consideration when selling shares or a business.

Cash: Money in hand or in a bank account.

Cash book: A record of all cash receipts and payments.

Cash flow: The money coming into and going out of a business in a given period. Cash flow may be positive (if more comes in than goes out) or negative.

Cash-flow forecast: A projection of what a business expects its cash income and cash payments to be in a given period of time. Business plans should include a cash-flow forecast to indicate how much working capital needs to be made available if negative cash flow is expected at any stage.

CHAPS: Clearing House Automated Payment System, a same-day method of transferring funds in pounds sterling and euros between bank accounts. As it is quicker than BACS (see above), CHAPS is expensive.

Collateral: An asset pledged as a guarantee to a lender until a loan is repaid. If the borrower defaults on their loan payments, the lender has a right to sell the collateral asset to recover their loan.

Consolidated accounts: The accounts of a parent company or holding company, which combine the accounts of all subsidiary companies.

Consumer credit: Provision of credit to retail customers. An example is hire purchase or deferred payment. Businesses providing consumer credit must comply with the Consumer Credit Act 1974 (as amended).

Contingent liability: Liabilities that may be incurred by a business which depend on the outcome of a forthcoming event, such as a court case, which may or may not happen. This should be recorded in the notes to the accounts.

Contribution: The difference between the price charged and the direct costs involved in making a product. This 'contributes' to covering the fixed costs or overheads and, once all the fixed costs are covered, contributes to the net profit.

Corporation tax: The tax on a company's trading profits, charged as a percentage of the profits made during its accounting period.

Cost of sales (also known as direct costs): The cost to a business of producing goods. In the case of a retail or distribution business, cost of sales is the cost of purchasing goods prior to their resale.

Credit: In banking terms, credit is a facility that allows a business or individual to borrow money. In bookkeeping terms, a credit balance in a business' accounts reflects a liability, because the business owes money to its creditor. In the trading terms between businesses, credit is the value of goods which one business will supply to another before payment is required.

Credit limit: A limit on borrowing from a bank, or a limit that a business imposes on how much its own customers can purchase on account.

Credit note: A note, issued to a person or business when goods are returned by them, which cancels or modifies the original invoice.

Credit period: The time allowed between the provision of goods or services and when they have to be paid for.

Creditors: People or businesses who are owed money. Suppliers who are owed money are described as 'trade creditors' to distinguish them from other creditors, such as banks. They are usually shown separately on the balance sheet.

Creditors' turnover ratio: An average measure of how long it takes a firm to pay its creditors. This is calculated as purchases divided by average number of creditors. Dividing 365 by the result gives the average payment period.

Current assets: Assets in a cash or near cash state, such as debtors and stock.

Current liabilities: Debts owed by a business which have to be paid back in less than 12 months.

Current ratio: A financial ratio that measures the ratio of current assets to current liabilities. The ratio indicates whether a business has sufficient working capital to operate.

D

Debenture loan: A type of long-term loan taken out by a business, which it agrees to repay at a specified future date. The business will usually pay a fixed rate of interest to debenture holders each year until maturity. If it fails to pay either the interest or the principal amount of the loan when the time comes, the debenture holders can force the business into liquidation and recover their money from a sale of the assets.

Debit: An entry on an account statement used to designate a payment or sum owed, as opposed to a credit (which is a receipt).

Debt: Money that is owed to a person or business.

Debtors: Businesses or individuals who owe a business money, usually resulting from the purchase of goods or services.

Debtors' turnover ratio: A measure of how quickly debtors pay their debts. This is calculated as total sales divided by the average number of debtors. Dividing 365 by the result gives the average debt collection period.

Depreciation: The charge in a business's accounts that reflects the reduction in value of a tangible asset over time, as its useable life is exhausted (see Amortisation). Depreciation is charged before calculation of profit, on the grounds that the use of capital assets is one of the costs of being in business and one of the contributors to profit.

Direct costs: Sometimes known as cost of sales, these are the costs that can be directly attributed to the production of a particular product or service (for example, raw materials and direct labour).

Disbursement: Money paid out for incidental expenses.

Discount: A deduction from the recommended price of an item, or a bonus for prompt payment.

Discounted cash flow: Technique for comparing projects to see which may give the best return on investment. It is used when comparing two projects that will generate income at different times, as it makes allowance for the fact that money now is worth more than money in the future.

Dividend: Payment made from net profits to the shareholders of a company.

Double entry: The method of bookkeeping where every transaction is entered as a debit to one account and a credit to another account. The totals of debits and credits are always equal.

Drawings: Money that self-employed people withdraw from their businesses to cover their monthly living costs. Drawings are regarded as an advance against the profits of a business, not as a business expense. This is unlike a salary paid to an employee, which is allowable as a company expense (although the salary attracts tax and NI under the PAYE scheme).

E

Equity: The capital which shareholders own in a company.

Expenses: General term which can mean all the costs of a business, but is normally used to signify overhead expenses (as opposed to direct costs).

F

Factoring: Specialised companies (factors) which will pay a business a proportion of the amount it is owed, in return for the right to collect debts from customers. The factors charge the business fees and interest.

Finance house: A company whose business is lending money. It also accepts deposits from savers.

Financial services: Term covering areas like banking, building societies, insurance, loans and pensions.

Financial Services Authority (FSA): Government body undertaking regulatory responsibilities for the UK financial services industry.

Financial year: The 12-month period which a business chooses for its accounting year.

Finished goods: Stocks of goods that are ready to sell.

Fixed assets: Assets with a life of longer than one year (such as buildings and machinery).

Fixed costs: Costs which are fixed for a business for a reasonable length of time, and not dependent on the number of units produced (such as rent, rates and salaries).

Fixed rate: A loan in which the interest rate does not change during the entire term of the loan.

Flotation: Term used to describe the entry of a company to the stock market.

G

Gearing: A measure of debt as a proportion of total finance. It is usually expressed as the ratio of debt to capital employed.

Goodwill: The value of a business to a purchaser over and above its net asset value. It reflects the value of intangible assets like reputation, brand name, good customer relations, high employee morale and other factors that improve the firm's performance.

Grants: Financial assistance given to a business by a third party (such as the Government). Grants do not usually have to be repaid provided agreed terms are met.

Gross profit: The difference between turnover and the cost of making a product or providing a service, before taking into account overheads, indirect salaries and interest payments.

Gross profit margin: Gross profit divided by sales, usually expressed as a percentage.

Guarantor: A person who commits to guarantee the debts of another. If, for example, an individual fails to meet their obligations on hire purchase repayments, the guarantor will be obliged to make those repayments.

H

Hire purchase: An agreement to hire goods for a period of time, with the option of purchasing them at the end of the agreement for a reduced sum.

HM Revenue and Customs: Government department responsible for the collection of tax and customs duties. This includes income, corporation, capital gains, inheritance and environmental taxes; and value added tax (VAT), National Insurance and excise duties. The department was formed after the merger of the Inland Revenue and HM Customs and Excise.

I

Income tax: Tax on an individual's income.

Indirect costs: Business costs that cannot be attributed directly to the production of a particular product or service (such as bank charges or rent).

Inflation: The overall general increase in the price of goods and services in an economy. Traditionally it has been measured by the Retail Price Index (RPI), which is a domestic measure of inflation in the UK. The measure of inflation for macroeconomic purposes and for the Government's current inflation target now comes from the Consumer Prices Index (CPI), which is known internationally as the Harmonised Index of Consumer Prices (HICP).

Inheritance tax: Tax payable by the new owner (or the transferrer) on assets transferred upon the death of the previous owner.

Input tax: The VAT that a business pays on supplies (inputs) required for it to produce goods or services.

Insolvency: The situation in which a person or business is unable to meet debts when they fall due.

Intangible assets: Assets that are non-physical in form. Examples include patents, goodwill, trade marks and copyrights.

Interest: The amount charged by a lender on borrowed money, usually expressed as an annual percentage.

Interest cover: Measure of the ease with which a business can meet its interest payments out of profit. It is calculated as profit before interest and tax (PBIT) divided by interest paid.

Inventory: Stock items or a list detailing them. In accounting, inventory is the sum of raw materials, components, work in progress and finished goods still not sold.

Investment: Using money (to buy assets, for example) in the hope of receiving income or a larger repayment in return. Return on investment is a measure of business performance.

Investment appraisal: Evaluation of any investments or potential investments to be made, usually in profit terms.

Invoice: A bill issued for products or services provided to a customer.

Invoice discounting: A commercial arrangement in which a third party (the discounter) pays an advance on the value of an invoice which is not yet due for payment. Interest and fees are charged by the discounter for this service.

L

Lease: A contract in which the legal owner of property or another asset agrees to allow another person to use that property or asset in return for a regular specified payment (known as rent) over a set term. In addition to buildings, other items such as cars and computers are often leased in order to avoid capital costs in the running of a business.

Lease purchase: A variation on leasing. At the end of the lease period the goods become the lessee's property.

Leverage: The ratio of total finance to equity. This term is more commonly used in the US; in the UK, the popular term is 'gearing'.

Liabilities: Combined debts owed by a business, whether short- or long-term.

Liquid assets: Cash or items such as debtors and finished stock that can readily be converted into cash.

Liquidation: Formal closing down of a company. Any assets are sold and used to pay off some or all of the firm's debts.

Liquidity: Measure of the working capital or cash available to a business to enable it to meet its liabilities as they fall due. Liquidity ratios include the current ratio and the quick ratio (also known as the 'acid test').

Loss: Where expenditure exceeds income in a given period.

M

Management accounts: Detailed financial accounts normally prepared monthly for internal use by a business.

Management buy-in: The purchase of a business by outside investors who bring with them a new set of managers.

Management buy-out: Purchase of all or part of a business by its existing managers, often with the backing of venture capitalists.

Margin of safety: Describes how far above break-even point a business is operating.

Marginal costing: The amount spent on producing one extra unit. The marginal cost is the increase in total cost when one more unit is produced. Marginal costing compares the marginal revenue (the extra income) of selling the extra unit with the marginal cost.

Mark-up: The profit margin on goods or services, expressed as a percentage of the product's cost.

Maturity: The date on which a debt becomes due for payment.

N

National Insurance (NI): NI contributions are deducted from wages by a business on behalf of its employees, and are paid to the state to cover various insurance benefits including sickness, unemployment, maternity cover and a state pension. Employers also make contributions on behalf of their employees.

Negative cash flow: Where more money is going out of a business than is coming in.

Net current assets: Current assets minus current liabilities. This should normally be positive; otherwise a business may not be able to meet its debts as they fall due.

Net present value: The value of a business' future trading, expressed in today's money. In the discounted cash flow method of evaluation, the comparison between two commercial projects is based on their net present value.

Net profit: The gross profit of a business less all expenses. In business accounts, the word 'net' is often dropped, so that you simply have 'Profit before tax' and 'Profit after tax'.

Net profit margin: Measures trading profit relative to sales revenue. It is calculated by net profit divided by sales and expressed as a percentage.

Net worth: Total assets less total liabilities.

O

Operating profit: Actual profit made by a business after the deduction of all expenses except interest. For self-employed people, drawings are not regarded as an expense; however, salaries and wages for company directors and staff are allowable as expenses.

Output tax: The amount of VAT a business adds to the price of its product or service.

Overdraft: A flexible form of bank lending on a current account, allowing the customer to overdraw money to a certain limit. Banks may agree an overdraft limit (the maximum amount by which they will allow the customer to overdraw), but will charge interest and may require additional fees. An overdraft is often used as a short-term business finance facility, but it can be cancelled by the bank at any time.

Overheads: All operating costs that are not directly linked to a product and which, generally speaking, are fixed costs (such as rent, utilities and insurance).

Overtrading: When a business is selling more products or services than the working capital facilities can cope with, which is often the result of poor planning.

P

PAYE (Pay As You Earn): Income tax on salaries and wages. All employers are required to deduct income tax from employees' pay. The system uses tax codes to adjust the level of deductions from each employee's wages.

Payroll: The financial record of employees' salaries, wages, bonuses, net pay and deductions.

Personal expenses: Expenses incurred by an individual while on business, and normally reclaimable as business expenses.

Petty cash: A small amount of cash kept on hand by a business for incidental expenses.

Positive cash flow: The situation in which more money is coming into a business than is going out of it.

Pricing: Goods and services can be priced by taking the cost of making or providing them and adding a mark-up for profit. Some businesses add a fixed percentage.

Profit: Level by which income exceeds expenditure in a given period.

Profit and loss account: A set of accounts, usually prepared annually or monthly, which depict a business' trading performance. This is normally read in conjunction with the balance sheet and cash flow statement.

Profit margin: Ratio of profit to sales; calculated using either gross profit (gross profit margin) or profit before interest and tax (net profit margin). Often expressed as a percentage (profit divided by sale x 100). It shows how profitable a business is.

Purchase ledger: Used to record all suppliers' invoices and payments to suppliers, and to show which invoices remain unpaid.

Q

Qualified accounts: Audited company accounts where the auditor has expressed doubts or disagreement over the information shown in the accounts.

Quick ratio: A financial ratio that measures how readily a firm can pay off its debts. It is the ratio of cash plus debtors to current liabilities, and is also called the 'acid test ratio'.

R

Ratio analysis: This is a tool for analysing the financial performance of a company by calculating ratios from its published accounts. These ratios can help to give a more in-depth picture of how the company is managing resources. Four main types of ratio look at liquidity, solvency, efficiency and profitability. The Centre for Interfirm Comparison (**www.cifc.co.uk**) publishes average ratios for particular industries.

Raw materials stock: Stocks of materials required to manufacture products, held by the manufacturer for future use.

Receivership: When a company cannot meet its financial commitments, one or more of its main creditors may appoint a receiver. The receiver takes over the day-to-day running of the company, doing whatever they think is best to help the creditors get their money back.

Reducing balance depreciation: Where depreciation on a fixed asset is calculated by applying the depreciation rate to the net book value.

Reserves: The retained profits of a business that form part of its capital.

Return on investment: Amount of money generated by a capital investment in a given period of time expressed as a percentage of the total amount invested.

Revenue: Income generated by a business for a specific period.

S

Salary: The gross amount of money paid to an employee in return for their labour. It is usually paid monthly (unlike wages, which are usually paid weekly) and expressed as an annual sum. It is subject to PAYE and NI deductions by the employer, and the employer is also liable for additional NI contributions based on the employee's salary.

Sales ledger: Record of every invoice issued, the amount of cash received and the amount owed to a business by its customers.

Security: An asset that is offered by a borrower to a lender to safeguard a loan.

Self-assessment for tax: The Government has now made many individuals responsible for calculating their own tax liability and reporting the details annually to HM Revenue and Customs.

Shareholders: Owners of a company's shares or stocks.

Shares: The ownership of a company is divided into shares, each representing a part of the equity capital invested in the business.

Soft loan: Loan made at an interest rate below the market rate or with lenient repayment terms.

Solvency: Measure of a business' ability to pay its bills as they fall due. If it cannot pay, then it is insolvent. A negative net worth indicates that a business is insolvent.

Staged payments: Payment by instalments. This may be a normal condition in a contract or arranged as a way of improving cash flow where a customer cannot pay the full amount due in one payment. Total charge can be subject to the addition of interest.

Start-up costs: Costs specifically associated with setting up in business.

Stock: An asset of a firm held for sale in the ordinary course of business. Raw materials, components and consumables may also be held in stock. You should remember to write off 'dead stock' periodically so as not to be lulled into a false sense of security by this figure.

Stock exchange: A financial centre where shares in public companies are traded.

Straight line: Method of accounting for the depreciation of a fixed asset across its estimated useful life in equal instalments.

T

Tangible assets: Physical assets owned by a business or individual that can be seen or touched, such as stock and machinery.

Tax avoidance: Reducing or deferring the amount of tax that needs to be paid by making best use of available allowances and claiming for all allowable expenses.

Tax evasion: Illegal attempts to pay less tax than required (for example, by forging expenses or hiding income).

Taxable supplies: Goods and services supplied to a customer that are liable for VAT (even if zero rated).

Taxable turnover: The total value of taxable sales for VAT purposes.

Trial balance: In double entry bookkeeping, checking to see if all debit and credit items in a ledger have the same total.

Turnover: Total sales income. Net turnover is calculated by total sales income less returns. VAT is not included in turnover figures.

U

Unsecured loan: A loan under which the lender has no entitlement to any of the borrower's assets in the event of the borrower failing to make the loan repayments. Such a loan normally carries a higher interest rate than a secured loan.

V

Value Added Tax (VAT): VAT is a tax on consumer expenditure, and is collected on business transactions. The VAT that businesses pay to HM Revenue and Customs is equal to their output tax minus their input tax.

Variable costs: Costs that vary with production levels (for example, direct costs such as raw materials). In some businesses, however, costs such as power consumption may also vary substantially depending on output; these would then be regarded as variable.

VAT registration: Businesses whose annual turnover exceeds a certain threshold must register with HM Revenue and Customs to become a VAT vendor. Businesses with a lower turnover than the threshold can still register voluntarily.

Venture capital: Funding which may be made available to companies with good prospects of growth but which are unable to get funds from standard lenders such as banks. Venture capitalists (VCs) supply capital to companies in return for an equity stake in the company.

W

Wages: Regular money payments to an employee in return for their labour. They are usually paid weekly and based upon an hourly wage rate. Wages are also subject to PAYE and NI deductions.

Wages book: Records wages and salary payments made to employees, as well as PAYE and NI deductions, commonly known as the payroll.

Winding up: Voluntary or compulsory liquidation of a company.

Work in progress: Raw materials, components and products that are within the production process but are not yet finished goods.

Working capital: The difference between current assets and current liabilities. This capital is used to run the business.

Write off: To reduce the value of an asset in the books to zero (for example, to record a debt as being a bad debt).

Written down value: When the book value of an asset is reduced to take depreciation into account, the new value is the written down value or net book value.

Z

Zero-based forecasting: Forecasting that starts from a zero base rather than from the previous year's actual performance figures.

GETTING OFF THE GROUND

Sources of finance for small firms

GETTING STARTED

Before you begin trading, you need enough money both to set up your business and to cover your initial running costs (for example, buying office equipment and paying for any licences you need). There are a number of options for finding finance for your business, including loans, credit cards, overdrafts, private equity and grants. And it's important to consider all the options. Your business adviser and bank manager will be essential sources of help and advice about available sources of funding in your area.

This actionlist provides a brief introduction to the main types of financial support available to small businesses and start-ups, and lists the most important organisations offering funding. It also provides guidance on where to obtain further information about applying for the different types of support listed.

FAQS

What can I do to increase my chance of success in getting some funding?

Before you begin investigating your financial options and applying for funding, it's essential that you do your market research thoroughly. You need to be able to demonstrate a comprehensive understanding of your target customers and how you'll reach them before you can convince a financier to support your idea. Market research will also help you with your business plan, which is often an essential requirement when you're trying to secure finance.

Remember that funding for small businesses is frequently raised most effectively as a package of support from several sources. Backing from one source can inspire the confidence of another and help you build up momentum. The best way to get financial support in this way is through an experienced business adviser who'll act as an intermediary. Financial assistance, especially for business start-ups, is often associated with business skills courses. So it's probably worth undertaking some business training not only to improve your personal skills, but also to increase the confidence of potential investors in your business.

MAKING IT HAPPEN

There are a variety of funding options open to small business owners in the UK, as explained below.

Loans

Debt finance may be in the form of a loan, which is an amount of money you borrow and pay back over an agreed period, at an agreed rate of interest.

There are two types of loans: commercial loans, which are borrowed from banks or building societies; and non-commercial or 'soft' loans, which are schemes managed by enterprise or local development agencies.

Advantages of taking out a commercial loan from a bank include the fact that loans can be flexible; you can choose a repayment period that suits you; and you can shop around for good deals. The main drawback is that commercial loans are usually secured against a personal asset, such as your house or car.

Many 'soft' loan funds are managed at a local level, by enterprise or development agencies. Terms and conditions often depend on the region or area in which your business is based, while interest rates for these loans are often fixed for the period of the loan or charged at below bank rates. There's usually less security required for this type of loan, and repayment periods are often more flexible in comparison to the loans offered by banks and building societies.

Some 'soft' loans are available only to businesses that are viable but can't raise all the finance they need from banks. Most funds require borrowers to be monitored for the period of the loan, and some integrate loan finance with business advisory or training schemes.

Business advisers are usually familiar with application procedures and will be able to advise you on the most suitable loan schemes to apply for.

Bank overdraft

An alternative to arranging your debt finance via a loan is to obtain an overdraft, which is when your bank agrees to let you withdraw more money than you actually have in your account. Your bank will set a maximum level of overdraft.

You only have to pay interest on the amount you're overdrawn, so overdrafts can be a good option if you only need small amounts of extra cash regularly. However, the interest you pay is often higher than the rate you'd pay for a loan.

Grants and awards

Grants are sums of money that usually don't have to be paid back. They tend to be available only in certain regions or for certain business sectors, or for specific types of people (for example, unemployed or young people) or projects (for example, marketing or buying IT equipment).

Many new start-ups think they'll automatically be able to apply for a grant or similar award to help fund their venture. While the main advantage of grants and awards is that they don't usually need to be repaid (unless the money is misused), many agencies offering such funding only do so for specific purposes. Grants also often come with restrictions and conditions, and many require you to match the funding given using your own resources.

Your chances of successfully applying for this type of financial support will depend largely on how well your business or project fits the profile of a particular grant funding scheme.

Sometimes the most useful advice a small business looking for grant finance can be given is to target its applications at support programmes that are relatively undersubscribed. As most grant initiatives only have limited amounts of money to hand out,

a business is more likely to be successful in obtaining the funds it requires by targeting new schemes early in their lifespan.

The Government, European Union (EU) and many local authorities provide grants to encourage small firms. There are also specific award schemes for particular areas, such as the Shell LiveWIRE scheme for young entrepreneurs.

Private equity

This form of funding is invested into your business by a third party. In many cases, that could be someone you know, such as a member of your family, a friend or personal sponsor. Alternatively it could be a venture capitalist or a business angel.

Venture capital

Venture capital is a means of financing a business where a portion of your firm's share capital or equity is sold in return for a major investment in the enterprise. It means that some measure of control over your business has to be conceded to the new shareholder, but the amount of finance gained can be very large. Most venture capitalists will only invest in established businesses or those looking to raise sums of over £250,000. The British Venture Capital Association publishes a list of member firms and their contact details. See also pp. 241–62.

Business angels

Business angels are private investors who look for opportunities to put money into new or growing businesses in the hope of making a good return. Most regions of the UK now have business angel matching services, which encourage local investment and mentoring on a smaller scale. The Government-sponsored British Business Angels Association matches business angels with small businesses requiring equity finance of between £20,000 and £400,000.

Financing through credit cards

In recent years there's been an increasing tendency for entrepreneurs to finance their new businesses through the use of credit cards, encouraged by a growing number of cheap deals, such as introductory interest-free offers. While many credit-card companies discourage the use of personal credit cards for business purposes, there are now a number of credit-card offers specifically targeted at new business owners.

While using a credit card can help a business to raise initial low levels of finance, it doesn't make sense over the long term. Although initial interest rates may be attractive, the costs of long-term credit-card rates are usually relatively high.

Other sources of financial support

The information below is an introductory overview of other sources of financial support for small businesses, and is by no means exhaustive. Your business adviser or local enterprise agency should have details about what is available locally.

Business start-up

Local enterprise agencies administer a variety of schemes to help support new businesses. Each organisation uses its own discretion to determine how the scheme is run, and terms and conditions vary from region to region. Most schemes include business planning advice, training and some form of financial support. Go to **www. nfea.com** to find your nearest enterprise agency, or consult your business adviser (a directory of advisers is available at **www. iba.org.uk/aspx/advisersearch.aspx**).

The UK Government

The Government operates a variety of initiatives through its different departments, offering help to businesses in such areas as start-up, technology, research and development, and exporting. For example, the Department of Business, Enterprise and Regulatory Reform (BERR) runs the Small Firms Loan Guarantee (SFLG) scheme, which provides guarantees to approved lenders for funding start-ups and young

businesses that have problems accessing finance.

Organisations supporting young entrepreneurs

The Prince's Trust and the Prince's Scottish Youth Business Trust help young people aged 18–30 (18–25 in Scotland), who are unemployed or in an unfulfilling part-time or temporary job, to start up in business. The Trusts are aimed at disadvantaged young people who find it difficult to obtain finance from conventional sources. They operate from regional offices, arranging advice and training as well as grants and loans.

Shell LiveWIRE, sponsored by Shell UK, supports young people aged 16–30 who want to start their own businesses. Shell LiveWIRE Business Start Up Awards provide over £200,000 of cash and support to entrepreneurs aged 16–30 and in their first year of trading. Turn to pp. 33–35 for more information.

Organisations supporting older entrepreneurs

The Prince's Initiative for Mature Enterprise (PRIME) provides advice, support and loan finance to help entrepreneurs aged over 50 start up businesses. Loans of up to £5,000 are available for individuals (£10,000 for partnerships) who've been refused funds by other sources of finance.

The UK Government's New Deal 50 Plus (available through JobCentre Plus) can provide discretionary financial support to help people aged over 50 to get a business idea off the ground, and give them access to a personal adviser. Also see pp. 30–32.

European funding

Various European funding schemes are available to businesses, mainly supporting research and development. See the European Commission (EC) website at **http://europa.eu.int/grants/index_en. htm** for details about the grants and loans on offer.

USEFUL LINKS

British Business Angels Association:
www.bbaa.org.uk
British Venture Capital Association:
www.bvca.co.uk
Department for Business, Enterprise and
   Regulatory Reform
www.berr.gov.uk
European Business Angel
   Network:
www.eban.org
JobCentre Plus:
www.jobcentreplus.gov.uk/

PRIME:
www.primeintiative.org.uk and
   www.primebusinessclub.com
PRIME Cymru:
www.prime-cymru.co.uk
The Prince's Scottish Youth Business
   Trust:
www.psybt.org.uk
The Prince's Trust:
www.princes-trust.org.uk
Shell LiveWIRE:
www.shell-livewire.org
Welsh Business Angels Network:
www.xenos.co.uk

Approaching business angels

GETTING STARTED
Finding investment to start a small business can often be arduous and time-consuming, particularly if you have no trading history, few savings, poor credit ratings or no security.

Many small businesses turn to business angel investors for help, but only the strongest applications will succeed and the process is not easy. This actionlist looks at how to make the best use of this form of funding and what you will need to do to be successful.

FAQS
What are business angels?
Business angel funding is a private, unregulated source of investment which fulfils a need for capital that cannot be introduced by the business owners themselves, or be raised by way of loans.

Business angels are usually individuals with a high net worth. They are private investors, or groups of investors, looking for opportunities to invest money in enterprises with the aim of making a substantial financial return. However, research has shown that 40% of business angel investments don't succeed, so the risks of losing their money are potentially as high as the rewards. Visit **www. envestors.co.uk** for more information.

Typically, business angels may have owned a successful business in the past. They often assist businesses during the start-up or expansion phase, and may invest either alone or in networks. As well as money, they often have a wealth of commercial experience and if they have earned their fortunes by building businesses themselves, they may also bring industry contacts with them.

The Government has encouraged business angels through its Enterprise Investment Scheme (EIS), which allows tax relief on investments. They will need to invest for a minimum period of three years in order to qualify for this (**www. hmrc.gov.uk/eis/ eis-index.htm**), but will typically invest for a maximum of five years.

What sort of business do they invest in?
Business angel funding is the money that investors put into a private company in return for a share in the ownership of the company. (It's also referred to as equity finance.) This type of finance is therefore not available to businesses that operate under the legal status of sole trader or partnership.

Business angels will want to know how much money you are seeking, and that this is a realistic amount. They will also be looking for clear information and supporting evidence to demonstrate your strategies for marketing, achievement of targets and your management approach.

How much will business angels invest?
Business angels typically invest between £10,000 and £100,000, but may invest larger sums if they are part of a syndicate. The average amount invested is £25,000. This type of finance may be provided to start-up or expanding businesses—and because it involves the business angel temporarily buying a stake in the business, there are no monthly loan repayments to make or crippling debts to restrict the business.

MAKING IT HAPPEN
Understand what business angels look for
Every individual or group looking to invest in small businesses will be looking for a different range of investment factors, but businesses and entrepreneurs that appear to be innovative or stand out from the crowd will have a better chance of success. Investors are also likely to be attracted by:
- an enterprise with good prospects of rapid growth, but which needs money in order to create the conditions for that growth
- young businesses or even start-ups with the right management team

- companies with motivation, enthusiasm, a clear business plan and a thorough knowledge of the market

Business angel funding is most suitable for businesses that have high growth potential and whose owners are prepared to give up part-ownership in return for investment. It's not, then, suitable for businesses that:

- are seeking to address cash-flow issues
- have other chronic problems, such as no real market for their goods or services
- are lifestyle businesses with no real prospect of significant growth

There are many types of business angel, with dozens of different priorities and interests, but nearly all of them will be looking for the positive outcomes below.

Return on their investment

By taking an equity stake in your business, investors will clearly be looking for a significant return on investment. What sort of return this should be will vary according to the angel, the nature of the industry and the initial size of your business. The SME Statistics Unit reports that the average business angel would like to see an internal rate return of between 35% and 40% each year, but much of that return will arise on the sale of their shares.

Tax benefits

The Enterprise Investment Scheme offers income tax relief on investments in shares worth up to £400,000 in any one tax year. As long as the investor keeps their money in your business' shares for at least three years, they will be entitled to capital gains tax relief on any profits (and may also qualify for relief on losses).

Interest and excitement

Some business angels may choose to invest in unusual or risky enterprises. Knowledge of the sector they are investing in will be advantageous for all concerned.

Management involvement

Business angels may often require some involvement in running the venture. This is

not because they mistrust your abilities – in fact your management capability will be a major factor in their decision to invest. You should look beyond the financial aspects of the relationship, as many angels can offer a wealth of experience and commercial acumen.

Approach angels

According to statistics (see **www.envestors.co.uk**), a mere 2% of applicants are successful in raising finance from business angels, so to stand a chance of attracting investors, prepare thoroughly and hone your pitch carefully.

Do all you can to make sure that the first meeting goes well, and be aware that business angels will be evaluating how you present yourself and react to feedback. Personal chemistry between you and the investor, and the strength of your management team, will be crucial success factors.

You will need to demonstrate to a business angel:

- that you are a clear thinker and are well organised
- that your business is sustainable, can achieve significant growth and is not just a concept that will fail to return a profit
- how your business will achieve success and the returns on investment projected in the business plan
- that your management team is strong, with relevant previous experience and the capability to deliver results
- that your business has a unique selling proposition
- that your business would benefit from an angel's management skills and experience
- that you are prepared to sell shares to an outsider, give up a degree of control over the business, and submit the business to scrutiny from investors
- that you are confident yet honest, and that you are personally compatible with the business angel investor

For further information about the process of raising private investment, see pp. 12–15. Also turn to the Directory section at the back of this book, which lists the contact details of hundreds of UK-based business angels.

Finding a business angel

There are several different ways to get in touch with angels. You could simply ask your business adviser, bank, solicitor or accountant if they know of suitable people who might be interested in investing in your venture. Alternatively, tap into your own network and ask business contacts if they know of other firms which have benefited from private investment.

The government also offers some help, and funds various networks which aim to match businesses with suitable angels (privately funded networks exist too). The British Business Angels Association offers a directory of business angel organisations which can help match you with potential investors. All the networks will be different—some are limited to helping businesses from particular regions; others will be interested in certain industry sectors—so it pays to make sure they can match you up with the right sort of investor. See **www.bbaa.co.uk** for more details.

COMMON MISTAKES
Your business plan isn't up to scratch

Having an effective business plan is important not just for your business angel, but for the overall wellbeing of your business: it will help clarify your own thinking. You should also take advantage of professional advice from your lawyer or accountant, and the various support organisations set up to advise businesses in your position.

You forget it's a two-way street

As important as it is to secure funding, your own business is equally entitled to carry out a due diligence investigation of your potential investor (and future board-room colleague) as they are of you. Ask contacts about your prospect's previous track record as a business angel, their expertise and their ability to sustain long-term participation.

You don't think things through to their logical conclusion

Before drawing up an agreement, it is essential to consider what will happen at the end of the investment period. Who will purchase your investor's stake if they decide to sell it? What will happen if things go wrong and the value of their investment falls?

USEFUL LINKS

Angel Investment Network:
www.angelinvestmentnetwork.co.uk
Department for Business, Enterprise and Regulatory Reform (BERR):
www.berr.gov.uk
Envestors:
www.envestors.co.uk/investment-clinics.htm
Equity Entrepreneur:
www.equityentrepreneur.co.uk
Information on the Enterprise Investment Scheme:
www.hmrc.gov.uk/eis/eis-index.htm
VCR Directory Online:
www.vcrdirectory.co.uk

Understanding the Small Firms Loan Guarantee

GETTING STARTED

For many entrepreneurs, getting hold of the right type of funding to take their business further can be one of the biggest challenges they face. If, for example, you have a poor credit rating or no security or trading history, bank loans can be hard to come by.

To address this, the Department for Business, Enterprise and Regulatory Reform (DBERR) has teamed up with high street banks and specialist lenders to provide the Small Firms Loan Guarantee (SFLG). This helps start-up and early-stage businesses to gain access to the commercial funding they need to get their ideas off the ground.

FAQS

What are the aims of the Small Firms Loan Guarantee?

The SFLG is a tool which enables lenders to provide finance on commercial terms to early stage businesses with viable business plans but which otherwise would be prevented from borrowing because they lack the necessary security.

The SFLG guarantees loans of between £5,000 and £250,000 over terms of between two and ten years to start-ups and businesses that have been trading less than five years and which have an annual turnover of less than £5.6 million.

All decision-making and other administration is carried out by the participating lenders. The Government, through the SFLG, provides a guarantee to the lender.

MAKING IT HAPPEN

Understand how the SFLG works

The Government guarantees 75% of the loan and in return, businesses pay a premium of 2% per year on the outstanding balance. Banks and other financial institutions apply their usual commercial lending practices, including setting interest rates and other charges.

A lender may choose to offer a loan guaranteed under SFLG if:

- you are about to start, or already run, a qualifying business
- your proposed business activity is eligible for a loan

- the loan will be used for an eligible purpose
- your lender wishes to make the loan but is unable to do so because you do not have the security they would normally require

Qualifying businesses may include sole traders, partnerships, franchises, co-operatives and limited companies involved in commercial activities that have a viable business proposition and, which, in the lender's opinion, have the ability to repay the loan.

Most business activities are included, but there are some restrictions. This is not a definitive guide but some of the main areas of activity which are excluded include: self-employed artists, authors, composers, playwrights and musicians; activities involving granting finance or financial services to clients; betting and gambling; insurance; medical, health and veterinary services; and all publicly owned bodies.

Loans guaranteed by the scheme must be for:

- business development
- financing a project
- starting up trading
- expanding an existing business
- improving efficiency

Loans for research and development are only available to businesses carrying out commercial activities.

The SFLG can be used to finance a business acquisition, as long as both businesses satisfy the five-year age limit, but *can't* be used to:

- replace existing borrowing

- finance interest payments
- fund export promotion or a specific export order

Loans are available for terms of between two and ten years, including any 'capital repayment holidays' (periods agreed between the borrower and lender in which the borrower pays the interest and premium, but does not make repayments on the loan).

Access the loans

The SFLG is available, at the lender's discretion, in connection with eligible small business lending through a number of banks and other financial institutions, many of which are household names. For a full list of approved lenders, visit: **www.berr.gov.uk**.

Lenders must be satisfied that the only reason they cannot offer your business a conventional loan is because you do not have the necessary security. They will apply their standard commercial lending decision-making process to your application. You'll need to supply them with a business plan and financial projections for at least one year's future performance—together with supporting evidence, such as order books and customer enquiries.

You'll also need to detail the amount of funding required, the security available (if any), details of the accounting systems your business uses, and evidence that you can produce regular management accounts. Make sure that you can explain the areas of risk most likely to affect your business, and what you would do to address them.

Understand what happens after the loan is approved

Normally, loans have to be taken out within six months of the offer of the guarantee, or within a shorter period if specified by the lender. If the loan isn't used within this time, it will be withdrawn. Loans are usually drawn down in one lump sum, but your lender may be able to agree to (or on occasions require) it being drawn down in instalments if that is appropriate.

In return for the guarantee, you'll have to pay the Government a premium of 2% a year on the loan's outstanding balance. Premiums are paid quarterly in advance, through a payment collection service on behalf of the Small Business Service (SBS). They reduce as the loan is repaid.

Providing financial management information is a condition of almost any business loan. Your lender will advise what regular financial information they require you to provide, which could include cash-flow comparisons and profit and loss figures.

USEFUL LINK

Department for Business, Enterprise and Regulatory Reform (BERR):
www.berr.gov.uk

Financing your business with private equity

GETTING STARTED

When you're thinking about financing your new business, looking into the option of securing private equity may be what you need. Financing your business in this way involves attracting investment from either private individuals or a venture capital organisation, and it can enable your business to achieve rapid growth. If your business is not already set up as a private limited company, you will need to make this change to be eligible to receive this type of funding.

This actionlist provides an introduction to what private equity is. It explains the process involved in acquiring this type of investment, the changes in management approach you are likely to have to undertake, and the advantages and disadvantages of this approach to financing your business.

FAQS

What is private equity finance?

Private equity finance is the money that investors put into a private company in return for a share in the ownership of that business. It's often also referred to as 'venture capital' or 'equity finance'. This finance may be provided to start-up or expanding businesses, and is also used to help fund management buy-outs (MBOs) and management buy-ins (MBIs).

Private equity is not secured on a company's assets, so the investor faces the same risks as the other shareholders—and if the business fails, investors will lose their money. While interest is not payable for capital invested in ordinary shares, investors can expect to receive dividends, which may be paid to shareholders out of accumulated profits. Investors also expect to make a capital gain on the value of their shares when they sell them. Typically, they are looking for compound returns of at least 30% per annum.

Is private equity right for your business?

Many businesses may only consider private equity finance after their bank has decided not to give them a loan. While private equity investors do not require the level of security that banks commonly insist on, they do still have stringent criteria that must be met before they will consider investing; so not all businesses are suitable for this type of funding. The key criteria that investors will look for in your business are:

- a sound business model
- high growth potential
- a balanced and preferably experienced management team
- an achievable exit opportunity in three to six years

If you start your enterprise as a 'lifestyle' business (one that offers services such as wedding planning or life coaching, for example), or because you want to control what work you do and when you do it, you will not be attractive to private equity investors. Equally, this type of funding is not designed for businesses with chronic problems or for those that need temporary help with cash flow. It's well worth thinking about other sources of finance before you take the plunge: these include include grants, loans, overdrafts, factoring, leasing, hire purchase or personal funds.

MAKING IT HAPPEN

Think through the pros and cons for your business

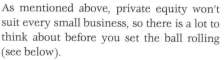

As mentioned above, private equity won't suit every small business, so there is a lot to think about before you set the ball rolling (see below).

The advantages of raising private equity finance are:

- investors will be keen to help you to succeed because their return is dependent on your company's success
- investors will provide valuable expertise and often have a network of useful contacts that you can tap in to
- private equity firms often work with other finance providers and may be able to construct a total finance package for your business
- the cash invested can be used fully for the benefit of growing the business (as dividends); the capital can be repaid when the business has been profitable
- risks are shared, and if the company runs into difficulties investors will work with you to achieve a successful turnaround
- according to research by the British Venture Capital Association (BVCA), companies that win private equity backing grow significantly faster than the average company in terms of sales, exports, investment and workforce

On the down side, you need to be sure that you're really ready to meet the demands of a private equity investor: the cash won't be given as a freebie. Disadvantages include the following:

- securing investors' backing can be both time-consuming and stressful
- there are many costs involved in the investment process—and you'll have to meet them
- your management structure may change and new people may be brought it at board level
- it opens up your business to outside scrutiny and controls
- your personal control of the direction of your business will be reduced
- the investment agreement will impose legally binding covenants to protect the investors' interests—for example, their approval may be needed for major business decisions, and caps could be placed on directors' salaries

Investigate the various sources of private equity

Finding the most appropriate sources of private equity will depend very much on how much money you're looking for. For example, for smaller amounts between about £5,000 and £20,000, you could approach friends and family. Having said that, funding from these sources will involve emotional decisions—and you run a very real risk of alienating people close to you if things go wrong and they lose their money. Don't see this as an easy way out.

For more objective financing, there are also wealthy individuals who are prepared to invest equity in businesses. Usually referred to as 'business angels', these people generally invest smaller amounts than private equity firms (usually between £10,000 and £100,000) and typically become involved at an early stage of a business's development (see also pp. 7–9). The British Business Angels Association (BBAA) can help in the search for an investor and their website address is given below.

According to the BVCA, about 80% of private equity firm financings are for more than £100,000, with most private equity firms preferring to make investments of more than £1 million. To help overcome this so-called equity gap, the Government has established Regional Venture Capital Funds (RVCFs) in England, which specialise in making investments of between £50,000 and £250,000. The Government is also in the process of setting up six Enterprise Capital Funds (ECFs), which will provide equity funding of up to £2 million.

Larger investments are preferred by many venture capital organisations because the time and effort required to carry out the investment process is similar whatever the level of funding, but the return on investment is likely to be greater and more reliable on larger investments. As a result, before you approach investors, try to find out beforehand whether they've invested previously in businesses like yours in terms of:

- the amount of money you're looking for
- the stage your business is at
- the sector it operates in

Secure professional support

Most entrepreneurs won't have a lot of experience of trying to raise private equity, so it's highly recommended that you take appropriate professional advice. Financial advisers, lawyers and accountants all have a role to play in the private equity process and can help you with the following areas:

- reviewing your business plan and its forecasts
- advice on valuing the business
- advice on how much funding is required and how the investment could be structured
- advice on tax implications and planning
- making introductions to appropriate sources of private equity and other finance
- reviewing offers of finance and helping you to negotiate the best terms for the deal

Although the costs involved with using professional advisers can mount up, the benefits are substantial—particularly if it allows you more time to concentrate on running your business. Use advisers who have experience of private equity investments in similar businesses to your own, and ask for fee estimates before engaging them.

Start to approach investors

An up-to-date and accurate business plan is an essential starting point for marketing your company to potential investors. Make sure that the plan:

- demonstrates that you have a realistic strategy to develop your business
- shows clearly how much money you need and for what
- provides detailed financial forecasts to show how your investors will be able to achieve a good return on their investment

You should also write a two- to three-page executive summary of key points, which can be sent out as a stand-alone document. Once you have written your plan, circulate your executive summary to a few potential investors initially and then ask for feedback. Take all comments on board—even negative ones—and be ready to reassess your strategy as appropriate.

If, after reading your plan, investors are interested in your business, they'll want to meet you and your management team to discuss the plans in more detail. This will be an important opportunity for you all to impress the investors with your knowledge

and understanding of your business. Also make sure that you're completely up to speed with your chosen market and any developments or trends in it, and double-check any assumptions that you've used in your financial forecasts.

Negotiate the investment deal

Once you get to the stage where you and your potential investors are ready to discuss business terms, you need to focus on:

- the amount of money to be invested and the percentage ownership that the investor will get. The key to this process is agreeing a current valuation for your business
- the structure of the funding package. Do the investors want different classes of shares to be issued, such as preference shares, and do they want another organisation to be part of the funding package?
- the key investment terms that the investor wants to impose
- the costs, such as due diligence and legal fees, that the investor expects you to pay for

Using experienced advisers can help you through this process, and you will be in a far stronger position to negotiate a more favourable deal if you have more than one investor interested in your business. When you have reached broad agreement, investors will draw up an offer letter outlining the main terms of their investment proposal, which will be subject to due diligence and contracts being signed.

Due diligence

Due diligence is a process investors undertake to check whether your business is suitable for them to invest in and that there are no nasty surprises lurking. It typically covers the verification of information in the following areas:

- current financial information and testing forecasts
- conformity with legal and tax obligations, such as VAT and PAYE
- contracts with customers, suppliers and employees
- review of assets and intellectual property rights (IPR) owned

■ business control processes

Due diligence is a key process for the investor and is frequently a stage at which a deal may fail—so prepare thoroughly for it, and make sure that your company's records are accurate and up to date. The process is usually undertaken by accountants who visit your premises—be prepared to devote a considerable amount of your time to them when they are on site.

The investment agreement

The investment agreement is a formal document that legally binds the two parties to the agreed terms and will be based on the offer letter. It is drafted by the investor's lawyer and changes are made as necessary as both parties work out the final terms. Take professional legal advice during this stage of the process to make sure that you are fully aware of the implications of the agreement's terms. The investment agreement will formalise:

■ the amount and form of the investment
■ the specific rights of the investor
■ warranties to confirm that the information you have provided to the investor is true
■ indemnities so that you accept liability if certain events happen
■ the obligations of the directors

If your business is already established as a company, it is likely that the terms of the investment agreement will require the company's Articles of Association and any existing shareholder agreement to be amended to reflect the specific rights of the new investor. The investment process is then completed when both parties sign the investment agreement and the funds are paid to the company.

COMMON MISTAKES
You don't plan for the investors' exit

Most investors will want to achieve a sale of their shares within two to six years of the deal being completed, so if you're in business for the long-haul, do make contingency plans so that you're not left high and dry if your investors decide to take their money before you're ready for them to go. If things go well and your business floats on the stock market, investors could exit via the following routes:

■ a trade sale of the company
■ sale of the investor's shares to a new investor
■ buy-back of the investor's shares by the company

You're careless about the phrasing of your business plan

Sending a business plan to potential investors counts as a financial promotion. Make sure that you're aware of the general requirements of the Financial Services and Markets Act 2000, and in particular, avoid misleading statements.

You hope for a quick fix

When you're in dire financial straits, it's natural that you want a speedy solution to your business's problems. The private equity process takes, on average, three to six months to complete: it can go more quickly than that, but can also take an awful lot longer, so do factor that into your business forecasts.

Your business isn't ship-shape

You'll get the most from the process if you make sure at the outset that you're managing your business in the best possible way. All investors will be looking for robust systems and procedures in place to maximise profitability and efficiency. Also remember that signs of extravagance, such as expensive cars and frequent holidays, are likely to discourage private equity firms.

USEFUL LINKS

British Business Angels Association (BBAA):
www.bbaa.org.uk
British Venture Capital Association:
www.bvca.co.uk
Envestors LLP:
www.envestors.co.uk
European Private Equity and Venture Capital Association (EVCA):
www.evca.com
HM Revenue & Customs (HMRC):
www.hmrc.gov.uk

Financial support for women in business

GETTING STARTED

If you're a woman thinking about starting up your own business, you're one of many. Recent figures have shown that the number of women going into business is increasing, with more women graduates starting businesses than men, and more unemployed females taking the journey into self-employment.

The Government has recognised that women's contribution to the world of business is important to the success of the UK's economy. Accordingly, policy-makers increasingly want to encourage more women to become entrepreneurial, and to give them the confidence and support they need to start up and run their own businesses.

This actionlist summarises the main sources of support, advice and finance for women business-owners in the UK. It includes Government-funded business support schemes, as well as independent and online organisations offering support to women in business.

FAQS

Where can you find help and support?

Given the current legislation, there's been a lot of effort to ensure that women get equal opportunities and aren't excluded from business and enterprise support. So there's now more open and accessible support for women, with extra incentives for them to move towards self-employment without being blocked by cultural and social barriers.

Government-funded business support

There are various Government-funded organisations committed to encouraging and supporting women in business across England, Wales, Scotland and Northern Ireland.

These organisations are a source of information for pre-start, start-up and growing businesses, covering access to finance and support networks, local business advice, and signposting to development programmes and training courses specifically designed for women.

Area	Organisation	Website
England	Business Link	**www.businesslink.gov.uk**
Wales	Business Eye	**www.businesseye.org.uk**
Scotland	Business Gateway	**www.bgateway.com**
	Scottish Enterprise	**www.scottish-enterprise.com**
	Highlands and Islands Enterprise	**www.hie.co.uk**
Northern Ireland	Enterprise Northern Ireland	**www.enterpriseni.com**
	Invest Northern Ireland	**www.investni.com**

Other sources of business advice and support for women

There's also a wide range of other groups and organisations throughout the UK offering support and advice to women wanting to start or develop their own businesses.

Area	Organisation	Services offered
UK	Prowess Ltd	Association of UK organisations providing support for women to start and grow their businesses. Provides a map to help women find a comprehensive range of support and services available across the UK and at local levels. Tel: (01603) 762355 Website: **www.prowess.org.uk**
	British Association of Women Entrepreneurs (BAWE)	Not-for-profit organisation for UK-based women business-owners, providing training, networking, mentoring and conferences. Tel: (01786) 446044 Website: **www.bawe-uk.org**
	The Women's Company	Networking group for women offering workshops, lunches and seminars. Tel: (020) 8650 8015 Website: **www.thewomenscompany.co.uk**
	Women in Rural Enterprise (WiRE)	Supports women in rural areas who want to start their own business. Also runs networking events, workshops, conferences and a business support network for rural businesswomen. Tel: (01952) 815338 Website: **www.wireuk.org**
England	Women into the Network (WIN)	Networking initiative helping to develop women's businesses in the north east through training, counselling, mentoring, networking, awards and workshops. Tel: (0191) 334 5502 Website: **www.womenintothenetwork.co.uk**
	Women in Business	Networking group for women in the south east offering support, training and contacts. Website: **www.wib.org.uk**
	Women's Employment, Enterprise and Training Unit (WEETU)	Helps women in Norfolk and Suffolk to develop enterprise skills and provides advice on setting up in business. Offers loans for new starts and developing existing ventures. Tel: (01603) 767367 Website: **www.weetu.org**

	Women's Business Development Agency (WBDA)	Helps women in Coventry and Warwickshire overcome business barriers. Provides business start-up courses and advice, business planning, market research, finance and legal advice. Tel: (024) 7623 6111 Website: **www.wbda.co.uk**
	Rural Women's Network	Provides business support and skills training to women based in Cumbria. Services include workshops, networking opportunities, one-to-one advice, and start-up and ICT training. Tel: (01768) 869510 Website: **www.ruralwomen.org.uk**
	Quaker Social Action	Helps women in east London who are on benefits or low income to start up small businesses through the Street Cred micro credit project. Tel: (020) 7729 9267 Website: **www.quakersocialaction.com/ streetcred.htm**
Wales	Chwarae Teg	Supports and promotes the role of women in the Welsh economy, offering skills development and training through the Ready SET Go project, and overseeing the provision of enterprise support to women in Wales. Tel: (029) 2047 8900 Website: **www.chwaraeteg.com**
Scotland	Association of Scottish Businesswomen (ASB)	Umbrella organisation for business and professional women's clubs in Scotland. Promotes women in business, and offers networking, an education programme, discussion forums and an awards dinner. Website: **www.businesswomenscotland.org/asbw**
	Enterprising Women	Provides training, support and guidance for women in the Glasgow area who are considering self-employment. Tel: (0141) 429 6314 Website: **www.enterprising-women.org.uk**
Northern Ireland	Women in Enterprise (WIE)	Non-profit-making company encouraging, supporting and empowering women into business and helping existing women entrepreneurs. Offers training, mentoring, advice and support. Tel: (028) 7136 6967 Website: **www.womeninenterprise.com**
	Women in Business Network	Networking organisation run by female business owners, offering information, training and discussion forums. Tel: 0845 607 6041 Website: **www.womeninbusinessnetwork.org.uk**

	Women into the Network (WIN) Ireland	Networking initiative based on the north east of England model, providing training, research, information and access to business support, and helping women return to work through self-employment. Website: **www.winireland.com**
	Aspire Micro Finance	Delivers micro loans and support services for women in disadvantaged rural areas who are interested in self-employment. Tel: (028) 9024 6245 Website: **www.aspire-loans.com**

What online help is available?

There are a number of Web-based online communities that can provide useful information, support and advice for women in business.

Organisation	Services offered
Aurora Women's Network	Provides networking events and services for entrepreneurial women. Tel: 0845 260 7777 Website: **www.network.auroravoice.com**
Everywoman	Online source of training, resources and support services for women in business. Tel: 0870 746 1800 Website: **www.everywoman.co.uk**
FunAfterBaby (FAB)	Online community for business mums to share ideas and expertise, including information on a number of business ideas, a discussion forum and tips on running a business. Website: **www.funafterbaby.co.uk**
Scottish business-women.com	Online community for advice on business start-up, networking, mentoring and information on women in business. Website: **www.bgateway.com/scottishbusinesswomen**
Women at Work	Online directory of services and products provided by women in the UK. Includes networking opportunities and events. Tel: (01223) 873349 Website: **www.womenatwork.co.uk**
Women Returner's Network	Online help and advice for women wanting to return to work or venture into self-employment. Website: **www.women-returners.co.uk**
Visible Women	E-business training and support for women aged over 50 who want to make the most of online business opportunities. Tel: (020) 8305 2222 Website: **www.visiblewomen.co.uk**

How can you find funding?

There are numerous funding schemes across the UK targeted specifically at women. There is no one single access point for these funding schemes, but for information on available Government-funded loans and grants, contact the organisations listed above under 'Government-funded business support'.

It's also worth contacting your local enterprise agencies for information on funding available in a particular area:

Area	Organisation	Website
England (and Wales)	National Federation of Enterprise Agencies (NFEA)	**www.nfea.com** (also includes a directory of enterprise agencies in Wales)
Scotland	Business Enterprise Scotland (BES) Highlands and Islands Enterprise	**www.bes.org.uk** **www.hie.co.uk**
Northern Ireland	Enterprise Northern Ireland	**www.enterpriseni.com**

COMMON MISTAKES
You lack basic business skills

Many women who start businesses often have useful experience, knowledge and contacts up their sleeves. However, if you lack basic business skills in areas such as marketing or IT, think about getting some extra training before you get too far down the line in setting up your business. Consult the Learndirect website at **www.learndirect-business.co.uk** to browse a directory of courses and find training opportunities which can be accessed online.

You don't ask for help

While there are lots of professional organisations that can give you help and support, don't forget to get extra advice from those living nearer to you. Try to join a local women's networking group so you can make useful contacts, gain confidence and learn from the experience of others.

USEFUL LINKS

Business Enterprise Scotland (BES):
www.bes.org.uk
Business Eye:
www.businesseye.org.uk
Business Gateway:
www.bgateway.com
Business Link:
www.businesslink.gov.uk
Enterprise Northern Ireland:
www.enterpriseni.com
Highlands and Islands Enterprise:
www.hie.co.uk
Invest Northern Ireland:
www.investni.com
National Federation of Enterprise
   Agencies (NFEA):
www.nfea.com
Scottish Enterprise:
www.scottish-enterprise.com
Women and Equality Unit:
www.womenandequalityunit.gov.uk

Business support for ethnic minorities

GETTING STARTED

If you want to set up your own business and you're from an ethnic minority, there's currently lots of business support available to you. It's estimated that people from ethnic minorities own and operate around 250,000 enterprises across the UK, representing about 12% of all businesses, and they contribute around £13 billion a year to the UK economy. Business start-up rates among ethnic minorities are generally higher than the general population. See **www.berr.gov.uk/files/file38528.pdf** for more information.

This actionlist looks at some of the initiatives aimed at supporting people from ethnic minorities who want to start their own businesses. It also signposts contact details of the organisations that can provide financial support, business advice and networking opportunities.

FAQS

Where can you get help and support?

When starting a business, people from ethnic minorities are more likely to turn to family members and friends for support or seek traditional bank finance, rather than investigate other forms of finance. But if you need funding for your business, think about contacting one of the many national support agencies specifically involved in supporting ethnic minority businesses (EMBs).

The Asian Business Federation (ABF) acts as a gateway for EMBs to access mainstream business support and training. It lobbies on behalf of Asian businesses and operates a number of initiatives, including the Food Smart Programme, a support programme for businesses in the food sector (**www. abfed.co.uk/index.asp?p=Business-Services&s=Food-Smart-Programme**) as well as other retail businesses (**www. abfed.co.uk**).

Black Enterprise helps EMBs to develop and grow through support, encouragement, education, training and finance. It publishes *Black Britain News*, the only regular publication for the African-Caribbean business community (see **www. blackbritain.co.uk/news**) and hosts the annual Black Enterprise Awards. It also aims to provide role models for other EMBs (**www.blackenterprise.co.uk**).

The Business Federation Partnership acts as a networking organisation for EMBs and advises the finance sector and national and local Government on their needs. Its training arm, the South London Ethnic Minority Business Association (SLEMBA) delivers training to EMBs and signposts other sources of support (**www. bem.org.uk**).

The majority of financial support schemes aimed at EMBs are run on a regional basis. The following outlines just some of the support that is available around the UK.

BABA (Birmingham Asian Business Association) provides a range of business development programmes and services to help Asian businesses make the most of opportunities for long-term survival and growth, including a group purchasing scheme that enables groups of similar businesses to purchase goods at a discounted price (**http://users. powernet. co.uk/baba/index.html**).

Black Business in Birmingham (3b) is an enterprise agency focused on the specific needs of African-Caribbean-owned businesses. It runs a range of programmes, including business support, start-up services, conferencing, IT facilities and enterprise development programmes. It also has a community-based finance initiative providing loans to start-ups and existing businesses (**www.3b.org.uk**).

The Ethnic Minorities Business Service provides business support for existing and start-up EMBs across the Bolton metropolitan area. It offers customised services to businesses in different sectors, with particular support programmes for businesses in the food, manufacturing, retail and service sectors. It also runs programmes to encourage enterprise among women and young people (**www.embs.co.uk**).

Business Works' Greenwich Business Development Centre provides a comprehensive range of business support for ethnic minority entrepreneurs who are thinking of starting a business in the boroughs of Greenwich, Bexley and Lewisham (**www.greenwich.gov.uk/ Greenwich/Business/ SupportAndAdvice/BusinessWorks/**).

The Ethnic Minority Enterprise Project offers business support services in the London borough of Tower Hamlets, including specialist support for restaurant businesses (**www.emep.co.uk/pnp_ restaurant_support.html**) and enterprises in the clothing sector (**www.emep.co.uk/ sew_east.html** and **www.emep.co.uk**).

The Gloucestershire Ethnic Minority Business Association promotes and supports the development of ethnic minority businesses in Gloucestershire. It provides business development training, seminars, and advice on all aspects of running a business. Its business centre also offers workspace on flexible terms (**www. gemba.org.uk**).

The Ethnic Business Support Programme (EBSP) helps entrepreneurs in Wales to set up and develop their businesses. It provides free advice and guidance to bridge the gap between established sources of business support and ethnic minority groups (**www.ebsp.org**).

The West Midlands Minority Business Forum is an independent advisory body representing the interests of enterprises owned and operated by people from minority ethnic communities across the West Midlands (**www.minority4business. co.uk**).

Enterprise4all North West provides a gateway to EMB support in the North West. It operates business support initiatives, including access to grants, training, export

advice and networking. It runs a number of specific programmes for start-up businesses, including a Business Plan assessment service and a business start-up toolkit and business directory (**www. enterprise4all.co.uk/ index.asp?p=New-Business-Start-Ups** and **www. enterprise4all.co.uk**).

MAKING IT HAPPEN

Whether or not you succeed in business should have nothing to do with your race and background. But it you're from an ethnic minority, it's worth contacting one of the above organisations for advice, support and possibly financial assistance as well.

COMMON MISTAKES
You have no clear business objective
Entrepreneurs are most likely to succeed if they have thought carefully about what they want to do, have a clear idea of their target customers, and have a complete understanding of the need of the market that they aim to satisfy. You need to know exactly what you want to achieve before you can make it happen. There is considerable support for EMBs, but getting the best advice for your own situation is often a case of a establishing a good personal rapport with someone within a supportive organisation.

You don't bother creating a strong business plan
Make sure you have a sound business plan from the outset. Recent research from Barclays Bank suggests that EMBs who have done the groundwork and developed their proposal with care are most likely to raise the finance they need. If you're trying to raise funds, you'll need to persuade a lender that you have a viable proposition and the determination to succeed. This means you need to carry out thorough market research, provide strong financial forecasts and be prepared to demonstrate your enthusiasm and personal commitment to any prospective lender.

USEFUL LINKS

Business Federation Partnership:
www.bem.org.uk

Commission for Racial Equality:
www.cre.gov.uk
ETHNOS:
www.ethnos.co.uk

Support for rural enterprises

GETTING STARTED

The UK's rural economy, and farmers in particular, are facing an unpredictable future, with an increasingly competitive global market affecting returns on food production. While agriculture remains essential to rural economies, its position in the overall economy is changing.

Residents of rural economies are responding to their changing economic circumstances by trying to enhance their income from sources other than traditional means. As a result, an increasing amount of support is being offered to rural businesses to help them maintain and diversify their operations, and create new opportunities to improve the countryside by creating sustainable enterprises.

This actionlist provides practical advice for rural enterprise owners, giving an overview of available sources of funding, details about specific funding schemes, as well as sources of further information.

MAKING IT HAPPEN

There are a number of UK-wide initiatives for small business owners working in rural communities, as detailed below.

Lantra is the Sector Skills Council for the environment and land-based sector. It's licensed by the Government to represent the interests of environmental and land-based industries in the UK. It works closely with industry employers to address a range of issues affecting businesses working in land management and production, animal health and welfare, and environmental industries. And it provides access to a range of qualifications and apprenticeships, plus National Occupational Standards: **www.lantra.co.uk**

Ruralnetuk is a rural regeneration charity that promotes living and working in the countryside by finding ways to help rural communities improve and strengthen their local economies. It works with support agencies to alleviate disadvantage and create social enterprises. It promotes collaboration, research and consultancy projects, and has specialist skills in Information Communications and Collaboration Technologies: **www.ruralnetuk.org**

Women in Rural Enterprise (WiRE) is a UK-wide networking and support organisation for women running rural enterprises. Its website features a rural marketplace where female entrepreneurs can market their products and services. It also provides access to networking events and news and views from women working in rural enterprises: **www.wireuk.org**

England

In England, the Department for Environment Food and Rural Affairs (Defra) operates numerous initiatives aimed at supporting rural enterprises.

The England Rural Development Programme is a European Community initiative to help rural communities improve the quality of life and economic prosperity in their communities. The programme provides support to help farmers diversify their activities and become more competitive, and to conserve and improve the environment: **www.defra.gov.uk/erdp/schemes/default.htm**

Under the Grants for Parish Plans initiative, **parish councils** can apply for grants to help them identify the needs of their communities. Funding is administered by the Rural Community Councils. For more information contact Defra (**www.defra.gov.uk/rural/communities/parish-planning.htm**) or Action with Communities in Rural England (ACRE) at: **www.acre.org.uk/zPROJECT_ParishPlans.htm**

Natural England was created by the

amalgamation of: English Nature; the landscape, access and recreation elements of the Countryside Agency; and the environmental land-management functions of the Rural Development Service. Its main objectives are the creation of a healthy and natural environment for England, sustainable use of the natural environment and a secure environmental future for rural economies. It delivers a number of programmes, outlined below:

Environmental Stewardship provides funding to farmers and other landowners to promote biodiversity, maintain and enhance landscape quality, protect historic and natural environments, and promote public access to, and understanding of the countryside: **www.naturalengland. org.uk/planning/grants-funding/ default.htm**

The **National Farm Attractions Network** is a co-operative group that provides assistance and support to farm and rural diversification enterprises. It offers guidance on issues such as planning legislation and business rates, marketing, promotion and publicity, grant aid and health and safety issues: **www. farmattractions.net**

The **Rural Crafts Association** organises exhibition space at agricultural, equestrian and horticultural shows that highlights the work of its members: **www. ruralcraftsassociation.co.uk**

An executive summary of the report 'Crafts in the English Countryside' can be downloaded from **www. craftsintheenglishcountryside.org.uk**.

Local and regional

Local and regional funding advice is also available from a number of sources, including Business Links, local authorities, regional development agencies and the Welsh Assembly Government. Examples of this support include the following:

The **Forestry Commission's English Woodland Grant Scheme** offers six grants designed to sustain and increase the public benefits of existing woodlands, and to help create new woodlands. The grants include support for planning, assessing, regenerating, improving, managing and creating woodland. Depending on your activities, you may be able to apply for grant funding of between £300 and £1,800: **www.forestry.gov.uk/forestry/ infd-6dccen**

Each **Regional Development Agency (RDA)** in England has some form of rural strategy to help rural enterprises trying to find information, advice, grants and other sources of funding in their particular area. A full list of RDAs is available at **www. englandsrdas.com**

The **Commission for Rural Communities** tackles rural disadvantage. Its website is a useful resource which publishes information, news and details of events relating to rural issues: **www. ruralcommunities.gov.uk**

Business Link Devon and Cornwall operates a number of grant schemes for rural businesses. Its Capital Grants programme provides funding for food and drink businesses in Cornwall and the Isles of Scilly. The Grants provide up to 50% of eligible project costs of food and drink producers and primary agricultural producers. Grants of up to £75,000 are available: **www.bldc.co.uk/downloads/ CFDPS_21.02.05.pdf**

Cumbria Rural Enterprise Agency provides free business advice and support for people in rural communities aiming to start a business in the Eden & South Lakes district. Training consists of five full days or ten evening sessions. Topics covered include business planning and financial management, promotion and sales, taxation, and health and safety: **www. crea.co.uk/startup_training.htm**

The **Rural Enterprise Gateway** is a one-stop shop service for rural businesses in Cheshire, Warrington and Halton. It works with partner organisations to provide support services, from architects and planners to environmental experts: **www.ruralenterprisegateway.co.uk**

There are numerous **smallholders' associations** across the UK. They provide advice and information for their members, including providing outlets for their produce. A directory of smallholding organisations can be found at: **www.blpbooks.co.uk/smallholding_ organisations. php**

Smallholders Online provides information and advice about operating a smallholding, from a garden to a family farm. It's particularly aimed at those interested in sustainable food production: **www.smallholders.org**

Wales

The **Welsh Assembly Government** provides a range of advice services and grants to support rural businesses and communities; including a Processing and Marketing Grant, a Farming Advisory Service, Quality Food Scheme, and plans to develop the supply chain: **http:// new.wales.gov.uk/topics/ environmentcountryside/food_and_ market_development/rdpschemes/ ?lang=en**

A number of local authorities and enterprise agencies offer support schemes and grants to rural enterprises. Visit **www.direct.gov.uk** for a list of local authorities in England and **www. direct.gov.uk/en/Dl1/Directories/ DevolvedAdministrations/DG_10014393** for details of devolved administrations in Scotland, Northern Ireland and Wales. Visit **www.nfea.com** for the contact details of your nearest enterprise agency in England.

Don't forget there's general Government support available to businesses in the form of grants to encourage capital investment, the employment of graduates, assistance with research and development costs, and exporting. Details of these schemes can be found at **www.berr.gov.uk/bbf/BSS/ page28879.html**

Successful diversification projects can help to attract new people and businesses into rural areas, helping to build your potential customer base. There are also bound to be publicity opportunities in certain activities in rural communities that'll bring attention to your business and help to attract customers from further afield.

USEFUL LINKS

Commission for Rural Communities:
www.ruralcommunities.gov.uk
The Country Land and Business Association:
www.cla.org.uk
Department for Environment, Food and Rural Affairs (Defra):
www.defra.gov.uk
Farmers' Markets.net:
www.farmersmarkets.net
National Farmers' Union (NFU):
www.nfuonline.com
The Tourism Society:
www.tourismsociety.org
Women in Rural Enterprise (WiRE):
www.wireuk.org

Support for social enterprises

GETTING STARTED

Social enterprises are organisations which fulfil a social purpose and which earn all of their income through trading. Examples of social enterprises include community businesses and credit unions.

According to the Government's Annual Small Business Survey 2005 quoted by the Social Enterprise Coalition, there are at least 55,000 social enterprises in the UK, with a combined turnover of £27 billion a year. They account for 5% of all businesses with employees. See **www.socialenterprise.org.uk/page.aspx?SP=1345** for more information.

This actionlist provides details of support agencies and organisations, and sources of finance for social enterprises, with details of specific funding schemes.

FAQS

I run a social enterprise: who can I approach for support?

Like any business, social enterprises need access to high-quality business support, advice and training. Many social enterprises are under-funded, particularly at start-up, and making sure they have enough funds to grow and develop should be an important priority for owners.

A number of regional and national organisations and agencies currently provide support and funding to help social enterprises.

National funding is available through the following sources.

- **Loan finance** may be more easily available to social enterprises from community development organisations and micro-finance institutions, including Community Development Finance Institutions (CDFIs), rather than from conventional sources such as banks and building societies. CDFIs specialise in providing finance to new and growing businesses, including social enter-prises and firms in disadvantaged areas. Most CDFIs are members of the Community Development Finance Association (CDFA) which can provide further information. Con-tact them by phone on 020 7430 0222 or online at: **www.cdfa.org.uk**
- **Backscratchers** is a support network for social enterprises, offering networking and expertise-sharing opportunities. Registra-tion is currently free but in future a £10 membership charge will apply (see the website for up-to-date information). Eligible projects may also qualify for help with online promotion, web design and finding resources. Contact them by phone on 07763 664845 or online at: **www.backscratchers. org**
- The **Community Action Network (CAN)** is a social franchising organisation for the development, promotion and support of social enterprises. The CAN Pilot toolkit helps social entrepreneurs to plan, monitor and evaluate the potential success and profitability of their ideas. Based in London but with regional associates in Wales and Northern Ireland as well as some other areas in England, CAN also runs a social franchising programme that allows social enterprises to have their ideas replicated by other social entrepreneurs. For more information, contact them by phone on 0845 456 2537 or online at: **www.can-online.org.uk**
- The **Social Enterprise Unit** acts as a focal point and a co-ordinator for policy making on social enterprise, addressing the bar-riers to growth faced by social entre-preneurs, and identifying and spreading examples of good practice. Contact them by phone on: (020) 7276 6400 or online at: **www.cabinetoffice.gov.uk/third_sector/social_enterprise**
- The **Esmee Fairbairn Foundation's** 'Social Change: Enterprise and Independence' programme helps social enterprises to improve their performance. See **www. esmeefairbairn.org.uk/programmes/sd.**

html for further information and to check on current availability of funding programmes. For more information, call 020 7297 4700.

- The **School for Social Entrepreneurs (SSE)** is a UK-wide programme that provides training to enable people to use their entrepreneurial abilities for social benefit. For more information, call 020 8981 0300 or go to: **www.sse.org.uk**
- The **Small Firms Loan Guarantee (SFLG)** is a form of debt finance aimed at businesses that have problems raising loan finance because they are unable to offer any security. Under the scheme, the Government guarantees 75% of loans of between £5,000 and £250,000. In return for the guarantee, the business must pay the Government a 2% premium per year on the outstanding balance. Call 020 7215 5000 for more information, or visit online at: **www.berr.gov.uk/bbf/small-business/ info-business-owners/access-to-finance/ sflg/page37607.html**
- **Social Firms UK** aims to generate jobs for disabled people through the creation of social firms. It currently has more than 300 members and plays an important role in lobbying and disseminating news. Visit online at **www.socialfirms.co.uk** or call 01737 764021.
- The **Social Enterprise Training and Support Consortium (SETAS)** is a nationwide source of information and support for social enterprises. Its website offers a directory of business support for social enterprises in the UK. See **www.setas.co.uk** for further information.
- The **UK Social Investment Forum (UKSIF)** is a membership network for socially responsible investment. It has more than 200 members, including CDFIs, banks, law firms, fund managers and consultants. Call 020 7749 9950 for more information, or go to: **www.uksif.org**
- **UnLtd**—the Foundation for Social Entrepreneurs—supports social entrepreneurs across the UK. Its UnLtd Millennium awards offer practical support and funding for social entrepreneurs in the UK. Call 020

7566 1100 for more information, or visit: **www.unltd.org.uk**
- The **Big Boost** award provides finance of between £250 and £5,000 to help young people aged between 11–25 deliver projects with social benefits for their area. Find out more online at **www.thebigboost.org.uk** or call 0845 410 20 30.

Funding via the regions has become more robust in recent years, and current sources include:

- the **North East Social Enterprise Partnership**, which works to support the development of support agencies for social enterprises in the north east of England. They can be reached on the phone on 0191 427 2150, or online at: **www. nesep.co.uk**
- the **Adventure Capital Fund**, which provides finance and support packages to businesses in England that work to improve their local communities. It provides seed capital for start-ups of between £25,000 and £100,000, working capital of between £25,000 and £100,000 and major investment capital of up to £400,000 for the purchase of buildings and refurbishment costs. See **www.adventurecapitalfund. org.uk** for further information on funding criteria and availability, or call 020 7488 3455.
- **RISE-South West**, a membership organisation open to anyone working in the social enterprise sector which promotes the development of sustainable social enterprises in the south west of England. Its website, **www.rise-sw.co.uk** includes a directory of agencies providing advice and support. Alternatively, call them on 01392 435775.
- the **South East Social Enterprise Partnership**, which brings together social enterprises, development trusts and co-operatives, helping them to pool their knowledge and resources for the benefit of the social enterprise sector in the region. See **www.sesep.org.uk** for further information.
- **Social Enterprise East of England (SEEE)**, a network of social enterprises, advice and support organisations in the region. It promotes the establishment of social enter-

prises and lobbies key decision makers on policy affecting the sector. For more information, call 01234 834 711 or visit: **www.seee.co.uk**

- **Social Enterprise East Midlands (SEEM)**, which brings together key stakeholders in social enterprise in the region, to create an environment in which social enterprises can grow, and provides details of funding initiatives. Call on 0115 845 6434 or go to: **www.seem.uk.net**
- **Social Enterprise London**, which provides services aimed at building capacity, spreading best practice and creating a supportive infrastructure for social enterprises in the city. It operates free open surgeries for start-up social enterprises, and fee-based services for established businesses. For more information, go to **www.sel.org.uk** or call them on 020 7022 1920.
- **Social Enterprise Yorkshire and the Humber**, which represents the needs of social enterprises in the region to Government. Its membership is made up of social enterprise development agencies across the region. See **www.seyh.org.uk** for further information.
- **Senscot**, an independent network for social enterprises and their support organisations in Scotland. It provides information and support services to ventures that aim to tackle the country's social problems, particularly in deprived areas. You can contact them by phone on 0131 220 4104 or online at: **www.senscot.net**

- the **Scottish Social Enterprise Coalition**, which lobbies the Scottish Parliament with regard to policy affecting social enterprise. Its membership comprises both social enterprises and business support organisations. Find out more online at **www. ssec.org.uk** or by phone at 0131 557 1516.
- **Co-operatives UK**, a membership organisation for co-operative enterprise throughout the UK. See **www.cooperatives-uk.coop/ live/welcome.asp** for more details.
- the **Development Trusts Association (DTA)**, the representative body for the UK's development trusts. You can call 0845 458 8336 for more information or go to: **www.dta.org.uk**

USEFUL LINKS

Development Trusts Association (DTA): **www.dta.org.uk**
Directory of Social Change (DSC): **www.dsc.org.uk**
Social Enterprise Coalition: **www.socialenterprise.org.uk**

Business support for the over-50s

GETTING STARTED

If you're over 50 and thinking of going into business, you're not alone. Figures from the Office of National Statistics (ONS) have shown that the number of people aged 50 plus who are doing just that is on the increase. In fact, according to the ONS, self-employment among those aged over 50 is now more common than among those under 50 (see **www.statistics.gov.uk/cci/nugget.asp?id=1266** for more information).

Though most 'olderpreneurs' are in their 50s, a number of people in their 60s and even 70s also set up new businesses. Many over-50s decide to go it alone after being made redundant and around 43% of those seriously considering starting a business after 50, go on to do so (see the PRIME report at **www.primeinitiative.org.uk/newsmaster03/docs/ PRIME_interim_report_on_olderpreneur_outcomes_2006.pdf**).

This actionlist summarises the main sources of support, advice and finance for older business owners in the UK. It includes Government-funded business support schemes, as well as independent and online organisations offering support to older people in business.

FAQS

Where can you get help and support?

A number of schemes specifically provide business support for the over-50s. Legislation introduced in the UK on 1 October 2006 has made it illegal to discriminate against a worker under the age of 65 on the grounds of age. So making someone redundant or barring them from training or promotion because they're too old (or too young) is against the law.

Efforts have been made to ensure that business and enterprise support doesn't exclude the over-50s from these services. And there's now more open and accessible support for the over-50s, with incentives to encourage people to think about self-employment.

There's a wide range of help for older business owners from many groups and organisations throughout the UK. They'll offer support and advice to anyone over 50 who wants to start or develop their own businesses. These organisations include:

- PRIME (The Prince's Initiative for Mature Enterprise)—a not-for-profit organisation helping those aged over 50 into self-employment in England and Northern Ireland. PRIME Cymru is a sister organisation providing similar support in Wales. PRIME provides guidance and information about networking and sources of funding available to the older entrepreneur who's thinking about starting their own business. PRIME also provides awareness workshops for over-50s toying with the idea of possibly working for themselves. The organisation's website features discussion forums and a business club that has listings of events and case studies for the self-employed. It can also refer people to a network of advisers in partner organisations, a list of which can be found at **www.primeinitiative.org.uk/ prime_locations.php**.

- New Deal 50 Plus is part of the Government's New Deal initiative and helps people over 50 to find employment or training, or to start their own business. It's available to individuals in the UK who've been receiving Income Support, Jobseeker's Allowance, Incapacity Benefit, Severe Disablement Allowance, Pension Credit, or a combination of benefits in the previous six months.

  Those who join the programme, available through JobCentre Plus, are put in touch with an adviser who will provide support and advice while you look for work, or get your business started. Website: **www.jobcentreplus.gov.uk/JCP/ Customers/New_Deal/New_Deal-_50_plus/index.html**

What online help is available?

There are a number of web-based online communities providing information, support and advice to the over-50s thinking of starting a business:

- Seniority UK (**www.seniority.co.uk**) is a forum for people over 50 that enables them to share experiences and knowledge. It includes articles on a range of subjects, like starting a business and trading online.
- The DirectGov Internet portal has a section dedicated to the over 50s (**www. over-50.gov.uk**). It provides practical guidance and resources covering working, learning, retirement and pensions, benefits, travel and leisure and home, care and community. The Working to Suit You section includes information on becoming self-employed after 50. Details can be found at **www.direct.gov.uk/en/Over50s/Working/ WorkingToSuitYou/DG_10027003**
- Saga also provides online information for the over-50s who are thinking about starting a business. Visit **www.saga.co.uk/ magazine/lifechanges/startabusiness/ RightBusinessForSelf-Employed.asp** for further information.
- The Olderpreneur is another network forum for those over 50 wanting to start or who are already running their own business. See **www.olderpreneur.net**

Other sources of support

There are a number of sources of financial support that provide funding for businesses started by entrepreneurs of all ages. However, Enterprise agencies and local authorities in some areas run schemes, events and provide support specifically for those aged 50 or over.

The National Federation of Enterprise Agencies (NFEA) is a network of independent local enterprise agencies that gives advice and support to pre-start, start-up and micro businesses, including: those started by the over 50s across England. It runs a number of schemes, including the New Entrepreneurship Scholarship programme, which aims to remove barriers to starting up a business in the most disadvantaged parts in the country; and the Small Business Advice Service, which provides Internet-based advice to entrepreneurs, owner-managers and the self-employed of all ages. In conjunction with Barclays Bank, it runs a series of half-day events across England aimed at helping people to develop their business ideas, as well as supporting those who are almost ready to start trading (**www.nfea.com**).

Inbiz is a network helping individuals in England and Scotland, including those aged over 50, to develop entrepreneurial skills. It focuses on enterprise creation with start-up, micro and established small businesses, and its website features information on planning, getting started and obtaining further support. Its BusinessClub365 offers a range of useful online services, such as a panel of experts, online business tests, a Virtual PA, bookkeeping and secretarial services (**www.inbiz.co.uk**).

Invest Northern Ireland's Start a Business Programme is available to individuals of any age who want to start a business. The programme is free and provides an advisory service, a financial planning service, and a business course focusing on sales and marketing, financial management, legal issues, ICT and general business practice (**www.sabp.co.uk**).

Scottish Enterprise is the economic development agency for Scotland, working with 12 enterprise agencies. Scottish Enterprise and its local partners run the Business Gateway, which provides support for start-up businesses, including those started by the over 50s. It also signposts sources of grants and other financial support (**www.scottish-enterprise.com/ sedotcom_home/services-to-business/ how_to_start_a_business.htm? siblingtoggle=1**).

Highlands and Islands Enterprise provides business support, training and learning opportunities to businesses and community projects in the Highland and Islands of Scotland. Its website gives access to a range of information on starting a business, and signposts sources of financial support for all businesses (**www.hie.co.uk**).

COMMON MISTAKES
You start up a business without basic skills

'Olderpreneurs' tend to start up businesses based on a hobby or interest, so they can be thwarted by a lack of basic business skills in areas such as marketing or IT. Don't forget your aim is to make your business a success—so you need to know how to balance the books, prepare accounts and so on. Local colleges often run courses in basic business management, providing guidance for those with little practical experience. Consult the Learndirect website at **www.learndirect-business.co.uk** to browse a directory of courses.

You give up before you get started

If you're over 50 and want to set up your own business, remember that there's a great deal of support available. Contact the organisations above, concentrating at first on those that look as though they best suit your circumstances and might be able to help. Think about what you want to achieve and why: being over 50 is not a barrier to business success.

Also, these days the law is on your side if you want to get funding to set up your business. In other words, no one can deny you just because of your age—even though others might be starting to think about retirement. So if you come up against a brick wall when trying to get your business off the ground, keep going. And don't be surprised or upset if you find yourself taking advice from someone half your age!

USEFUL LINKS

Business Gateway (Scotland):
www.bgateway.com
Enterprise Northern Ireland:
www.enterpriseni.com
Highlands and Islands Enterprise:
www.hie.co.uk
Invest Northern Ireland:
www.investni.com
National Federation of Enterprise Agencies (NFEA):
www.nfea.com
PRIME:
www.primeintiative.org.uk and **www.primebusinessclub.com**
PRIME Cymru:
www.prime-cymru.co.uk
Scottish Enterprise:
www.scottish-enterprise.com

Business support for the under-30s

GETTING STARTED

Starting a business can be a daunting prospect at any age, but for young entrepreneurs, it can be an even greater challenge. The lack of practical business experience, knowledge and contacts is often directly responsible for the failure of many fledgling ventures set up by young people.

However, according to research from national business education and enterprise charity Business Dynamics (**www.businessdynamics.org.uk**), the number of young people choosing to work for themselves has risen rapidly since 2000, with a particular rise in the number of young women starting their own businesses.

This actionlist looks at the enterprise initiatives aimed at supporting young people starting their own businesses. It also signposts contact details of providers of business support and advice for young entrepreneurs and gives useful links to sources of further information.

FAQS
Where can you get help and support?

A number of agencies and initiatives will provide support, encouragement and advice for young entrepreneurs planning to start their own businesses. Although most concentrate on offering training and support programmes so that young entrepreneurs gain the basic skills they'll need, some specialise in helping them to find finance.

The Prince's Trust

The Prince's Trust is aimed at young people aged 18–30 who've come up with an idea for a business, but can't raise sufficient funds from other sources. In England, start-up support includes low-interest loans of up to £4,000 for sole traders and £5,000 for partnerships. Grants of up to £1,500 are also available in special circumstances. In Scotland, financial support is offered to 18–25-year-olds through The Prince's Trust partner charity, The Prince's Scottish Youth Business Trust. These grants and loans aren't currently available in Wales.

Grants for test marketing are also available in England and Scotland. These provide up to £250 to help entrepreneurs find out whether there's a market for their product or service.

The Prince's Trust will also put you in touch with a business mentor who'll provide advice, and give you access to legal and other helplines. It publishes a range of start-up guides, with topics ranging from writing business plans, finding premises and managing finances to understanding tax, and sales and marketing. The Prince's Trust has offices in England, Northern Ireland, Scotland and Wales (**www.princestrust.org.uk** and **www.psybt. org.uk**).

Young Enterprise

Young Enterprise provides young people with a taster of what it would be like to run their own business. Through a series of programmes in schools, colleges and universities, this UK-wide charity helps people under 25 to engage in business through the 'learning and doing' principle.

The Company Programme gives students aged 15–19 the chance to set up their own company over the course of an academic year. Similarly, the Graduate Programme provides students in higher education with the opportunity to set up and run their own company, enabling them to consider self-employment as a future career option (**www.young-enterprise.org.uk**; **www.yeni.co.uk**; **www.yes.org.uk**).

Shell LiveWIRE

Shell LiveWIRE provides free advice and support for young people aged 16–30 across the UK who are interested in starting their own business. It also hosts a national competition, the LiveWIRE Young Entrepreneur Awards, for new business start-ups, with a first prize of £10,000 to help develop business ideas. See **www.shell-livewire.org** for more information.

New Deal

New Deal for Young People provides the opportunity for applicants to trade as self-employed for up to 25 weeks, without losing current State benefits entitlements. The programme provides training towards accredited qualifications and is designed to stimulate and develop entrepreneurship among people aged 18–24. It's not available in Northern Ireland.

The programme also provides access to a business adviser, help with funding applications, access to office resources and continued support for the lifetime of your business. See **www.jobcentreplus.gov.uk/ JCP/Customers/New_Deal/New_Deal_ for_Young_People/index.html** for information.

The Big Boost

The Big Boost is part of the Big Lottery Fund's Young People's Fund. It assists entrepreneurs in England, aged 11–25, to set up projects that have social benefits, by providing grants for revenue and capital projects. Awards of between £250 and £1,000 are available to those aged 11–15, and those aged 16 in full-time education. For young people aged 15–25, those aged 16 in Year 12, or those who have left education, awards range between £500 and £5,000 (**www. thebigboost.org.uk**).

Connexions

Connexions provides advice and support to youngsters aged 13–19 (25 if disabled) in England, providing them with the information they need to achieve their goals. Its 'Start your own business' section should be their first port of call (**www. connexions-direct.com/ index.cfm?pid= 78&catalogueContentID= 121**).

Graduating to Enterprise

Graduating to Enterprise is a Welsh Government-funded initiative providing free support services to graduates starting a business in Wales. Its Small Business Programme includes business skills training, mentoring, consultancy and advice on grant availability (**www.g2e.co.uk**).

Other sources of support

There are a number of sources of financial support that provide funding for businesses started by entrepreneurs of all ages, but which may be of specific interest to the under-30s. These include:

- The National Endowment for Science, Technology and the Arts (NESTA), which runs the Insight Out programme aimed at the creation of creative businesses. In England, Wales and Northern Ireland, successful applicants receive business and professional development training. Those who complete the training can then apply for up to £5,000 of business start-up funding from a total of £20,000 per region. See **www.nesta.org.uk/programmes/insight-_out/index.aspx** for further information.

- In Scotland, NESTA operates the Starter for 6 programme, which provides training for innovative business start-ups and a facility to apply for up to £10,000 of grant funding. See **www.nesta.org.uk/programmes/ starter_for_6/index.aspx** for further information.

- In conjunction with The Prince's Trust and the Association of Business Schools, The National Federation of Enterprise Agencies (NFEA) manages the New Entrepreneur Scholarship programme (**www.nesprogramme.org**). This offers start-up funding of up to £1,500, aimed at people from disadvantaged areas who want to start a business, including those under 30.

- Although the Citizens Advice Bureau (CAB) serves people of all ages, it can provide young people with useful advice. It provides a self-employment checklist available at: **www.adviceguide.org.uk/index/life/ employment/self-employment_checklist. htm**

- Enterprise Northern Ireland's Start a Business Programme provides advice, training and support to would-be entrepreneurs, including those aged under 30. This free programme provides advice on sales and marketing, financial management, legal and statutory requirements, ICT and general business practices. It also provides access to grant support and small business loans. Visit **www.enterpriseni.com/Content.asp?nSectionId=92**

- Finance Wales provides access to loans, equity, mezzanine finance and management skills for small businesses in Wales. It operates a number of funds available to all businesses, but may be of specific interest to those started by the under-30s. These include the Wales Creative IP fund for creative businesses in the media and new media sectors, and the Wales Spinout Programme for businesses created as the result of research in universities. See **www.financewales.co.uk/eng/support.php/c_type=content~c_id=29~sM_id=10** for further information.

- Inbiz is a network helping individuals, including those aged under 30, to develop entrepreneurial skills. It focuses on enterprise creation with start-up, micro and established small businesses. Its website features information on planning, getting started and obtaining further support. Its BusinessClub365 offers a range of useful online services, such as a panel of experts, online business tests, a Virtual PA, bookkeeping and secretarial services. Services are currently available across England and Scotland (**www.inbiz.co.uk**).

MAKING IT HAPPEN

Young entrepreneurs should always consider gaining some relevant experience before starting a business, so if you're at the beginning of your business career, try to get some hands-on experience.

Successful businesses are usually started by people with some suitable knowledge or experience about their specific business activity and type of product or service. The information, experience and contacts that young people can gather from studying a relevant course, volunteering or taking a work-experience placement in a related business or field can be invaluable.

Once you're sure you want to start up your own business, contact the organisations above which seem most appropriate to you and best suited to your needs—regardless of whether you're after funding or just some helpful advice.

COMMON MISTAKES
You lose sight of your target market

Market research is vital for all entrepreneurs. Before you even think about getting your business off the ground—or writing your business plan—focus on which customers your proposed product or service is targeted at. You need to get this right before you do anything else.

You lack basic training

It's no good having a brilliant business idea if you lack the basic skills to put your proposal into action. Local colleges often run useful courses in basic business management—covering budgeting, writing a business plan, customer service, managing staff, marketing and so on. Consult the City and Guilds website at **www.city-and-guilds.co.uk** to browse courses.

USEFUL LINKS

The Big Boost:
www.thebigboost.org.uk
Business Dynamics:
www.businessdynamics.org.uk
InBiz:
www.inbiz.co.uk
National Endowment for Science, Technology and the Arts (NESTA)
www.nesta.org.uk
The National Federation of Enterprise Agencies (NFEA):
www.nfea.com

Applying for grants

GETTING STARTED

Business support in the form of grants to help you start a business or develop specific projects can provide much-needed finance, and sometimes expertise, to help your business grow.

You can get a grant for a number of business activities or projects around the UK. Grant funding is intended to support and develop enterprise in the hope that it will also provide a boost to employment and the local economy. A variety of organisations and Government departments offer grants—and as a small business, you may be eligible to access some of these.

This actionlist describes how grants work and the types of grant that are available. It also provides information about where to find grants and how to apply for them.

FAQS

What is a grant?

A grant is financial assistance, usually to start a business or for a specific project, which is given to your business by an awarding body. The finance provided by a grant means that your business may be able to undertake a specific project that otherwise wouldn't have been possible. Such a project might involve the initial business start-up, developing a new product or buying equipment.

A grant is usually a one-off payment and provides funding that covers a percentage of the costs of the project—normally, you or your business will have to meet some of the costs too. Unlike a loan, a grant doesn't usually have to be repaid, unless you don't keep to the specific terms and conditions under which it's been given.

What can you get a grant for?

Grants are available for a variety of projects, but each individual scheme will offer funding for a specific purpose. Whether you qualify for a grant can also depend on factors such as the type of business you run, the size of your business, whether the project you want the funding for will create jobs, and where your business is based.

Grants may be available to cover one or more of the following activities:

- advertising, marketing and promotion
- business expansion and relocation
- business start-up and market testing

- investment in capital equipment
- co-operatives and community enterprises
- product design
- environmental improvements
- exporting
- improving business premises
- information technology (IT) and e-commerce
- new technology and innovation
- recruitment and training
- research and development (R&D)
- security

Note that you're most unlikely to get a grant just to increase your working capital or provide a lump sum towards the organic growth of your business.

Will you be eligible for a grant?

If you don't ask, you don't get! But most grants in the UK have strict eligibility criteria or specific exclusions—for example, for certain locations or industry sectors. Although individual schemes vary, there are a few common themes across most grants.

Some areas of the UK have their own grants or specific schemes targeting social deprivation or high unemployment. Other grants are only available to businesses of a certain size, measured by turnover or the number of employees.

Certain sectors, including shipbuilding, coal, steel, agriculture and transport, are subject to special restrictions. Manufacturing businesses are more likely than others to qualify for grant support, while retail businesses are probably least likely to qualify.

The other thing to remember is that most grants aren't available retrospectively. For instance, if you are planning to start a new business you should apply for any appropriate grants well before you intend to begin trading. You won't usually be eligible for this kind of funding if you've already started to trade, and if you've already bought the equipment you want a grant for, it's unlikely that your application will be successful.

Who offers grants?

A large number of publicly funded groups provide financial assistance to businesses. And the awarding bodies for grants may be European, national or local organisations. At a local and regional level, grants may be available from organisations such as:

- local authorities (go to **www.direct.gov.uk** for contact details)
- Enterprise agencies (see **www.nfea.com**, **www.bes.org.uk** and **www. enterpriseni. com**)
- Government Offices (GO) for the English Regions (**www.gos.gov.uk**)
- Business Link (England—**www.businesslink. gov.uk**)
- Business Gateway (Scotland—**www. bgateway.com**)
- Business Eye (Wales—**www.businesseye. org.uk**)
- Invest Northern Ireland (**www.investni.com**)
- Highlands and Islands Enterprise (HIE— **www.hie.co.uk**)
- Regional Development Agencies (RDAs— **www.englandsrdas.com**)
- Chambers of Commerce (**www. chamberonline.co.uk**)
- Learning and Skills Council (LSC— **www.lsc.gov.uk**)

Nationally, grants are available from various Government departments and agencies, such as:

- The Department for Business, Enterprise and Regulatory Reform (DBERR—**www. berr.gov.uk**)

- UK Trade & Investment (UKTI— **www.uktradeinvest.gov.uk**)
- The Department for Environment, Food and Rural Affairs (Defra—**www.defra.gov.uk**)
- The Scottish Executive (**www.scotland. gov.uk**)
- The Welsh Assembly Government (**www. wales.gov.uk**)

Grants are also available for business owners aged 18–30 from organisations like the Prince's Trust (**www.princes-trust. org.uk**), and for businesses in specific sectors from organisations such as the UK's Arts Councils (**www.artscouncil.org.uk**, **www.scottisharts.org.uk**, **www.artswales.org.uk** and **www.artscouncil-ni.org**).

MAKING IT HAPPEN

How you should apply for a grant will vary from scheme to scheme. However, these are some of the general stages that will apply to most situations.

Before applying:

- To find out what grant funding is available in your area and for your particular project, the best places to start are your local Business Link, Business Gateway, HIE, Business Eye or Invest Northern Ireland office. Most will have a directory of assistance available locally, nationally and at a European level. Advisers will be able to put you in touch with the relevant grant-awarding bodies and to help you through the application process.
- Contact the awarding body and check your project meets the specified eligibility criteria of the scheme, to see whether it's actually worth applying. As grant application forms can be very long and may take a lot of time and effort to complete, it's worth finding out about your chances before you spend hours filling in forms. So ask the awarding body for more detailed information about the grant before they send you an application form.
- Remember you'll have to prove that your business has a genuine need for grant assistance.

Most schemes will require you to supply a project plan or proposal, or frequently a business plan, providing information such as:

- a project description detailing the aim of the project and how it will benefit your business
- who will run the project, and what experience, knowledge and skills they have
- the total cost of the project, and how much money you're asking for
- the length of the project and key deadlines
- the location of the project
- why the project needs grant funding and what would happen if the support wasn't provided
- how you intend to fund your share of the project's costs
- how the project complies with any criteria set by the grant provider
- details about your business, when it was set up, its activities and so on
- financial information about your business—possibly including accounts and forecasts

When making the application, keep the following points in mind:

- If you're after funding from a new scheme, apply as soon as possible after it's launched as the chances of a successful application are always highest then.
- Read any guidance notes that are supplied with the application forms. These will tell you how to complete each form and could save you a lot of time and effort in the long run.
- Application forms vary from grant to grant. Make sure you follow the format required, are clear and concise, and include all the information relevant to the grant you are applying for.
- For national and European grants, you may have to submit two forms. First, you'll have to fill in a short form for a basic assessment of your eligibility for the grant. Then you'll need to fill in a second form which will be much longer, providing detailed information about your business and the project you intend to undertake.
- If you can, speak to someone involved with administering the grant to get help with completing the form. Alternatively, depending on how complicated the form is, it may

be worth asking your business adviser or accountant for help with your application.
- Remember that your business plan should provide a lot of the detail for your grant application. Make sure the plan is up to date, and includes information about your experience, future proposals and financial requirements.

When you've completed the application form, check it over and make sure you've supplied all the information required. If your application is incomplete, it will take longer to process and is more likely to be rejected. Also, if you provide incorrect information, any grant may subsequently be reclaimed.

If your grant application is declined, ask for feedback about why it failed, so you've got some ideas on how to improve your future applications.

COMMON MISTAKES
You expect immediate funding

After you've submitted your grant application, you'll probably have to wait some time before you get a decision, ranging from a few weeks for local grants to a year for national or European grants. So don't forget to consider this when applying for funding. If you need immediate cash for your project, applying for a grant is probably not your best option.

You don't take care with your application

Don't forget to contact the grant provider before pursuing an application, and check whether you're eligible or not. Make sure you can prove you have a genuine need for a grant—and that without the grant the project would be unable to proceed. Write your application proposal to match the awarding body's objectives. Many awarding organisations prefer to see specific targets and results that are compatible with their own objectives. If possible, mention any benefits your project will bring—whether to your local community, the economy or the environment.

You forget your own cash contribution

Remember that you'll probably be required to meet some of the costs of the project (usually at least 50%), so check you're able to provide the extra finance. Send in a detailed business and project plan and wait until you've received written confirmation that your application has been successful before you start committing finance to a project.

You lose sight of your business focus

Too many businesses put all their efforts into chasing grant aid, neglecting their core business purpose in the process. This is a big mistake. The first step is to decide what your business needs, then look at what this might cost to put into place. Finally, explore whether grant aid might contribute towards the cost. Talk to your business adviser and people from businesses similar to yours for more advice about whether applying for a grant is a good idea.

USEFUL LINKS
Business Enterprise Scotland (BES):
www.bes.org.uk

Business Eye:
www.businesseye.org.uk
Business Gateway:
www.bgateway.com
Business Link:
www.businesslink.gov.uk
Enterprise Northern Ireland:
www.enterpriseni.com
Highlands and Islands Enterprise:
www.hie.co.uk
Invest Northern Ireland:
www.investni.com
National Federation of Enterprise
   Agencies (NFEA):
www.nfea.com
The Prince's Trust:
www.princes-trust.org.uk
Scottish Executive:
www.scotland.gov.uk
Welsh Assembly Government:
www.wales.gov.uk

Benefiting from grants for developing new products

GETTING STARTED

Innovation is the successful exploitation of new ideas, and is regarded as a key business process that helps UK businesses compete in the global marketplace, and to research and develop new products. The government is understandably keen to make sure that innovation, research and development play a role in businesses of all sizes, and as this actionlist explains, offers support to help them develop new product ranges.

The Department for Business, Enterprise and Regulatory Reform (DBERR, formerly the DTI) and a number of other organisations provide a range of grants and assistance that offer practical support and encouragement to businesses at all stages of the innovation process. They are available to assist research and development of new technologies and to encourage collaborative development projects. Support is also available for businesses located in 'assisted areas' and technical academic expertise can be accessed by businesses through Knowledge Transfer Partnerships (KTPs).

FAQS

What type of grants are available to assist innovation?

Innovation is often under the spotlight these days, and there are a good number of sources of financial assistance to support it, ranging from local authority grants to Government support and European Union (EU) initiatives. As you may imagine, competition is high and these grants often come with strict and challenging criteria.

MAKING IT HAPPEN

The Technology Programme

The Technology Programme is a government initiative which aims to help businesses with research, development and innovation activities. Up to 2006, £320 million has been made available to businesses in the form of grants to support research and development in technology areas identified by the Technology Strategy Board (which is made up of experienced business leaders). A further £100 million was announced in the 2007 Budget to help UK business develop new technologies as part of a Collaborative Research and Development competition.

The programme enables businesses to exploit technologies by providing some of the funding, and sharing some of the risk, of taking new technologies to market through collaborative research and development. It also develops communities of interest around emerging technologies, to help businesses spot opportunities to meet potential collaborators and identify potential threats, through Knowledge Transfer Networks (KTNs). To find out more visit: **www.berr.gov.uk/files/file18830.pdf**

Grant for Research and Development

The DBERR's Grant for Research and Development is available to individuals and small and medium-sized enterprises (SMEs) in England. It is administered by the Regional Development Agencies, which should be your first point of contact for application details. The grant can be used to fund projects involving the research and development of innovative products and processes. There are four types of grant, each supporting different forms of research and development.

1. **Micro projects**: Grants of £20,000 are available to businesses with fewer than ten employees, for projects lasting no longer than 12 months.

2. **Research projects**: Grants of up to £75,000 are available to businesses with fewer than 50 employees to investigate the feasibility of innovative technology.

3. **Development projects**: Grants of up to £250,000 are available to SMEs for the development of new prototypes over a period of 6 to 36 months.
4. **Exceptional development projects**: Businesses that qualify can obtain up to £500,000 of funding for projects that are strategically important to their particular sector.

For further information, visit:
www. berr.gov.uk/innovation/randd/support-for-business-randd/page11353.html.

Research and Development Tax credits

Research and Development Tax Credits are available for both large and small businesses. They provide tax incentives for research and development activities. Eligible companies can deduct up to 150% of qualifying expenditure on research and development activities when calculating their profit for tax purposes. SMEs, in certain circumstances, can surrender this tax relief to claim payable tax credits from HM Revenue & Customs (HMRC). For details of how the system works, visit **www.hmrc.gov.uk/randd/**

Office of Science and Innovation

The Office of Science and Innovation (OSI) supports the Government in developing and implementing domestic and foreign policy for science and innovation. The seven research councils work together to enhance the overall effectiveness of their research, training and innovation activities. The UK Research Councils are:

■ Arts and Humanities Research Council (AHRC)
■ Biotechnology & Biological Science research Council (BBSRC)
■ Engineering & Physical Sciences Research Council (EPSRC)
■ Economic & Social Research Council (ESRC)
■ Medical Research Council (MRC)
■ Natural Environment Research Council (NERC)
■ Science and Technology Facilities Council (STFC)

Knowledge Transfer Partnerships

Knowledge Transfer Partnerships (KTPs) help businesses to grow by giving them access to the expertise in the UK's universities and colleges. For more information, visit **www.ktponline.org.uk**.

Knowledge Transfer Networks

Knowledge Transfer Networks (KTNs) have been developed to increase the speed at which new technologies are transferred into UK businesses, to deliver improved industrial performance and provide opportunities to network with businesses and individuals in the UK and abroad. They also provide a voice for business to inform the Government of technology needs and about issues such as regulation. For more information visit: **www.berr.gov.uk/files/file35678.pdf**

National Endowment for Science, Technology and the Arts

The National Endowment for Science, Technology and the Arts (NESTA) focuses on support for innovative products. Support is provided through a variety of investment programmes, including NESTA Ventures, which invests up to £500,000 in eligible companies. To find out more about supported programmes, visit: **www. nesta.org.uk**

Department of Health

The Department of Health (DH) commissions research and development programmes that are considered vital to improvements in medicine and health. For more information on these programmes, visit: **www.dh.gov.uk/en/Policyandguidance/Researchanddevelopment/index.htm**

Regional Development Agencies

Regional Development Agencies (RDAs) evaluate applications for support under Selective Finance for Investment (SFI) in England, for businesses located or moving to 'assisted areas'. To find out if your business is in an assisted area, visit: **http://217.154.27.195/regional-aa/index.asp**

Grant requests for over £2 million are evaluated by the BERR. Some local authorities also issue grants or loans to help local businesses. More information can be found at **www.berr.gov.uk/regional/ investment/sfi-intro/page28441.html**

Framework Programmes

The Framework Programmes are the EU's main scheme for funding research and technological development. The Seventh Framework Programme started at the beginning of 2007 and will run for seven years. It is a competitive programme, with the largest amount of funding for research projects involving transnational co-operation. For details of the programme, visit: **www.berr.gov.uk/science/uk-intl-engagement/euro-programmes/fp7/ page8390.html**

EUREKA

EUREKA is a pan-European network for encouraging market-oriented, collaborative research and development projects that lead to the development of innovative products, processes and services. Project ideas are submitted to the EUREKA website, where they are advertised and circulated on the network. The EUREKA website can be searched for potential project partners. Visit **www.eureka.be** for further details.

Regional Funds

There are numerous regional innovation funds. The following list is just a sample of the many programmes available. There are also sector-specific funds, such as the eContent programme.

- Innovation Networks encourage groups of three or more small businesses to collaborate to develop new products or services, providing grant support of up to £15,000. For example, for information on funding available to businesses in the West Midlands see **www.2wm.co.uk/innovation-networks**
- Medilink (**www.medilink.co.uk/home.html**) is a national network providing services to the bioscience and healthcare sectors.

- The Lachesis Fund (**www.lboro.ac.uk/business/Lachesis/**) provides venture capital to transform innovative research into commercial products.
- The eContent Programme (**http://cordis. europa.eu/econtent/**) provides funding to support the growth and development of the digital content industry across the whole of Europe.

COMMON MISTAKES
You don't check if you're eligible before you apply for a grant

Collecting and drafting a top-notch grant application can take a good amount of time and concentration, so do check first that your business will qualify before you put all that hard work in. Most grants have strict eligibility criteria in terms of the types of business that can apply and what the money can be used for, and if you're at all uncertain about your company's status, contact the awarding organisation to double-check.

You completely under-estimate the competition

As you'd imagine, most grant schemes are extremely competitive, and it's often the case that applications are entered into a regional competition, with closing dates advertised nationally and locally. To give yourself a good chance of success, find out as much as you can about the award and how it will be judged, and be sure to give the awarding bodies all the information they need. They will usually expect you to provide plans or proposals giving details of the project, and the knowledge and skills of the people running it—along with a compelling case about why your project needs the support and what will be done with any award.

You assume the grant will pay for the entirety of your pet project

Sadly, it's uncommon for grants to be awarded to cover the whole cost of a project: your business will usually be expected to match the funding or contribute a portion of the cost.

USEFUL LINKS

Business Link:
www.businesslink.gov.uk
Department for Business, Enterprise and
  Regulatory Reform:
www.berr.gov.uk/innovation
Cordis, for help searching for partner
  businesses:
**http://cordis.europa.eu/partners-
  service**

Department of Health (DoH), for useful
  information about research and
  development projects in the health
  service:
**www.dh.gov.uk/PolicyAndGuidance/
  ResearchAndDevelopment/fs/en**
UK Intellectual Property Office:
www.ipo.gov.uk

Accessing expertise through Knowledge Transfer Partnerships (KTPs)

GETTING STARTED

Knowledge Transfer Partnerships (KTPs) support innovation by encouraging partnerships between businesses and the UK's further and higher education establishments.

Businesses are given access to knowledge and expertise to help them develop products and services, while academic institutions gain new source material for use in teaching, evidence of practical application and the commercial value of their research work.

This factsheet explains what KTPs are, how they work and the types of businesses they help. It provides details of the costs and benefits to businesses and academic institutions and provides statistics about the benefits of involvement in a KTP.

FAQS

What is a Knowledge Transfer Partnership?

KTPs are the successor to the Teaching Company Scheme (TCS) and were officially launched in 2003. They help businesses to access expertise in the UK's higher and further education institutions to help them develop new products and ideas.

KTPs also enable the transfer of knowledge between businesses and universities, colleges and other research organisations through the recruitment of recently qualified people (KTP Associates), who work for the business on challenging or high-profile projects, lasting between one and three years. Associates are supported by experienced members of staff from the business and the further and higher education establishment (Knowledge Partner).

What kind of businesses take part?

Business of all sizes in most industries and commercial sectors can apply, and you do not have to be a limited company to take part. There are limitations surrounding the type of project and business that can be supported; for example, a KTP may not be appropriate for a very small business (with fewer than five employees) as it may not have the resources to provide adequate support to the KTP Associate.

To take part in a KTP, you must be able to provide a supportive environment for a recently qualified person who may not have previous experience of working in the private or public sector. Your business must be financially viable and able to sustain the project until completion. You may be required to provide proof to the KTP adviser.

Business taking part in KTPs should be able to afford the direct and indirect costs of participating through the lifetime of the partnership, but also to sustain growth beyond that in order to benefit from the investment of public sector funds.

Interested businesses can discuss their project with a KTP adviser. For advice, call the dedicated KTP helpline (0870 190 2829) or visit the website (**www.ktponline. org.uk/ ktpadvisers/advisers.aspx**).

MAKING IT HAPPEN

Understand the role of the KTP Associate

KTP Associates are postgraduate researchers, university graduates or recently qualified people with a minimum NVQ Level 4 or equivalent, recruited to manage projects put forward under the KTP programme. The university or college and the partner company jointly undertake the recruitment of the KTP Associate. Details of the latest positions for KTP Associates are advertised on the KTP website. Associates are recruited for a period of between 12 and 36 months to work on a range of challenging strategic projects.

KTPs are designed to help deliver real business solutions central to the needs of the business. While Associates own their projects, staff within the business and from the Knowledge Partner help the Associates to develop them.

Typical challenges faced by KTP Associates include designing new products, introducing new systems, and developing strategies to help the business break into new markets. In return, Associates receive a competitive salary and ongoing training. The majority of the Associates' time is spent on their personal project, with around 10% spent on their own personal development and training. The main benefits for them are gaining business experience and personal development opportunities, but they also have access to a wide range of training opportunities, including:

- an Associate Development Course on project management, people skills and leadership
- an NVQ Level 4 in Management accredited by the Chartered Management Institute (CMI)
- a training budget of £1,750 per year per Associate to further develop their skills
- higher degree qualifications, dependent on the project being undertaken

KTP Associates receive a competitive salary in excess of £18,000 per year, depending on their expertise.

Understand how Knowledge Transfer Partnerships are funded

KTPs are part funded by the Government, which reimburses some of the knowledge partners' costs. While the budget for an individual KTP, and a business's contribution to it, depends on the details of the specific partnership, a small business with fewer than 250 employees could expect to contribute a third of the annual costs, while a large business could be expected to contribute half of the annual costs. The average cost of a project is around £60,000 per year. The business will have to meet its own overheads, including management and supervisory and capital equipment costs.

The work of KTPs is funded through a variety of sponsors, including:

- The Arts and Humanities Research Council
- The Biotechnology ad Biological Sciences Research Council
- The Department for Environment, Food and Rural Affairs
- The Department of Health
- The Department for Business, Enterprise and Regulatory Reform
- The Engineering and Physical Sciences Research Council
- The Economic and Social Research Council
- Invest Northern Ireland
- The Natural Environment Research Council
- The Scottish Executive
- Science and Technology Facilities Council
- The Welsh Assembly Government
- The European Social Fund
- Regional Development Agencies
- The Northern Way

Consider the benefits of starting a Knowledge Transfer Partnership

KTPs are designed to benefit all parties involved. The business acquires new knowledge and expertise, while the KTP Associate gains valuable business-based experience. The Knowledge Partner will improve the commercial relevance of research and teaching.

According to KTP figures for 2006, the average business benefits achieved by KTP projects were:

- an increase of over £290,000 in annual pre-tax profits
- the creation of eight jobs
- an average investment in plant and machinery of £220,000

Put another way, every £1 million invested in a KTP by the Government has led to a £4.2 million increase in annual pre-tax profits for participating firms, and the creation of 112 new jobs.

Although KTPs are not directly about skills enhancement, experience shows that in addition to the skills learnt by the KTP Associate, the skills of many of the business's existing staff are also enhanced.

Around 70% of KTP Associates are offered full-time employment by the business on the completion of the project.

Finding out about government support for exporters

GETTING STARTED

Breaking into overseas markets is the ultimate goal for many small businesses, and the UK government actively supports companies hoping to do just that via a variety of schemes. It helps them make contact with potential customers or intermediaries abroad, and provides information or support to enable businesses to make better decisions on selling in unfamiliar markets, so reducing the risks.

FAQS

Who can I contact for assistance?

Most of the support available to potential exporters falls into one of the following four categories:

1 advice and support on preparing to trade and on the export process
2 provision of information on target markets and tailored sales leads
3 market sector research
4 financial subsidies and assistance; for example; with attending international trade shows

The following government departments or agencies also provide support:

- Export Credits Guarantee Department (ECGD) (**www.ecgd.gov.uk**)
- UK Trade & Investment (**www. uktradeinvest.gov.uk**) is the government body that helps UK-based businesses to succeed in the global economy by helping them to grow internationally. It is the trade development arm of the regional development agencies (RDAs; see **www. englandsrdas.com**).

Your first point of contact for assistance through UK Trade & Investment is your local Trade Team in England, Scottish Development International (**www. sdi.co.uk**); International Business Wales (**www.walestrade.com**); or Invest Northern Ireland (**www.investni.com**). In certain areas, UK Trade & Investment offices are located in local Chambers of Commerce (**www.chamberonline.co.uk**) or the relevant RDA but you can find your local office through the UK Trade & Investment website (details above).

Once in touch, new and inexperienced exporters can ask an international trade adviser for advice on export documentation, events, using websites to attract overseas customers, marketing abroad, training and researching a market. There is some funding available for certain activities such as an export communications review but you will have to contribute towards the cost—this is known as matched funding.

UK Trade & Investment operates a number of programmes and services specifically for small and medium-sized businesses (SMEs), such as the Tradeshow Access Programme (TAP) and Passport to Export. Other services aim to work with intermediaries such as trade associations, which help businesses explore opportunities in overseas markets.

Some services are free, others are charged for. You should check with your local trade team for up-to-date costs.

For more information you can download a guide to trade and investment services, 'Your Springboard to Global Growth' from **www.uktradeinvest.gov.uk/ukti/ ShowDoc/BEA+Repository/345/401911**

MAKING IT HAPPEN

Understand the types of support available

Passport to Export is the primary UK Trade & Investment initiative bringing together many types of advice and resources into a single process for new-to-export SMEs. It includes an export 'health check', mentoring, training, a market visit, and help with promotion and market research. There is some matched funding available for activities such as a first visit to an overseas market which are agreed with the International Trade Adviser. You need to meet certain criteria to be eligible for Passport to Export, however, such as not having more than 250 employees and an annual turnover of no more than €50 million. For more information, visit the Business Link site (**www.businesslink.gov.uk**).

Passport to Export operates on a local level within the English regions only. Scotland, Wales and Northern Ireland have similar all-in-one packages (see **www. uktradeinvest.gov.uk/ukti/support-_to_succeed** for contact details).

There are a number of services available to help would-be exporters assess overseas markets for their products or services. Again, the UK Trade & Investment website is a good starting point, providing a wide range of information, useful links and contacts, checklists for new exporters, an events list, an enquiry service, and sales leads from around the world.

UK Trade & Investment offers:

- **reports** on countries and sectors in many countries, which provide a description of the services and publications available to assist with exporting to a certain country, and your particular business sector. The agency also produces *Overseas Trade* magazine (**www.overseas-trade.co.uk**), which provides exporting information to small businesses.
- '**Market Desks**', which provide collated market advice and information on specific countries. The Export promoter Initiative helps small firms to win business overseas. Export Promoters are industry or market specialists, or general advisers, working with UK Trade & Investment.
- **Export Marketing Research**, a service enabling a business with 250 employees or fewer to access the services of experienced market researchers. Subsidised market research can also be carried out, with UK Trade & Investment meeting up to 50% of the cost. The scheme is managed by the British Chambers of Commerce (**www. chamberonline.co.uk**).

- an **export information service**, which alerts UK businesses to opportunities around the world, by matching them with opportunities noted by UK trade missions and embassies. See **www.uktradeinvest.gov.uk/ukti/ appmanager/ukti/ourservices?_nfpb= true&_pageLabel=opportunities&_nfls= false** for details.
- **British Expertise**, a service which can also highlight overseas business opportunities provided by the development arms of major non-governmental organisations (NGOs) or other trans-national organisations such as the United Nations, European Commission and World Bank.

A broad range of assistance is available to help with the promotion of your goods or services abroad. Support includes:

- the **Export Communications Review**, a fee-based UK Trade & Investment service for businesses with 250 or fewer employees offering an on-site assessment of your firm's ability to communicate with overseas customers and representatives. It makes recommendations on how you and your staff can become more aware of the languages and cultures of your target markets and deal with contacts accordingly. Again, the scheme is run through the British Chambers of Commerce (see **www. chamberonline.co.uk/c0aoX_to2c5pNA.html** for details).
- **commercial officers** at British embassies and other missions overseas, who can produce tailor-made country reports. They assist with identifying potential contacts in your target country to act as representatives for your business. Help can include basic market information, identification and assessment for potential agents or distributors, customised local contact lists, market assessments for products and services, advice on market approach, information about potential local business contacts and general information on local investment opportunities. Face-to-face help and advice is also available. The service can be accessed from your local trade team, which you can find at **www.uk tradeinvest.gov.uk**. If you need help while overseas, the Foreign and Commonwealth

Office (FCO) produces a directory of British embassies who can also commission this service for you (see **www.fco.gov.uk/ servlet/Front?pagename=OpenMarket/ Xcelerate/ShowPage&c=Page- &cid=1007029395231** for details).

UK Trade & Investment sponsors an information service about trade fairs and exhibitions held in the UK (see **www. exhibitions.co.uk**), which can help you identify contacts, business opportunities or potential export partners.

You're bound to encounter language and other cultural barriers when you export. The National Centre for Languages (CILT) can help you develop an effective approach to contacting customers in non-English speaking countries. It includes practical services to enable you to make more informed choices about communications needs, such as a national database of language trainers, translators and interpreters, how-to guides, and expert software.

COMMON MISTAKE
You don't check your eligibility

Most support offered by the government, financial or otherwise, usually comes with conditions attached. Before you invest time and money in any plans that would be dependent on government support, do double-check that your business is eligible for help from this source.

USEFUL LINKS

BERR Export Control Organisation:
www.berr.gov.uk/europeandtrade/ strategic-export-control
British Chambers of Commerce:
www.chamberonline.co.uk
The National Centre for Languages (CILT):
www.cilt.org.uk

MANAGING YOUR MONEY

Choosing a small business bank account

GETTING STARTED

Having a business bank account is an essential part of running a credible and professional business. You need it not only for processing all your payments and receipts, but also for making use of several other essential banking services for businesses, such as overdrafts and other sources of finance.

It's important you take time to select the right bank to provide these services, because you'll typically enter into a long-term relationship with the bank and be able to take advantage of a range of other services it provides.

This actionlist looks at the various services provided by banks to their business account customers, and what you need to consider when choosing the bank that's best for you. It includes useful hints and tips as well as links to online sources of further information.

FAQS

What does a business bank account offer?

A dedicated business bank account offers a host of benefits for you and your business, including:

- the credibility you need—by allowing you to use your business trading name to collect cheque payments from customers who would otherwise have to pay your personal account
- access to business banking services, such as overdrafts and loans
- a bank reference, which you often need when obtaining credit terms from suppliers
- a way of keeping separate business and personal accounts, which helps your accountant work more efficiently
- less likelihood of problems with HM Revenue & Customs (HMRC) should any tax queries arise, because you're keeping separate accounts
- having a partner in developing a viable, long-term plan for your business by involving your bank from the outset

How do you choose the best account for your business?

Banking services, and the charges associated with them, vary enormously. The answer is to choose the bank and cost/service package that most suits your particular business needs. You need to find an account where the charges are lowest for your most frequent banking activities. For example, if your business receives many small payments by cheque, you will want to avoid a bank which charges a fee for each deposit or demands a very high fee for processing cheque receipts.

To do your research thoroughly, look at the accounts offered by all the major high street banks as well as one or two smaller ones before you make your decision.

Each bank will usually provide you with a 'starting up' pack, containing general information relevant to starting a business. But there's no substitute for visiting the bank in person and talking in depth to the bank's Business Manager so you can discuss your particular circumstances and requirements. Start by talking to whichever bank you have a personal account with, and then talk to at least one other, so that you can compare their services.

Carefully consider the following issues when evaluating how suitable and cost-effective each bank is likely to be:

- Is there a dedicated small-business team or manager?
- Can you speak to an individual in a local branch, or does the bank only provide access to a call centre?
- What exactly do you need? Obviously, you should review what your likely business requirements will be before talking to the banks. This will help you identify which bank will give you the best service.
- What's the rate of interest payable on your credit balance?

- What are the charges—are there fees for every transaction or is there a monthly account maintenance charge?
- Are there additional general fees, such as charges for status enquiries?
- How much does it cost to use any additional services?
- What's their policy towards overdrafts? If your cash flow is seasonal, you may need an overdraft when money is coming into the business slowly and an account that pays good interest for the rest of the year.
- Will you be running a retail business? If so, you're likely to have a lot of cash transactions and you'll also need to think about the payment options you offer customers. You may need to be able to accept credit or debit card payments, for example, and it'll be more convenient if there is a local branch of the bank so you can easily pay in cash.
- Are you likely to have a small number of large transactions or a large number of smaller ones?

What are the basic services you'll need?

When choosing a bank account for your new business you should look for:

- a current account for your day-to-day payments and receipts. This should include a chequebook and may offer interest on credit balances.
- an interest-bearing deposit account for any cash not needed for day-to-day operations. There are two types:
  - a demand deposit account where funds can be transferred immediately into the current account at any time. Under this arrangement you'll be given instant access to your funds but at lower rates of interest.
  - a term deposit account for funds you're unlikely to need at short notice. Your money will be tied up for a fixed term or the bank will only release it after a notice period, but you'll receive higher rates of interest.
- an agreed overdraft facility. This is a flexible borrowing facility set at an agreed limit so you can borrow funds up to that amount and only be charged for what you borrow.

Although useful to cover cash-flow fluctuations and often quick to arrange, overdraft facilities usually have to be renegotiated annually and an arrangement fee may be charged as well as interest on the outstanding balance. The bank might also need you to provide personal guarantees or security—and if you go over your overdraft limit, charges can be high.

- a loan account for major business purchases, or to get your business started. If you need to purchase assets or equipment or require start-up capital, it may be wise to consider applying for a loan rather than an overdraft. Loan accounts are usually repaid over a period of three to ten years and interest rates, which may be fixed, are often negotiable. Banks may need security against a loan.
- a mortgage facility if you are buying premises. In this case, you'll have to apply for a commercial mortgage. Interest rates are usually higher for these than for domestic mortgages. You're likely to be asked for a substantial deposit—possibly in the region of 25% of the purchase price of the premises.
- a business credit card. Some banks will only issue these after you've held a business account with them for a specified period of time, often a year. Credit cards can help you manage cash flow and may also help to reduce your bank charges if you use your credit card instead of writing a cheque. Using a credit card may also mean that you can avoid using your overdraft facility, but credit cards will often be subject to an annual charge in the region of £25–30.
- a merchant account so you can accept payments from customers by debit and credit card. To accept card payments you'll need an electronic point of sale (EPOS) terminal which you can get through the bank. There's usually a monthly fee for this service and you may have to enter into an agreement for a minimum period (often a year).
- a local branch, if you'll need to deposit cash regularly.
- a foreign currency account for trading overseas, if appropriate.

- as your business grows, you may need more sophisticated banking services, such as access to factoring and invoice discounting or lease finance.

What are the benefits of online banking?

The main advantage with online banking is that it gives you greater convenience and speed at reduced charges for many of the services offered by traditional banking. Most banks now provide an online service which enables you to make transactions over the Internet and view the current status of your account at any time. This can include making payments to suppliers and employees by BACS rather than by cheque, and checking that customer payments have been received into your account.

What charges and fees do banks apply?

Unlike many personal accounts, most business bank accounts charge for transaction services, such as deposits and payments. However, they frequently offer free banking for an introductory period, usually up to 18 months. And most banks also offer lower costs for using online banking services, so the cost of running the account may not be as high as you might anticipate.

Bank charges are usually taken from your account on a monthly or quarterly basis. Check your statements regularly to ensure that no other fees are being levied. Here's a list of typical bank services and charges, although the actual amounts may vary considerably between competing banks:

- service charges, which may include a monthly account charge
- transaction charges—per cheque, for direct debits and standing orders, and for credits to the account which may include an additional charge per cheque or for cash paid in
- general charges—for unpaid cheques, status enquiries, CHAPS, bank drafts
- cash withdrawal facility set up—at another branch or bank
- authorised and unauthorised overdraft fees

You should also compare bank accounts in relation to the amount of interest they pay if your account balances are in credit, as well as to the charges they make.

What is the business banking code?

This is a voluntary code followed by UK banks in their dealings with customers. The business banking code covers small businesses with an annual turnover of less than £1 million and includes current accounts, personal loans, savings and credit cards. It is a good mark of quality if your bank, building society, card issuer or merchant service provider subscribes to this code.

Apart from laying down general principles of good banking practice, the code sets out how customers are to be dealt with in the following areas:

- opening a new account
- marketing of services
- information on interest rates
- bank charges
- lending
- confidentiality
- handling financial difficulties

Which main banks offer services to small businesses?

All the main banks listed below provide services to small businesses. You can expect a period of free banking for new business start-ups, usually between 12 and 18 months. And some will provide free accounting software, guides to starting up in business, business advice clinics and specialist services such as factoring or Islamic business accounts. Banks regularly update their charges and interest rates, so for up-to-date information on current services, it's best to contact your local branch or visit the bank's website:

Abbey Business: **www.anbusiness.com**
Alliance Leicester Commercial Bank: **www.alliance-leicestercommercialbank.co.uk**
Allied Irish Bank: **www.aibgb.co.uk**
Bank of Ireland: **www.bankofireland.co.uk/business_banking**
The Bank of Scotland: **www.bankofscotlandbusiness.co.uk**
Barclays: **www.barclays.co.uk/business**
Clydesdale Bank: **www.cbonline.co.uk**

The Co-operative Bank: **www.co-operativebank.co.uk**
HSBC: **www.hsbc.co.uk**
Islamic Bank of Britain: **www.islamic-bank.com**
Lloyds TSB: **www.lloydstsbbusiness.com/**
NatWest (Part of the RBS group): **www.natwest.com/business.asp**
The Royal Bank of Scotland: **www.rbs.co.uk**
Yorkshire Bank: **www.ybonline.co.uk**

✔ MAKING IT HAPPEN

Don't forget that banks are competing for your custom, so consider all the above information before you open a business account. It's also worth talking to your accountant to check whether there are any specific banking services that you might need.

Some bank charges are negotiable, but the best time to negotiate is before you formally open an account and while the ball's still in your court—although you'll be lucky if charges aren't reviewed and increased annually. Remember that banks don't like processing cash so will probably have high charges for this, which is a good reason to think about having credit and debit card payment facilities for your customers.

✘ COMMON MISTAKES

You choose the wrong bank for your business

If your business is in a particular sector, it makes sense for you to open an account with a bank that has a reputation for expertise in that particular field. Don't be afraid to ask your contacts, including your accountant or business adviser, whether they can recommend a bank that might best suit your needs. Word of mouth is often the easiest way to find a solution, especially if you trust and respect the person making the recommendation.

Similarly, remember to review your bank account regularly to make sure you're paying competitive rates, and if not then renegotiate or think about moving your account to a bank offering a better deal. You can compare business accounts and find the best one for you by looking at the money-facts website at **www.moneyfactsonline.co.uk/mfBAF/root.asp**.

You don't keep the bank informed

If you run into financial difficulties, perhaps experiencing an unexpected cash-flow problem, always tell your bank as soon as possible. And if you can foresee potential problems, then forewarn your bank. If you exceed the limits on your credit or overdraft arrangements without authorisation, it will be expensive for you and bad for your relationship with the bank. Banks like to lend money—so if you need additional funding, talk to them before things get out of hand.

USEFUL LINKS

Banking Code Standards Board:
www.bankingcode.org.uk
The British Bankers' Association:
www.bba.org.uk
Ethical Investment Research Services (EIRIS):
www.eiris.org
Financial Ombudsman Service:
www.financial-ombudsman.org.uk

Choosing and using an accountant

GETTING STARTED

Whatever business you're in, you need to make sure your financial records are in order and that payments (both in and out) are up to date. An accountant will carry out audits to show how much profit or loss a business is making and whether tax needs to be paid. Accountants can also give you advice on how to keep the tax you pay to a minimum, and can help growing businesses with financial issues relating to the takeover of another firm.

In practice, most businesses use external accountants to provide services ranging from basic bookkeeping to tax advice or strategic business planning. Your accountant is likely to be your most trusted business adviser, so it's worth taking the trouble to find the best individual or business when you're first choosing one.

This actionlist explains the services offered by accountants, what to look for when choosing an accountant and how to engage one. It covers how to monitor and assess the service you receive, and indicates likely costs. It also provides useful sources of further information.

FAQS

What services does an accountant offer?

An accountant can help you with several aspects of your business. These include:

- Start-up advice. An accountant can advise on the best legal status (such as whether you set up as a sole trader, partnership, limited company etc.) for your business, and can help with other legal and taxation issues.
- Bookkeeping. Many businesses take care of day-to-day bookkeeping themselves, but an accountant will tell you which records you need to keep and whether it's OK for them to be manual or should be computerised. If you don't do the books yourself, you'll need to keep receipts, invoices and records of all income and expenditure to pass on to your accountant.
- Value Added Tax (VAT). If you are doing your own bookkeeping and are VAT-registered, you'll have to prepare VAT returns. An accountant can advise you on which scheme is best for your business and also outline the VAT rules you may need to be aware of.
- Preparing annual accounts. Many small businesses use an accountant to produce key annual financial statements, such as their profit and loss (P&L) account and the balance sheet. These are then submitted to HM Revenue and Customs (HMRC) and used in calculating tax due. Unlike bookkeeping or VAT returns, professional judgement is needed when deciding how various items of income and expenditure should be classified, and which tax allowances can be claimed. This can make a difference to the amount of tax due. Limited companies have to file accounts with the Registrar of Companies and accountants can help with this too.
- Preparing tax returns. Good accountants—using their working knowledge of the rules, regulations, exceptions and case law that apply to your business sector—can often achieve tax savings. Plus, if your tax return is queried, your accountant will know how best to present your case to HMRC.
- Business advice/management accounting. Once your business is up and running, a management accountant can set up systems that will monitor performance and budgets, and generally improve efficiency. They can also provide specialist advice and an independent perspective on how your business is doing, whether you should expand and so on.

What type of accountant do you need?

You need to hire the right accountant for your business. There are three main types of accountant:

- A chartered accountant is a practitioner who's a member of one of the UK's chartered institutes for the profession. They work in many different settings, including as sole traders and partners within large accountancy firms, and may work for anyone from private individuals through to large commercial organisations.
- A chartered certified accountant also works within private practice, industry and the public sector. They are responsible for issues such as future forecasting and auditing, and may also develop financial management systems.
- Chartered management accountants help organisations in the private and public sectors with planning and financial protection. They also develop financial policies and management systems. Their focus is on future planning rather than auditing.

MAKING IT HAPPEN

Before you choose and hire an accountant, make sure you do the following:

- Check that the accountant is suitably qualified and belongs to an approved accountancy body. Look for the letters ACA or FCA after a chartered accountant's name, ACCA or FCCA in the case of a chartered certified accountant, or ACMA or FCMA for a chartered management accountant. These qualifications mean the accountant has passed numerous exams before qualifying and has several years' practical experience. Using an unqualified accountant might seem cheaper, but could cost you money in the long run if their work is below standard or they give you poor advice.
- Remember that members of leading accountancy firms and associations keep their technical knowledge up to date by attending regular courses and seminars, as well as following a programme of continuing professional development (CPD) throughout their career.
- It's crucial that your accountant understands the sort of business you are in—so if you have a mail-order service, check your accountant has experience of that sector.

- It's also worth making sure your accountant has experience of working with small-business clients. In fact, many small businesses find it helpful to work with small accountancy firms because they'll understand their problems and will be more likely to provide a personal service. When considering an accountancy practice, find out how many partners there are and who exactly would be looking after you.
- Accountancy associations recommend that you contact six accountancy firms before you choose one, and you should try to have face-to-face meetings with three of them. You need to find someone you trust and feel comfortable talking to.
- Some accountancy firms will waive the fee for an initial meeting unless specific advice is given at that meeting, so check beforehand whether the consultation will be free.

Finding the right accountant for you

Investigate and, if possible, choose an accountant before you start your business. Ask your friends and business contacts for recommendations. Your local enterprise agency or your bank manager may also be able to suggest some possible names.

You can also check out the following directories held by professional bodies:

- The Institute of Chartered Accountants in England and Wales (ICAEW—**www. icaewfirms.co.uk**).
- The Institute of Chartered Accountants of Scotland (ICAS—**www.icas.org.uk/ directory**).
- The Institute of Chartered Accountants in Ireland (ICAI—for both Northern Ireland and the Republic of Ireland—**www.icai.ie/General/gi-links.cfm**).
- The Association of Chartered Certified Accountants (ACCA—**www.acca-business.org/dom/**).
- The Chartered Institute of Management Accountants (CIMA—go to **www. cimaglobal.com** and click on 'Find a practising accountant').
- The Association of Accounting Technicians (AAT—**www.aat.org.uk/home/findanaccountant**).

Briefing your accountant

At the first meeting, describe your business and discuss whether the accountant can offer the specific services you need. Explain how you currently keep records and ask whether the firm could make improvements. Take along a copy of your business plan and details of areas in which you would like the accountant to be involved—business advice, financial reporting, tax or auditing work. If you haven't yet got a business plan but want to raise finance, you'll need help with drafting a plan, which an accountant may be able to provide.

You need to know not just how much the accountant charges, but what the fees are based on, and what services they include. Some will have a fixed annual fee to complete business tax calculations and file documents, while others will charge by the hour. Fees may vary depending on the seniority of the person doing the work. If the bill isn't fixed, get an estimate of what the annual fee will be—and be prepared to challenge the final invoice if the amount exceeds this.

Find out who'll be looking after your business and whether they are a partner or a junior member of staff. Also check how quickly you can expect them to answer your queries and how long it's likely to take them to prepare your accounts.

You should also ask whether the firm provides any additional services, such as advice on future tax planning or, for example, whether they offer any form of insurance cover against tax investigations by HMRC. You could also find out whether they'll send you reminders about up-coming deadlines, or regularly update you on changes to financial and law.

Finally, don't be afraid to ask to speak to existing clients before you sign up. A refusal should set alarm bells ringing.

Your contract with your accountant

When you appoint an accountant, they will issue a letter of engagement. This is the contract between you and your accountant, and should set out:

- the accountant's responsibilities
- your responsibilities
- the fees and how they will be charged

Make sure you keep in regular touch with your accountant, to allow the relationship to grow and so that you can both keep each other informed about any issues that arise. Always keep adequate records and pass on any information to your accountant well in advance of deadlines. This should give you plenty of opportunity to discuss any tax implications and enable you to plan the future strategy of your business.

How much your accountant charges you will vary according to your location, the size and complexity of your business, and the size of the accountancy firm you have chosen. Fees are likely to start from around £500 for preparation of annual accounts and tax computations, if you are a sole trader and not registered for VAT. Larger, more complex businesses that deal in cash, and are registered for VAT, should expect to pay at least £2,000 a year and often more.

Dealing with disputes

With any luck, your accountant will stay in touch and continue to give your business the attention it needs. However, your business may outgrow your accountant, or your accountant may outgrow you. In either case, the best plan is to find a new accountant.

Similarly, if your accountant is difficult to contact, or fails to provide information or produce your accounts in good time, you may wish to hire another one. But do check whether the contract with your current accountant includes a notice period.

Accountants should co-operate with you, if you decide to move your business elsewhere. Obviously, you should end the agreement with your existing accountant before entering into a contract with a new one. Always set out a clear timetable for the transfer and make agreed payments to your accountant on time. If you don't, they have the right to withhold your figures and other data they have on record about your business until payment is made. The exception to this is limited company accounts that must be filed with Companies House.

Accountants who break the law or their professional codes of conduct are liable to disciplinary action by their professional body. Contact the relevant organisation for advice if you are unsure whether your complaint is valid. Most practising accountants must hold indemnity insurance, which will protect their clients, in most circumstances, from loss caused by negligence. You should consult a lawyer if you have suffered substantial loss, however, as the professional bodies won't help you seek compensation.

The professional bodies don't usually involve themselves in disputes about fees, which will have to be resolved via the small claims court. If larger sums are involved, contact the ICAEW (**www. icaew.co.uk/index.cfm?route=139191**, the ICAS (**www.icas.org.uk/site/cms/ contentCategoryView.asp?category=3970** or the ICAI who will help with fee arbitration and who have complaints-handling schemes (**www.icai.ie/general/ gi-compliants.cfm**).

✘ COMMON MISTAKES
You hire the first accountant you find
Often you can find an accountant through word of mouth, but do check that they're the right accountant for you. If you want them to do audit, investment business or insolvency work, make sure they're authorised to undertake that type of work. Also, ask around to check their reputation and that they'll be acceptable to finance providers and shareholders before you sign on the dotted line. Finally, if you think you're going to have overseas operations, you might want an accountant with overseas links.

You don't keep your accountant informed
Accountants aren't mind-readers. Remember to let your accountant know as soon as possible if there are any major changes in your business, including cash-flow problems, hiring or firing of key personnel or if your circumstances improve or get worse. Accountants need to be kept fully in the picture.

You forget to ask about charges
Remember to discuss fee arrangements when you're choosing an accountant, and before you sign up, ask for a guarantee that charges won't rise steeply after a year. But you should review your accountant's charges annually and remember to make an allowance for these fees in your financial forecasts.

USEFUL LINKS
Association of Accounting Technicians (AAT):
ww.aat.org.uk
Association of Chartered Certified Accountants (ACCA):
www.acca.org.uk
Companies House:
www.companieshouse.gov.uk
HM Revenue & Customs (HMRC):
www.hmrc.gov.uk
Institute of Chartered Accountants in England and Wales (ICAEW):
www.icaew.co.uk
Institute of Chartered Accountants in Ireland (ICAI) (Belfast office):
www.icai.ie
Institute of Chartered Accountants of Scotland (ICAS):
www.icas.org.uk

Choosing and using accounting software

GETTING STARTED

One of the most important aspects of running any business is making sure you have up to date and accurate records of the cash flowing in and out of the company. Tracking the money in your business can be done with very few tools, but the age-old 'invoices in a shoebox under the bed' method isn't the one to choose! Today, you are spoilt for choice when it comes to choosing accounting software and there are systems to suit just about every business. Accounting software can offer your business the following advantages:

- cash and credit can be easily tracked throughout your business
- payroll is efficient to set up and administer
- tax returns can be completed quickly as all the relevant information is to hand
- 'what if . . .?' scenarios can be tested to see if new projects are cost-effective and viable before you plough time and money in to them
- the accounting system can expand as your business does

FAQS

How can accounting software make my life easier?

Accounting packages can be a great help to a small business in particular as they enable it to track each of its different financial components easily. These can include suppliers' invoices, stock, outstanding credit and the current level of debts that are owed. Think of your accounts package as having a financial adviser permanently on your staff.

Businesses use accounting software to help them perform a number of tasks that would normally be time consuming and prone to inaccuracies if done manually, such as:

- preparing financial records for each year's tax return
- illustrating to a financial backer that the business is on a firm economic foundation if it requires extra capital to expand or buy new plant and machinery
- tracking the money that is owed to your business
- the efficient issuing of invoices and payment reminders
- enabling the monitoring of the business' cash situation at any given time

Are there different types of accounting software products?

The size and complexity of your business will have a bearing on which accounting application is right for you. It can be easy to get carried away and buy the most complex accounting system that is available, but remember that the accounting software is there to help you run your business more effectively and if you're only using ten per cent of the software's features—or find you're continually consulting the manual to operate the package—you may have chosen an application that is too complex for your needs.

Ask yourself these questions before you decide on which application to buy:

- Does your business have specialist needs? Some applications are designed especially for certain businesses such as retailers.
- Does your accountant favour a particular application? Using the same one can save time and money.
- Do you have—or plan to have—any employees? Packages that have payroll modules are available.
- Do you need to interface with any of your suppliers systems? Some retailers require that your financial systems can accept purchase orders for instance in a particular electronic format.

How do I choose which software package is best for my business?

When choosing accounting software you will need to think about what you want to get from it. Do you just want to be able to raise and post invoices and calculate your VAT return, or do you want to be able to manage your stock and forecast your future turnover? All accountancy software can do the basics of raising and posting invoices, but if you want to do more with your software then you will need to look at the additional features offered and consider the following:

- Do you require just basic bookkeeping?
- Do you want to be able to calculate and record your VAT returns and process your payroll?
- Do you want to be able to provide reports so you can easily see your debtors and creditors, or how the business stands financially at a moment in time?
- Do you want to be able to send your invoices by secure e-mail?
- Do you want to be able to submit your payroll, VAT and Construction Industry Scheme (CIS) information to HM Revenue & Customs?
- Can you upgrade the software to grow with your business?
- Do you want to be able to link up your accounts software with your online banking?

There is also help and advice on the website of the Institute of Chartered Accountants in England and Wales (ICAEW). They have a guide to choosing the right accounting software that you can download at: **www.icaew.com/enterprise/db/pdf/it2accs.pdf**

Also, when choosing which accounting software to buy you should check to see if the Business Application Software Developers Association (BASDA) has accredited the product. You can download the BASDA guide to choosing business systems from this link: **www.comrange.net/cr/basda/downloads/DL04/BASDA%20Selecting%20a%20Business%20System.pdf**

Do I need any financial knowledge or training?

All of the accounting packages that are aimed at the smaller business are designed to be used right out of the box, and they all contain extensive help and tutorial files that you can use. However, all accounting software is based on the same financial management systems like double-entry bookkeeping. If you have no experience at all of handling accounts, it's a good idea to look for a local course that will introduce you to the basic concepts. Contact Learn Direct for available courses at: **www.learndirect-business.co.uk**

MAKING IT HAPPEN
Choose an option that offers good value for money

When you're mulling over which accounting software is right for your business, cost will, of course, be a major factor, but it should be balanced with ease of use and the available features each application offers. Think carefully about the following factors before making your final decision.

Features

Again, this is a bit of a balancing act. If your business's needs are relatively straightforward, choosing an accounting package full of 'bells and whistles' that you just won't use will use up cash you could usefully plough back in the company. On the other hand, if your business does have specialist needs, not being prepared to pay extra for a package that can address these specifically may mean that you waste money on a basic program that just doesn't cut the mustard and then have to buy another one that does. As you consider your options, ask yourself:

- What features does the software provide?
- Do I really need the features or is it just something I would like?
- Will the features save me time and therefore money?

Support

Most software packages have a support option that you usually have to pay for on top of the initial purchase price of the software itself (although often you'll get a limited time of free support, after which you may to pay for additional services). Look closely at these costs as they can add significantly to the purchase price of the application. Consider these points:

- What support do I get and are there different levels?
- Am I likely to use the support?
- Will I be tied in to a fixed-term contract if I opt for the support?

The different levels of support can range from online help files on the software provider's website to telephone or e-mail support. Telephone support is often a boon, as you can have your query explained to you without having to trawl through help files and guidance manuals. However, telephone support is commonly only available during normal office hours and can be very expensive: it's often charged at premium rates.

Software providers are always looking to improve and add extra features to their product. They will continually bring out new versions for you to upgrade to, so it is worth seeing if you can receive free upgrades if you have paid for support. On that note . . .

Upgrades

As your business grows, you'll need your accounting software to grow and fulfil your requirements, so make sure that you can easily upgrade your software without additional time-consuming paperwork or punitive costs. Most of the major accounting application developers have packages aimed at every size of business—so factor in future plans as you make your decision. You're better off choosing a supplier that has more sophisticated applications you can upgrade to when your business demands this.

Additional points

Do your homework before you take the plunge and buy an accounting application. The software you select will be operating right at the heart of your business, so it must be stable and offer you all the features you need to run your business efficiently. For example:

- can your existing computer run the software efficiently? Check that your computers meet the minimum system requirements, which will be listed on the supplier's website.
- do you have a regime in place to back up your business' data? This is essential, as you must keep account records for several years. Make sure you have in place a robust data back-up system to protect this valuable financial information.
- your business's accounting system may have to interface with several others, most notably the HMRC. This is particularly important if you have a payroll system, so choose an accounts package that conforms to an accredited standard. You can read more about the Payroll Standard Accreditation Scheme on the HMRC website at: **www.hmrc.gov.uk/ebu/acclist.htm**

Investigate the costs

Your final spend will depend on the type of software you purchase, as well as any additional support or stationery. The initial purchase of the software is often a one-off fee, which can range from £45 for start-up packages aimed at the very small business up to £500+ for professional applications aimed at larger businesses.

Support contracts are usually an ongoing cost and can range from £60 for start-up packages up to £350 for software aimed at small and medium-sized businesses (SMEs). Also, before buying the software check whether it has any ongoing licence fees (do you need to renew every year, for example?).

The table below lists some examples of popular software packages and their guide prices.

Make the purchase!

Once you've zeroed in on the package you want, get yourself down to a computer retailer such as PC World, or buy direct from the software's developer. If your accountant uses software from the same provider, it's usually possible to send your data to them so that they can produce your annual accounts. Alternatively, your accountant may be able to supply you with a software package, and may also offer training in how to use it.

Name	Details	Description
Excel	**http://office.microsoft.com/en-us/excel/default.aspx** Price £170 (Excel only)	Suitable for micro businesses that have few transactions to keep track of. You may already have Excel, as it is included in the Microsoft Office suite of applications.
Microsoft Money 2007 (Home & Business)	**www.microsoft.com/money/default.mspx** Price £60	Designed for personal finance, the home and business version has some business accounting features such as invoicing. Money is ideal if a spreadsheet would be too simplistic, and you only need very basic account tracking.
TAS Books	**http://shop.tassoftware.co.uk** Price £128	This system of bookkeeping is easy to learn.
Sage Instant Accounts	**http://shop.sage.co.uk/instantaccounts.aspx** Price £129	This package enables you to manage suppliers or customers and can connect you to your accountant via the Internet.
MYOB (Business Basics)	**www.myob.co.uk** Price £79	MYOB BusinessBasics helps you process sales, manage your VAT and track who owes you money.
Simply Books	**www.simplybooks.net** Price £99	This software can handle sales, purchase orders and petty cash as well as produce profit and loss reports. It's also a fully accredited double entry system.
QuickBooks (SimpleStart)	**www.quickbooks-software.co.uk** Price £50	This application includes interactive tutorials and includes reporting functions to help develop your business.
IRIS Bookkeeping	**www.iris.co.uk** Price £160	This accounts package includes a full set of accounting features including payroll.

COMMON MISTAKE
You get put off too easily

Using an accounting application to help you operate your business is absolutely essential these days, so much so that you'll be at a competitive disadvantage if you don't have comprehensive accounting and financial forecasting in place from day one of trading. Even if accounting baffles you, don't be put off by what appear to be complex systems; you'll soon realise that your accounting software is a boon.

USEFUL LINKS

Accounting Web (publishes online information on financial topics, including articles about choosing accounting software):
www.accountingweb.co.uk
Association of Accounting Technicians (AAT):
www.aat.org.uk

Keeping a manual cash book

GETTING STARTED

A cash book records all the money that comes into and goes out of your business. Although it's called a cash book, the transactions recorded in it needn't be in cash but can be in any form including those made by cheque and by electronic forms of payment.

This actionlist explains what you use a cash book for. It shows how income and expenditure are entered so that all transactions are recorded. The treatment of VAT is discussed, as well as the actions you should take at each month end. How the cash book fits into the overall accounting system of your business is also examined, as well as how to carry out a bank reconciliation—comparing your cash book with your bank statement.

FAQS

What's a cash book?

A cash book is simply where you record the flow of cash in and out of your business. Any transaction that involves the inflow (receipt) or outflow (payment) of money from your business should be recorded in the cash book.

How do you complete a cash book?

You should start by buying a simple cash analysis book from a stationery supplier. This will be laid out with a number of columns across each page where you can log your income and expenditure. The first thing you should do is head up one page 'Payments' and the opposite page 'Receipts'. It's conventional for receipts to be recorded on the left-hand page and payments on the right-hand page. Use these pages to record the cash coming into and out of your business for the month ahead.

How you choose to record your income and expenditure will depend on your individual business circumstances, as not all businesses will incur the same types of costs. However, the following columns should be included in every cash book:

- date
- details of transaction—i.e. what was bought or sold
- reference—type of transaction, ie cash or cheque, plus an identifying number
- total cost

To the right of these columns, you can then analyse the payment or receipt by category. The number of categories of payment or receipt you have is up to you, but as a general rule of thumb, you should have a category for the types you're most likely to incur regularly, such as wages or stock. The final column should be labelled 'Other' and this will capture any income or expenditure that doesn't fit into any other classification. This immediate analysis will help you to monitor the major and the most important items of payment and expenditure.

In order to complete your cash book, you'll need the following items of paperwork:

- purchase invoices received from suppliers
- sales invoices raised to customers
- details of cheques written and cancelled
- cash received and payments made
- bank statements and paying-in book

MAKING IT HAPPEN
Record payments made (outgoings)

An example of a cash book entry is shown below. This is the payments page for the month of July and includes all transactions that involve money being paid out of the business:

- A payment was made to Jones Fabrics for £150 by cheque (cheque number 1041) on 11 July. The entry in the cash book therefore includes these details under the appropriate headings and then allocates the payment to the payment category, which in this case is 'Stock'.
- The payment made on 15 July was also by cheque, and this was to KH Leasing. The total paid was £350 and this has been

				PAYMENT TYPE		
DATE	DETAILS	REFERENCE	TOTAL	Stock	Motor	Wages
11/07	Jones Fabrics	Cheque 1041	£150	£150		
15/07	KH Leasing	Cheque 1052	£350		£350	
25/07	July wages	BACS 4253	£1,500			£1,500

Cash book page showing payments made July — Payments

classified to the payment type 'Motor' as this relates to a vehicle lease.

- The July wages were paid on 25 July by BACS, and totalled £1,500. In the cash book, this payment has been logged in the wages column.

To ensure that you've allocated the total income and expenditure for the month, you should check that the total of all the payment type columns equals the sum of the total column.

Record payments received (incomings)

An example of the receipts page of a manual cash book is shown below. As you can see, it's very similar to the payments page, with the types of income analysed in the columns on the right-hand side.

Every time a cheque is received, the total amount should be entered in the column headed 'Total' and then analysed into the appropriate columns. Income received by standing order or BACS should also be recorded in this way.

In the example below, revenue has been received from two customers and interest was received from the bank. The revenue received is recorded in the column headed 'Income'. It's possible to have more than one income column if your business receives revenue from different sources (for example, if you sell to different geographical areas you may wish to analyse them on this basis). Again, the 'Other' column is included to ensure all revenue can be recorded.

Sales and purchase ledgers

When your business offers credit to customers (i.e. they pay you 30 days after the invoice date) and you in turn benefit from a credit account with your suppliers, you'll need to keep separate sales and purchase-ledger books in addition to your cash book.

The sales ledger details the sales invoices raised, income received and amount outstanding from customers. The purchase ledger details all the payments you make against invoices you receive from your suppliers.

When cash is received or a payment is

				INCOME TYPE		
DATE	DETAILS	REFERENCE	TOTAL	Income	Rent	Interest
05/07	Invoice 255 (Brown's)	Cheque 0842	£425	£425		
18/07	Invoice 276 (J Jackson)	Cheque 7826	£645	£645		
31/07	Bank interest	00152405	£12			£12

Cash book page showing income received July — Receipts

made and the invoice is included in the sales ledger or purchase ledger, this should be logged in the sales ledger or purchase ledger column in your cash book.

Understand how VAT is treated

If you're VAT-registered, you should include a column in the income and payments pages of your cash book for VAT, and separate this element from your receipts and payments.

If you've registered to account for VAT using the cash-accounting scheme, you need to total up the VAT column on the receipts and payments pages of the cash book each quarter and enter these figures on your VAT return. However, if you account for VAT on a tax point basis, you need to look at the sales invoices raised and the purchase invoices received in the relevant return period, rather than the cash movements.

Month end

At the end of every month, all the columns in your cash book should be totalled and you should check that the sum of the analysis columns equals the sum of the 'total' column to make sure there aren't any discrepancies.

At the end of each month, deduct the payments from the receipts to give the net cash flow for the month. Then add the figure carried forward from the previous month to give the 'carry down' figure. This is also the balance that should be in your bank account. If the figure is negative—i.e. you have an overdraft—you should carry it forward on to the payments page for the next month. If the figure is positive, carry it forward to the receipts page.

Bank reconciliation

After you've totalled the monthly figures, you should undertake a bank reconciliation. This is the process of comparing your cash book with your bank statement to make sure that they match. This acts as a means to check your bookkeeping is accurate and also checks that there aren't any discrepancies with the balance shown on the bank

statements, and any cash held by your business.

The bank reconciliation should start with the closing balance as per the cash book, and then you adjust for uncleared cheques that have been issued or received but haven't cleared the banking system at month end. Thus, any cheques issued but not cleared should be added to the cash-book total, and cheques received but not yet cleared should be deducted. The revised balance should then be calculated and this should equal the balance shown on the bank statements. For example:

Closing cash book balance at 31 July	23,045
Add uncleared payments	726
Deduct undeared receipts	(1,425)
Revised cash book balance	22,346
Balance as per bank statements at 31 July	22,346
Difference	0

If the figure you get isn't the same as on your bank statement, you've got an error somewhere. Perhaps a payment or receipt has cleared sooner than expected? It's essential that a bank reconciliation is undertaken every month so that any mistakes are identified and rectified. The sooner you sort out any discrepancies the better.

Start as you mean to go on

Get into the habit of keeping your cash book up to date on a regular basis: it should be something that you regularly do at a specific time, rather than a chore that needs to be squeezed in with the rest of your business.

It makes good business sense to compare your cash-flow forecast to your actual cash balance often, so you can examine your results and identify any potential cash-flow problems before they arise.

It's also sensible to ask your bank to send your statements at the end of each month, so they coincide with the end of each of your accounting periods. Most importantly, do try to find time to carry out a bank reconciliation every month. Not only will this help you keep track of your bank balance, but it's far easier to identify the source of errors when you know that they can't be more than a month old.

COMMON MISTAKES
You don't do regular bookkeeping

Keep your cash book up to date by recording every transaction immediately after it's made. Don't put it off to do later—you may forget the details, and this will mean a time-consuming task every month end. Keeping on top of your bookkeeping also helps you identify problems early.

You don't keep the appropriate records

Don't forget that you must keep all your accounting records for a minimum of six years, as this is a legal requirement. If HMRC want to check anything and you can't produce your financial records, life becomes unnecessarily complicated—and you could find yourself having to pay fines and penalties.

USEFUL LINK
Business Link:
www.businesslink.gov.uk

Keeping sales and purchase ledgers

GETTING STARTED

Sales and purchase ledgers can be maintained in a simple cash analysis book available from any office stationer's. Computerised accounts packages are widespread and user-friendly, but it's important that you understand the basic process of maintaining the sales and purchase ledgers.

This actionlist explains what sales and purchase ledgers are and what you should use them for. It also explains how transactions should be recorded and looks at the information that ledgers must include. Plus there's information on how sales and purchase ledgers fit into the overall accounting system of your business.

FAQS

What's a sales ledger?

A sales ledger records each sale that you invoice for during a month, and each of the payments you receive from your customers.

Every time an invoice is issued, it should be recorded in the sales ledger. A copy of the invoice should be retained, showing:

- the date the invoice was issued
- the details of the customer and the work for which the invoice has been issued
- a unique invoice number
- the amount charged

If your business is registered for VAT, you must also include the following:

- the VAT rate applied
- the amount of VAT
- your VAT number

A typical format for a manual sales ledger is shown below. There's a column to enter the date when an invoice is paid, so it's easy to

see which invoices are outstanding and which need to be chased at the end of the month.

Adding up the total invoices and the outstanding debtors (customers who haven't yet paid you) at the end of each month will help in the preparation of your management accounts (that is, the financial information you need to help you make decisions from month to month).

Debtors who are still outstanding at the end of the month should be carried forward by recording the amount they owe at the bottom of the page. It'll be helpful at the end of the following month to add a further line for the debtors who are still outstanding. Unless you find yourself with 'bad debts', eventually the number of debtors for any one month will reduce to zero.

The figure for total invoiced sales should be copied to your profit and loss (P&L)

Date	Customer	Invoice No.	Net amount	VAT	Total	Date paid
1 Sept	Jones Wood	9101	1,000	175	1,175	
4 Sept	Nail & Co	9102	2,000	350	2,350	25 Sept
7 Sept	Bioggs	9103	1,000	175	1,175	26 Sept
12 Sept	Mask Ltd	9104	1,000	175	1,175	
Totals			5,000	875	5,875	
Outstanding debtors at the end of September					2,350	

Date	Supplier	Ref No.	Total	VAT	Materials	Travel	Premises	Date paid
1 Sept	Northern Electric	991	94	14			80	
5 Sept	Premier Paper	992	235	35	200			
7 Sept	Andy's garage	993	48	8		40		25 Sept
12 Sept	Rent	994	500				500	26 Sept
Totals			877	57	200	40	580	
Outstanding creditors at the end of September			329					

account, while the figure for outstanding debtors should be copied to your balance sheet. You can also use the totals in the net amount and VAT columns to complete a VAT return speedily and accurately.

If it helps, you can add extra columns to differentiate between various types of sales (net amounts). You can also keep separate records by customer, although if you've reached the stage where this level of record-keeping is necessary, it makes more sense to put your sales and purchase ledger on a computer.

What's a purchase ledger?

A purchase ledger is used to record all your purchase invoices and to show those which are still unpaid. It also allows you to account for any VAT that you could claim back. As with the sales ledger, you can quickly extract the VAT figures when you need them.

Many people are rather cavalier with purchase invoices (or bills), often tossing them in a desk drawer until the end of the month. While this is an easy habit to fall into, it's bad practice. Instead, if you make a note of bills in a purchase ledger, you'll be able to see at a glance how much you owe to suppliers and which bills are still

outstanding. This means you're less likely to miss a payment accidentally.

While it isn't essential to use purchase order numbers in your purchase ledger, it makes good sense. You should number the bills as they are received and record the number in the purchase ledger so you can easily retrieve the bill if a query arises later.

As with the sales ledger, every time you make a payment, you should note it in the 'date paid' column. It's then very easy, at the end of each month, to note all those purchase invoices which are still outstanding. This will help you with your management accounts.

Finally, you should copy the total net amounts to your P&L account, where they can be recorded under their individual headings. And copy the figure for outstanding creditors to your balance sheet.

COMMON MISTAKES
You're not organised

If you keep on top of you sales and purchase ledgers and update them regularly, you'll have a much better idea of your cash flow and will be in better control of your finances.

Make a note of all purchases in the purchase ledger as soon as you receive the purchase invoices (in other words, bills). If there's likely to be a delay before you receive a bill, it's a good idea to enter the amount into the ledger as soon as the order is placed—then you won't forget to make provision for paying it.

You don't update your ledgers on a regular basis

If you want to run a tight ship, it's vital that you make a note of sales in the sales ledger as soon as the invoice is written and by the same token make a note of receipts in the sales ledger as soon as invoices are paid by your customers.

You don't reconcile your ledgers

Assuming that you make sure your sales and purchase ledgers are kept accurate and up to date, then you should reconcile the two at the end of every month. In other words, check that the amounts invoiced match up with the payments received. That way, you'll be able to spot any potential cash flow problems and take the necessary action to recover any outstanding debts sooner rather than later.

USEFUL LINK
Business Link:
www.businesslink.gov.uk

Costing and pricing a product or service

GETTING STARTED

Working out the right price for a new product or service can be one of the biggest problems faced by small business owners. The price needs to cover costs and make a profit, but must also take account of what competitors are charging and what customers will be prepared to pay.

Setting too high a price can lead to lost sales. Undercharging will lower your profits and possibly result in your business failing. Prices charged should reflect costs on the one hand, and the strength of the market on the other.

Pricing is also crucial to business success because it affects the image you present to the market. Pricing communicates messages about the quality of the products or services offered, and positions your business in the marketplace. You also need to understand the impact of pricing on profitability, and to be able to choose the best pricing strategy for your business.

FAQS

I'm often a bit flummoxed by some of the terminology related to price setting. What are the most important terms?

Here are some of the most common terms and phrases you'll come across, split across the key related areas.

Cost terms

- **Direct costs**
  The direct cost of a product or service is the specific cost incurred in producing and supplying the product or service. These costs are also known as variable costs, because they vary in direct proportion with the number of units produced.
- **Fixed costs**
  All businesses have costs that are incurred regardless of whether any products are sold. These fixed costs are also known as overhead costs, and include items such as your salary or drawings, employee costs, rent, rates, insurance and depreciation in the value of fixed assets such as machinery and equipment.

Pricing terms

- **Cost plus pricing**
  This is a traditional method of calculating the price to charge, and is often used in pricing products rather than services. It is based on applying a percentage mark-up on

top of the cost of producing a product in order to make the desired profit.

- **Value-based pricing**
  This is based on what the market will bear—the price level that can be achieved is affected by the impact of factors such as fashion, convenience and monopoly.

Profit terms

- **Gross profit**
  Gross profit is the selling price less the direct costs involved in making a product or delivering a service.
- **Operating profit**
  A business' operating profit is the gross profit minus the fixed costs.
- **Gross profit contribution**
  As long as a business sells a product for a higher unit price than its direct cost, the income that is received from the sale of the product will make a contribution to the fixed costs of the business—and hopefully to the generation of an operating profit. If you sell a range of products, you should look at the gross profit generated by each of them to compare their contribution and therefore their importance to the business. The product that has the highest volume of sales may not contribute the greatest gross profit, but could be useful in marketing terms to attract and retain customers.
- **Breakeven point**
  The breakeven point is the stage at which

income from sales exactly equals all the costs incurred by a business. More sales than this level will result in a profit; fewer sales will result in a loss.

MAKING IT HAPPEN
Understand your costs

In essence, costing and pricing is very simple. You work out all of your costs and then charge a price that is higher than your costs. In practice the process is a bit more complicated. It is sometimes difficult to identify what are variable and what are fixed costs. Your costs also need to be absorbed by all the products you sell—so that the more you sell, the less you need to add to each unit to cover your overheads. Your costing will therefore depend on your estimate of how many products, or hours of your time, you think you can sell.

Calculate costs for a production-based business

If you have a production-based business it is possible to calculate the total cost per item produced, but you need to know the direct costs for each product as well as your actual or expected fixed costs for the business. For a business producing just one product, you will need to divide your total fixed costs by the number of units that you expect to produce. Add this figure to your direct cost to obtain your total cost. If your business produces a number of products you will need to apportion your fixed costs to each product.

As an example, consider a cabinet maker's business that makes bespoke desks. The business expects to make and sell 100 desks during the year. The direct costs of the materials used to make each desk such as wood, glue, screws and packaging are £50. The total fixed costs or overheads of the business (which include the value of your time) for the year have been estimated at £30,000, which gives a fixed cost to each desk of £300. The total cost to produce each desk is therefore £350.

The table below shows the effect on the total cost for each desk if the business increases the number of units made.

Assuming that there are no additional costs incurred, you can dramatically reduce the cost of producing each desk by increasing the number made. This allows you to consider either selling the desks at a lower price if you adopt a cost plus pricing approach; or if you adopt a value based pricing approach you will maintain your price and achieve a much higher profit.

Calculate costs for a service-based business

If you provide a professional service, you need to be able to calculate your average daily or hourly cost. In making the calculation it's important to remember that not all working hours will be productive and that most service businesses have low direct costs and high fixed costs.

You will need to consider the amount of time that will be required for promoting your business, buying supplies, and doing the books and other administrative jobs. You will also need to make an allowance for holidays and other time off, such as for illness. To calculate your daily cost you should divide the annual business fixed costs by the number of productive days you

Number of Desks made	100	150	200
Direct (variable) cost per desk	£50	£50	£50
Total Fixed (overhead) costs	£30,000	£30,000	£30,000
Fixed cost per desk	£300	£200	£150
Total cost to produce a desk	**£350**	**£250**	**£200**

expect to work. You can get an hourly cost by dividing this figure by the number of hours you expect to work each day.

As an example, let's say Kirsty works as a photographer. Her total overheads for the year are £30,000, which include her salary and vehicle running costs. After allowing for holidays and illness, she estimates that around 200 days of her time will be sold every year. Kirsty expects to average five hours per day, which will leave her time to do her marketing and administration and this equates to 1,000 productive hours per year. Therefore her daily cost is £150 and her hourly cost is £30. In order to be able to work out a selling price, she'll also need to add her direct costs (film, developing and printing), a profit margin and VAT (if applicable).

Working out how much to charge

There are two main steps in setting a price:
1 determine the costs of producing and delivering a product or service
2 setting a price that is high enough to cover the costs, but low enough to be competitive

In the example above of Kirsty the photographer, we were able to identify her average hourly cost at £30. If she adopted a cost plus pricing approach for a one-day assignment (of 7.5 hours), she will charge her time (£225) + direct costs (say £40) + profit (say 20%) + VAT (17.5%). This would give a total price of £374.

However, if Kirsty's market research has revealed that the going day rate for photographers in her area is £500, she could charge on a value-based approach at a rate that the market would bear, and earn considerably more that way.

You need to research your market carefully to determine the price range that you will be able to charge. This is difficult for start-up businesses, since they have little information on which to base their pricing decision. They can only examine the prices charged by their competitors and compare these with the market research they have carried out with potential customers.

Once you are in business, pricing becomes easier since you can adjust your prices up and down and review the effect this has on demand.

The price can always be changed, but there will be customer resistance if an increase is too great or if it is changed too frequently. Ultimately, the price that is charged depends on what the market will stand—that is, on how much the customer is prepared to pay. By understanding your costs, you are in a position to decide whether it is cost effective to sell your goods or services at that price.

Understand how price affects your profit

It is important to understand the impact that charging different prices for a product or service can have. The table below shows the effect on profitability of a 10% change in the price of a product at the same volume of sales.

At the lowest selling price of £45, the business is operating at its break-even point. It generates a small operating profit at a selling price of £50, but it can increase its operating profit by 100% if it can sell the product at £55.

Look at how sales volumes and price interact

The price at which you decide to sell your products will have an impact on the number of units that you are able to sell. However, just selling a greater volume of products does not mean that the business will generate a higher profit. The table below shows the number of products that need to be sold at different prices to achieve a gross profit of £35,000, which generates an operating profit of £10,000.

In this example, you have to sell 40% more units at a price of £45 to achieve the same level of profitability that you can achieve by selling 1,000 units at £55. This may be an important consideration if your business has a production capacity constraint, which may be determined by the maximum output that can physically be produced by a machine or a person.

Selling price	£45	£50	£55
Revenue from sales of 1,000 units	£45,000	£50,000	£55,000
Direct (variable) costs	£20,000	£20,000	£20,000
GROSS PROFIT	**£25,000**	**£30,000**	**£35,000**
Fixed (overhead) costs	£25,000	£25,000	£25,000
OPERATING PROFIT	**£0**	**£5,000**	**£10,000**
Selling price	**£45**	**£50**	**£55**
Number of units sold	1,400	1,167	1,000
Revenue from sales	£63,000	£58,350	£55,000
Direct (variable) costs	£28,000	£23,350	£20,000
GROSS PROFIT	**£35,000**	**£35,000**	**£35,000**

Understand the risks involved in charging less than your competitors

Many new businesses have difficulty calculating the direct costs of their products or services before they start trading and, as a result, let their competitors effectively set the price. They think that as long as they undercut that price, they will succeed. But this approach to pricing is a strategy that often fails for small businesses. Because you lack the economies of scale necessary to make the price really competitive, you end up not being able to make a profit, which is necessary to sustain the business.

Customers frequently quote price as their main buying criterion, but often there are many other factors involved, such as the service and support you provide to your customers. Try to differentiate your product or service in comparison to your competitors, as this will reduce the importance of price in the buying decision of your customer.

Look at the various pricing strategies

When you're working out the prices for a product or service, always have an objective in mind. Being clear about what you're trying to achieve will have a huge impact on the final price that you set. The following list includes five pricing strategies designed to meet certain objectives. Each strategy may result in a very different price for a product to meet the objectives of the business.

Strategy 1—Pricing low to penetrate the market and gain customers

Objective: you are just entering the market with a new product and want to gain as many customers as possible.

When to use: if you have a big 'back-end' product that you plan to sell as a follow-up to a lower-priced 'front-end' product. Or you may have a consumable product that people will buy repeatedly, so you want to gain customers, get them hooked and then slowly raise the price.

Strategy 2—Pricing high to gain maximum profits (price skimming)

Objective: to gain the maximum amount of profit per unit in the shortest amount of time.

When to use: when a product is unique and new, with no competition, and you have a short window to skim the maximum profits before copycat products start flooding the market.

Strategy 3—Pricing to make a 'normal' profit
Objective: to set a price that is seen by the customer as honest and reasonable.
When to use: if you want to develop long-term relationships with your customers. In this case, you might use a cost-plus pricing strategy.

Strategy 4—Pricing to be competitive in the market
Objective: when you want to be competitive and considered for any tenders, proposals, auctions or other competitive pricing situations.
When to use: when your product is very similar to the competition, and you are limited in the methods you can use to differentiate it.

Strategy 5—Pricing for maximum profit and maximum sales
Objective: you want to get the maximum amount of profit possible but not at the expense of losing customers.
When to use: after the initial introduction when you have the ability to differentiate your product.

Other pricing considerations
There are a number of other issues that may affect the prices that you charge.

Flexible pricing
You may wish to offer special prices across a range of products.

Volume discounts
There may be a number of advantages to offering price discounts for customers who make bulk purchases.
- The lower gross profit per unit sold is offset by the higher total gross profit generated by the total bulk order.

- You will have lower costs associated with supplying one larger order to one customer.
- By achieving higher total sales for a product, you may be able to achieve lower unit costs for each product, due to increases in your productivity and buying power. This reduction in cost can allow you to increase your gross profit, even though your average unit-selling price is lower.

Total customer value
By understanding the total potential value to their business of an individual customer, you may be able to achieve a higher gross profit by selling a range of products to that customer at lower prices than you typically charge for each individual product.

You may negotiate fixed prices for the products that you supply (based on your customer committing to purchase a minimum volume of the products over an agreed term), or they will treat you as their sole or preferred supplier for those products.

Although you will generate a lower gross profit on individual products sold, the total gross profit generated from the full range of products sold to that customer will be greater, so the business will be more profitable.

Variable prices
Depending on the industry you work in, it may be possible to charge different prices for providing premium services at unsociable hours (if you are a plumber or electrician, say), or variable rates depending on the season (if your business is in the tourism sector, for example).

COMMON MISTAKES
You don't do any market research
Price is primarily a perception of value, and if you build value, you can charge higher prices. Make sure that you test price points for your products, or you might miss out on a lot of additional profit. You could do this by carrying out market research to establish your customers' perception of possible price points, both before you start trading and

once your business is established in the marketplace.

You pitch your price too low

Many people don't charge enough when they set prices for the first time. Raising a price is always more difficult than lowering one, so the more you can do to get it right first time, the easier you'll find it to manage your customers' expectations. Yes, at times you will feel tempted to undercut the competition, but it's unlikely that you'll be able to do this all the time and still make any money. Proceed with caution.

You forget price isn't everything

Price is important, but it's often not *the* most important issue for a customer. Even if you have a product that is regarded as a commodity, there may be ways to differentiate it so that you can charge a higher price than other similar products.

USEFUL LINKS

Chartered Institute of Purchasing and
  Supply (CIPS):
www.cips.org
Office of Fair Trading (OFT):
www.oft.gov.uk

Putting together a budget

GETTING STARTED

Every business needs to plan its spending on the basis of what it expects from sales income; without this tool, you can't be sure that your business will survive. Budgeting is simply the name given to the process of working out what you expect your business to earn and spend in a given period. It also gives you the ability to check how the business is doing from week to week, or month to month; without this check, you can easily overspend. This actionlist explains how you can make use of your budget, and how to draw one up.

FAQS

What can I use a budget for?

It's important that you use your budget as a control mechanism. At the end of each month, you should enter the actual figures for sales and expenses next to the figures that were forecast. If there are substantial differences between the budgeted figures and the actual figures, then you need to do something about it. For instance, if your sales are too low, you may need to reconsider your marketing strategies. If sales, on the other hand, are higher than planned, then you may need to reconsider your staffing levels or raw material supplies, in order to cope with the rising demand. Also, if your expenditure is too high, you'll need to find ways to bring costs down.

How do I estimate sales and expenditure?

The starting point for drawing up a budget is for you to estimate future sales and expenditure. The sales budget can be split into: the number of different products your business plans to sell; the number of units of each product that you plan to sell; the price that you plan to sell each unit for; and the place or area where you plan to sell them.

You'll need to split your expenditure budget into: production costs or variable costs (such as materials, power, and subcontractors); overhead costs or fixed costs (such as rent and salaries); and capital costs (equipment).

MAKING IT HAPPEN

Create a sales budget

Forecasting sales is particularly difficult for brand new businesses, because they don't have any historical data on which to base expectations. Thorough market research can help you fill in the gaps, however, as you'll see on pp. 71–76. Also make sure that your predictions are tied in closely to a realistic marketing plan that will help you generate the sales you expect. In short: don't just guess your sales figures; you're on the way to cash-flow crisis that way. Also, don't start by looking at your planned expenditure and then just calculating sales that will cover the cost.

Go into as much detail as you can with your sales budget, and be very clear about what you plan to sell, and at what price. Set out your expected sales on a monthly or quarterly basis. If your business sells a range of products, draw up sales budgets for each of them: this will help you monitor performance more easily, and will also help you see at glance how the overall mix of products is working. If you sell items in more than one market, it's worth creating a sales budget for each.

Look at your expenditure

Once the sales budget is done, you have the foundations in place to calculate your expenditure. For your purposes, the expenditure budget can be split into a production budget and an overheads budget. Now that you know who many products you expect to sell, you can work out the direct costs of producing them. These direct costs will then make up the production budget, and will vary with the level of production. The overhead costs will stay more or less constant, though.

The production budget

The production budget details the materials or components that go into the products you make. If you have a sales team, you also need to include commission paid to them (if sales people earn a regular retainer as well, this retainer would normally be regarded as a fixed cost). Make sure that you include the cost of subcontractors, where people are being paid as independent contractors to perform a certain, defined job.

Discounts are usually shown in the budget as a direct cost. Some expenses, such as depreciation, are usually treated as fixed overheads, but if you want to be particularly accurate with your production budget, you could include these, especially if you can clearly associate them with specific products.

The overheads budget

Once you have prepared the production budget, you'll need to consider the other costs that the business will incur. These will include the salaries for you and your staff, National Insurance contributions, pension contributions and so on. You'll also need to include rent and company insurance, and telephone, Internet, and e-mail account costs. Any interest on money that you have borrowed will also need to be included in your overheads.

If you operate a manufacturing business, it's likely that the above will represent a relatively small proportion of the total costs. In service sector businesses on the other hand, overheads will probably represent a very high proportion of the cost. Include all overhead costs, including interest payments and drawings (how much money you plan to take out of the business). Remember that you are taxed on the total profit (if you are self-employed), so allow for this too. If your business is registered as a company, and you expect to take high dividends, make sure that you budget for this as well.

Your business may aim to allocate the overheads to each product, or may prefer to retain overheads as a single budget. Whichever path you choose, it's important that you ensure that the price for each product makes a reasonable contribution to the overheads.

Budget for the full cost of production

You're now in a position to pull together the production budget and the overheads budget into a single production cost budget. If there is more than one product or service, then there will be a production budget for each. There will also be variable overheads for you to add for each product. There is no need for you to split fixed overheads across products at this point, since the object of this exercise is for you to be able to determine the *total* costs.

Capital expenditure budget

If you expect to buy capital equipment, you'll need to decide how you'll pay for it (whether in cash or through a loan), and make sure that you budget for these payments in the relevant months. This is essential information if an accurate forecast is to be prepared, particularly where the business may have to take out a loan to finance the purchase and meet a repayment schedule that includes interest. The Internal Revenue Service doesn't consider an operating lease to be a purchase, but rather a tax-deductible overhead expense. Lease payments can therefore be deducted from the corporate income.

If the business decides to lease equipment, it's important to make sure that you read all the small print of the lease agreement.

Cash flow

If you operate your business on a cash basis—in other words, take in cash for sales and then pay it out again for purchases—then it's fairly easy to see if you are on the right track: if you're making a profit, you'll have cash left over at the end of the month. Very few businesses, however, operate like this. It's far more likely that you'll be selling goods or services in one month, and not receiving payment until the following month, or the month after that. Similarly, you may be buying raw materials one month, but not paying for them for at least another four weeks. A budget will help you keep track of how cash is moving in and out of your business, and to feel more in control.

Once the budgets have been prepared, don't let all the useful data you've gathered go to waste. Use it to prepare financial forecasts, such as a cash-flow forecast, a profit and loss statement, and the balance sheet. The cash-flow forecast should set out, on a month-by-month basis, all cash inflows and outflows from the business for the following 12 months—which will help you to determine your working capital needs. The profit and loss forecast will help you to check that your business remains profitable. See pp. 112–121 for more information.

COMMON MISTAKES
Your targets are unrealistic
Forecasting means treading a sometimes uneasy path between pragmatism and optimism: if you set your goals too low, your sales team may not feel inspired to do their best, but if you go over the top completely and you base your financial commitments on ridiculous figures, your business will quickly go the way of the Dodo. Be as realistic as you can and monitor your figures closely so that if something does go wrong, you'll be able to take action quickly to address the issue.

You can't be bothered to prepare a cash-flow forecast
It's important to remember that a cash-flow forecast is as important as the budget itself. While the budget can tell you if your business is generally profitable, it might not alert you to cash flow problems.

USEFUL LINK
Business Link:
www.businesslink.gov.uk

Forecasting sales

GETTING STARTED

Forecasting future sales is a crucial part of setting up and running a business, as well as an essential part of business planning. The future will, of course, always be unpredictable to a certain degree. But being able to make reasonable, evidence-based projections will help you create your business strategy.

In this actionlist, we'll look at the importance of sales forecasting, various methods of doing it, and how you can interpret and use the results.

FAQS
What is a sales forecast?

A sales forecast is a month-by-month financial projection of the amount of revenue that a business expects to generate from the sales of its products or services. While (ideally) a forecast should be based on real data and previous sales history, that's not always possible for start-ups. It should, however, take into account not just sales potential but also detailed consideration of various external market issues affecting the business. In a way, forecasting is both an art and a science!

Do I really need to forecast sales?

Yes! Forecasting sales will help you:

- work out whether your business is viable. You need to know whether it is likely to make enough sales to be able to function. This is especially important in the case of start–ups, where you're looking for reassurance that the company will eventually reach profitability even if it takes some time to get there.
- plan and manage cash flow. You can use the forecast as part of your business plan if you need to apply for funding, and it will also help you avoid unforeseen cash-flow problems by establishing whether you need to inject capital or borrow funds.
- plan future resource requirements. Once you have the forecast in place, you'll be able to work out, for example, the number of staff needed to achieve your planned sales. It will also help you order the correct amount of stock.
- plan production and marketing activities. The forecast will show which products are the most popular, flag up sales trends and help you to decide where to direct future investment.
- set goals and targets for the business.
- compare your actual sales with your forecast, understand the differences and use this information to produce new, increasingly accurate forecasts.

Sound market research will always form the foundation of your business plan, and this will be a crucial factor in obtaining funding: potential backers will want to know how the market you operate in has been functioning.

MAKING IT HAPPEN
Consider key factors as you prepare a sales forecast

A sales forecast in a business plan should show sales by month for at least the next twelve months, and then by year for the following two years. Three years in total is generally enough for most business plans.

Before you pull all the necessary information together, think carefully about the following issues:

Market awareness

- Is there an established market for your product?
- What is the size of the market?
- Is the market growing or declining, and if so, by what percentage each year?
- Which factors are currently influencing that market?
- What may influence it in future?
- How do seasonal factors affect purchases of your product or service?

- Which trends or fashions are relevant to the sector?

Customer knowledge

- Develop a clear picture of your existing and potential customers.
- Be realistic about how many of these customers will wish to purchase your product.
- Detailed customer profiling can help determine strategy by enabling you to focus on niche markets; and hence affects pricing policy and sales forecasts.

Capacity

- Make sure that the sales forecast is within the limits of your production capacity.
- How will any possible future changes in personnel or the size of marketing budget affect future capacity to produce or to meet sales targets?

Competition

- How many competitors do you have? Even if your business is unique at the moment, new competitors are likely to enter the market once you have done the groundwork to raise market awareness. If there are already many competitors, this will probably indicate that there is an established market for your services.
- Be clear about how your products and services fit into the marketplace. How can you differentiate your business from your competitors' businesses?
- You may need to be flexible with regard to pricing and the range of products and services offered.

External factors

- Political, economic, socio-cultural, technological, environmental and legal (PESTEL) factors—such as energy prices, seasonal trends, interest rates, legislation, political and health issues—may all have an impact on your future plans.
- How do the economic climate and other external factors impact on your business; and on your customers' attitudes and inclination to buy your type of product or service?

Prepare the forecast

Preparatory steps

The way you'll go about creating your forecast will depend to a large extent on how established your business is, but as a general rule, all forecasts should be based on accurate and current market research.

All businesses need to base their forecasts on certain assumptions regarding potential changes that may take place in the future. Ideally, you need to quantify them (in other words, flesh out predictions with some reasonable numbers), as in the following examples:

- an expectation of market growth or decline by a certain percentage, say 10%.
- a planned expansion in the number of employees to generate an expected 15% increase in production
- a move to a new and better location that should produce a 50% increase in sales

It will also be useful to break down projected sales by market, product or geographic region, and to consider the likely conversion rates from enquiries to orders.

New businesses

New business don't have any historical data on which to base a forecast. This adds a layer of complexity, as many formal methods of estimating future sales are really only useful if the business has been running for some time and has a history of sales trends from which to work. Accurate market research is crucial to the start-up business, as your projections need to have some basis in fact.

Secondary or 'desk' market research can be helpful, however. For example, if you wanted to open a bed and breakfast, you could get hold of historical data on bed occupancy levels or visitor numbers from your local tourist board or Regional Development Agency (RDA). You can then project sales by multiplying average occupancy levels by price per-person per-night (remembering to make some allowances for seasonal peaks and troughs).

If you don't have access to either documentary research or historical sales records, you can still carry out primary or field research among your target customer group. Interviewing potential customers, obtaining 'letters of intent' and testing the market with some advance/prototype products or services can provide useful information to estimate potential future sales. For instance, a person opening a restaurant or café could approach potential customers to ask:

- how often do you eat out?
- on average, how much do you spend on a meal?

Existing businesses

Forecasting can be easier for businesses which are already trading; not only do they have a clearer picture of the market as a whole, but they also have historical sales data on which to base their forecast. Make sure you keep accurate and up-to-date figures of previous sales on a monthly basis, and compare these with the targets you have set so that you can monitor your progress (and adjust your sales forecast as necessary).

Future sales can be estimated on the basis of current trading levels, that is, on existing customers continuing to buy from your business for the foreseeable future. However, your business may be in a position where sales have been growing, or even declining, steadily. In this case, you should identify the main trend in past sales, and then project this forward to give a general picture of future sales.

Talk to key customers about any potential changes in purchasing patterns and review market trends regularly, so that you can reflect them in your forecast. Also take into account the likely effect of any changes in sales strategy, such as additional marketing and price increases or decreases.

When your business is up and running, it can be tempting to think that all your market research has been done and dusted. Actually, the opposite is true: if you don't keep on top of what the market wants (and this will change over time), both your product offering and your forecasts will be completely out of step with your customers' needs. Do make some time regularly to look at what your competitors are doing and what your customers really want. This is the only way you'll keep your competitive edge, and will also make sure that the forecasting process is based on accurate information and market intelligence.

Prepare your forecast

If you sell more than one product or service, prepare a separate forecast for each item in your range. Each forecast needs to take into account:

- the volume you expect to sell; for example, how many units of the product will be sold per month? Product-based businesses sell in units, but so do many service businesses—accountants sell hours of their time, and restaurants sell meals.
- the price at which you expect to sell. The price charged will have an impact on the volume of sales, and the total revenue earned by the business is therefore equal to the volume of units sold, multiplied by the price of each item. Some industries (such as publishing) have a history of selling products at a discount, so remember to factor this in if it applies to you.
- the number of customers to whom you expect to sell. Do your sales tend to be one-offs, or do you achieve regular repeat business from each customer?

Sales in a restaurant can be forecast by looking at a reasonable expectation of the number of tables that will be occupied at different hours of the day, and then multiplying the percentage of tables occupied by the average estimated revenue per table, based on assumptions about the number of meals sold and the average price paid.

Think about your pricing policy

By considering both volume and price, you can decide on a pricing strategy. To continue the restaurant example, if you run a fast-food restaurant, you'll be selling a large volume at a low price. If you own a higher-end French restaurant, on the other hand, you'll be selling a relatively low volume at a premium price. As you set your prices (or revise them), think about:

- what the market will bear (again, make sure you've checked out what your competitors are doing)
- the costs of producing your goods and services
- what you'll need to charge to make a profit

To help you calculate how often your product will be bought, and how much you could charge for it, work out how many customers who fit the customer profile live in your local area. This task may have been onerous before the Internet, but thankfully sites such as **www.upmystreet.com** and **www.checkmyfile.com** are a boon for this type of research.

Raising or lowering your prices could have a significant impact on sales. When preparing your forecast, you will need to consider the impact of any decisions on total revenue and profitability. From this, you can estimate the total number of sales per week/month/year for your business. These figures can be saved in a spreadsheet and plotted on a simple graph against high, medium and low monthly sales expectations.

Remember to compare forecasts (and sales records, if you have any) against potential capacity to make sure that what you are forecasting is achievable. You must have enough staff and resources to meet the expected production and sales targets or to provide the level of service required. Factors such as location, the quality of your products and services, and your target market's needs and expectations should also go into the mix.

Choose a forecasting method

There are several methods of preparing your forecast (see below), and the right one for you will depend on the information your business wishes to gain from the process. For example, if you have been trading for some time, you can use the data from past sales periods as a starting point and base your forecasts on these. New businesses will be able to use these techniques after the first few weeks or months of trading, and can

then compare the *actual* sales figures with the projections made after carrying out initial market research.

Graphical analysis

If you find visual representations of facts and figures useful, plotting past sales data on a line graph will give you a picture of seasonal patterns and general direction. You can use this method to plot different sales figures for different scenarios, which will enable you to 'test out' various scenarios. What would happen, for example, if sales grew or declined? How might your new discounting strategy impact on the business?

You can also choose to plot sales levels by volume or value, or to calculate a percentage increase for annual sales.

Moving averages

A moving average is an indicator that shows the average level of sales over a given period of time. It can be a useful tool for forecasting, but you'll need to use historical sales data to predict future increases or decreases. You'll then be able to forecast sales for the year ahead so that a three-month and twelve-month moving average can be calculated and plotted on a line graph (see below).

The three-month moving average smooths out large monthly fluctuations, but still gives seasonal variations. The twelve-month moving average, however, gives a general trend line.

The forecast three-month moving average for each month can be obtained by adding the expected sales figures for the current and previous two months and dividing by three. The twelve-month moving average can be calculated by adding the forecast sales figures from the current month to the previous eleven months and dividing by twelve (see below).

COMMON MISTAKES
You leave the forecast in the filing cabinet

Once you've put in all the work to create your sales forecast, don't file it away neatly

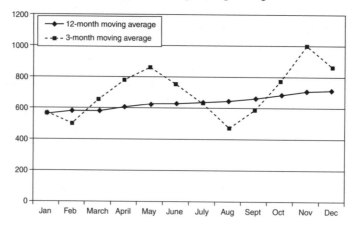

Sales Forecast using Moving Average

and forget about it. Put it to good use and see it as a 'living' document. You can use it to set targets, prepare budgets, raise finance, and work out staff and resource requirements if necessary. The forecast will also give clues about how your business can shape its future strategy, by correlating sales with promotional spending or pricing.

In addition, you should compare actual results with the forecast, revise the forecast regularly as a result of this comparison, and carry out sensitivity analyses to consider the 'what if?' scenarios, such as what would happen to the forecast if customer numbers dropped by 10%.

You don't see the forecast's links to all parts of your business

Many of the elements involved in sales forecasting are inextricably linked with other parts of the business planning process, so be careful how you arrive at your assumptions. Follow the checklist below to avoid common pitfalls when forecasting sales:

- Is the forecast based on verifiable, realistic and unbiased market research information?
- Have you been tempted to ignore the implications of the research if it came up with negative results?
- Don't make projections solely on the basis of historical performance. Keep looking at what else might affect your sales in the

future and adjust the forecast accordingly.

- Is it physically possible to produce the amount of sales being forecast with the personnel, equipment and financial resources available to you, or is the forecast based on wishful thinking? That is: do you understand your capacity limits?
- Does the pricing policy used in calculating the sales forecast relate to what is really achievable, or conversely, have the prices been set too low so that either way the forecast is unrealistic?
- Do you understand the link between sales and costs, and hence the meaning of profitability? Remember the maxim that 'turnover is vanity, while profit is sanity'.
- When you prepared the sales forecast, did you also carry out sensitivity analyses?
- If you have just started up in business, have you considered that it may take longer for your enterprise to become established— and therefore for sales targets to be achieved—than you would like?
- Have you allowed for the possibility that high sales based on an initial promotional surge may drop off afterwards, leading to a need for more intensive marketing and higher ongoing costs?
- You should review your sales performance every month and compare this with the targets. This will help you to anticipate cash flow requirements and will also be useful when adjusting future forecasts.

- Computer spreadsheets and specialist software packages can make the forecasting process much easier.
- Can you identify and justify the assumptions you have made in reaching the forecast, and explain them to interested parties if necessary?

USEFUL LINKS

Chartered Institute of Management Accountants (CIMA):
www.cimaglobal.com
The Chartered Institute of Marketing (CIM):
www.cim.co.uk

Forecasting cash flow

GETTING STARTED

A cash-flow forecast shows how and when you expect money to be received and paid out by your business. Cash is the lifeblood of any business, so it's vital that you know your business will have enough cash to pay your creditors and meet expenses when payments fall due. A cash-flow forecast is usually projected over a period of 6 or 12 months, although you can look at a shorter timescale (such as a week or month) if this is necessary. A cash-flow forecast is a useful management tool that will help you to plan ahead, so you can make important strategic decisions about the way your business operates.

This actionlist explains how to prepare a cash-flow forecast and then use the information to demonstrate the viability of your business. It also considers how you can use the forecast to monitor your cash flow on an ongoing basis.

FAQS

What is a cash-flow forecast and why is it important?

A cash-flow forecast enables a business to project its future cash income (receipts) and cash expenditure (payments) over a given period of time. You can use forecasts to make management decisions about the business and, in particular, a forecast will enable you to identify:

- how much initial cash investment a start-up business requires.
- when other finance, such as an overdraft or loan, may be needed
- what level of loan repayments you can afford
- when your business will be able to spend cash in the future, such as when taking on a new employee, paying for a marketing campaign or buying new capital equipment
- what sort of salary you can pay yourself
- when cash-flow problems may occur once your business is trading and as it grows

If you want to apply for a grant or borrow money either in the form of an overdraft facility or a loan from a bank, the cash-flow forecast is a critical document that you'll need to provide with your application because it shows in cash terms how the business will operate.

Cash-flow forecasts can be drawn up in various ways. This is a commonly used layout, with data that could relate to a start-up business.

Note that figures in brackets indicate a negative balance and that the forecast consists of three main sections—receipts, payments and net cash flow (or cash-in-hand).

Receipts

This section gives details of the sales income the business receives. Cash sales generate immediate income, whereas with credit sales there will be a delay before the money comes in depending on what credit period you've agreed with your customers. If we assume that all customers will pay within 30 days, the money from credit sales invoiced in January will be received in February. If your business is registered for Value Added Tax (VAT), the VAT charged on your sales and paid by your customers should be included in the receipts. (Remember, VAT is money you have collected on behalf of HM Revenue and Customs (HMRC) and you need to put it aside and account for it later when you submit your VAT return.)

The forecast can also record under 'other income' any cash that is received from non-trading sources such as bank loans, business investments, Government grants and bank interest for cash on deposit.

Payments

This section details all the cash payments made by your business. You need to record when you expect to pay your suppliers for their goods and services, which may be on a

Receipts	January	February	March	April	May	June
Cash sales	£2,000	£4,000	£6,000	£7,000	£8,000	£8,000
Credit sales	£0	£8,000	£12,000	£15,000	£18,000	£20,000
Other income	£10,000	£0	£0	£0	£0	£0
Total receipts	**£12,000**	**£12,000**	**£18,000**	**£22,000**	**£26,000**	**£28,000**
Payments						
Credit purchases	£7,000	£9,000	£12,000	£14,000	£16,000	£17,000
Wages	£3,000	£3,000	£5,000	£5,000	£5,000	£5,000
Office expenses	£2,000	£1,000	£1,000	£1,500	£1,000	£1,000
Finance and tax payments	£0	£500	£500	£650	£650	£650
Capital expenditure	£3,000	£0	£0	£0	£0	£0
Total payments	**£15,000**	**£13,500**	**£18,500**	**£21,150**	**£22,650**	**£23,650**
Net cash flow	(£3,000)	(£1,500)	(£500)	£850	£3,350	£4,350
Opening cash balance	£0	(£3,000)	(£4,500)	(£5,000)	(£4,150)	(£800)
Closing cash balance	(£3,000)	(£4,500)	(£5,000)	(£4,150)	(£800)	£3,550

cash-with-order basis, or on agreed credit terms.

The example above gives five payment categories, but you may want to change or add to these categories to suit your particular business. For example, you could further divide these categories to help you identify the different costs you have as follows:

- credit purchases—payments to suppliers and subcontractors, and marketing activities

- wages—production and admin staff, Pay As You Earn (PAYE) and National Insurance (NI), and training costs
- operating expenses—rent, business rates, telephone and Internet, utilities, insurance, stationery and post
- finance and taxes—bank charges, loan repayments, quarterly VAT payments and lease payments
- capital expenditure—office equipment, furniture and cars

Net cash flow/cash-in-hand

At the end of each month, you need to calculate the net cash flow (i.e. add up the total receipts, and from this subtract the total payments).

Net cash flow is added to the opening balance to give the closing cash balance at the end of each month. The closing cash balance is the amount of cash your business has available at that given point in time, and should correspond with what you expect to see on your bank statement.

In this example, the business receives £2,000 of sales income in January as well as a £10,000 capital injection, but pays out £15,000 in costs, resulting in a negative (or overdrawn) balance of £3,000 at the end of January. As the business continues to trade, it suffers a negative cash flow over the next two months and shows a maximum cash deficit of £5,000 at the end of March. It is only in April that receipts start to exceed payments and the business begins to generate a positive cash flow, and it takes until June before there's a positive cash balance. For this business to be able to trade successfully, it would need to have an extra £5,000 invested when it starts trading or to have an alternative source of funds, such as an agreed overdraft facility for at least this amount.

✔ MAKING IT HAPPEN

There are a number of things that you need to think about when preparing a cash-flow forecast—ranging from your projected sales to your working capital requirement:

Sales forecast

To forecast your cash receipts accurately, you need to forecast what your sales will be on a weekly or monthly basis. For a start-up business this will be based on your market research and your business plan, while if you've been trading for a while, you'll be able to look at your actual trading performance and link this to your current marketing plan. How quickly sales are then turned into cash will depend on whether or not you give your customers credit (and on what terms).

Credit terms

While few retail businesses offer their customers credit, many others do offer some form of trade credit to their customers. Don't forget that how long it takes your customers to pay you will have a significant bearing on your cash flow, with most trade accounts operating on a 30- to 60-day credit period. Just as you may offer your customers credit, your business may also be able to obtain credit from your suppliers. You need to define your credit policy clearly to your customers, and understand what credit terms you may be able to get from your suppliers, so you can predict when you will receive cash and when you need to make payments.

Cash is not the same as profit

Profit is an accounting concept and, in terms of running a business on a daily basis, having sufficient cash to pay for purchases and expenses is always the most important single issue.

Let's assume that Mr Jones runs a furniture store. He pays £250 in cash for a table and sells it to a business customer for £500 on credit. On this transaction, Mr Jones has a made a gross profit of £250—that is, the difference between the cost price of the item and its selling price. However, his business can only benefit from this profit when and if the customer actually pays him cash for the goods.

Working capital requirement

In the example above, Mr Jones has paid £250 to his supplier, but he also has to fund the daily costs incurred in running his business and paying for further stock until his customer pays him. If we assume that these costs amount to £200, he will need a total of £450 to operate his business before his customer pays him. This is the working capital required by his business, and equates to the cash needed to fund its day-to-day operations. When the customer pays him the £500 owed, his closing cash balance is only £50 better than when the transaction first started, even though the gross profit was £250!

Cash cycle

'Cash cycle' is the term used to describe the connection between working capital and cash movements in and out of a business, and it's usually measured in days or months. Businesses typically purchase goods and services before they're in a position to make a sale to their customers; this is particularly evident in production-led businesses. Suppose that a firm buys raw materials on one month's credit, and then holds them in store for a further month until they're used by the production department. The production cycle is very short, but finished goods are typically held for one month before they are sold. Customers then usually take two months to pay these invoices.

The cash cycle would be:

	Months
Raw material stock turnover period	1
Less: credit taken from suppliers	(1)
Finished goods stock turnover period	1
Debtors' payment period	2
Cash cycle	3

So there's a gap of three months between paying your supplier for the raw materials and receiving cash from your customer. A few dates will help to clarify this point. Suppose the business buys its raw materials on 1 January. The sequence of events would then be as shown in the diagram below.

In this example, the cash cycle is the three-month period between 1 February, when payment is made to suppliers, and 1 May, when cash is received from debtors. And it's this period that will determine the amount of working capital required by the business. If you can shorten the cash cycle, you can reduce the amount of money

Event	Date
Purchase of raw materials	1 January
Issue of materials to production (one month after purchase)	1 February
Payments made to suppliers (one month after purchase)	1 February
Sale of finished goods (one month after production begins)	1 March
Receipt of cash from customer (two months after sale)	1 May

needed by your business to fund its working capital.

Types of business costs

When preparing your cash-flow forecast, you need to be aware that there are four main types of costs for which your business makes payments:

- variable costs, which vary directly in relation to the sales that you make. These include raw materials used in your production processes, or the goods you may buy in and then resell—all of which can be linked to your sales forecast.
- fixed costs, which don't vary directly in relation to your sales. These costs may be incurred on a regular monthly basis, such as wages and salaries, insurance, rates or a car lease; or they may be paid quarterly in advance, which is more typical for property rental payments.
- capital costs, which relate to the purchase of business assets (such as computers or a vehicle) and occur relatively infrequently.
- Government taxes, where businesses have the responsibility to collect and pay a range of taxes covering employee PAYE deductions, NI contributions, VAT if they are registered for it, and corporation tax for companies.

How to set up the forecast

You can use various methods to set up your cash-flow forecast, the most popular being:

- manual preparation
- spreadsheets (such as Excel or Lotus 123)
- forecasting tools
- accounting software

The most commonly-used method is to set up your forecast in a standard spreadsheet, which allows you to change the numbers quickly and easily as you refine and tweak the figures. There are seven key steps to take when setting up the forecast:

1 produce a sales forecast for the next 12 months. Estimate the split between credit and cash sales, and the credit period taken by your customers so you put receipts in the correct month.

2 check whether any other cash income is due over the year ahead. This will include money you are investing in your business, as well as any loans and grants you might have in the pipeline.

3 think about the purchases you'll need to make for goods/stock to allow you to achieve your sales forecast. At first, your suppliers may want to receive cash payments when your order is delivered, but after a month or two you should be able to set up a trade account and benefit from credit payment terms.

4 identify your other regular monthly cash payments. These will include your employees' salaries, marketing costs, operating costs, vehicle running costs, and any other sundry expenses.

5 include any one-off big payments, such as fixed asset purchases.

6 set out the cash-flow forecast month by month for a full year. Check carefully that your figures tally with when you expect payments will actually be made.

7 list your assumptions as a reminder of how you've derived your figures—for example, make a note of any payment terms and what cash cycle length you're using. Most lenders will look at your assumptions quite closely, as doing this will help them to spot whether your figures have been thought through in detail.

How to use the forecast in practice— variance analysis

Once you've completed your cash-flow forecast, you need to compare it with what happens in reality. Typically at the end of each month you should compare your forecast values with your actual results.

In the cash-flow forecast below, you'll see there's a column for the difference (variance) between the forecast value and actual result for receipts and payments. Where the actual result is worse than the forecast value, this is shown as a figure in brackets.

By comparing your actual cash flow with the forecast figures, you'll be able to see whether your assumptions remain valid. If there are significant differences, you should revise your assumptions and then re-forecast your cash flow—trying to be more realistic this time!

When you first start trading, you should think about revising your cash-flow forecast every month to reflect what is actually happening. If you're running an established business, you'll still want to look at revising your forecast every three to six months to reduce the risk of cash (or, more specifically, lack of it) becoming a problem.

COMMON MISTAKES
You ignore your cash-flow forecast

It's important to keep referring to your cash-flow forecast and revising it when you need to. Try using 'what if' scenarios to see what happens to your cash flow if sales are 10% higher or lower than your forecast.

You're over-optimistic about customers paying you

Be cautious, especially in the first few months of trading, about how quickly your customers will pay you. It's better to expect slow payment and then actually receive the cash more quickly than you expected than to anticipate immediate payment and have to wait for months before the cash is forthcoming! For this reason, try to have a contingency reserve of cash to cover unexpected costs or a sudden shortfall in receipts.

Cash-flow forecast	January			
	Forecast	**Actual**	**Variance**	**Notes**
Receipts				
Cash sales	£2,000	£1,500	(£500)	Started trading a week later than expected.
Credit sales	£0	£4,000	£4,000	Early payment discount offered to customers.
Other income	£10,000	£10,000	–	Start-up capital.
Total receipts	**£12,000**	**£15,500**	**£3,500**	
Payments				
Purchases	£7,000	£11,000	(£4,000)	Credit accounts slow to establish with suppliers.
Wages	£3,000	£3,000	–	
Office expenses	£2,000	£3,000	(£1,000)	More sundry items needed than expected.
Finance and tax	£0	£300	(£300)	Overdraft arrangement fee from bank.
Capital expenditure	£3,000	£2,500	£500	Negotiated better deal on office furniture.
Total payments	**£15,000**	**£19,800**	**(£4,800)**	
Net cash-flow	(£3,000)	(£4,300)	(£1,300)	
Opening cash balance	£0	£0	–	
Closing cash balance	(£3,000)	(£4,300)	(£1,300)	

You forget that months can vary

Bear in mind that a monthly forecast doesn't take account of timing issues within each month. In other words, during a month that shows a small positive cash balance at the start and finish, you may suffer a large negative balance in the middle if a large payment has to be made before sales income has been received.

USEFUL LINK
Business Link:
www.businesslink.gov.uk

Avoiding cash-flow problems

GETTING STARTED

Running out of cash is one of the main reasons why small businesses fail. There are many scenarios when you could face a cash crisis, but if you're aware of these and know how to prevent a short-term problem, you should be able to prevent your business from collapsing through lack of cash. No matter how healthy your balance sheet may seem to you (in terms of physical assets and the money owing to your business), your ability to convert this into actual cash at critical times may make the difference between your business's survival or failure.

This actionlist looks at the situations that can lead to cash-flow problems and the steps you can take to avoid running into trouble.

FAQS

Why is cash so important?

Your business can only continue to trade if you can pay your bills as and when they fall due. So you need to have a really good grasp of how and when money flows in and out of your business.

Cash obviously flows into your business through the money that you invest in it and the money that is paid to you by your customers when you've made a sale of some sort. Cash flows out of your business whenever you pay suppliers, employees, overhead costs, taxes and so on.

Problems arise when the outflows are greater than the inflows and reach a critical point when you've used up all your available cash. So it's essential to address any cash-flow problems before you reach this stage.

What are the main causes of cash-flow problems?

Late payment by your customers
Don't forget that a sale is only completed when your invoice has been paid in full. Many businesses concentrate on generating new sales, but fail to set up credit-control procedures until they run into cash-flow problems.

A key customer becomes insolvent
If your business is dependent on a few major customers, you'll be exposed to the risk of one of them having financial problems, which could result in you not

being paid. This can be disastrous if the income from the client concerned makes up a large proportion of your overall revenue, and you're relying on that money to pay your own creditors or employees.

Insufficient working capital
Working capital is the money that funds the day-to-day running of your business. Most businesses incur significant costs when they're set up, and they then have to pay suppliers and staff regularly before they actually receive any money from their customers. If you don't invest enough money in your business from the outset, you'll be in danger of having cash-flow problems once you start to trade—cash tends to flow out much faster than it comes in!

You can also run into problems with working capital if your business expands very quickly. This is because, as your sales grow, your working capital requirement also grows. Money becomes tied up in stock and you'll end up being owed an increasing amount of money by your customers, who may pay you more slowly than you need to pay your suppliers. This situation, commonly known as 'over-trading', can usually be avoided if you keep an eye on your cash-flow forecasts.

Focusing on turnover instead of profit
Everyone wants to see their sales grow as quickly as possible but you need to remember that long-term sustainable cash-flow into your business is only generated

through making profits. So, always cost the products you're supplying carefully to make sure they'll generate a profit for your business at your expected selling prices. Focusing on high-volume but low-profit margin sales can also lead quickly to a position of over-trading, if you've under-estimated how much working capital your business needs.

Poor financial planning

Not surprisingly, problems can occur when you don't plan for certain payments, such as Value Added Tax (VAT), Pay As You Earn (PAYE) income tax contributions, business rates and personal or business tax bills. You need to build such payments into your cash-flow forecast and check that sufficient funds will be available at these key times. Make sure that, if you're investing in equipment, you buy it when your cash flow is healthy, or else try to structure any repayments over a longer period to reduce the impact on your finances.

Buying too much stock

Many suppliers will offer you discount incentives when you agree to buy their goods in bulk. While this may look attractive, you need to think carefully before committing to large orders of stock, particularly while you're establishing your business. If you order bulk purchases only to find that the items quickly go out of fashion or have a short shelf life, you could be left with stock that you can't sell, but which you still have to pay for.

MAKING IT HAPPEN

Preparing cash-flow forecasts and putting them to good use is the key to avoiding many financial problems. They can help you anticipate working-capital shortfalls and most cash-flow difficulties that might crop up during the normal course of running your business. Cash-flow forecasts also allow you to do a sensitivity analysis, which enables you to see what effect lower sales or slower payments will have on your cash movements. Try to do your forecasts with lower-than-expected sales income and higher-than-expected costs—that way you'll see how cash flow makes an impact on your business's financial position.

The key ways to reduce cash-flow problems are as follows:

Adopt tight credit-control procedures

Set up procedures for managing how and when you give your customers credit. Start by providing credit only to approved customers and make a note of when their accounts are due for payment, checking that they pay according to your agreed terms. Make sure you've got efficient administration procedures in place for preparing your invoices promptly and sending statements to your customers, so you don't unwittingly add to payment delays.

Offer incentives for early payment

Consider encouraging your customers to pay more quickly by offering a discount if they pay either on delivery or within a certain timescale (typically 7–14 days) from the invoice date. Discount levels are usually 2–5%, but before you agree an amount, check what effect it will have on your profit margins and think about how important early payment is to you.

Consider debtor finance

If your business is growing rapidly, you might want to use an invoice discounter or factoring service. These firms will provide your business with a cash advance (usually 80–85%) against the value of your invoices as soon as they are raised. In return, you'll be charged interest on the advance, plus a service charge. You can also ask factoring firms to take direct control of collecting payments from your customers, which can save you the cost of using your own staff to manage this process.

Negotiate better credit terms with your suppliers

As your business grows, you may be able to negotiate better credit terms with your suppliers. Initially, you might do this by delaying payment from when you make a purchase to having a 30-day credit account. If the majority of your customers expect to have 60-day credit accounts, try to agree 60-day payment terms with your suppliers.

Set up a bank overdraft facility

An overdraft allows you to borrow money as and when you need it from your bank, up to an agreed limit. It's a relatively cheap way to finance working capital if you have large variations in cash flow during the course of a month, or if your business is very seasonal, because you only pay interest on the amount actually borrowed.

However, if you're continually relying on your overdraft, it can become expensive. More importantly, it may also highlight that your business needs additional working capital, or a longer-term form of finance. With an overdraft, you're also exposed to 'repayment on demand', which means that your lender can ask for full repayment at any time. A 'term loan' with fixed monthly instalments is safer from your point of view, as the lender can only demand full repayment if you default on your instalments.

Asset financing

If your business needs to invest in new equipment but doesn't have the cash, you can fund this either with a term loan, a hire purchase loan or a leasing deal. This gives you a fixed level of regular repayments over a set period (usually two to five years). In situations where the asset is being used as security for the finance, you'll probably still need to provide at least a 10% deposit.

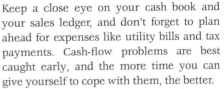

COMMON MISTAKES
You think your cash flow will look after itself

Keep a close eye on your cash book and your sales ledger, and don't forget to plan ahead for expenses like utility bills and tax payments. Cash-flow problems are best caught early, and the more time you can give yourself to cope with them, the better.

You don't forecast your cash flow

If you take the trouble to calculate your future cash-flow requirements, you'll be able to act quickly when you expect a shortage of cash in the future. Talk to your bank and your suppliers as soon as you think there might be a problem. If you don't take action in good time, you run the risk of affecting your relationship with your bank, suppliers and customers. Your bank will be far more receptive to dealing with your cash-flow difficulties if you talk to them before the problem occurs.

USEFUL LINK
BusinessLink:
www.businesslink.gov.uk

Controlling costs

GETTING STARTED

The basis of any successful business is that income should exceed expenses. One way to improve profitability is to increase the sales of your business, but you can also enhance profitability by cutting down on your costs. A business that can do this will be able to release more resources for growth in the good times, and will be in a better position to survive in recession. This actionlist gives some suggestions on ways to control (and in some cases reduce) the costs of your business.

FAQS

Which costs do I need to control?

To be able to *control* costs, you first have to know exactly what they are. Start by identifying each cost clearly, and make sure that you keep records of all bills, receipts, and so on. Review your costs regularly, basing the timing on when your accounts are normally completed. It is not enough to calculate whether the business is in profit or loss, important though that is; you also need to be aware of what normal costs are, so that you can spot anomalies and take action to address them. Some costs will be more important to control than others, so you need to work out what the *business's* critical costs are, and concentrate on reducing them.

Who is responsible for controlling costs?

Cost control is the responsibility of everyone working in the business. If you have a team of people working for you, all your employees have countless opportunities to affect costs throughout each day. You need to be aware that if employees are unhappy at work, they are in a position to do a lot of damage, if only through what they *don't* do. For example, if they're bored, frustrated or feel undervalued, they're less likely to feel that the business's welfare is their focus. If they're motivated and feel part of the business on the other hand, they'll work economically without supervision. Rising to the challenge of providing this kind of environment for your employees is a test of good management; one approach is to involve employees by asking them to come up with ideas to reduce costs. As your staff are on the 'front line', they're bound to have some practical suggestions that may really have a significant impact. If you do decide to ask your staff for their input, though, be careful with the way you phrase your request. Unless the company is in dire straits and you are genuinely thinking of making redundancies, don't give them the impression that their jobs are on the line as part of this cost-cutting measure!

Many people assume that because the volume of expenditure is so much larger than they are used to in home life, any savings they might make are insignificant. Every little does help, though, so let your team know that cutting back on what look like insignificant costs will help the business overall.

MAKING IT HAPPEN
Use cost control measures

One effective cost control measure is to carry out a cost–benefit analysis. Try to build in cost awareness as part of your general planning processes across all areas of the business. Whether you're planning ways to develop yourself, your staff, or the company's direction in general, think of how the overall impact of any decision should be understood in terms of business profitability. In other words, the benefits of a particular course of action should be set against the cost. For example, a person may be assigned to carry out a piece of research that could, in fact, be done quicker by a consultant, or bought off the shelf. It can be hard to keep a professional distance when you have to make hard decisions about a project or issue that you have invested a lot in personally, but this is exactly what you have to do if money is tight: you must be pragmatic.

Another method of cost control is value analysis (VA), which involves a detailed examination of each part of a product, service or system to work out if there is any way in which its costs could be reduced without affecting quality. Value analysis is usually done as a group exercise, and is therefore a good way to involve employees and increase general awareness of cost control. Each aspect of the product should be brought under the spotlight. The group has to decide, for example, whether the product is really necessary; whether it can be made with cheaper materials; whether it is actually cheaper to buy than to make; whether it can be made more quickly; or whether it can be simplified to reduce potential faults. Other aspects to look at might be reducing the material that is used to make it, or reducing wastage. Economizing on the use of raw materials can be a very effective cost-saving measure.

Also look at your company's purchasing methods and as a first step, see if you could get a discount from buying in bulk from your suppliers if you don't do this already. Be prepared to haggle and regularly review the cost of supplies and suppliers. In fact, no bill or invoice that your business receives should be taken for granted. For example, if you rent your business premises and you feel the rent is too high, don't just accept the status quo but talk to your landlord about the possibility of reducing it. Alternatively, if you feel that rates are too high, your local property valuation service may be able to help you with your property's assessment value.

Stock control is another potential area for savings, as accurate control will reduce storage and working capital costs. Providing effective security should reduce the cost of stock lost through theft. For example, if your business manufactures products that have a high market price (or if you're a wholesaler), do check that you're protecting your stock well. For example, electronic equipment, pharmaceuticals, alcohol and cigarettes are the type of thing that people might try to steal. Your insurance should cover theft, of course, but it's much better to keep your stock secure so that you don't lose money as a result of someone else's actions.

Look at potential areas for cost savings

Staff costs often offer the greatest potential scope for savings, although it would be wise not to launch wholesale into redundancies until you've thought through your actions to their logical conclusion. You may be able to manage with fewer people on your team, but then again there's a risk you could pare back your staff numbers so much that the business just can't function. It's perfectly valid to investigate whether your staff are delivering value for money, though. Are they being motivated and managed well? Also check that their pay is appropriate for the work they do. You are trying to cut costs, of course, and too much is clearly expensive, but if salaries are too low, you'll end up with a high staff turnover rate that may ultimately damage performance.

One environmentally-friendly way of making your business run more leanly is to cut down on energy costs. Encourage your employees to use energy as responsibly at work as they do at home (where *they* are paying the bills). Many people today are concerned about the environment, and this can motivate them to save energy. It's easy to forget that some of the biggest savings available to businesses lie within some of their most basic costs, such as gas and electricity. Have your meters double-checked, especially if the business uses a lot of energy, and set thermostats correctly. Something as basic as insulation can really help you shrink your bills and produce long-term savings, and you may even be eligible for a grant to help pay for it.

Telephone calls are another basic company cost offering potential savings. Some private phone calls made from the office are necessary, but don't allow staff to take advantage. Make sure that you outline a policy for the use of phones for personal calls and agree and circulate it. Staff should also be made aware of any possible disciplinary action that could be taken against them for breach of the policy. It is possible to get itemised bills for each extension, which should discourage misuse of phones. Staff should also be trained in the efficient use of the telephone, to reduce the length of calls.

Photocopiers are easy to use and the expense can soon get out of control if usage is not monitored. Make sure that all copies are logged, allocated to a cost centre, and that the initials of the person taking the copy are recorded. Staff should be charged for personal copies, and discouraged from making unnecessary copies. Someone should be made responsible for monitoring copying, and usage should be reviewed regularly. Make sure that all staff know exactly how to use all the facilities on the copier. This in itself can reduce cost—for example, printing double-sided copies can save time and money.

Some staff may be tempted to take office stationery home for their own use, so it might be worth keeping the stationery cupboard locked, and making someone responsible for issuing materials. Recycling can again play a useful role here: scrap paper can be recycled as stapled writing pads, for example, and used laser printer cartridges can be sent off to be refilled at a discount price. In fact, all waste should be considered for potential recycling or resale to recycling companies. For example, there are companies who will buy industrial plastic waste for recycling.

Finally, make sure you have a clear expenses policy. It is possible to reduce misuse of expenses by drawing up guidelines so that everyone understands what is, and is not, acceptable. Expense claims should be cleared by a manager before being paid. Make sure that expenses for individuals are reviewed periodically, and anomalies investigated.

COMMON MISTAKES
You make false economies

Don't cut back on the wrong things. If you reduce the level of service your customers are used to, you'll probably end up losing money instead of saving it. Similarly, if you make working conditions too harsh (for example, by cutting back on pay, benefits, or training), your staff will become de-moralised and won't perform as well as they could—indeed, you run the risk of them leaving.

You ignore rising costs

Confront cost problems immediately, rather than put them off and hope they'll go away. They won't go anywhere. It's much better to act sooner and to stop the problem from escalating.

USEFUL LINK
Business Link:
www.businesslink.gov.uk

Reducing energy costs

GETTING STARTED

As energy prices have steadily spiralled higher, more and more businesses have been looking at ways of becoming more environmentally friendly in order to save money. There's also been a lot of pressure on businesses to reduce the amount of power they use, and the Government is introducing stringent targets with the aim that companies should do all they can to minimise their environmental impact.

By following simple, practical measures such as switching off equipment when it's not in use and turning down heating, the Government estimates that you could make a 20% annual saving on your energy bill. A bonus is that if you can be seen to be making your business more environmentally responsible, you may also improve your reputation—because an increasing number of consumers are keen to buy from firms with 'green' credentials.

FAQS

Why is energy efficiency so important?

Businesses are looking more closely at their energy consumption for two main reasons: rising fuel costs and the impact on the environment. The rise in the price of wholesale gas bought by UK energy suppliers over the past two years is widely blamed for the soaring cost of bills. There are a number of reasons why prices have risen, including:

- North Sea gas supplies have declined faster than expected
- the rocketing cost of oil (in Europe, gas prices are linked to oil prices)
- the UK doesn't have adequate facilities for importing and storing gas
- gas is used to make a significant proportion of the UK's electricity, so electricity bills have risen too

The environmental impact of inefficient energy use is also prompting many business owners to take active steps to improve their energy efficiency. Working towards a more environmentally-friendly workspace can have a number of business benefits, such as:

- saving money on fuel bills
- increasing productivity because people are working in a more comfortable environment, and processes are streamlined and more efficient
- boosting your firm's 'green' image, which may be useful for your PR and marketing
- not falling foul of the law—legislation in this

area is getting more stringent, and even small businesses must comply or risk heavy fines

What targets has the Government set for energy efficiency?

Reducing energy usage is high on the Government's agenda. Many of the schemes now in operation have sprung from the Kyoto Protocol, signed in 1997. It committed the UK to cutting its greenhouse gas emissions by 12.5% on 1990 levels between 2008 and 2012.

The Government has set itself even tougher targets—it wants carbon dioxide emissions to be at least 20% below 1990 levels by 2010, and in the longer term, it wants a 60% reduction by 2050. And it's targeting both small firms and large companies through new legislation. Small businesses are affected by:

- the **Climate Change Levy**, which is a tax on business consumption of electricity. All businesses that use more than the 'domestic level' of energy are liable for the levy, which is added directly to your fuel bills (see **www.netregs.gov.uk/netregs/ 275207/1018642/1415034/1415084/ ?version=1& lang=_e** for more details). You can avoid paying this if you have signed up for a 'green tariff'—which means you've instructed your supplier to provide you with electricity sourced from a renewable source (see below for more on green tariffs)

- the **Climate Change Programme 2006**, which sets targets for reducing emissions of carbon dioxide. See the whole programme at **www.defra.gov.uk/ENVIRONMENT/climatechange/uk/ukccp/pdf/ukccp06-all.pdf**
- the **Landfill Tax**, which levies a tax on businesses sending waste to landfill. At the time of writing, this is £2 a tonne for inert waste, with rates for other types of waste varying up to £18 per tonne

MAKING IT HAPPEN

There are numerous cheap, easy and practical ways you can reduce your business energy costs—many of which can be done immediately, without having to invest in expensive equipment. For example:
- don't automatically switch on lights; natural lighting is often perfectly adequate
- switch off lights in unused rooms
- fit low-energy light bulbs or strips. They cost more to buy, but use 80% less energy than normal ones and last a lot longer
- consider fitting a timer or infrared sensor to control lighting
- switch off PC monitors overnight—this can save enough energy to microwave six dinners, or laser print 800 A4 copies. Switching off the monitor when you are at meetings or at lunch can save around £100 per computer per year
- when buying new computers, think about replacing PCs with laptops—they use a tenth of the energy of PCs with large monitors, and also mean that people can work from home more easily—which will in turn cut down on the amount of energy they expend getting to work
- turn off other office equipment when not in use. Check whether the equipment has an energy-saving 'standby' or 'sleep' mode, which it will automatically switch to when idle
- consider installing smarter energy displays and meters, so you can monitor how much power you are using
- reduce the thermostat on your radiators by one degree centigrade—this can reduce the power used for heating by 10%
- check whether your building is insulated,

and if it isn't, fit insulation in the loft cavity and around hot-water pipes. If you rent your premises, ask your landlord about getting this type of work carried out
- ensure draught proofing is fitted around windows and external doors
- think about using fans instead of air-conditioning—an air-conditioning system uses around ten times as much power as a single fan
- if you run company vehicles, remember there are tax breaks for businesses that use cars with low carbon-dioxide emissions (see below)

Tap into support

The high cost of buying and fitting equipment to harness renewable energy is hampering its adaption according to the Carbon Trust, which works with businesses and the public sector to cut greenhouse gas emissions.

However, there are number of grants and tax breaks available to help businesses become more environmentally friendly:
- the Government's Low Carbon Buildings Programme, which replaced the Clear Skies and Solar PV programmes in 2006, will run for three years. It has a pot of more than £80 million from which to make grants to businesses and householders installing micro-generation equipment such as wind turbines or solar panels. Go to **www. low-carbonbuildings.org.uk** for more details.
- Energy-Efficiency Loans are available from the Carbon Trust to replace old equipment such as lighting, boilers or insulation with energy-efficient versions. Small businesses in England and Wales can borrow up to £100,000 unsecured and interest-free (up to £200,000 in Northern Ireland). See **www.carbontrust.co.uk/energy/takingaction/loans.htm** for more details. The Carbon Trust also provides free advice and information on energy efficiency.
- Enhanced Capital Allowances (ECAs) enable firms to claim a 100% allowance in the first year against taxable profits on a variety of energy-efficient equipment. This includes boilers, combined heat and power systems, compact heat exchangers, lighting, pipe-

work insulation and solar thermal systems. ECAs are also available on cars with low carbon-dioxide emissions. See **www. eca.gov.uk** for full details.

Use renewable energy

In the UK, it just isn't practical for a business to rely solely on a self-generated alternative source of energy. However, increasing numbers of firms are starting to generate part of the power used by their business. This is usually done via a wind turbine or solar panels.

You can either store this energy in batteries or, as is more usual, set up a National Grid connection with your power supplier. The power you generate via your alternative energy source is fed into the National Grid, and its value is deducted from your energy bill. You will continue to pay for your power in the usual way but will benefit from these energy credits.

The advantages of this approach include:

- you'll receive smaller energy bills
- in the long run, greater use of renewable energy will help to stabilise energy prices
- renewable energy won't run out and causes less pollution
- there are grants available to buy power-generating equipment
- solar panels and wind turbines have a life-span of at least 20 years

There are, however, some drawbacks:

- without grants, power-generating equipment is expensive—£2,000 upwards to buy, install and connect a basic system to the National Grid
- you won't be able to generate sufficient energy to totally fulfil your needs. For example, a wind turbine might perhaps generate about 10% of your annual electricity
- you'll need planning permission for a wind turbine, and in some cases, for solar panels (if the panel is not flush with your roof, if you work in a listed building or a building located in a National Park, for example.) If you rent your business premises, you'll need authorisation from your landlord

If you don't want to generate your own electricity, you can still use renewable energy and save money by signing up for a 'green tariff'. This means your electricity supplier is obliged to provide you with power from a renewable source. Firms that sign up for a green tariff will pay less to the Climate Change Levy. There are two types of green tariffs:

- renewable tariff—if you sign up for this, all the power you use is provided from renewable sources
- eco-funds tariff—this is a more expensive option, where part of your money goes towards developing new renewable energy projects

The majority of the UK's electricity companies allow businesses to sign up to green tariffs. However, you can also switch your account to companies that were set up expressly to supply and invest in 'green' energy. These include:

- Ecotricity (**www.ecotricity.co.uk**)
- Good Energy (**www.good-energy.co.uk**)
- Green Energy (UK) plc (**www. greenenergy.uk.com**)

COMMON MISTAKE
You don't involve your staff

It's a good idea to appoint a 'green co-ordinator' to take responsibility for ensuring that all members of staff are playing their part. Make sure that everyone has an input into your 'green policy' and understands your position on the environment. According to Friends of the Earth, this can be a 'positive, team-building' exercise.

USEFUL LINKS
The Carbon Trust:
www.carbontrust.co.uk
The Energy Saving Trust:
www.est.org.uk
Energywatch:
www.energywatch.org.uk
The Green Energy Marketplace:
www.greenelectricity.org
The National Energy Foundation:
www.nef.org.uk

Controlling your stock levels

GETTING STARTED

Keeping a careful eye on your stock—so that you can balance your customers' orders without loading yourself up with so much that you can't shift it—is an important part of successful cash management. In this actionlist, we'll look at how you can control your stock levels (this is sometimes also referred to as 'inventory management'), and also at how you can account for the stock you hold on your balance sheet.

FAQS

Can you give me a simple definition of stock and inventory?

Stock is the supply of goods or materials that your business holds to be sold on. For example, a traditional manufacturing business will hold stock in the following categories:

- **raw materials**: supplies to be used in the production process
- **work in progress**: items *in* the production process
- **finished products**: goods available for sale to customers

A retail or wholesale business will hold a range of products appropriate to its customers. Greengrocers will stock fruit and vegetables, newsagents sell papers and magazines, and a mechanic will sell spare car or bike parts. Essentially, any saleable item you use in the course of your business may be regarded as stock.

Items such as machinery, tools and computers *aren't* classified as stock unless they are for resale. They are assets of your business and are neither consumed in any process nor sold to customers.

Inventory is both a list of your stock items and the act of checking your physical stock against your record of stock in hand. Inventory management is vital to help manage your ordering process and to help you control stock loss (through wastage or theft, for example).

MAKING IT HAPPEN
Decide on the quantity of stock you need

Judging the right level of stock for your business is a fine balancing act, in which you need to minimise the costs of holding stock but still make sure that you can meet customer demand. There are bound to be times where you don't get it right, especially if your business is young, but you will soon get a feel for it. That said, make sure you don't get into the habit of ordering stock as a matter of course: it's wise to review your order sizes and suppliers regularly.

When you're working out how much stock is right for your business, think about the following core stock levels:

- **maximum stock:** the most stock that you should keep on hand
- **minimum stock:** the lowest stock level for any given item
- **re-order level:** the point at which you need to place an order for new stock
- **re-order quantity:** the amount of any item to be ordered at the re-order level

It may be time-consuming, but it's important that you review your stock levels regularly and that you also think about the context in which you're selling. A number of factors may drive the orders that you place, and not all of them may relate directly to the sales history of the item in question: you need to look at the whole picture. For example, if you're a retailer, there'll probably be a point when you decide to run down stock of one particular item in order to free up space for a new product line. Also, stock levels for some products will fluctuate greatly on a seasonal basis; there won't be much call for sun hats in November, for example, or heavy sweaters in July.

Put stock control methods in place

Having too much or too little stock can have real knock-on effects for your business.

Overstocking can lead to:
■ stock loss as the result of damage or waste
■ your working capital (cash) being tied up
■ soaring storage costs

On the other hand, understocking can result in:
■ lost orders
■ damaged customer goodwill over time
■ high handling/transport costs if you have to rush new stock in
■ lost output (if you run a manufacturing business and you don't have key items to hand, you won't be able to meet orders on time)

Juggling so many balls at once is tricky, especially if your business holds stock lines. Putting in place the right stock control methods and systems will get you on track and will help you reduce costs, improve efficiency and make sure you can give your customers what they want—when they want it. Some of the most common systems used include:

Par method

If your business has a high turnover of perishable goods—for example, a restaurant or food retailer—the 'par' method would be a good choice. A regular manual stock check is reconciled against a par sheet, which lists ideal levels for particular items. All you need to do then is place an order that will bring your stock back up to the suggested optimum level.

First in, first out

This method is also used often in businesses trading in perishables. Stock is identified by the date it is received and used in strict order to make sure that wastage is kept to a minimum.

Just in time

The 'just in time' concept aims to reduce costs by cutting stock levels to a minimum. Items are delivered when they are needed, rather than stockpiled in a warehouse, and then used immediately. This method does carry the risk of running out of stock items, though, so is best used if you are confident about the reliability of your suppliers.

Batch control

If you are a manufacturer, this method is probably most appropriate for you. By managing the production of goods in batches, you know the precise amount of materials and components you need for each batch. This has two advantages: first, when an order is placed you can buy enough stock to fulfil the order; second, if there is a quality control issue it's much easier for you to identify the supplier of any faulty or sub-standard items.

Fixed quantities

Ordering fixed quantities at regular intervals is another option, but is only beneficial if you know that you are going to use the stock ordered within a particular timeframe—if you have a have a regular customer with an ongoing order, say. The advantages of this method are that it's likely you'll be able to get a discount from suppliers because you're ordering regularly, and you'll also know that you have enough stock to fulfil repeat orders.

Set up systems for stock control

All stock control systems have the same aims. They will help you to:
1. place orders
2. track stock levels
3. identify trends
4. improve processes
5. reduce costs
6. prevent losses
7. meet customer demand

Perhaps the simplest stock control system is the paper-based stock book, which is best suited to a small business with few stock items. It is a 'profit and loss' record of stock received and stock issued, and works well when used with the 'two-bin' system: when one bin is empty, the second stock bin is brought into use and more stock is ordered to fill up the empty one.

A more detailed paper-based system may involve coding stock items to indicate the supplier, unit cost and location of the stock in your warehouse. While this is a straightforward method, it soaks up a lot of time and labour and severely limits your ability to analyse trends in any but the most basic stock control scenario.

For more complex situations, multiple product lines or multi-site operations, computerised stock control systems offer much greater flexibility and ease of use. Modern computerised inventory and stock control systems allow records to be updated automatically when goods are received and sold by using bar codes or Radio Frequency Identification (RFID) technology.

Most computerised systems will show your actual stock holding and alert you when lines are under- or over-stocked. Some programmes allow turnover and profit analysis by product, helping you to identify trends and improve efficiency. They will also:

- show a valuation of your current stock
- integrate with accounting and invoicing systems
- trigger orders when the re-order level is reached
- identify your best suppliers

Protect your stock

Once you've chosen the right stock control method and system for your business, you'll also need to know that your system is reporting accurately on the physical stock you are holding.

The only reliable way is to count your stock, and reconcile actual stock levels with those recorded by your system by taking an inventory. A discrepancy can indicate there is a security issue or that your system is not recording your stock use correctly.

If you're rolling out a new stock control system, it's essential that you take an accurate inventory before the system goes live. Also keep your previous stock control system running for a short time, so that you have a back-up in case of disaster while you're getting to grips with the new system and sorting out any blips.

If you're certain that your stock control system is accurate but there are still discrepancies in stock levels, you'll need to investigate to work out whether theft is at the root of the problem. If this is the case,

there are several methods you can use to safeguard your stock, such as:

- regular and ad hoc stocktaking
- use of CCTV and/or a security firm
- regular reviews of procedures
- recruitment and training of staff
- use of electronic technology

Take pro-active measures to protect your stock from theft (or 'shrinkage'). The only way to discover if theft is occurring is by carrying out a physical stock-take on a random basis: if someone is stealing, he or she has probably noticed when you do your stock-take normally, and will be caught off guard if you appear unexpectedly.

Deterrent measures such as the use of CCTV and/or a security company can go a long way in preventing loss by theft. Back this up by making sure that basic paperwork and security measures are understood by all staff and followed without exception. For example:

- is the burglar alarm set?
- is there tape in the CCTV recorder?
- are the entrances and exits properly secured?
- are visitors and contractors regularly logged in and off the premises?

Many of the problems associated with shrinkage come down to staff dissatisfaction, or just plain dishonesty. When you're taking on staff, *always* check personal references before making an offer of employment. If existing staff are unhappy and raise legitimate grievances with you, do as much as you can to make changes to correct them. Making sure that you offer induction training and ongoing staff development are also positive ways of building loyalty among your team.

If you operate a rapidly growing business, the introduction of RFID technology may be the best way to control stock loss. While this may seem a drastic step to take, the cost of RFID has fallen considerably, and it enables the tracking of even the smallest item of stock throughout the entire process— from supplier to stockroom, to sale and beyond.

Stock loss can occur from the showroom as well as the stockroom, and well-placed

CCTV and the use of RFID—particularly on high-value items—has reduced pilfering levels in many businesses.

Account for stock

Once you have stock control systems and security measures in place, you should also be able to accurately record the amount of stock you hold in your business accounts. Take an inventory every quarter, not only for security purposes but also to produce financial reports and tax records.

If you use a paper-based system, you'll need to reconcile your sales ledger with your purchase ledger. All purchase orders, which should be filed securely, must tally with their corresponding delivery dockets. If you have robust stock control systems in place, this task should be relatively straightforward. A computerised system, particularly one that is integrated with your accounting and invoicing systems, will make the task simpler still. One word of caution, however: never keep just one copy of this business-critical data. Back it up regularly and also keep copies of all your important data and documents somewhere safe: preferably off site.

Value stock for a balance sheet

For accounting and tax purposes, your inventory of stock will appear on your balance sheet as assets. Stock may generally be valued on a 'first-in first-out' (FIFO) or 'last-in, first-out' (LIFO) basis for the purposes of your balance sheet.

FIFO accounting presumes that the next item you sell will be the oldest of that type in stock. As the older and cheaper goods are sold, the newer and more expensive stock items remain as assets on your books. In LIFO accounting, last stock purchased is recorded as the first stock sold. Therefore the older, and cheaper, stock remains as an asset on your books.

The choice between FIFO and LIFO can significantly affect your profit and loss statements: one shows greater assets, the other greater profits. For tax purposes, however, LIFO is *not* an allowable method for valuing stock. It's a good idea to take professional advice from a qualified accountant to determine the best accounting practice for your business.

COMMON MISTAKES
You don't help yourself

Stock control systems are only as good as the data entered into them. These should include:

- up-to-date inventory
- costs of purchase, transportation and storage
- historic and predicted trends
- seasonal variations
- product life cycle

Your stock is high, but sales are low

You probably will over-order at some point: it's virtually inevitable. If you find that you have some items that just aren't shifting, take it on the chin and offer some incentives to purchase. Discounts, sales, special offers, 'bundling' items together and so on should help you get your stock on the move.

USEFUL LINKS
British Retail Consortium (BRC):
www.brc.org.uk
British Shops and Stores Association (BSSA):
www.british-shops.co.uk
HM Revenue & Customs (HMRC):
www.hmrc.gov.uk
Manufacturing Advisory Service:
www.mas.berr.gov.uk

Understanding depreciation

GETTING STARTED

If you want to calculate the overall profitability of your business, you need to be able to determine all your costs. Most costs, such as your time, rent, materials and so on, are relatively straightforward to assess. However, it's more difficult to evaluate the cost of assets, which are expected to have a useful life of more than one year (usually known as fixed assets). You need to allow for the fact that your business's assets lose value due to obsolescence, general wear and tear, or the passing of time and they'll need to be replaced.

This is referred to as 'depreciation' and is a critical part of understanding business finance and your balance sheet.

FAQS

What is depreciation?

Depreciation is an allowance for wear and tear to fixed assets and is shown as a cost in the businesss profit and loss (P&L) account. Equipment, machinery, vehicles and industrial buildings (but not land) can be used again and again over time, until they wear out. During this time the value of these assets will fall. Since fixed assets generally have a life greater than one year, it would be unreasonable to attempt to charge the entire cost of an asset in the year of acquisition. Instead, the cost is spread over the expected life of the asset by charging a proportion of the cost each year. The aim is to calculate a fair charge for the use of the assets, to ensure that you cost your products or services accurately and provide a realistic profit figure in your P&L account.

When you buy items of equipment, their value is shown as a fixed asset in the balance sheet. Depreciation reduces the value of these assets; it's shown as a cost in the P&L account, and the balance sheet shows a corresponding reduction in the value of the fixed assets.

MAKING IT HAPPEN
Understand the two main methods of calculating depreciation

To calculate depreciation, you need to be able to estimate the expected life of the asset and what you expect to be able to sell it for at the end of its useful working life (residual value). Note that this residual value is often zero!

The two main ways of working this out are:

1 straight-line method
2 reducing-balance methods

Straight-line depreciation

This assumes a constant annual depreciation charge over the course of the asset's life, which means that the original cost of the asset is written off in equal amounts over the course of its working life. Using this method, the annual depreciation charge is calculated by taking the original value of the asset, taking away its estimated final residual value, and dividing this amount by the estimated life of the asset.

For example, a new piece of equipment is purchased for £30,000. It's estimated that it will last for seven years, and will be sold at the end of its working life for £2,000. Therefore the total depreciation is £28,000. The equipment is expected to last for seven years so the depreciation figure works out at £4,000 per year (£28,000 divided by seven).

Reducing-balance depreciation

The second way of working out depreciation is the reducing-balance method. This assumes that depreciation in the early years of an asset's life is higher than during its later years. This gives a fairer reflection of the real value of the equipment, as anyone who's ever bought a new car will know.

To calculate the depreciation charge using this method, a constant percentage rate is applied to the residual value of the asset every year. This has the effect of reducing the amount charged as depreciation over the course of the asset's life. The table below demonstrates how this set percentage reduces the depreciation figure charged over the period of the asset's life, leaving (as in the previous example) an expected final residual value of £2,000 for which the asset can be sold. Therefore, using the same example as before, the equipment purchased for £30,000 is charged at a 32% depreciation rate over the seven years of its expected life.

Pounds (£)

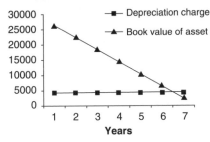

Using this method, your accountant or business adviser will be able to advise you on a suitable percentage rate to be applied as a depreciation rate.

MAKING IT HAPPEN

When you come to dispose of an asset at the end of its useful life, your accounts will show a residual book value. In the example used above, the value was £2,000. However, if the asset is actually sold for £3,000, for example, a profit of £1,000 will need to be shown in your P&L account. Similarly, if an asset is sold for less than its book value, the loss will need to be shown on the P&L account.

You should be careful not to confuse depreciation with capital allowances for tax purposes. You may choose any level of depreciation that you think is appropriate. When you submit your accounts to HM Revenue & Customs (HMRC), depreciation will be removed completely from its calculations of your net profit for tax purposes. HMRC then allows a capital allowance, generally of 25%, on a reducing

balance basis. For industrial buildings, 4% per annum is allowed. There's no allowance for commercial buildings.

Making allowances for depreciation doesn't involve any transfer of money or build-up of reserves to replace equipment in the future. Therefore, if possible, you should aim to put aside a cash sum at least equal to the annual depreciation, preferably higher, to allow for inflation, to ensure that you have the cash available when equipment needs to be replaced.

COMMON MISTAKES
You miscalculate the value of an asset

When estimating the useful life of an asset, remember to consider possible changes in technology and changing market requirements. Also, don't forget that it can be difficult to estimate the residual value of an asset. Where the value is likely to be small in relation to the cost, it's best to record it simply as being zero.

You fail to get advice

It can be quite tricky to calculate depreciation, so do seek guidance from your accountant or business adviser, if you need help with working out depreciation rates to use for your business. The more accurately you can reflect depreciation in your budget, the more accurately you'll be able to cost your product or service.

USEFUL LINKS

HM Revenue & Customs (HMRC) (for information on capital allowances):
www.hmrc.gov.uk/capital_allowances/ investmentschemes.htm
Institute of Chartered Accountants in England and Wales (for Guides to Statements of Standard Accounting Practice):
www.icaew.co.uk
Institute of Chartered Accountants in Ireland:
www.icai.ie
Institute of Chartered Accountants of Scotland:
www.icas.org.uk

Leasing business equipment

GETTING STARTED

If your business needs a piece of equipment or an asset such as machinery for your factory, a motor vehicle, IT equipment, office furniture or a photocopier, you might simply decide to buy the item outright.

Splashing out on a major piece of equipment can soak up a great deal of the working capital of a small or growing business. Buying equipment means that once you have paid the supplier's invoice, that cash has gone and can't be put to work in other parts of the business. Leasing the asset instead could be an attractive option.

FAQS

How do leasing arrangements work?

In a leasing arrangement, a finance company purchases the asset and then enters into a contract with you which allows you to use the asset for a period of time (known as the term of the lease). In return you make regular rental payments to them, usually on a monthly or quarterly basis. This gives you the advantage that the payments are made over the period when you are using the asset and you avoid paying the total purchase price upfront.

Bear in mind that under a lease, while you may be both using and paying for the asset, the finance company always remains its owner; if you don't keep up with the lease payments, the finance company can repossess it.

Various forms of leasing provide ways of obtaining the use of assets that your business needs, without the disadvantages of buying them outright. This is particularly useful where:

- you may only need the asset for a short period and will then get rid of it
- you can avoid the risk that the asset (such as IT equipment) will become obsolete
- as a small company, you don't have the bargaining power to get as good a price as a large company
- the tax deductions you can claim may be less than if you had leased the equipment
- your cash is tied up in the asset when it might be better used in growing your business, negotiating better supply terms, or clearing expensive loans

The best type of leasing arrangement for you will depend largely on whether you want to have the item for the whole of its useful life or for only a part of it. Long and short-term leasing differ significantly. For example, in short-term leasing arrangements, the finance company may take responsibility for insuring or maintaining the asset (and sometimes even both).

Having said that, any form of leasing—other than for relatively small amounts—may be difficult to obtain for start-up businesses, as finance companies will often want to look at several years' accounts before they'll lend to you. It's still worth having a go at leasing for small sums, such as for a forklift truck (which might cost £10,000 to buy outright), as this could make quite a difference to your business's finances. To use this example, if you take a simple lease—over three years, say, and with no initial deposit—it'll probably cost you about £330 per month, which means that in cash terms you are £6,040 better off during your first year of trading.

Leases are drawn up to run over a set term, so you also need to ensure that the term is appropriate for your use. Most will contain penalty clauses covering early termination of the arrangement.

MAKING IT HAPPEN
Understand short-term leasing arrangements

Short-term leases are designed to allow you flexible use of assets so that you keep them only for the period that you think you will need them, rather than the whole life of the asset. They're very commonly known as 'operating leases'.

Under this type of lease, you're simply renting the use of an asset in much the same way as you might rent a car, although you will be committing to longer periods of rental (typically from one to three years). As opposed to hiring a car from a pool of cars that the hire company already owns, you decide the asset you need and the finance company acquires it specifically in order to rent it to you.

Contract hire arrangements are a type of operating lease often used, for example, with motor vehicles where the leasing firm is also responsible for ongoing servicing and repairs. This type of lease is often used for motor vehicles and for technical equipment or items which require a high degree of servicing and support, such as photocopiers.

However, with contract hire, the choice of asset can be limited to those items which the leasing company is willing to stock or supply, such as a particular range of vehicles. It's likely that you may also face some restrictions on your use of the asset—only being able to use a vehicle for a set number of miles annually, for example—and you'll end up paying a penalty if your usage exceeds the agreed amount.

At the end of the lease, the underlying asset will normally still have a 'residual value', which the finance company can realise by re-renting the asset to you for a further term or by selling it (either to you or in the second-hand market).

As you are clearly not going to benefit from the asset's full life or any value it may have at the end of your lease, for accounting purposes the asset is never yours—and so the item will not be recorded as an asset on your balance sheet, nor will the lease be recorded as a liability. This makes the tax treatment easy in that you will be able to regard all the rental payments (net of any VAT) as tax-deductible expenses.

Understand long-term leasing arrangements

Long-term leases are designed to enable you to have access to the item involved for the whole of its useful life and they're a way of enabling you to finance what would otherwise be purchased. As a result, this type of lease is known as a 'finance lease' as its purpose is purely to provide the finance with which to acquire the asset.

Under this type of lease you decide, say, the type of machine that you need for your factory. However, instead of placing the order yourself, the finance company buys the machine on your behalf. They then rent the machine to you over a long enough period so that the instalments you pay cover the cost of the machine the finance company has to meet (known as the principal or capital), as well as the finance company's leasing charges and interest.

In practice, you'll need to treat the asset as something you've bought yourself, as you'll be responsible for servicing and insuring it. This also applies to accounting for it. Your accountants will apply a test known as 'substance over form—while *legally* you do not own the asset, it will be shown on your books as though you did (as a fixed asset), while the principal due will be shown as a matching liability.

Lease payments will partly cover the interest and charges, which are written off as expenses in the profit and loss account and can be allowed against tax, and also repay the principal which will reduce the lease liability due.

Despite the fact that you will be recording the item as an asset, you cannot claim capital allowances for tax purposes as you would if you owned it. Instead you have to depreciate the asset by an equal amount each year (known as 'on a straight-line basis') over the life of the lease. This depreciation charge is allowable as an expense for tax purposes. As this tax treatment may be less favourable than if you had bought the asset, you should always take advice from your accountant when deciding whether to buy or lease equipment in this way.

Once you reach the end of the lease term, sometimes known as the principle term, the financing company has, in effect, been repaid for a quasi loan. Usually you can continue to rent the asset for a secondary term at a nominal or 'peppercorn' rent, or you may have an agreed option to purchase the asset for the equivalent of, say, a further month's instalment.

Hire purchase agreements are an alternative form of financing where the finance company acquires the asset and you pay rental instalments until you exercise an option to buy the asset outright. By being flexible about the structure of the deal, such as having a large option payment being required at the end of the term, the level of regular instalments can be made lower than the equivalent payments under a finance lease.

Assets acquired under hire purchase arrangements are also recorded as fixed assets on your balance sheet, and you can claim capital allowances on them for tax.

Both finance leases and hire purchase arrangements will normally require you to pay some level of deposit at the outset.

Using leasing to raise cash

Sometimes established businesses will use leasing arrangements as a way of raising cash against equipment that they already have.

To do so they will enter into a 'sale and leaseback' agreement, where they sell their equipment to a finance company—receiving between 70% and 100% of its current second-hand value—and lease it back over a period of three to five years.

These types of deal may include not only equipment owned outright, but also equipment under existing finance leases in which the business has some 'equity'. The current value of the asset exceeds the outstanding balance due to the finance company—so settling the existing lease can free up cash.

These types of transaction can be put in place quickly and are therefore often used in business rescue refinancing. However, there are a limited number of finance companies which undertake this type of work and their terms vary widely, so you should take advice from a reputable finance broker.

COMMON MISTAKES ✗
You forget that you can make money from leased items

You don't have to own an asset to both use it and make money from it. UK businesses tend to own their assets but this is not necessary. Leasing assets as you need them may be more flexible and less restrictive in the long term.

You don't read the 'small print'

Lease agreements can be lengthy and complex, but do take time to read them carefully before you sign anything. There are some potential pitfalls, particularly in areas such as the option price in hire purchase agreements, the costs of extending the lease at the end of its term, the method of returning the item and the condition it must be in on return. Most people lease items to make their life (and cash flow!) easier, but if you're unaware of important terms and conditions you run the risk of making it a lot more complicated. For example, if you decide not to renew your agreement in future, make sure you give the notice required in the contract: if you don't, you'll probably have to pay a penalty. On a related theme, if you're asked to give a personal guarantee (PG) to the finance company, seek professional legal advice before you sign.

You don't explore other options

Interest rates on leasing are usually higher than the rates charged for mortgages on commercial property. If you are thinking of leasing a piece of equipment, it may be worth exploring the option of raising the finance more cheaply by borrowing against your premises instead.

You don't plan for future needs

If you are leasing IT equipment or any other technology that may become obsolete, make sure your leasing terms allow you to upgrade the items without incurring hefty additional costs.

You don't synchronise multiple lease agreements

If you have more than one item leased through the same finance company, try to make sure that all the leases end at the same date, to make renewing or switching to a new finance company as easy as possible at the end of the term.

USEFUL LINKS

General
Finance & Leasing Association (FLA):
www.fla.org.uk
Leasing Life:
www.leasinglife.co.uk

Leasing firms
Car Leasing Directory:
www.carleasingdirectory.co.uk/

Halo Corporate Finance (leases of all sorts of equipment and services, from agricultural machinery to vending machines):
www.hcfl.co.uk/ whatwefinanceindx.htm
Applegate (lists a number of businesses providing leasing services):
www.applegate.co.uk/products/psz/ 39632.htm
Technology Leasing (leases IT equipment):
www.technologyleasing.co.uk
The OER group (an office equipment supplier):
www.oergroup.co.uk/
Creative Business Finance Limited (a full service asset finance brokerage and a member of the National Association of Commercial Finance Brokers):
www.creativefinance.co.uk

Reading a balance sheet

GETTING STARTED

A balance sheet tells us something about the financial strength of a business on the day that the balance sheet is drawn up. That situation changes constantly, so you could say it is more like a snapshot than a film. Although the method of producing a balance sheet is standardised, there can be a certain element of subjectivity in interpreting it. Different elements of the balance sheet can tell you different things about the how the business is doing.

This actionlist gives an overview of a balance sheet and looks at a brief selection of the more interesting figures that help with interpretation. It's important to remember that a lot of these figures do not tell you that much in isolation—it is in trend analysis or comparisons between businesses that they talk more lucidly.

FAQS

What is a balance sheet?

A balance sheet is an accountant's view, showing the book value of the assets and liabilities of a business at a specific date and on that date alone. The term 'balance' means exactly what it says—that those assets and liabilities will be equal. In showing how the balance lies, the balance sheet gives us an idea of the financial health of the business.

What does a balance sheet not do?

A balance sheet is not designed to represent the market value of a business. For example, property in the balance sheet may be worth a lot more than its book value. Plant and machinery is shown at cost less depreciation, but that may well be different from market value. Stock may turn out to be worth less than its balance-sheet value, and so on.

There may also be hidden assets, such as goodwill or valuable brands, that do not appear on the balance sheet at all. These would all enhance the value of the business in a sale situation, yet are invisible on a normal balance sheet.

MAKING IT HAPPEN

Here is a very simple company balance sheet:

Define the individual elements

- *Fixed assets*—items that are not traded as part of a company's normal activities but

Fixed assets		1,000
Current assets	700	
Less current liabilities	400	
Net current assets		300
		1,300
Less long-term loans		200
Net assets		1,100
Profit and loss account		500
Share capital		600
Shareholders' funds		1,100

enable it to function, such as property, machinery or vehicles. These are tangible assets (meaning you can kick them). This heading can also include intangible assets (you cannot kick them). A common example is 'goodwill', which can arise upon the acquisition of one business by another.

- *Current assets*—items that form the trading cycle of the business. The most common examples are stock, debtors, and positive bank balances.
- *Current liabilities*—also items that form the trading cycle of the business but represent short-term amounts owed to others. Examples will be trade creditors, taxes, and bank overdrafts—broadly, any amount due for payment within the next 12 months from the date of the balance sheet.
- *Net current assets*—not a new figure, but simply the difference between current assets and current liabilities, often shown

because it may be a useful piece of information.

- *Long-term loans*—debt that is repayable more than one year from the date of the balance sheet.
- *Net assets*—also not a new figure, but the sum of fixed assets plus net current assets less long-term loans. In other words, all of the company assets shown in its books, minus all of its liabilities.
- *Profit and loss account*—the total of all the accumulated profits and losses from all the accounting periods since the business started. It increases or decreases each year by the net profit or loss in that period, calculated after providing for all costs including tax and dividends to shareholders.
- *Share capital*—the number of shares issued, multiplied by their nominal value. The latter is the theoretical figure at which the shares were originally issued and has nothing to do with their market value.
- *Shareholders' funds*—not a new figure, but the sum of the profit and loss account plus the share capital. It represents the total interest of the shareholders in the company.

Learn to interpret them

Note that balance sheets differ between one industry and another in the sense of the range and type of assets and liabilities that exist. For example, a retailer will have little in the way of trade debtors because it sells for cash, and a manufacturer is likely to have a far larger investment in plant than a service business like an advertising agency. So the interpretation must be seen in the light of the actual trade of the business.

Reading a balance sheet can be quite subjective—accountancy is an art, not a science and, although the method of producing a balance sheet is standardised, there may be some items in it that are subjective rather than factual. The way people interpret some of the figures will also vary, depending what they wish to achieve and whether they see certain things as being good or bad.

Look first at the net assets/ shareholders' funds

Positive or negative? Our example, being a healthy business, has net assets of a positive £1,100. Positive is good. If there were 600 shares in issue, it would mean that the net assets per share were £1.83.

If it had negative assets (the same thing as net liabilities), this might mean that the business is heading for difficulty unless it is being supported by some party such as a parent company, bank, or other investor. When reading a balance sheet with negative assets, consider where the support will be coming from.

Then examine net current assets

Positive or negative? Again, our example has net current assets of a positive £300. This means that, theoretically, it should not have any trouble settling short-term liabilities because it has more than enough current assets to do so. Negative net current assets suggest that there could be a possible problem in settling short-term liabilities.

You can also look at NCA as a ratio of current assets/current liabilities. Here, a figure over one is equivalent to the NCA having a positive absolute figure. The ratio version is more useful in analysing trends of balance sheets over successive periods or in comparing two businesses.

A cut-down version of looking at NCA considers only (debtors + cash)−(creditors) thus excluding stock. The reasoning here is that this looks at the most liquid of the net current asset constituents; again, a figure over one is the most desirable. This is also a ratio that is more meaningful in trends or comparisons.

Understand the significance of trade debtor payments . . .

Within current assets, we have trade debtors. It can be useful to consider how many days' worth of sales are tied up in debtors—given by (debtors × 365)/annual sales. This provides an idea of how long the company is waiting to get paid. Too long, and it might be something requiring investigation. However, this figure can be misleading, where sales do not take place evenly throughout the year. A construction company might be an example of such a business: one big debt incurred near the year end would skew the ratio.

...and trade creditor payments

Similar to the above, this looks at (trade creditors × 365)/annual purchases, indicating how long the company is taking in general to pay its suppliers. This is not so easy to calculate, because the purchases for this purpose include not only goods for resale, but all the overheads as well.

Recognise what debt means

Important to most businesses, this figure is the total of long and short-term loans. Too much debt might indicate that the company would have trouble paying the interest in a downturn. It's difficult to give an optimum level of debt because there are so many different situations, depending on a huge range of circumstances.

Often, instead of an absolute figure, debt is expressed as a percentage of shareholders' funds and known as 'gearing' or 'leverage'. In a public company, gearing of 100% might be considered pretty high, whereas debt of under 30% could be seen as on the low side.

✗ COMMON MISTAKES
You think that balance sheet figures represent market value

Don't assume that a balance sheet is a valuation of the business. Its primary purpose is that it forms part of the range of accounting reports used for measuring business per-formance—along with the other common financial reports like profit and loss accounts and cash-flow statements. Management, shareholders, and others such as banks will use the entire range to assess the health of the business.

You forget that the balance sheet is valid *only* for the date at which it is produced

A short while after a balance sheet is pro-duced, things could be quite different. In practice there frequently may not be any radical changes between the date of the bal-ance sheet and the date when it is being read, but it is entirely possible that some-thing could have happened to the business that would not show. For example, a major debtor could have defaulted unexpectedly. So remember that balance sheet figures are valid only as at the date shown, and are not a permanent picture of the business.

You're not sure whether all assets and liabilities are shown in the balance sheet

Some businesses may have hidden assets, as suggested above. This could be the value of certain brands or trademarks, for example, for which money may never have changed hands. Yet these could be worth a great deal. Conversely, there may be some substantial legal action pending which could cost the company a lot, yet is not shown fully in the balance sheet.

USEFUL LINK
Motley Fool:
www.fool.co.uk

Creating a balance sheet

GETTING STARTED

A balance sheet measures the financial standing, or even the net worth or owners' equity, of a company at a given point in time—typically at the end of a calendar or fiscal year.

FAQS

What can a balance sheet help me do?

The balance sheet will show you what your company owns (assets), what is owed (liabilities), and what is left (owners' equity). It will give you a concise snapshot of your business's financial position.

MAKING IT HAPPEN

The format of a company's balance sheet is strictly defined by the 1985 Companies Act. Essentially, assets must be in balance with liabilities and shareholders' equity. In other words, assets must equal liabilities and owners' equity.

Assets include cash in hand and cash anticipated (receivables), inventories of supplies and materials, properties, facilities, equipment, and whatever else the company uses to conduct business. Assets also need to reflect depreciation in the value of equipment such as machinery that has a limited expected useful life.

Liabilities include pending payments to suppliers and creditors, outstanding current and long-term debts, taxes, interest payments, and other unpaid expenses that the company has incurred.

Subtracting the value of aggregate liabilities from the value of aggregate assets reveals the value of owners' equity. Ideally, it should be positive. Owners' equity consists of capital invested by owners over the years and profits (net income) or internally generated capital, which is referred to as 'retained earnings'; these are funds to be used in future operations.

As an example:

COMMON MISTAKES

You read too much into it

Remember that:

- The balance sheet does *not* show a company's market worth, nor important intangibles such as the knowledge and talents of individual people, nor other vital business factors such as customers or market share.
- The balance sheet does not express the true value of some fixed assets. A six-year-old manufacturing plant, for example, is listed at its original cost, even though the price of replacing it could be much higher or substantially lower (because of new technology that might be less expensive or vastly more efficient).
- The balance sheet is not an indicator of past or future performance or trends that affect performance. It needs to be studied along with two other key reports: the income statement and the cash-flow statement. A published balance sheet needs to include prior period comparatives.

ASSETS £

Current:

Cash	8,200
Securities	5,000
Receivables	4,500
Inventory & supplies	

Fixed:

Land	10,000
Structures	90,000
Equipment (less depreciation)	5,000

Intangibles/other

TOTAL ASSETS	129,000

LIABILITIES £

Payables	7,000
Taxes	4,000
Misc.	3,000
Bonds & notes	25,000
TOTAL LIABILITIES	39,000
SHAREHOLDERS' EQUITY (stock, par value × shares outstanding)	80,000
RETAINED EARNINGS	10,000
TOTAL LIABILITIES AND SHAREHOLDERS' EQUITY	129,000

Reading a profit and loss account

GETTING STARTED

A profit and loss account is a statement of the income and expenditure of a business over the period stated, drawn up in order to ascertain how much profit the business made. Put simply, the difference between the income from sales and the associated expenditure is the profit or loss for the period. 'Income' and 'expenditure' here mean only those amounts directly attributable to earning the profit and thus would exclude capital expenditure, for example.

Importantly, the figures are adjusted to match the income and expenses to the time period in which they were incurred—not necessarily the same as that in which the cash changed hands.

FAQS

What is a profit and loss account?

A profit and loss account is an accountant's view of the figures that show how much profit or loss a business has made over a period. To do this, it is necessary to allocate the various elements of income and expenditure to the time period concerned, not on the basis of when cash was received or spent, but on when the income was earned or the liability to pay a supplier and employees was incurred. While capital expenditures are excluded, depreciation of property and equipment is included as a non-cash expense.

Thus if you sell goods on credit, you will be paid later but the sale takes place upon the contract to sell them. Equally if you buy goods and services on credit, the purchase takes place when you contract to buy them, not when you when you actually settle the invoice.

What does a profit and loss account not show?

Most importantly, a P&L account is not an explanation of the cash coming into and going out of a business.

MAKING IT HAPPEN

Here is a simple example of a profit and loss account for a particular year:

Sales		1,000
Opening stock	100	
Purchases	520	
	620	
Closing stock	80	
Cost of sales		540
Gross profit		460
Wages	120	
Other overheads	230	
		350
Net profit before tax		110
Tax		22
Net profit after tax		88
Dividends		40
Retained profit		48
Retained profit brought forward		150
Retained profit carried forward		198

Note that the presence of stock and purchases indicates that the business is trading or manufacturing goods of some kind, rather than selling services.

Define the individual elements

- *Sales*—the invoiced value of the sales in the period.
- *Stock*—the value of the actual physical stock held by the business at the opening and closing of the period. It is always valued at cost, or realisable value if that is lower—never at selling price.
- *Purchases and other direct costs*—the goods or raw materials purchased by the business for resale—not capital items used in the business; only items used as part of the direct cost of its sales. In other words, those costs which vary directly with sales, as distinct from overheads (like rent) which do not.

Where a business holds stock, the purchases figure has to be adjusted for the opening and closing values, in order to reach the right income and expenditure amounts for that period only. Goods for resale bought in the period may not have been used purely for that period but may be lying in stock at the end of it, ready for sale in the next. Similarly, goods used for resale in this period will consist partly of items already held in stock at the beginning of it. So take the amounts purchased, add the opening stock and deduct the closing stock. The resulting adjusted purchase figure is known as 'cost of sales'.

In some businesses there may be other direct costs apart from purchases included in cost of sales. For example, a manufacturer may include some wages if they are of a direct nature (wages of employees directly involved in the manufacturing process, as distinct from office staff, for example). Or a building contractor would include plant hire in direct costs, as well as purchases of materials.

- *Gross profit*—the difference between sales and cost of sales. This is an important figure as it measures how much was actually made directly from whatever the business is selling, before paying for overheads.

The figure is often expressed as a percentage ratio, when it is known as the 'gross profit margin'. In our example the GPM is 460:1,000—or 46%. Ratios are really only useful as comparison tools, either with different periods of the same business or with other businesses.

- *Overheads*—the expenses of the business which do not vary directly with sales. They include a wide range of items such as rent, most wages, advertising, phones, interest paid on loans, audit fees and so on.
- *Net profit before tax*—the result of deducting total overheads from gross profit. This is what the business has made before tax is paid on that profit.
- *Tax (or corporation tax)*—This will not actually have been paid in the year concerned, but is shown because it is due on the profit for that period. Even then the figure shown may not be the actual amount due, for various reasons such as possible over-payments from previous years. Tax can be a very complex matter, being based upon a set of changeable rules.
- *Net profit after tax*—the result after deducting the tax liability—the so-called bottom line. This is the amount that the company can do with as it wishes, possibly paying a dividend out of part of it and retaining the rest. It is the company's reward for actually being in business in the first place.
- *Dividends*—a payment to the shareholders as a reward for their investment in the company. Most publicly listed companies of any size pay dividends to shareholders. Private companies may also do so, but this may be more for tax reasons. The dividend in the example shown is paid out of the net profit after tax, but legally it is not permitted to exceed the total available profit. That total available profit is comprised of both the current year's net profit after tax and the retained profit brought forward from previous years.
- *Retained profit*—the amount kept by the company after paying dividends to shareholders. If there is no dividend, then it is equal to the net profit after tax.

- *Retained profit brought forward*—the total accumulated retained profits for all earlier years of the company's existence.
- *Retained profit carried forward*—the above figure brought forward, plus the current year's retained profit. This new total will form the profit brought forward in the next accounting period.

Interpret the figures

A lot of accounting analysis is valid only when comparing the figures—usually with similar figures for earlier periods, projected future figures, or other companies in the same business.

On its own a P&L account tells you only a limited story, though there are some standalone facts that can be derived from it. What our example does show, even in isolation, is that this business was successful in the period concerned. It made a profit, not a loss, and was able to pay dividends to shareholders out of that profit. Clearly a pretty crucial piece of information.

However, it is in making comparisons that such figures start to have real meaning. The example figures reveal that the gross profit margin was 46%, an important statistic in measuring business performance. The net profit margin before tax was 110:1,000, or 11%. You could take the margin idea further and calculate the net profit after tax ratio to sales as 88:1,000, being 8.8%. Or you could calculate the ratio of any expense to sales. In our example, the wages:sales ratio is 120:1,000 or 12%.

If you then looked at similar margin figures for the preceding accounting period, you would learn something about this business. Say the gross margin was 45% last year compared with 46% this year—there has been some improvement in the profit made before deducting overheads. But then suppose that the net profit margin of 8.8% this year compares with 9.8% last year. This would tell you that, despite improvement in profits at the gross level, the overheads have increased disproportionately. You could then check the ratio of each of the overheads to sales to see where this arose, and find out why. Advertising spending could have shot up, for example, or perhaps the company moved to new premises incurring a higher rent. Maybe something could be tightened up.

Another commonly used ratio

Another ratio often used in business analysis is return on capital employed. Here we combine the profit and loss account with the balance sheet by dividing the net profit (either before or after tax as required) by shareholders' funds. This tells you how much the company is making proportionate to money invested in it by the shareholders—a similar idea to how much you might get in interest on a bank deposit account. It's a useful way of comparing different companies in a particular industry, where the more efficient ones are likely to derive a higher return on capital employed.

COMMON MISTAKE
You assume that the bottom line represents cash profit from trading
It doesn't! There are a few examples where this is the case: a simple cash trader might buy something for one price, then sell it for more; his profit then equals the increase in cash. But a business that buys and sells on credit, spends money on items that are held for the longer term such as property or machinery, has tax to pay at a later date, and so on, will make a profit that is not represented by a mere increase in cash balances held. Indeed, the cash balance could quite easily decrease during a period when a profit was made.

USEFUL LINK
Motley Fool:
www.fool.co.uk

Creating a profit and loss account

GETTING STARTED

A profit and loss account (P & L) is an important financial tool. It looks at a company's sales revenues and expenses over a period, providing a calculation of profits or losses during that time.

FAQS

What is the benefit of doing a P & L?

Reading a P&L is the easiest way to tell if a business has made a profit or a loss during a given month or year. The most important figure it contains is net profit: what is left over after revenues are used to pay expenses and taxes.

Companies tend to produce P&L reports monthly. It is customary for the reports to include year-to-date figures, as well as corresponding year-earlier figures to allow for comparisons and analysis.

HOW IT WORKS IN PRACTICE

A P&L adheres to a simple rule of thumb: 'revenue minus cost equals profit'.

There are two P&L formats, multiple-step and single-step. Both follow a standard set of rules known as Generally Accepted Accounting Principles (GAAP). These rules generally adhere to requirements established by governments to track receipts, expenses and profits for tax purposes. They also allow the financial reports of two different companies to be compared.

The multiple-step format is much more common, because it includes a larger number of details and is thus more useful. It deducts costs from revenues in a series of steps, allowing for closer analysis. Revenues appear first, then expenses, each in as much detail as management desires. Sales may be broken down by product line or location, while expenses such as salaries may be broken down into base salaries and commissions.

Expenses are then subtracted from revenues to show profit (or loss). A basic multiple-step P&L looks like this:

MULTIPLE-STEP PROFIT & LOSS ACCOUNT (£)

NET SALES		750,000
Less: cost of goods sold		450,000
Gross profit		300,000
LESS: OPERATING EXPENSES		
Selling expenses		
Salaries & commissions	54,000	
Advertising	37,500	
Delivery/transportation	12,000	
Depreciation/store equipment	7,500	
Other selling expenses	5,000	
Total selling expenses		116,000	
General & administrative expenses		
Administrative/office salaries	74,000	
Utilities	2,500	
Depreciation/structure	2,400	
Misc. other expenses	3,100	
Total general & admin expenses		82,000	
Total operating expenses			198,000

OPERATING INCOME		102,000
LESS (ADD): NON-OPERATING ITEMS		
Interest expenses	11,000	
Interest income earned	(2,800)	8,200
Income before taxes		93,800
Income taxes		32,360
Net Income		**61,440**

P&Ls of public companies may also report income on the basis of earnings per share. For example, if the company issuing this statement had 12,000 shares outstanding, earnings per share would be £5.12—that is, £61,440 divided by 12,000 shares.

COMMON MISTAKE
You don't realise what a P & L *can't* do

Although P & Ls can shed a lot of light on a company's health, they don't give the 'story' behind the figures: you can't see how a business earned or spent its money, for example. Also, one month's P&L can be misleading, especially if a business generates the majority of its receipts in particular months. A retail establishment, for example, usually generates a large percentage of its sales in the final three months of the year, while a consulting service might generate the lion's share of its revenues in as few as two months, and no revenues at all in some other months.

Invariably, figures for both revenues and expenses reflect the judgements of the companies reporting them. Accounting methods can be quite arbitrary when it comes to such factors as depreciation expenses.

USEFUL LINK
Biz/ed:
www.bized.ac.uk

GETTING PAID ON TIME

Setting up a trade credit policy

GETTING STARTED

While it's true that, in the words of the business saying 'a sale isn't a sale until it's been paid for', in practice most businesses find they have to give some level of credit to their customers so they don't lose sales to competitors who *will* allow the customer time to pay.

Allowing customers a period of credit is, however, a business risk as the cash from sales is the lifeblood of your business. If customers delay paying you for the goods or services you've supplied to them, it could cost you money, especially if you have to borrow on overdraft to fund your business while waiting for payment. At worst, it could stretch your cash flow so much that your business may go under. And if the customer fails to pay you at all, your business will be faced with a bad debt.

To help you avoid these financial crises, this actionlist will help you create a trade policy, understand frequently used trade credit terms, and evaluate customers for credit worthiness.

FAQS

What is a trade credit policy?

Simply put, a policy of this type is made up of the processes and practice your business uses to make sure that you only extend credit where it's appropriate, and that you get paid.

Remember that if you allow customers credit, you are, in effect, lending those customers money until they've settled their bills. You have to choose whether or not to allow a customer credit, and part of that decision will be based on your sense of whether or not your loan will be repaid. At the same time, you'll probably want to keep your customers with a view to making future sales, so while your debt collection process needs to be effective, it mustn't be so intimidating that it scares people away.

Why do you need a trade credit policy?

Your trade credit policy should be clear and unambiguous so that both your staff and your customers can get to grips with it quickly. Make sure you set out:

- how you are going to 'do business'
- the terms on which you are prepared to give customers credit
- how the process is to operate, including any penalties for late or non-payment

By doing so, not only can you minimise your risks, but also you can make the process of collecting your cash as efficient as possible. It will also mean that you can focus your sales effort on the customers that you have identified as being most profitable and reliable.

MAKING IT HAPPEN
Draw up the policy

The policy should also cover the way in which new accounts are opened with your business. Make sure that:

- your credit terms are built into your contracts with any new customers and are non-negotiable
- you ask for references and other supplementary information (if appropriate) before you give credit. If you decided to ask for security before extending credit to customers, explain what documentation is necessary and what the next steps in the process are
- you explain who can set the initial credit limits and payment terms and on what basis these are to be arrived at

It's important to agree these key issues, but the policy shouldn't end there. If you do decide to give a customer credit, the policy will need to be adapted if business conditions or the customer's circumstances change. Think about:

- how the customer's account and credit-worthiness will be monitored
- the responsibilities for making any subsequent changes to credit limits or payment terms, and who has the authority to override these in certain circumstances

- how credit limits are to work, and the actions to be taken if a customer exceeds their limit

The day-to-day details also need to be spelled out. Make clear who is responsible for issuing invoices, statements and reminders, and also think through the escalation process for reviewing and taking action to recover overdue debt. This should include a set of standard letters so that your company's approach is consistent.

Finally, there's no point spending hours slaving over a trade credit policy if you don't tell anyone about it! Make sure all your staff are aware of it and that they understand it; and post a copy on your company's intranet (if you have one) so that they can refer to it if they need to. Also make sure that you stick to the policy yourself. If your sales team are eager to close a deal and hear you giving someone else better terms that the policy allows, they'll follow suit—so you'll need to lead by example here.

Understand trade credit terms

The UK accounting terms 'debtors' and 'creditors' can cause confusion in comparison with their American equivalents of 'receivables' and 'payables'.

When you allow someone time to pay, you're offering them credit. Your *debtors* (or receivables) are the people or businesses to whom you have given credit, so they are the people who owe you money. Don't mix them up with your *creditors* (or payables), who are the people who have given *you* credit and to whom you owe money.

There is a variety of commonly used invoice payment arrangements:

- **pro forma**, where the customer has to pay on an invoice raised in advance of shipping the goods
- **on presentation**, where the invoice is due for payment as soon as it is received
- **'X' days net**, which simply means payment is needed within the specified number of days after the date of the invoice
- at the **end of the month in which the invoice is issued**
- on a **net monthly account basis**, which means at the end of the month following

the month in which the invoice was issued
- on a **specified day** of the month following the invoice

Typical terms that you could include on an invoice might be:

- **30 days' credit** from the date of the invoice. For example, if the invoice is dated '15th May, you should expect to be paid by 15th June
- **30 days' net monthly**. Any invoices raised in the month of May are expected to be paid by the end of June
- **60 days' net monthly**. Any invoices raised in the month of May are expected to be paid by the end of July

Some businesses offer customers a discount if they pay quickly, usually within 7 to 14 days of the invoice being issued. This may be 1%–2% of the net price. Full payment will still be due within 30 days (or whatever you have defined as your standard term) if they don't want to take advantage of your discount. (Discounting can be a good incentive, but it's wise not to use it all the time, or your customers will begin to expect it.)

In addition to these terms which define how quickly the invoice is due for payment, you should also set credit limits—in other words, the maximum amount of credit you are prepared to allow that customer. As a result there may be occasions where, in order to remain within a monetary credit limit, the customer will have to pay an outstanding invoice before it is actually due.

If you also buy materials or services from one of your customers, you may agree a 'contra' arrangement, where the sums due between each party are offset against each other without cash actually changing hands.

Evaluate customers for credit

Before you lend money to your customers by giving them credit, it is *essential* that you research them thoroughly beforehand. Finding that you've given credit to a company with a poor trading history can be soul-destroying.

First of all, you need to check that your potential new customers really are who they say they are. Ask them to complete and return a signed credit application form which details all the following information:

- full name and address, including any trading names
- the trading status of the business (whether a sole trader, partnership or limited company) and company registration number and registered office address, if appropriate
- invoicing and delivery addresses if these are different
- contact details for the individual with whom you will need to deal
- details of two trade references and permission to obtain bank and credit references

This form is also a great early opportunity for you to make your terms of business crystal clear. Incorporate them in the paperwork and explain that in singing and returning the form, customers are accepting the terms.

It's crucial that you also check customers' creditworthiness. This normally involves three areas.

1. Taking up references

To obtain any references for a customer, you need to have their permission. Ideally, you'd be able to choose any of their suppliers at random to get objective references, but in reality you'll be limited to the ones that they suggest. Since they are unlikely to suggest dissatisfied suppliers, the value of these references may be limited.

Banks are very cautious in providing any references as they are always concerned about their risk, so it is normally very difficult to obtain any meaningful information from them.

2. Reviewing published accounts

Looking at the published accounts of a potential customer sounds like an excellent tack to take, and in some cases it can yield useful results, but the odds are stacked against you to a certain extent. If the customer is a limited liability company (designated by the word Limited or PLC in its name) or limited liability partnership (designated by LLP in its name) you will be

able to obtain its last filed accounts from Companies House. However, accounts do not have to be filed by the company until many months after the year to which they relate, and so the information can be significantly out of date.

There are also exemptions that allow small and medium-sized companies to file abbreviated sets of accounts with very limited information, while for larger companies the accounts can be complex and difficult to interpret. Of course sole traders and most partnerships do not have to file accounts at all.

3. Checking public sources of adverse credit information

A number of public registers can be accessed to check for adverse information:

- The Register of County Court Judgements maintained by Registry Trust Ltd, which gives details of judgements against individuals and companies over the past six years (see **www.registry-trust.org.uk**).
- The Register of Individual Voluntary Arrangements (IVAs) kept by The Insolvency Service. IVAs are agreements supervised by a licensed insolvency practitioner between insolvent individuals and their creditors (for settlement of their debts).
- The Bankruptcy Search Room, also maintained by The Insolvency Service (website address given below).

Credit reference agencies, insurers and factoring firms

Undertaking work to check references will soak up both time and money, so it may be worth your using other agencies to help.

Credit reference agencies

Credit reference agencies can give independent assessments of customers' financial health and suggest appropriate trade credit limits, so they should be able to supply you with commercial credit scores or ratings online or by fax. Alternatively, organisations such as Dun & Bradstreet (**www.dnb.co.uk**) may be able to help.

These references are based on

information held by the agencies about trends of payment and business performance by sector, together with information gathered over the length of time it has been operating:

- financial performance as shown in its published accounts
- County Court Judgements
- other adverse credit information included in the public sources

Credit insurance

If you take out credit insurance, you'll get cover if your customers don't pay, as well as an early warning about customers who are in difficulty—their insurable limits will start to reduce. Once you're aware of this problem, you can reduce your exposure to them and concentrate your sales efforts on profitable and stable concerns instead. Having insurance in place will also provide greater security to any lenders to the business, and can make accessing finance easier. For more information on credit insurance, see **www.payontime.co.uk/collect/tradeins.html** and contact the British Insurance Brokers' Association (**www.biba.org.uk**) for advice on finding an insurance broker.

Factoring

A factoring firm will advance you money against your outstanding debtors. This will help your cash flow and also transfer responsibility for setting credit limits and collecting your debts. There is a catch, however: as factoring companies will charge you for their services, the costs make this an expensive way of borrowing money and does not eliminate the credit risk unless you opt for non-recourse (insured) factoring. The latter guarantees protection against bad debts, but is even more expensive than other types of factoring.

✗ COMMON MISTAKES

You set unrealistic credit levels

When you create your trade credit policy, make sure it's appropriate for your business and the levels of credit you can afford to give. This can be a tricky balance to strike, so it may be worth taking the advice of other business owners in your network, or a contact from your local chamber of commerce. Your policy also needs to be appropriate for your market and the levels of credit offered by your competitors: the time customers to pay will be a factor that they bear in mind as they place their business.

You let credit levels drift

Consider having a fast-track procedure to allow new customers a limited amount of credit while you complete your checks to set up a normal account; or having a limited discretionary level of credit on account for new or small customers. While this means taking a limited risk, this approach avoids losing new sales unnecessarily or incurring unnecessary credit checking costs. You must follow up and complete the checks to open a normal account, or do so when a customer's business gets beyond the discretionary limit—do not simply allow the account's level to drift upwards.

You don't get all the information you need about potential new customers

Ensure that your credit application form enables you to collect all the relevant information about sole traders and partnerships as well as limited liability companies. This will include the full names and home addresses of the owners or partners as well as their dates of birth. You may require this information if you have to take court action against them as individuals to recover your debt.

USEFUL LINKS

Better Payment Practice campaign:
www.payontime.co.uk
Companies House:
www.companieshouse.gov.uk
Credit Services Association (CSA):
www.csa-uk.com
Insolvency Service:
www.insolvency.gov.uk
Institute of Credit Management (ICM:
www.icm.org.uk
Registry Trust Limited:
www.registry-trust.org.uk

Understanding credit control

GETTING STARTED

Before you start trading, you need to appreciate the basics of credit control, as it's a vital part of your business's operations. It's through credit control that you can maintain your cash flow—by ensuring that you receive payment as quickly as possible from customers. And credit control also prevents you from losing money by providing credit to people who can't or won't pay.

Credit control needs to work closely with your sales, helping to keep your sales effort concentrated on good, profitable customers.

Poor credit control leads to cash being tied up in sales made to customers who don't pay on time, either because they don't realise payment is due, or because they're waiting until they're chased to pay, or simply because they're unable to pay. Your business will suffer if your customers don't pay you on time as you'll then be unable to pay your own suppliers and staff.

FAQS

How does credit control fit in with the sales process?

Credit control isn't just about collecting late payments from overdue debtors. It's an integral part of the sales process in determining:

- the terms on which you're prepared to sell to a customer
- how that sale is to be processed and documented
- how the cash is to be collected

All staff, including everyone in sales and credit control, should be responsible for ensuring payments are made by customers— they need to work together, presenting a united front, when dealing with any queries or disputes.

MAKING IT HAPPEN

Establish your credit-control system

When you're setting up a credit-control system, it can be useful to divide your customer base into those with higher- and lower-value accounts. For example:

- concentrate on your major customers and tailor your efforts to their circumstances. Check you've got their up-to-date credit ratings, prioritise dealing with their queries, and make sure you've got good personal contact with their staff so they'll pay you on time.
- for lower-value accounts, you can take a more standard approach to setting credit limits and collection procedures. Simply establish good contact with each customer at the outset, and have a robust process for issuing and chasing invoices as necessary.

Credit limits can be based on those recommended by a ratings agency, or if you're satisfied with their credit checks, you can set your own limits. This might represent two months' worth of the customer's normal level of sales, or perhaps no more than 10% of the value of your balance sheet for any one customer.

Whatever the level of credit, the credit terms must be made clear to the customer throughout sales negotiations. And you should repeat the terms on all order acknowledgements, account applications, invoices and statements.

When you first start trading with a customer, you need to have a formal account-opening process that requires them to complete an application form. This should enable you to collect all the information you need for credit checking, as well as obtaining the customer's acknowledgement of your terms and conditions.

Always issue your invoices promptly after the sale. To minimise disputes and queries, invoices should contain all relevant payment details including the due date and any customer order number. They should also accurately describe the goods or services, the agreed price and the invoice value.

Check that invoices and payments are entered on to your accounting system swiftly so you always have a clear and up-to-date view of your current position. You'll find it really useful if you have 'aged debtor reports' regularly produced. Ideally these lists should itemise invoices outstanding in order of debtor due date ('aged') rather than invoice date, and preferably sorted by size of outstanding debt (from largest to smallest).

You should set targets for cash to be collected and the acceptable levels of outstanding debt (such as debtor days, which is the ratio of your debtors to your total sales) and measure trends and the business's performance against these targets. Also establish a standard timetable of actions to follow up invoices to ensure payment. These might include:

- phone calls before the due date to ensure payment is going to be made
- regular issuing of statements
- a standard set of follow-up letters on over-due debts involving one or two reminder letters, escalating to named individual senior managers before issuing a final warning that you will take further action to recover payment
- a procedure for placing overdue accounts on hold until they are paid

If you have a large debtor book, you may need to have someone dedicated to chasing cash payments who is separate from the person maintaining ledgers, as the skills required are very different.

Recover debts

Once you're satisfied that there aren't any real disputes concerning the debt and that the customer should be able to pay, you need to move into debt-recovery action.

The first stage is often referral to a third-party debt-collection agency or a solicitor. This is often successful—when people receive a letter from a collection agency it's often enough to show them that you're serious about taking action to recover the money.

If the first stage is unsuccessful, you may then choose to go to court, either directly or using your solicitor, to obtain a judgment against the customer. This will enable you, for example, to instruct bailiffs to seize and sell the customer's assets in order to clear the debt.

If your customer is a company and has a debt over £750, you could threaten to move directly to insolvency proceedings, either by issuing a statutory demand (which if not paid within 21 days entitles you to apply for a winding-up petition), or by seeking the appointment of an administrator.

Understand factoring

A factor is a finance company that takes over the management of your debtor book. Once they receive an invoice you've raised with a customer, they'll typically advance you up to 85% of its value depending on the approved credit limit that they've set for that customer. The factor will then chase the customer for payment of the debt, paying to you the balance of the amount—less their charges—once it's been collected.

Invoice discounting provides a similar type of funding against debtors, but still leaves you responsible for collecting the debts.

The advantages of factoring are that, in addition to the cash-flow benefits of the immediate advance, your credit control is being handled by a professional process that specialises in checking the creditworthiness of customers and in collecting debts systematically.

The disadvantages of factoring are:

- a third party becomes responsible for chasing your customers for payment, which can affect your relationship with them
- the factor will want to approve all your major customers before advancing funds, which can delay your receipt of an advance
- some types of debt are not suitable for factoring
- some factors may impose 'concentration limits' where they will limit the advance given against larger debts

There are over 60 active lenders in the factoring and invoice discounting market, so it can be difficult to choose the best factor for your business. Contact a trade body such as the National Association of Commercial Finance Brokers for advice. See **www.nacfb.org/leasing_asset.asp** or the Factors and Discounters Association **www.thefda.org.uk** for more details.

Credit control risks when exporting

Not surprisingly, exporting carries with it some specific risks that require additional research if you're to manage them effectively. These include the following:

- customer risk can be higher as it can be more difficult to credit check a customer overseas than at home. You can obtain a limited customer status check through the DTI's UK Trade and Industry (UKTI) Overseas Market Introduction Service. See **www.uktradeinvest.gov.uk/ukti/fileDownload/OMIS(July2006).pdf?cid=391808**
- some countries carry specific risk relating, for instance, to political or economic instability. Some also have serious commercial issues such as whether the banking sector is efficient and reliable enough to enable payment actually to be made.
- foreign exchange ('Forex') risk if your sales are to be made in the customer's currency, where the rate of exchange to Sterling may wildly fluctuate.
- communication difficulties due to differences in language and time zones or problems with the customer country's communications infrastructure.

When it comes to managing the risk of not getting paid, there are a number of trading arrangements that you could adopt. The safest approach when selling overseas is to require payment in advance from foreign customers. However, this may restrict your levels of sales.

If you do decide to give credit to foreign customers, then you can minimise your risk by using documentary credits or collections:

- a letter of credit is an agreement from your customer's bank or finance house to pay you once you've supplied them with the correct documentation to show that you've supplied the goods. The risk here is that you must supply the exact documents

specified in the letter of credit—within the specified timescale—and you must also obtain the customer's agreement to accept any discrepancies.
- a bill of exchange is an agreement setting out the amount due for payment. Once this is accepted by the customer, they've accepted ownership of the goods and are liable to pay the sum due. The bill is then passed to the customer's bank for payment to you, in return for which you or your bank then releases the documents needed for the customer to collect the goods.

As these methods rely on matching the details in the documents to what has actually been supplied, it's vital that the documentation is both complete and accurate. This is a complex area and you'll need to give your staff the necessary training in handling and processing these documents.

The documentation can state that the cash due is payable immediately (or 'on acceptance') or at some stated interval after acceptance.

The terms of the underlying contract must be clearly stated in a contract that sets out what is to be supplied and the terms of payment, as well as who is to be responsible for any bank charges involved. To facilitate international trade, a set of internationally agreed terms called Incoterms 2000 has been developed. These define the relative responsibilities of the seller and buyer and these terms should be specifically incorporated into any contract.

Finally, the approach with the highest risk is to allow overseas customers normal credit terms ('trading on open account'). If you do this, you should look into taking out credit insurance on overseas customers or factoring with one of the lenders which will fund overseas debt. As insurers and lenders may vary depending on which regions they have strength in, it's worth taking advice from a broker.

If you're exporting some types of capital equipment, you may be able to take advantage of insurance offered by the Government's Export Credit Guarantee Department.

Protect yourself

You need to be sure that your customers will pay their bills before you start to trade with them. However, it can be difficult to assess the creditworthiness of start-up businesses as they have no trading history and there may be little other information available. Try obtaining the partners' or directors' details and checking at Companies House to see whether they've got other companies that you can credit check. If you've got any concerns, and substantial amounts of cash are involved, ask the principals of the company to give personal guarantees of payment. Be warned that these can be difficult to enforce, so you should take legal advice on how to put this in place.

It's also worth asking your lawyer to draw up a Reservation of Title clause (also known after a case as a 'Romalpa') for inclusion in your terms of business, so that the goods you've supplied remain your property until all sums due to you have been paid.

✗ COMMON MISTAKE
You don't carry out credit checks

You've got only yourself to blame if you trade with customers and don't bother to check their creditworthiness. As well as carrying out credit checks before trading and rechecking at regular intervals, you could also subscribe to a monitoring service that will alert you if, for example, your customer receives a County Court Judgement (CCJ) or fails to file their accounts on time.

USEFUL LINKS

@ rating (for country profiles):
www.trading-safely.com
Better Payment Practice Campaign:
www.payontime.co.uk
Chartered Institute of Arbitrators:
www.arbitrators.org
Credit Services Association (CSA):
www.csa-uk.com
Experian:
www.experian.com
Export Credit Guarantee Department:
www.ecgd.gov.uk
The Factors and Discounters Association:
www.thefda.org.uk
HM Courts Service:
www.hmcourts-service.gov.uk
HM Courts Service Money Claim Online service:
www.moneyclaim.gov.uk
The Insolvency Service:
www.insolvency.gov.uk
The Law Society (for finding a lawyer):
www.lawsociety.org.uk/choosingandus-ing/helpyourbusiness/foryourbusiness.law
Northern Ireland Court Service:
www.courtsni.gov.uk
Registry Trust Limited:
www.registry-trust.org.uk
Scottish Court Service:
www.scotcourts.gov.uk
SITPRO (for information about international trading terms and payment methods):
www.sitpro.org.uk

Issuing invoices and receipts

GETTING STARTED

When you start trading, you need to provide your customers with an invoice or receipt as evidence of your trading transactions, and you also need to keep copies for your own records. This actionlist looks at what invoices and receipts are and why they are important to your business. It considers different types of invoice and what information they need to contain; when you should issue invoices; and some of the commonly used processes for managing invoices in your business.

FAQS

What are invoices and receipts?

An invoice is a formal record of trading between either you and your customers or you and your suppliers, and it contains the details of the goods or services that have been supplied and the prices charged. If you give your customers credit—in other words, allow them to defer payment—the invoice becomes particularly important. From the date that the invoice is issued to the date it is paid, the value of the invoice is regarded as a debt to the business.

Receipts are a simplified form of invoice and are predominantly used in retail businesses. Whilst the main use of a receipt is to act as a proof of purchase for the consumer, receipts may also be issued to business customers when they are making infrequent or urgent purchases from retail businesses.

Invoices and receipts are key documents for all financial management and accounting processes in a business, and are vital documents in business tax records. They provide a record of income as well as a record of expenditure for your business. Without the evidence for your business' expenditure, legitimate expenses may not be allowable for tax purposes, which will result in you paying more tax.

What are the different types of invoice?

The main types of invoice document issued are:

Pro-forma invoice

This is an invoice provided by a supplier to their customer, usually in advance of supplying the goods or services to that customer. It acts as a formal request for payment and details what will be supplied, and usually has the same format as standard invoices. It is frequently used before credit facilities have been set up when you first start trading with a new customer. Although a pro-forma invoice may detail the Value Added Tax (VAT) due on a sale, it is not considered to be a tax invoice and should state: 'This is not a tax invoice'.

Sales invoice

This is the standard invoice document issued by a supplier to a customer to confirm a trading transaction. When an invoice is issued by VAT-registered businesses, it is called a VAT invoice. Sales invoices detail the income that a business receives from its trading activities, and for accounting purposes are recorded in the business' sales ledger.

Purchase invoice

The sales invoice that is issued to a customer is in turn regarded as a purchase invoice by that customer. The purchase invoice details the goods or services that are supplied to the business, and is evidence of the trading costs and expenses for that business. Purchase invoices are recorded in the business's purchase ledger.

Credit note

A credit note is issued to offset against an original sales invoice (or part of an invoice) when goods are returned, or a pricing error has been made. If the sales invoice has been paid before you issue the credit note, your customer will be entitled to a refund or alternative goods up to the value of the credit note. If your customer has an account, then they can deduct the value of the credit note from their next payment.

Self-billing invoice

These are purchase invoices issued by the customer to the supplier, under an agreed self-billing arrangement. The customer prepares and provides the self-billed invoice to the supplier and then pays the supplier the amount due—normally when the customer has control over the use of goods or services that the supplier provides. For example, if a business pays royalties to a supplier based on the sales of an item that it makes, then it may produce a self-billed invoice to account for the royalties due on those sales every month.

MAKING IT HAPPEN
Include the right details

All invoices need to have certain key pieces of information as supporting evidence for tax and VAT purposes. When starting your business, speak to your accountant or HM Revenue & Customs (HMRC) to make sure you know which details should be shown on your invoices and receipts, particularly if you are registered for VAT. Some of the information required is dependent on the legal status of your business, as shown below.

Sole traders and partnerships

If the name of the business is *not* the surname of the trader, you need to include the business name and its full trading address. For example, if Joe Brown trades as ABC Carparts, his invoices should show just 'ABC Carparts' or 'Joe Brown trading as ABC Carparts'.

Limited companies

A limited company must detail the following on its invoices:
- the full company name and registration number
- any trading name that the company may be using relevant to the transaction
- the address of the company

General information required

All invoices should also detail the following:
- the name and address of the customer
- an identifying number for the invoice
- the date of supply (the tax point)
- a description of the goods or services provided
- the gross amount due to be paid
- the payment terms for this invoice and ideally a due date for this

VAT invoices

Once your business is VAT registered, there are additional requirements for your invoices.
- Your VAT number must be shown.
- A unit price must be given if there are multiple units supplied.
- The VAT rate applicable to the goods or services supplied.
- The net amount charged for the goods or services excluding VAT.
- The amount of VAT charged at each rate.
- The rate of any cash discount offered.

Other information you may want to include

Depending on your business, you may also want to include some of the following on your invoices.
- A customer reference or order number.
- Your bank account details to facilitate your customers paying by BACS.
- A reservation of title clause, which means that ownership of the goods supplied does not pass to your customer until they have been paid for.
- Reference to the fact that you are entitled to charge interest and costs for late payment.
- A reference to your terms and conditions of trade which have already been made available to your customer. Alternatively you can print terms and conditions on the back of each invoice.

Include the right details on receipts

Retail businesses typically provide customers with a receipt produced by a point-of-sale till. If your business is VAT registered and you have signed up for one of the specialist retail schemes, there's no obligation to issue your retail customers with a VAT invoice unless you are asked for one. Most retailers provide receipts which show simplified VAT information, and this is acceptable as evidence of expenditure for VAT-registered customers for sales up to a value of £250.

Each receipt should show:
- the name and address of your business
- the VAT number if the business is VAT-registered
- the date of supply
- a description of the goods purchased and the price paid, inclusive of VAT
- the rate of VAT charged (if applicable)

(Note that if your business is going to export goods or services, there are additional requirements for the treatment of VAT on your invoices. It's worth seeking professional help to make sure you comply with the regulations.)

Retailers do not need to keep copies of individual receipts issued, but they do need to have a record of their daily gross takings, which should normally be supported by a till roll print-out and copies of sales vouchers.

Issue invoices at the right time

It's always good to invoice customers promptly—as soon as possible after the delivery of goods or completion of a service, in fact. This will help to avoid queries from your customer because they cannot remember receiving your goods, and also means that you're likely to get paid earlier, which will be good for your cash flow.

Sometimes the arrangements for invoicing are negotiated and agreed as part of the sale process. For example, a software company may want their customer to pay for a combined software and hardware package when the order is placed, while the customer wants to pay for everything 60 days after the order is completed. An agreed compromise could be as follows:
- Invoice for hardware when the order is placed—payment terms 7 days.
- Invoice for software licence one month later—payment terms 30 days.
- Invoice for customisation and installation of software when delivered—payment terms 30 days.

A common request from customers who buy lots of small value items regularly is to receive a consolidated invoice once a month. This will detail all items purchased in the month on one invoice, which reduces the number of invoices issued by the supplier as well as processed by the customer.

If you are providing regular services that are for a fixed monthly amount and are liable to VAT, you may consider providing your customer with an annual tax schedule, rather than issuing individual invoices each month. The schedule details the tax points for each monthly payment (usually collected by direct debit or standing order), and the net amounts for the services supplied and VAT charged.

Choose an invoicing system

If your business only issues a small number of invoices, you can write them out manually (for example, for one-off requests in a retail business), or use a computer, word-processing or spreadsheet package to generate more professional-looking invoices. This simple approach can work well, but once you start to offer credit, you'll have the complication of being VAT-registered and will need to produce many invoices a month—so it will make much more sense to use an integrated accounts system which manages both invoicing *and* credit control.

You can give invoices to customers when goods are delivered, but more typically they're sent out in the post or by e-mail after the goods or services have been provided. E-mail is an increasingly common method for sending invoices, but make sure that if you use this method, you send the invoice in a format that cannot be manually altered by the recipient. PDF files are a good option, and many accounting systems allow invoices to be generated in this format, which you can then send as an attachment in an e-mail. When your customer receives the e-mailed invoice, they will still have to print it out and enter its details into their accounting systems.

E-invoicing

This is the process which allows invoice data to be sent directly from your business to your customers' accounts systems, without the need for the manual re-keying of data. It is increasingly being demanded by large organisations trying to reduce the administrative costs of processing invoices onto their accounting systems.

The process usually starts with your customer raising and sending an electronic purchase order. Once you have provided the goods or services as normal, you then raise an invoice either on your own accounts system or on a third-party platform, which then sends an electronic file to your customer. This file is then uploaded automatically on to their accounts system, being identified against the original purchase order.

Keep track of outstanding payments once the invoice is issued

If you offer credit to your customers, the issuing of a sales invoice is only a part of the sales process: the transaction isn't completed until the invoice has been paid in full. Many businesses are very successful at selling their goods or services and yet still fail, because they are unable to collect the money owed to them by customers. It's essential that you set up processes which minimise the risk of your customers failing

to pay you. See pp. 125–128 (Setting Up a Trade Credit Policy) for further information.

COMMON MISTAKES
You don't give customers the information they need to pay you

Many organisations require their purchase orders (POs) to be printed on all invoices that they receive. If you don't include the PO number, you payment could be delayed and the invoice could even be sent back to you.

You lose track of key dates

The tax point of an invoice is regarded as the date when a supply of goods or services is treated as taking place, so for most businesses, the tax point for an invoice will coincide with the date of issue. However, some invoices are supplied significantly before or after the goods or services are supplied, and this will have an impact on how you account for these goods or services. Your accountant or HMRC will be able to provide advice on how you should treat these invoices and identify the correct tax point.

USEFUL LINKS

Bacs Payment Schemes Ltd for information on both Bacs and Direct Debit:
www.bacs.co.uk
Better Payment Practice Group:
www.payontime.co.uk
HM Revenue & Customs (HMRC):
www.hmrc.gov.uk
Open Business Exchange (OBE):
www.ob10.com/Country/UK

Recovering an unpaid debt

GETTING STARTED

No matter how good your credit control procedures are, at some point you're bound to have a debtor who just won't pay you—no matter how many reminders and statements you've sent them, or how often you've tried to get in touch to sort things out.

In cases like these, you may have to consider threatening to take recovery action and then following this through. In this actionlist, we'll look the issues you'll need to think through before you instigate legal proceedings, the basics of late payment legislation, and some options for debt recovery.

FAQS

I'm thinking about taking action against a non-payer. Will it be worth my time and trouble, however?

Dealing with a customer who has failed to pay can be extremely stressful, but deciding to take recovery action is a commercial decision, and shouldn't be a knee-jerk reaction made in anger. Weigh up the business issues involved *before* committing to any course of action by asking yourself the following questions:

- Why hasn't this customer paid? Is the debt, or part of it, disputed on some reasonable grounds? If so, how strong is the customer's claim and how strong is your case that the debt is actually due? Is there a danger that the debtor may have a valid counter-claim against you?
- What is the value of debt (or the disputed element)? How does this compare to the value of your relationship with the customer?

Commencing legal or other recovery action or starting insolvency proceedings will usually end any relationship with that customer. So if the value of the debt is small and the value of the relationship great, you may decide that it is worth writing this item off in view of the future profits to be made.

If this is a large debt, however, and the prospect of taking legal action is looming, you have to ask yourself: do you want that customer anyway?

- How much will it cost you to pursue the debt compared to its size?
- Is the debtor likely to be able to pay the debt and the associated recovery costs?

There is no sense in sending good money (and time) after bad if the customer has no assets or is clearly not going to be able to pay.

- If you go to court, how easy will it be to enforce any judgement achieved? It is no good appointing bailiffs for example, if the debtor has no identifiable assets in the UK for them to seize.

In some cases of course you may decide that irrespective of the merits of a particular case, it may still be worth pursuing in order to establish a reputation in the marketplace and encourage other debtors to pay. But again it should be a commercial decision that this is in the business' interests, not simply a point of principle or personal satisfaction.

MAKING IT HAPPEN
Investigate late payment legislation

Since the introduction in 1998 and then 2002 of laws and regulations covering late payment of commercial debts, you have a statutory right to claim interest at a rate of 8% above the Bank of England's base rate (unless you have separately agreed some substantial contractual right to interest in your terms of business). The base rate at 31 December is the reference rate for the following six months, while the base rate at 30 June is the reference rate for the other six months of the year.

Interest runs from 30 days after the date of delivery or invoice, whichever is later, unless other terms have been agreed explicitly or established through a course of dealings.

You also have the right to claim compensation for late payment of:

- £40 for debts under £1,000
- £70 for debts of £1,000 to £9,999
- £100 for debts of over £10,000

Again, whether or not to use these rights in respect of some or all creditors will be a commercial decision for you to take and you may also want to check what your competitor's policy is. If you are going to raise charges you also need to be efficient at chasing your debts, as customers may resent being charged where this is partly due to your failure to collect.

To claim, you should notify your customers of your policy and ensure that your right to charge interest is included on all relevant documentation, such as invoices and statements. You should then notify individual customers once interest charges start to accrue.

You can pursue these debts through the courts in the same way as any other claim, and once paid you should send the customer a bill or receipt documenting the interest and compensation paid.

Think about your debt-recovery options

If negotiation with your customer does not succeed, your options are:

- Debt recovery agency

  These agencies (some of which are operated by specialist solicitors) specialise in collecting debts and are therefore set up with staff and processes dedicated to doing so, which means that they are likely to be more expert and efficient at it than you are.

  A letter from a specialist agency (which is set up to follow through on chasing debt and taking recovery action) is often enough to generate payment from many debtors.

  Agencies charge a commission (usually around 10% of the sums recovered). Always use one that is registered with the Credit Services Association.

- Alternative Dispute Resolution (ADR)

  In order to avoid unnecessary cases clogging up the courts, the Court Service greatly encourages parties to try to resolve cases without court proceedings

(which may also be in your interests by avoiding unnecessary legal costs).

Trained mediators can be found through the Law Society who may be able to help you resolve your differences with the customer, and may therefore also help retain the relationship.

- Court proceedings

  Claims should be filed with your local County Court, or can be started directly on the Money Claim Online website up to a value of £100,000.

  The Court will allocate the claim on one of three tracks:

  1 Simple cases of up to £5,000—the small claims track. This is a relatively informal process where each side is expected to represent itself (therefore you will not be able to recover any lawyers' costs) or cases may be heard on written evidence alone.

  2 £5,000 to £15,000—the fast track.

  3 Complex cases and all cases over £15,000—the multi-track. Both the fast and multi track processes are more formal procedures and involve full hearings where you are expected to be represented by lawyers.

Whichever track you are on, you will need to pay court costs such as filing fees as you go through each stage of the process. If the case is for over £15,000 and complex, it may be transferred to the High Court where you will need to be represented and therefore are likely to incur much higher costs.

In Scotland claims are made to the Sherriff Courts and there are lower limits for small claims.

Once you have your judgement you will then need to enforce it, which can involve seeking further Court orders (and incurring further costs):

- Examination, where the debtor is required to attend court and answer under oath questions about their assets so that you can then decide how you want to enforce judgement.
- Warrant of execution, where bailiffs are instructed to seize assets to be sold to recover your money.

- Third party debt order, where cash due to the debtor from someone else is frozen to be used to pay you instead.
- Charging order, where your debt is secured on a piece of property so that you have to be paid when it is sold (although this does not force the debtor to sell).
- Attachment of earnings, which only applies to individuals and involves their employer being ordered to pay you directly by deductions from the debtor's wages.
- Insolvency proceedings

  If you can prove that the debtor is insolvent and that you are owed over £750, then you can petition for the court to liquidate the debtor's assets if they are a company or file for their bankruptcy if they are individuals.

  Failure to satisfy a judgement debt, or failure to pay within 21 days of a Statutory Demand for payment, are taken as proof of insolvency by the courts.

  This can be a powerful threat but there is a danger that you may run up costs in pushing a debtor into insolvency, because if they are liquidated or bankrupted this will not ensure that you get paid (other than for your petitioning costs, which will normally rank as an expense of the liquidation or bankruptcy). This is because there will be insolvency fees and secured creditors to pay before whatever is left is available for the normal trade creditors. Take advice from a licensed insolvency practitioner or your solicitor before taking this option.

Hints and tips

- Have good credit policies and procedures in place (see the guides noted below). By ensuring your billing arrangements and terms are clearly documented and accepted by the customer, invoicing regularly and closely monitoring your customers' payments, as far as possible you:
  - avoid problems arising in the first place
  - identify problems early for action
  - are as well prepared for taking action as possible.
- Consider factoring your debtors on a non-recourse (insured) basis, so that the factoring company has responsibility for

taking this type of action and you are covered against bad debts.

- If you are having difficulty in collecting a debt, start preparing the ground for later action if required as part of your normal chasing procedures. Seek confirmation from the debtor that the balance is acknowledged as being due (even if they are seeking to delay payment). This can then be used to challenge any later attempt to dispute that the debt is payable, or as evidence to support a claim of insolvency (that the customer is unable to pay its debts as they fall due).
- Always send a final notice stating that action will take place if payment is not received within a specified time, as this gives a clear point from which you may then start to claim costs (if appropriate).
- Consider whether you should mitigate your loss by seeking to recover your goods under your Reservation of Title clause (this should be made clear in your terms and conditions of trade and means that ownership of the goods does not pass to the customer until they have been paid for).
- If you obtain judgement and then a warrant of execution, seek advice from your solicitor about the appropriate type of bailiffs to use to enforce this, as some are much more proactive then others.
- As a creditor you can petition for an Administration Order which can be put in place much more quickly than obtaining an order for a compulsory liquidation. Speak to an insolvency practitioner or to your lawyer about using this as a threat to put maximum pressure on the debtor for settlement.

USEFUL LINKS

Better Payment Practice Campaign;
www.payontime.co.uk
Credit Services Association (CSA):
www.csa-uk.com
Experian provides credit reports, information and analysis to businesses, consumers and the public sector:
www.experian.com
HM Courts Service:
www.hmcourts-service.gov.uk
The Insolvency Service:
www.insolvency.gov.uk

Understanding factoring and invoice discounting

GETTING STARTED

Factoring and invoice discounting are financial services that allow your business to be paid in advance against your invoiced sales issued under credit terms. The advantage of this service is that you receive the money without having to wait for your customers to pay, which can be particularly useful when your business is growing and you need to maintain a positive cash flow.

This actionlist explains how factoring and invoice discounting work, and looks at the difference between the two. It explains the situations when these services could be useful to your business and offers practical hints and tips. It also provides guidelines on how to decide whether these services would be cost-effective for you and lists sources of further information.

FAQS

How does factoring work?

When you use a factoring service, it essentially takes over your sales ledger and pays you a proportion of what's owed by customers as soon as you've completed the delivery of a product or service sold under credit terms.

The factor takes on the responsibility of collecting payment from your business's debtors and frees up your time so you can focus on running your business. Your customers will pay the factoring firm, which will then charge a market-related interest rate (normally similar to bank overdrafts) and a fee depending on the level of service provided. Costs can vary enormously but they'll usually be between 1–4.5% above the base rate of interest. Factoring firms can provide various services—the main ones (full-service factoring, export factoring and invoice discounting) are outlined below.

Depending on your agreement, the factor will normally pay between 80–85% of the amount owed by customers as soon as they receive a copy of the invoice. The balance—less fees and interest—is paid to you when the invoice payment from the customer is received by the factor. Debts over a certain age, or customers considered a credit risk, may be excluded.

Factors will only pay out on 'approved invoices' which are agreed in advance between you and the factor. If you get a new customer and are going to offer them credit, they must first be approved by the factor.

Will factoring work for you?

For fast-growing businesses, factoring can make good financial sense. It speeds up cash flow, and reduces the amount of money you may need to borrow to cover the day-to-day costs of running your business. If your customers are reliable and you have few or no bad debts, then factoring can be cost-effective. Cash-based industries, such as retail, can't use factoring as it's linked purely to credit.

Factoring is an expensive form of finance, and is really only cost-effective if you would otherwise have to employ a credit clerk to monitor and chase payment of your invoices. The market is currently very competitive, and some banks or factoring companies might try to push you into factoring when it may not be the best option for your business.

Factoring provides funds in proportion to sales, so the amount of finance available becomes greater as your business grows—this makes it particularly helpful if your business is growing quickly. It also safeguards your business, since the factor will want to undertake credit checks before granting factoring arrangements for your new or existing customers.

MAKING IT HAPPEN

There are various factoring and discounting options for you to consider; think through the options carefully to find the one best suited to your business's circumstances.

Full-service factoring

In full-service factoring (sometimes called managed debt factoring), the factor will assume responsibility for both the sales ledger and credit management. The range of services available from a factoring agency varies and can be tailored to meet the needs of individual businesses. Generally, you can choose from the following services:

- **non-recourse factoring**: provides 100% cover against bad debt, although there's usually an excess of between £500 and £1,000 on each claim. If your customer fails to pay a debt, the factor will credit you with the amount due. In this case, the factor will be more selective about the debts taken on. Some smaller, independent factors don't offer this insurance themselves, but will arrange for this type of protection through a trade credit insurance agency.
- **recourse factoring**: in the event of bad debt, the factor will recover any advance payments made to you.
- **confidential factoring:** in this instance, the factor will not disclose the use of its services to your customers. However, confidential factoring is very uncommon and businesses tend to use invoice discounting instead.

Invoice discounting

You'll find invoice discounting attractive if you want to improve your cash flow but don't want any outside interference with your own credit management. Invoice discounting leaves all sales ledger management in your hands, while making similar payments to those offered by full-service factoring (that is, 80–85% against approved invoices).

Your customers also don't need to know that you are using a discounting agency, as you'll invoice them in the usual way. At the same time that you invoice your customers, you also provide a copy to the discounter, who'll then advance you the agreed portion of the invoice's value. Payments from your customers go into a bank account administered by the discounter, who then credits the remaining value of the payments to your account, less their charges.

Invoice discounting is most traditionally used by larger businesses (that is, firms with an annual turnover of at least £2 million). In recent years, however, the service has been made available to businesses with turnover as low as £250,000 a year. The main thing invoice discounters look for is a proven ability to run your own sales ledger. Unlike standard factoring, invoice discounting generally doesn't provide for protection against bad debts.

Export factoring

If you're an exporter who needs finance, credit management or bad debt protection services for overseas deals, you could use export factoring. A factor based in the UK, known as an export factor, takes responsibility for your sales ledger and for selecting a factoring agency in your overseas customer's home country. This factor serves as the import factor; they collect payment from your customer and pass it on to the export factor.

Export factoring allows you to offer potential customers in overseas markets the same terms and conditions as your competitors who are based in those markets. It makes business transactions with a foreign-trade partner more efficient by using the services of an expert in the local market, and it can offer protection against bad debts caused by export and foreign exchange risk. Factor services can also be provided to overseas businesses that are exporting to the UK.

Many factors who specialise in helping exporting businesses offer the following services:

- export credit assessment of customers
- advice on trading terms in export markets
- local collections and assistance with dispute resolution
- protection against foreign exchange risk
- faster transfer of funds to the UK

- expert local knowledge of overseas buyers' creditworthiness
- financial facilities available in major currencies
- export credit-guarantee insurance
- full responsibility for bad debt
- multi-currency and multilingual sales accounting

Alternatives to factoring

The main alternative to factoring is to negotiate an overdraft with your bank. However, if your business is growing quickly, it may be difficult to agree the level of overdraft that you need, or you may find that you have to keep going back to your bank to renegotiate.

Other options include applying to your bank for a loan, but newer businesses may find that banks are risk averse or require security to be given.

Take professional advice

Before you take the plunge, discuss your options in detail with your bank manager, accountant or business adviser, and explore all the implications involved in factoring or invoice discounting. It's important to be clear about how cash advances will be used and to know what the long-term effect of factoring will be on your business's finances.

Draw up a shortlist of possible factoring firms before making any decision. Remember that some factors specialise in a particular business sector and might understand your specific business needs better than others. And carefully consider the terms, cost and suitability of any arrangement before you enter into an agreement.

COMMON MISTAKES
You're bullied into factoring

If your cash flow isn't as healthy as you'd like it to be, factoring might seem like the perfect answer. But don't allow yourself to be talked into factoring by your bank manager without considering all the implications carefully. It may be simply that the bank is keen to reduce the level of your existing overdraft.

Remember that once you've committed to factoring or invoice discounting arrangements, it can be difficult to change because of the large amounts of working capital required to buy yourself out of the service.

You fail to establish areas of responsibility

When you're entering into an agreement with a factor, make it quite clear from the outset as to whether you or the factor will chase particular debts. Don't forget to think about how this will affect your relationship with your customers. So you need to decide whether you want to factor all of your debts or whether some (key) customer accounts should be excluded.

USEFUL LINKS

Department for Business, Enterprise and Regulatory Reform (BERR):
www.berr.gov.uk
Factors and Discounters Association:
www.factors.org.uk

Choosing and using a debt collection agency

GETTING STARTED
Chasing up unpaid debts is a time-consuming business, and for some small companies, engaging a debt collection agency to do that work for them could be a sensible option. Agencies take on the burden of encouraging debtors to cough up outstanding money, and are likely to have access to more ways of finding debtors who have been difficult to track down.

This actionlist describes the services that debt collection agencies offer and explains how to find the right agency to suit your business' needs.

FAQS

What services does a debt collection agency offer?
While not appropriate for every business, asking a debt collection agency to chase late-paying customers can save you a lot of time and money. You can engage them on an ad hoc basis (when your business has a specific problem), or on a type of retainer, where they regularly look for customers who have reneged on their normal payment terms.

Most debt collection agencies offer a range of services, including collecting debts owed by retail and business customers, and undertaking legal action on your behalf when debts remain unpaid and all other routes to prise the money from the errant customers have been exhausted. They can also:

- collect money from businesses or individuals overseas. Understandably, this is more time-intensive than retrieving debts within the UK, and as a result is more expensive.
- trace missing debtors. In some cases a debtor may be difficult to trace and an agency can be employed to investigate their whereabouts.
- offer advice on cases where there is little chance of debt recovery, such as when a company goes into administration
- in some cases, purchase your customers' debt from your business at a large discount, which gives you a guaranteed part-payment.

Areas of specialism can vary widely between agencies: some cover the whole gamut of debt collection, while others focus on just one area (such as collection from domestic customers). Some firms may operate on a regional basis, while others have a network of branches and provide national or international coverage.

How is a debt collected?
As a first step, the collection agency will send a letter to debtors informing them of the agency's involvement in the case, and requesting that the outstanding balance be paid immediately.

If there is no response, the correspondence will be followed up with a telephone call. If that route yields no results, the agency will then write again to the debtors, advising them that legal action will begin, usually in seven days' time from the date of the letter. Again, the threat of court proceedings can jump-start the repayment process, and often a representative of the agency can be sent to visit the debtor. If no money is forthcoming after these attempts, you'll need to decide whether to go ahead with the legal action or, in some cases, write off the debt if it looks extremely unlikely that it'll ever be recovered.

Engaging a debt collection agency can make some customers pay up there and then, as they think that non-payment will automatically result in court action. There is, however, sadly no guarantee that the agency will definitely be able to obtain payment from your customer, particularly if the customer is genuinely unable to pay.

MAKING IT HAPPEN
Find a debt collection agency

The Internet is a useful first port of call. There are many websites which can give you the contact details of debt collection agencies and link directly to their own websites. Visit some sites, comparing and contrasting the services they offer and any costs, so that you can work out whether they would be appropriate for your needs. The Credit Services Association (CSA) also lists its members online (see below).

Business directories such as Thomson and Yellow Pages can also provide listings, but don't engage an agency or hand over any money until you have thoroughly researched their methods, costs, and terms (see below). As ever, a personal recommendation is always valuable, so ask other businesses in your field to suggest effective, reliable and trustworthy agencies: you don't have to divulge details of the debts that need to be recovered to do this. If you're new to your local area or don't have many contacts in the business community, your trade association (see **www.taforum.org**) will be able to help you find details of member businesses in the area.

Choose the agency carefully

Just as you should check the credentials of new customers, it is always wise to find out more about a potential debt collection agency before you start to work with them. Bear in mind that:

- all collection agents must have a Consumer Credit Licence from the Office of Fair Trading (OFT; see **www.oft.gov.uk** for information). Any reputable agent or agency should be able to show proof of this licence.
- agencies must comply with the codes of conduct of both the Credit Services Association (CSA) and the Institute of Credit Management (ICM)—see below for their website addresses. If you feel that an agency hasn't complied with these codes, you may complain to these organisations.
- although qualifications are not essential, relevant professional training through an organisation such as the ICM will demonstrate that an agency has a high level of competence and is dedicated to keeping its staff up to date in terms of continuing professional development (CPD)
- agencies should have professional indemnity insurance, be financially sound, and have audited 'trust' accounts and their own legal staff

Ask as many questions as you need to of the agencies on your shortlist, until you're ready to make your final selection. Remember that you're looking for external help to *solve* a financial headache, rather than create a new one, so don't engage any agency you have misgivings or concerns about.

Be aware of collection agency fees

As part of your research, make sure you are very clear about the costs that you may incur if you ask an agency to help you. Because each debt recovery job can vary widely in terms of complexity, there is no set fee, but most agencies charge a fee of between 5% to 10% of the outstanding debt for their standard services and some may charge a minimum fee for small debts. You may also be charged a fee for each letter sent or phone call made, as well as for taking on legal action and tackling any particularly unusual circumstances. International work is also likely to be more expensive than debt recovery within the UK. Although ideally you will get paid on time in future, some agencies offer discounts to regular clients if you need to use their services again.

Brief your selected agency

Once you have chosen the agency you want to work with, you need to give them the information they'll need to chase up and (hopefully!) retrieve the money you're owed. They will need to know:

- the full contact details of the debtor
- the amount to be collected
- a description of the goods or services that have been charged for
- the date the balance was due
- the steps you have already taken to retrieve the debt

If you have any useful background information on the debtor, let the agency know. For example, they'll find it helpful to know about any work you've previously undertaken for the business or individual that owes the money, particularly if it is related to the current outstanding balance.

Monitor the agency's performance

Agencies should be able to give you regular updates on their progress with your case, so that you're fully in the loop. Some may only get in touch if significant progress has been made, so do be clear about how much information you will want if that doesn't sound like enough.

It's up to the agency to make sure that it is complying with all relevant legislation, the main regulation being the Consumer Credit Act 1974 and its various amendments, updates and additions. Make sure any agency you engage is fully compliant with all the current regulations and registration rules, and that you are personally satisfied with their approach.

The Office of Fair Trading will be able to advise on you on other regulations affecting debt collection agencies. For information about consumer credit licensing, see: **www.oft.gov.uk/ advice_and_resources/resource_base/ credit-licence**

COMMON MISTAKES
You go with the first agency you find

You may be lucky and find the best agency for your needs by clicking on the first link you find on Google, but any time and effort you spend on thoroughly researching an agency will be well spent. You'll be less likely to be stung for unexpected costs or disappointed by overly-optimistic predicted outcomes.

You expect a quick fix

Most debt recovery strategies take time: if it were easy, you'd have been able to get the money yourself in the first place! Be realistic and accept that it's unlikely you'll have any good news in the very short term. Also be prepared to draw a line under the whole thing at some point if it becomes apparent the debtor cannot be traced, or that he or she just doesn't have (now or in the near future) the money to repay you.

USEFUL LINKS
Better Payment Practice Campaign:
www.payontime.co.uk
Credit Services Association (CSA):
www.csa-uk.com
Insolvency Service:
www.insolvency.gov.uk
Institute of Credit Management (ICM):
www.icm.org.uk

Using the small claims court

GETTING STARTED

Small businesses are often affected by late payment, and in some cases this can become a serious problem. Being paid late (or not at all, in some cases) can affect your cash flow and make it difficult for you, in turn, to pay your suppliers. The good news is, however, that it's now much easier to make a claim in court to recover payment owed to you.

In England and Wales, a claim of under £5,000 is normally assigned to the Small Claims Court, a simple and informal way of resolving disputes before a District Judge in a County Court. Small claims are usually dealt with more quickly than other more complex cases. It's also less expensive, and the more informal nature of hearings allows claimants to present their own case without having to engage a solicitor.

If larger amounts are involved, claims are allocated to either the 'fast track' (up to £15,000 or the 'multi-track' (over £15,000). These cases are dealt with at a formal trial before a Circuit Judge and claimants typically prefer to use professional legal representation when they come to court.

A different system operates in Scotland, where small claims are limited to a maximum of £750 and are made to the Sheriff's Court. Claims over £750 and up to £1,500 must be started under a 'summary clause procedure', which is designed to let most actions be settled without the parties having to appear in Court.

This actionlist will show you how to recover debts through the civil claims procedure. It covers how to take court action and follow the small claims procedure, and also offers useful hints and tips and lists sources of further information.

FAQS

When is going to the small claims court the best option?

If at all possible, try to use other avenues to collect debts first, before you turn to the courts. You may save yourself a lot of time and stress in the process! For example, to encourage prompt payment:

- arrange payment schedules before starting work on a project or providing a service whenever possible
- send out invoices regularly and ensure that outstanding accounts do not accumulate
- put all job quotes in writing and sign a written agreement before you begin work
- carry out a credit check on new clients before you agree to take on work for them. This is a painless task you can do via the Companies House website where for a few pounds you can look at the latest set of accounts for every business registered in the UK (**www.companies-house.gov.uk**)

Before going to the small claims court, you should consider the following:

- try every other available option to resolve the matter amicably. Once a claim has been issued by the Court, customer relationships can be seriously damaged.
- ask whether the person owing you money may have any valid reason for disputing the claim.
- is the other party able to pay? Pursuing someone who is unemployed, or a business that is in financial difficulty, may be pointless. The Insolvency Service (**www.insolvency.gov.uk**) will be able to inform you if the person or business involved is bankrupt, and Registry Trust Ltd (**www.registry-trust.org.uk**) holds details of anyone who has previously failed to pay prior County or High Court judgements, orders and fines in England and Wales. For Scotland, go to the Accountant in Bankruptcy (AiB) site (**www.aib.gov.uk**), or see Northern Ireland's dedicated Insolvency Service site. **www.courtsni.gov.uk/en-GB/Services/Online_Services**

If it is now clear that legal action is the only way you're going to get the money you're owed, it's time to get the ball rolling. Advise the other party in writing that you are going to start proceedings, giving them one last chance to pay: if you haven't received the outstanding amount from them in seven days' time, the action will be going ahead.

How much does it cost to make a claim?
The fees involved depend on the amount of the claim, and the Court will tell you how much the total cost will be. See **www.hmcourts-service.gov.uk/info about/fees/county.htm** for a breakdown of current fees according to the amount claimed. Additional fees may be payable if: the claim goes to trial; you want to appeal against the decision; or to begin enforcement proceedings (see below).

MAKING IT HAPPEN
Starting a civil claim
It is up to you to initiate the claim and identify the defendant in question. To do this, go to the relevant Court and state that you wish to issue a claim for money owed to your business. Alternatively you can start a claim online at **www.moneyclaim.gov.uk**

The Court will provide a claim form, which must be completed with your business's details, the debtor's details, the amount claimed and how the claim arose. This is an opportunity for you to provide as much information as possible to demonstrate that your claim is reasonable. If the claim form is being used to demand a specified amount of money, this is called a liquidated claim, which is usually used if your business is recovering payments for goods or services. It is important to be specific about the value of the claim. Copies of the claim form and any particulars of the claim must be supplied to the Court, the defendant, and for your own records.

When you're describing the defendant, you must state their business status (sole trader, partnership or limited company). A claim should not be made against individual partners in a firm or directors of a limited company if the debt is against the business itself.

Claims can be made through any County

Court (or Sheriff's Court in Scotland), although you may find it most convenient to approach your local court. You can find your nearest Court using the HM Courts Service website (**www.hmcourts-service.gov.uk/ HMCSCourtFinder**).

If a claim is defended, the case may be transferred to another Court. This may occur, for example, if the defendant's address is in another Court's area.

Notification of a civil claim
You should receive written notification from the court stating that the claim has been issued and when the defendant received it. The defendant will than have 14 days from the date of receipt to respond. If you have given the wrong address for the defendant, the court will let you know, and you'll then have to serve the claim yourself.

If you or the defendant are based in Scotland, you should ask a Messenger-at-Arms or Sheriff's Officer to serve the claim. The defendant must receive the claim form within four months of the date of issue.

If the defendant does not respond
If the defendant does not respond to the claim form within 14 days, you can apply for judgement to be entered in 'default' (there is no additional fee for this). The Court will then send the defendant an order to pay the money your business is owed.

You can choose to be paid in full immediately, or to apply for an instalment order: if your tardy client hasn't paid because of cash-flow problems their end, it may be more likely that you'll get your money back if you ask for the debt to be paid by instalments. The defendant can suggest a schedule of payment terms, which you can then accept or reject. If you reject the offer, do indicate to the debtor what you *will* accept, rather than waste more time toing and froing. A Court officer will then assess the offer made by the debtor and decide an appropriate way for them to pay it.

Defences and counter-claims
Not all claims go through undisputed, and the defendant may file a defence or counter-claim (for which they'll have to pay a fee)

to your initial claim, which disputes the amount owed or even denies the existence of the debt at all.

The Court will then send you an 'allocation questionnaire' for completion. This helps the judge to allocate the claim to the appropriate track. For claims over £1,000, there is an additional court fee to pay. If the claim is allocated to the small claims track, you will be told when to come to the hearing and what you must do to prepare for it. These instructions are called 'directions': follow them carefully as they may affect the evidence that can be used.

That said, if your claim is disputed and a Court hearing arranged to decide the case, you don't necessarily need to attend provided that you inform the court of your absence in good time. Being there in person is preferable, but it may be possible to arrange a conference call hearing, involving the debtor, the judge and yourself.

Enforcing a judgement

Sadly, obtaining a judgement doesn't guarantee that you'll get paid, and the Court won't enforce the judgement *unless* you ask it to do so. Again, a fee is payable for this, which will be added to the amount to be recovered from the defendant.

A number of enforcement methods are available (see below) and you should decide which is appropriate, taking into consideration the size of the debt and your knowledge of the debtor and their assets. Some procedures involve only the completion of forms and paying the appropriate fees, while others are more complex.

- Warrant of execution against goods. This involves authorising a Court Bailiff or Sheriff to seize and sell goods belonging to the defendant to cover the debt and associated costs.
- Garnishee proceedings. You can request that the Court orders a third party who owes the defendant money to pay this directly to the Court. These are known as 'third party debt orders'.

- Attachment of earnings. If the defendant is in regular employment, this is the best method available to enforce the judgement. The Court will order the defendant's employer to make deductions from their wages to settle the debt.
- Bankruptcy or liquidation. If the debt is above £750 and the debtor is self-employed, the only way to obtain payment may be through a bankruptcy petition. 'Winding-up' or liquidation proceedings are the equivalent to bankruptcy where the defendant is a limited company.
- Oral examination. If more information about the defendant's financial situation is required, you can apply to have them questioned by an Officer of the Court. This is referred to as 'orders to obtain information from judgement debtors'.

Alternatives to court action

Taking a claim to court can be time-consuming, expensive and inconvenient for many small businesses. A useful alternative is HM Courts Services' Money Claim Online website, which enables you to make a claim, track its progress and receive a judgement over the Internet (**www.moneyclaim.gov.uk**).

COMMON MISTAKE
You think the small claims court is a quick fix

As with any legal process, cases heard in the small claims court can drag on for months, and in the long run costs will mount, if only for the amount of time you're away from your business. Weigh up the pros and cons of legal action carefully and consider whether court action really is the best way of recovering the debt.

USEFUL LINKS

Citizens Advice Bureau:
www.citizensadvice.org.uk/index/getadvice.htm
Scottish Court Service:
www.scotcourts.gov.uk
Better Payment Practice Campaign:
www.payontime.co.uk

Applying for a consumer credit licence

GETTING STARTED

Credit licences are a requirement of the Consumer Credit Act 1974 (as amended by the Consumer Credit Act 2006) and are administered by the Office of Fair Trading (OFT) Consumer Credit Licensing Bureau. Unlicensed trading is a criminal offence and your business may need to obtain a credit licence if you supply goods or services to consumers on a credit or hire basis.

In this actionlist, we'll look at whether you need a Consumer Credit Licence and how to go about applying for one.

FAQS
When would I need a consumer credit licence?

You will probably need a consumer credit licence if you:

- sell on credit to individuals
- hire or lease out goods to individuals for more than three months
- lend money to individuals
- issue credit cards or trading cheques
- arrange credit for individuals
- offer hire purchase arrangements to individuals
- collect debts arising from regulated agreements
- help people with debt problems arising from regulated agreements
- advise on an individual's credit
- provide credit information services.
- provide debt administration services

The licensing requirement applies to brokers and other intermediaries, as well as those who offer credit or lend money directly.

It's unlikely that you'll need a licence if you:

- only deal with limited companies as opposed to individuals
- offer no form of credit other than accepting credit cards issued by someone else
- simply allow customers to pay bills in four or fewer instalments within a year, beginning with the date of agreement

The Consumer Credit Act 1974 previously applied only to agreements where credit provided (or hire payments arranged) did not exceed £25,000. The 2006 Act removed this financial limit and all consumer credit or hire agreements are now regulated by the 1974 Act, unless specifically exempted.

What is a group licence?

A group licence may be issued where the OFT concludes that the public interest is better served by doing so (the public interest test). There are two broad categories of applicant that generally meet the criteria:

- advisory organisations with altruistic aims, and
- professional bodies, with established disciplinary arrangements, for whom credit is an adjunct to their prime business activity.

MAKING IT HAPPEN
Understand consumer credit licence categories

You can apply for different categories of licence depending on the nature of your business. Do check that your licence covers all the regulated business activities that you carry out, or you may be prosecuted for unlicensed trading. It may be worth applying for an 'all categories' licence, which covers your business for all credit activity.

Category A—consumer credit businesses

For businesses lending money, offering credit, or allowing people time to pay for goods and services. Examples of this include: cash loans, hire purchase, credit cards, trading cheques, personal loans, budget accounts, instalment sales, subscription accounts, overdrafts or personal loans. Types of business that might be affected include retailers, credit card companies and mail order firms.

Category B—consumer hire businesses

For businesses leasing, hiring or renting out goods for periods of more than three months. Examples include TV rental businesses, car rental and vending machines. This licence applies to hire agreements, but not hire purchase agreements, as they come under Category A.

Category C—credit brokerage

For businesses that do not offer credit or hire arrangements themselves but introduce their customers to traders who provide credit. A licence is still required even if no commission is received for the introduction. An example would be an estate agent arranging a mortgage for a client by introducing them to a building society.

Category D—debt adjusting and debt counselling

For businesses taking over other people's debts which have occurred as a result of credit or hire agreements and managing them on their behalf, or advising on how to discharge the debt. However, if a settlement figure is obtained with a finance house, it will be covered under Category C. Examples include social and consumer agencies advising on debt problems, accountants and insurance brokers.

Category E—debt collecting

For businesses collecting debts on behalf of other credit businesses (the debts must be as a result of credit or hire agreements). Examples include trade protection societies and debt collectors. A licence is not required for collecting your own debts or receiving due payments.

Category F—credit reference agency

For businesses that are involved in obtaining information about the credit status of customers to pass on to others. Simply providing personal customer references, however, does not make you a credit reference agency.

Canvassing credit using trade premises

For businesses calling uninvited on individuals to encourage the purchase of credit or hire agreement arrangements. The canvasser requires a licence to allow them to canvass from trade premises. The Consumer Credit Act is concerned with the canvassing of individuals: dealing with companies or other corporate bodies is outside the scope of the Act.

Investigate exemptions

Certain transactions are classed as exempt under the Act, such as agreements in which the debtor or hirer has a 'high net worth'. Also where agreements are entered into wholly for the debtor's business purposes, and where the credit provided or payments to be made exceed £25,000, they will be exempt from regulation under the Act. If you deal solely with these transactions, you will not need a licence. However, even if one transaction is not exempt but is used on a regular basis, a licence will be required, for example, if you regularly introduce customers to credit providers to help them purchase larger items.

'Occasional' transactions that require licences will be exempt if they are not part of your business' normal trading practice. Although the Act does not define 'occasional', a licence will not be required for things that are not part of the normal course of business, such as special agreements for relatives, friends or valued customers.

Apply for a Consumer Credit Licence

Application forms for businesses based in England, Wales and Scotland can be downloaded from the Office of Fair Trading (OFT) website (see p. 152).

In Northern Ireland, the Trading Standards Service is responsible for ensuring that businesses comply with the legislation (see **www.detini.gov.uk**).

Application forms differ depending on whether you are a sole trader, or operating as a partnership or limited company.

Licences are only issued to a business or individual that the OFT considers to be a 'fit person'. As well as your own activities, the activities of employees, agents or associates, (whether past or present) may be taken into account. When they're assessing your 'fitness', the OFT will consider:

- offences and convictions related to the business
- offences and convictions related to anyone involved in running the business
- evidence of discrimination
- failure to comply with any requirements of the Consumer Credit Act or regulations, as well as other consumer legislation
- consumer complaints
- evidence of business practices that damage, or could damage the interests of consumers
- insolvency, bankruptcy or disqualification as a director
- unauthorised use of the OFT name and logo

The application form asks for the following information:

- organisation name, trading names and legal status
- business and correspondence addresses and whether the organisation is based in the UK
- description of type of business
- company details—registration number, registered office
- which categories you want the licence to cover
- whether you want the licence to allow you to canvass away from your trade premises
- personal details, information and home addresses of owners or directors of the business
- previous names
- people who can influence the business, such as spouses and investors
- details of previous applications for Consumer Credit Licences
- details of bankruptcy, insolvency and disqualification of directors
- membership of trade associations and professional bodies, and whether any disciplinary action has been taken
- details of any County Court Judgments (CCJs)
- approvals and authorisations by the Financial Services Authority (FSA)
- VAT registration details
- criminal convictions

Some of the information applies only to sole traders, and some to partnerships or companies. The form also requests certain supporting documents, such as your certificate of incorporation, or copies of CCJs.

The licence application must to be made in the name of the business. All the names that your business trades under must be registered as part of the licence. You can check with the OFT to make sure the name you wish to register is not already in use. If your business is organised and registered as different companies or partnerships, separate licences will be required for each of those engaging in consumer credit or hire activity. A licence covers a business and not its premises, so you may trade from as many outlets as you like with the same licence.

When applying for a licence, you should complete the application form and enclose the correct fee. Failure to do so will delay the processing of the application. The OFT will acknowledge receipt of the form and give you an idea on how long it will take to process; it may also request further documentation. A decision will then be made about whether your business is fit to hold a licence. If there are any doubts about your fitness to hold a licence, you will be allowed time to make a representation to the OFT prior to an official refusal being made.

The OFT keeps a public register of all applications for Consumer Credit Licences and of all licences that have been issued. It also holds details of applications that have been refused and licences that have been revoked. This information is available to the general public.

Understand duration and cost of licences

Licences are valid for five years from the issue date. The OFT will notify you when your licence needs to be renewed.

You should inform the OFT of any changes to your business during the five-year licence period. It is a criminal offence not to do so. You must also indicate if the category of licence is to change. If changes to the licence category are planned, it is illegal to trade in new activities until the licence has been amended to include those activities. If you wish to alter the licence at the time of renewal, there will be no extra charge. A licence cannot be transferred to another person. Changing the status of the business, from a sole trader to a partnership for instance, always requires a new licence.

Fees

Fees are payable whenever you apply for a new licence, renew it or change it. Currently the fee for applying for a new licence or renewal is £135 for a sole trader and £335 for a partnership, company or other organisation. If you apply to alter your licence, you must pay £50 for the first change, £40 for subsequent changes and £50 for any number of category additions or deletions. Certain changes do not attract a fee, such as change of address or names of directors, but the OFT must be informed within 21 days of the change.

Debt counsellors and debt adjusters do not have to pay a fee, provided they don't charge a fee or commission for any of their services. Registered loan societies and credit unions are also exempt from paying the fees.

Consumer credit jurisdiction industry levy

As of April 2007, the OFT has been also responsible for collecting the industry levy which will fund the Financial Ombudsman Service's extended role in considering complaints about consumer credit products and services (see **www.financial-ombudsman.org.uk/faq/answers/consumer_credit_a2.html**).

The OFT will collect the levy at the same time as you apply to be licensed or make an application to renew your licence. Applicants whose licences are due for renewal now, have to pay the levy. The levy is payable in addition to the licence fee which must accompany the licence application, but you don't have to pay it if you are:

- a debt counsellor or debt adjuster—provided you do not charge a fee or commission for any services
- a registered loan society, credit union or registered under the Friendly Societies Act, or subject to the compulsory jurisdiction of the Ombudsman scheme

The levies payable are:

- applying for a licence (sole trader, partnership, company or other organisation)—£150.00
- renewing a licence (sole trader, partnership, company or other organisation)—£150.00

COMMON MISTAKE
You think you can get away without a credit licence

You can't. It's a criminal offence to carry out licensable activities without a licence, or to carry out activities not covered by the licence you have. Unlicensed trading can result in a fine, imprisonment or both.

Additionally, if any of your customers default on payment when you don't have a licence, you won't be able to enforce the credit agreement. This is also the case if an unlicensed broker is involved.

The OFT has the power to revoke, suspend or vary a licence if it feels that the holder is 'unfit' to hold one. It is possible to appeal against decisions made by the OFT to the Secretary of State for Trade and Industry, then to the High Court (or the Court of Session in Scotland).

Also remember that you must tell the OFT of any changes to your business during the five-year licence period. It is a criminal offence not to do so.

USEFUL LINK
Office of Fair Trading (OFT):
www.oft.gov.uk

A guide to the Financial Services and Markets Act 2000

GETTING STARTED

Businesses offering financial services (such as investment advisers, brokers and pension-fund administrators) must register with the Financial Services Authority (FSA). This is to ensure that individuals and firms have the qualifications and integrity as well as the financial back-up to deliver quality services.

The FSA was established by the Financial Services and Markets Act 2000, to replace the numerous organisations that previously regulated the financial service industry with a single regulator.

The FSA Register is a public record of financial services firms and other bodies that fall under its regulatory jurisdiction, as defined in the Financial Services and Markets Act 2000.

This actionlist looks at which businesses are affected by the Financial Services and Markets Act 2000, and outlines the responsibilities you have under this law. It also briefly describes the main responsibilities of the FSA and gives useful links to sources of further information.

FAQS

How do I know if my business is governed by the Financial Services and Markets Act?

Under the Act, the FSA is responsible for regulating:

- **dealing in investments.** This includes: stocks and shares; securities; units in collective investment schemes; Government and public securities; certain options; futures; long-term insurance contracts; contracts for difference (if their value is linked to property value or an index); interests in investments
- **people acting as investment advisers**, for example on pensions and shareholdings, those offering independent financial advice, and firms authorised to conduct investment business by professional bodies, such as chartered accountants and solicitors
- **people who manage assets for someone else** when these include, or probably include, investments
- **people who manage collective investment schemes**, which include unit trusts or in-house pension funds
- **other businesses** not strictly within the financial services sector, but which deal in investments regularly
- **mortgage advisers**

Why do I need FSA authorisation?

Under the Act, if you conduct business without authorisation you can be fined, imprisoned or both, and any contracts you make may not be valid. The FSA is the only body that can give authorisation to practise to individuals or businesses. You'll then be given a licence with a list of all the activities you and your business are allowed to carry out.

In order to be authorised, businesses or individuals must be 'fit and proper'. That means they should be qualified to provide the services and able to obey the rules, and that they have the financial back-up to do so.

What are my legal obligations?

- If you're running an investment business, you must register with the FSA. It's a criminal offence to carry out investment business or offer advice if you're unregistered and therefore unauthorised.
- If you're a financial adviser, you must declare whether you're independent or tied.
- Anyone giving advice must carry out a 'fact finding' exercise to gather details about clients before explaining why a particular product is suitable.
- You must give your clients a 'key features' document, which explains important

details including the level of risk involved in an investment.

- You must also offer your clients a 'cooling-off' period, explaining how long they've got if they want to opt out of the investment.

There's a central compensation scheme for anyone who receives negligent advice. There are also strict rules covering the financial resources that anyone wishing to carry out investment business must have.

Measures against 'insider dealing' are included, and there's close examination and monitoring of investment business and practice through financial returns.

MAKING IT HAPPEN
Understand what the Financial Services Authority (FSA) does

All investment businesses are subject to the FSA's ten high-level principles that cover matters such as market conduct and information for customers. The aim of the regulator is to raise and maintain standards in the industry. Minimum standards have been defined for regulated firms, and the FSA provides training for the industry, including workshops for small firms of independent financial advisers.

The FSA has four main objectives:

1 to maintain confidence in the market
2 to promote public understanding of the financial system
3 to protect consumers
4 to fight financial crime in this sector

The Act enables the FSA to have several responsibilities including those listed below.

Authorisation

The FSA authorises businesses working in insurance, investments and banking. Its entry assessment allows only businesses and individuals satisfying the necessary criteria—the 'threshold conditions'—to engage in regulated activity. The conditions include honesty, competence and financial soundness. The FSA also answers technical enquiries about whether businesses require authorisation or individuals require approval.

Regulation of investment firms

The FSA's Investment Firms Division regulates firms ranging from global fund management operations to individual financial advisers. It also directly regulates many professional firms—for example, lawyers and accountants—who carry out mainstream investment business such as giving clients direct advice on investment products.

Other professional firms that carry out investment business but which meet a set of detailed conditions are treated as 'exempt professional firms'. They're able to carry out certain regulated activities under supervision and regulation by their designated professional body, such as the Law Society for solicitors.

Enforcement

The FSA investigates when authorised firms breach the rules or the provisions of the Financial Services and Markets Act 2000. It can take such action as:

- withdrawing a business's authorisation
- disciplining authorised firms and people approved by the FSA to work in those businesses
- imposing penalties for market abuse
- applying to a court for injunction and resti-tution orders
- prosecuting various offences

Raising standards

The FSA aims to raise and maintain standards of competence in the financial services industry. It sets minimum standards for regulated firms and for examinations. It provides information and assistance to regulated firms on the implementation of training and competence requirements, and offers training and distance learning to improve the ability of a business to achieve compliance.

Targeted information for specific types of financial services firms such as Insurance Brokers and Mortgage Advisers is provided by the FSA and can be accessed via their website.

Do your bit

Make sure you get authorisation from the FSA and are complying with all the necessary regulations as soon as you can. The FSA produces a handbook of rules and guidance which contains details of the standards required, authorisation procedures and training requirements, which you can download from their website. They also run roadshows and one-to-one surgeries throughout the UK.

If you're unsure about the financial regulations that apply to your business, and your accountant and financial advisers can't help, don't forget to contact your relevant trade association or professional body for detailed information about how your industry is regulated.

COMMON MISTAKES

You don't get authorisation

If your business is in the financial services sector and you try to trade without authorisation from the FSA, you're likely to end up in serious trouble. So make sure you've done everything necessary before you start trading or take any clients onto your books.

You don't take a complaint seriously

If a customer's unhappy with the way you've handled a complaint, you could be referred to the Financial Ombudsman Service. This is the complaints-handling scheme for the whole financial services industry. The rules require firms in the sector to deal with consumer complaints accurately and promptly, as follows.

- If a consumer feels the advice they've received from an authorised firm is unsatis-

factory, they must complain to the adviser first. Firms must have a complaints procedure that consumers should be made aware of.
- Firms must aim to resolve complaints within eight weeks and must notify all consumers that if the complaint is not dealt with satisfactorily, they can take their complaint to the Financial Ombudsman Service.
- Firms must report information about their complaints handling to the FSA twice every year.
- The FSA can apply to the courts for an injunction to stop unauthorised persons carrying on business, and return their investors to their original financial position.

Access to the Financial Ombudsman Service is open to private individuals and small businesses with an annual turnover of less than £1 million. The Ombudsman can make a maximum award of £100,000, and may also dismiss certain complaints if appropriate.

USEFUL LINKS

Association of Independent Financial Advisers:
www.aifa.net
British Insurance Brokers' Association:
www.biba.org.uk
Council of Mortgage Lenders:
www.cml.org.uk
Financial Ombudsman Service:
www.financial-ombudsman.org.uk
Financial Services Authority (FSA):
www.fsa.gov.uk
The Personal Finance Society:
www.thepfs.org

COMPANY ADMIN, TAX AND PAYROLL

Preparing and submitting company accounts

GETTING STARTED

All businesses must keep accounting records for tax purposes, but if you operate your business as a limited company, the Companies Act 1985 requires you to prepare, maintain and submit accounting records to Companies House every year. While your accountant can carry out this function, you're still responsible for making sure it happens, so you need to be aware of what you're required to do by law.

This actionlist focuses on the accounting requirements for small companies. It explains when you need to submit your accounts, what you'll be required to submit and whether you'll qualify for any of the exemptions for small companies that allow you to submit less detailed information.

Note that accounts for companies based in Northern Ireland must be submitted to the Companies Registry, and are governed by the Companies (Northern Ireland) Order 1986. The requirements are very similar to those for the rest of the UK.

FAQS

What are a company's audit requirements?

All companies, regardless of size and whether or not they're trading, must prepare annual accounts that report on their trading activity during the year. The accounts produced and submitted by a company should be audited by a currently qualified auditor, unless your company qualifies for audit exemption and wants to take advantage of this (see below for audit exemption details). As long as your accountant has a current audit-practising certificate, they'll be able to fulfil this role if an audit is required.

The role of the auditor is to make an independent report to the company's members (i.e. shareholders) stating whether its accounts have been properly prepared in accordance with the Companies Act 1985. The report must also say if a company's accounts give a true and fair view of its affairs and whether the information in the directors' report is consistent with the annual accounts.

The company's auditor is initially appointed by the board of directors, and normally there's a motion at the annual general meeting (AGM) for the shareholders to reappoint them. The auditor can't be an officer or employee of the company or an associated company.

What are small company audit exemptions?

You may be exempt from having your accounts audited under the Companies Act 1985 (Accounts of Small and Medium-Sized Enterprises and Audit Exemption) (Amendment) Regulations 2004 and 2000 amendment.

There's total exemption from audit for certain small companies if they're eligible and wish to take advantage of this. To qualify for such exemption, a company must:

- have a turnover of not more than £5.6 million
- have a balance sheet total of not more than £2.8 million

Not all small companies are exempt from having an audit and many companies, even if they qualify as being exempt, may still be required to have an audit as part of the terms of their funding agreements.

What periods are covered by accounts?

The period reported on in your accounts is called the financial year. This starts on the day of incorporation for a new company, or on the day after the previous financial year ended for an existing company. A more precise term for a financial year is an accounting reference period (ARP). The ARP ends on the accounting reference date (ARD), which is the company's financial year-end.

For all new companies, the first financial year-end is automatically set as the first anniversary of the last day in the month in which the company was incorporated. For example, if your company was incorporated on 15 September 2005, its ARD would be set at 30 September.

The first accounts submitted would cover a period from 15 September 2005 to 30 September 2006. Although your ARD is set on incorporation, you can change it by completing Form 225 and sending it to Companies House.

What happens when accounts are delivered late?

There is an automatic penalty for late filing. The amount depends on how late the accounts arrive and whether the company is private or public. The fixed penalties are as follows:

Length of delay	Public company	Private company
3 months or less	£500	£100
3–6 months	£1,000	£250
6–12 months	£2,000	£500
More than 12 months	£5,000	£1,000

Failing to deliver accounts on time is also a criminal offence for which company directors may be prosecuted.

MAKING IT HAPPEN

If you prepare and use management accounts on a regular basis, then these will be the starting point when you prepare your annual accounts. Your accountant will also review all of your accounting records (bank statements, sales invoices, purchase invoices, payroll records and VAT returns) and make any amendments or adjustments necessary to your management accounts. Your accounts will then be presented in a format that corresponds to standards laid down in the Companies Act 1985.

Generally, your financial accounts must include:
- a profit and loss (P&L) account
- a balance sheet signed by a director
- assigned auditor's or accountant's report
- a directors' report signed by a director or the company secretary
- explanatory notes to the accounts
- group accounts (if appropriate)

Certain information can be omitted from the accounts of small and medium-sized companies prepared under special provisions in the Companies Act 1985.

File accounts at Companies House

All limited and publicly listed companies (PLCs) must send their accounts to the Registrar at Companies House.

If you're filing your company's first accounts and they cover a period of more than 12 months, they must be delivered to the Registrar within 22 months of the date of incorporation for private companies.

For subsequent accounts, the time normally allowed for delivering accounts to Companies House is:
- for a private company, ten months from the ARD
- for a publicly listed company, seven months from the ARD

All accounts submitted to Companies House are scanned so they can be stored electronically as public records. To get the best and most readable results, you need to submit your accounts on A4 documents, with black type printed on white paper.

Accounts don't need to have been approved by shareholders or HM Revenue and Customs before they are submitted to Companies House.

Submit abbreviated accounts if appropriate

Certain small companies may prepare and deliver abbreviated accounts to the Registrar. To qualify as a small company, you have to meet at least two of the following conditions:
- annual turnover must be £5.6 million or less
- the balance sheet total must be £2.8 million or less

- the average number of employees must be 50 or fewer

If you qualify, you can elect to submit abbreviated accounts, which will need to include:

- a simplified balance sheet signed by a director
- notes explaining the figures given in the balance sheet
- a special auditor's report, unless you are also claiming audit exemption

In the balance sheet, you must also include a statement that the accounts have been prepared in accordance with the special provisions relating to part VII of the Companies Act 1985.

Dormant companies

A company is classed as 'dormant' if it has no 'significant accounting transactions' during its ARP. If your company hasn't traded since incorporation, you should complete and submit form DCA, which is available from Companies House, as your record of annual accounts filing.

If your company has become dormant after trading, you only need to file simplified accounts. These accounts don't have to include a P&L account or a directors' report, but you'll need to show a balance sheet with associated notes.

If you manage a company that you think may be classed as dormant, discuss your specific circumstances with your accountant.

COMMON MISTAKES
You don't realise the importance of accounts

Banks and credit companies rely on information available from Companies House to assess a company's creditworthiness, and often require the reassurance of an independent audit. If your company qualifies for audit exemption, you'll need to decide whether unaudited accounts are appropriate to your circumstances. Remember that shareholders have a right to receive copies of annual accounts, which are normally presented at the AGM. If a shareholder owns more than a 10% stake in your company, they can also request a set of audited accounts.

You assume the accounts are your accountant's responsibility, not yours

The directors of a company are legally responsible for ensuring the accuracy of its accounts. So just because you're employing an accountant, it doesn't remove your responsibility. It's up to you to make sure that your accounts are accurate and are submitted before the relevant deadline.

USEFUL LINKS

Association of Chartered Certified Accountants (ACCA):
www.acca.org.uk
Business Link:
www.businesslink.gov.uk
Companies House (England, Scotland and Wales):
www.companies-house.gov.uk
Companies Registry of Northern Ireland:
www.companiesregistry-ni.gov.uk
Institute of Chartered Accountants in England and Wales:
www.icaew.co.uk
Institute of Chartered Accountants Scotland:
www.icas.org.uk

An introduction to Value-Added Tax (VAT)

INTRODUCTION

Value-Added Tax (VAT) is a tax levied on the supply of goods and services. It is one of the Government's major sources of tax revenue, and registered businesses are required to act as unpaid tax collectors. HM Revenue & Customs (HMRC) is responsible for ensuring that businesses comply with the legislation and that they regularly pay the tax due.

The legislation covering VAT is complex and therefore you should seek professional advice or speak to HMRC to ensure that you operate within the current law.

This factsheet introduces the basic principles of VAT, outlines when you need to register and the way the VAT system operates, and suggests ways of complying with VAT requirements efficiently. It also includes useful tips and sources of further information.

FAQS

What is Value-Added Tax?

VAT is a tax on consumer spending which applies to the value added to a product or service at each stage of its production and distribution. It is collected in stages by VAT-registered businesses (known as 'taxable persons'), but it is the consumer who ultimately pays the full amount of the tax.

The principles of VAT are:

- you buy goods or services from your suppliers at a price including VAT (the *input* tax)
- you sell goods or services to your customers at a price including VAT (the *output* tax)
- you deduct the input tax from the output tax and pay the balance to HMRC, or receive a refund if the input tax exceeds the output tax

Businesses are required to keep a record of their VAT transactions and at the end of each VAT accounting period (usually each quarter), they complete and submit a one-page summary form to HMRC known as a VAT return. This must be submitted within a month of the end of the VAT accounting period. Any VAT owed must also be paid at this time, although the exact date depends upon whether the payment is made by cheque, BACS or is collected by direct debit.

What is a taxable person?

A taxable person is any person operating a business (or separate businesses) who is either already registered for VAT, or should be registered for VAT. A taxable person is used to describe both individuals as well as separate legal entities, such as companies. Taxable persons can therefore be:

- individuals
- partnerships
- limited liability partnerships
- limited companies
- club, association, charities or trusts

VAT registration is by taxable person, not by business. So if you are a self-employed individual and own and operate more than one business venture and between them their taxable turnover exceeds the registration threshold, you must register for VAT.

What are taxable supplies?

All goods and services liable for VAT are called 'taxable supplies' and the total value of those supplied by your business is called your 'taxable turnover'. You may produce taxable supplies even if you're not registered for VAT, but you only become liable to charge VAT on your taxable supplies once the turnover of these supplies goes over the registration threshold.

Some specific supplies are exempt from VAT and if you supply them they do not form part of your taxable turnover. Exempt supplies normally relate to services and the most common ones are found in the following sectors:

- financial services
- insurance
- education

- health and welfare services
- some property transactions

It's essential that you find out whether the services you supply are exempt or not, so take advice from your accountant or the HMRC national advice service helpline (0845 010 9000).

What are the different rates of VAT?

There are currently three rates of VAT:

1. **the standard rate of 17.5%.** This covers all taxable supplies that are not reduced or zero rated.
2. **the reduced rate of 5%.** This is charged on certain specified products and services. The major ones are domestic fuel and power as well as other domestic energy saving products. The renovation and conversion of certain buildings is also subject to the reduced rate, as well as children's car seats and some health care products.
3. **the zero rate (0%).** This applies to specified categories of goods including children's clothes, exports outside the European Union (EU), food, but not fast food, restaurant meals or catering supplies, books and newspapers. The advantage to you of goods being zero-rated (as opposed to exempt) is that they are still included in your taxable turnover, so you can recover your input tax.

If your product consists of both zero rated *and* standard-rated goods (food in a decorative container, say), there may be occasions when VAT will be charged at a proportional rate. HMRC has special schemes to assist retailers selling a mixture of standard and zero-rated products, so ask them for advice early on about what you should do in these situations.

When do you need to register for VAT?

If in the course of your business you make taxable supplies above the VAT registration threshold (£64,000 from April 2007) then you become a taxable person and are legally required to register for VAT. Specifically you are required to register when either of the following occurs:

- your taxable turnover for the last 12 months exceeds the current registration threshold. In this case you must register within 30 days of the end of the month in which this turnover is achieved.
- when there is a reasonable likelihood that your taxable turnover will exceed the registration threshold during the next 30 days. In this case you must register within 30 days of being aware that this will happen. Examples of this occurring could be as a result of winning a large contract, or by the acquisition of another business.

You can also voluntarily register for VAT before your taxable turnover reaches the registration threshold. This is quite common when you set up a business that will primarily supply other VAT registered businesses and which is likely to exceed the registration threshold in the future. It has the advantage of allowing you to claim as input tax the VAT that you are charged by your suppliers when setting up the business, which reduces your costs and also improves the business's cash flow.

MAKING IT HAPPEN
Register for VAT

The good news is that registration is straightforward: simply complete form *VAT 1 – Application for Registration* which can be downloaded from the HRMC website (**www.hmrc.gov.uk**) and send it to HMRC. If you don't register at the correct time, you may be liable for a fine, as well as for any VAT that you would have charged.

Points to note about registration:

- you will be assessed for VAT from the time that your turnover exceeds the registration threshold, but you cannot start to charge VAT to your customers without a registration number. Don't delay your registration once you think that you will need to do it.
- if your business's taxable supplies are zero rated, you can apply for exemption from registration; this will mean, however, that you cannot recover input tax that you are charged by your suppliers.
- if your business makes taxable and exempt supplies, you may be 'partly exempt'. Input tax will only be reclaimable on the inputs that go towards the taxable supplies.

- Your business cannot register for VAT if it only makes exempt supplies.

Start charging VAT

VAT must be charged from the date your business becomes liable for registration, known as the Effective Date of Registration (or EDR), and not from the actual date of registration. When you complete the VAT 1 form, you'll be asked to put the date that you want your registration to be effective from.

Before you are issued with a VAT number, you are not able to issue VAT invoices and therefore should not show VAT separately on your invoices. While you're waiting for your registration form to be processed, you can instead issue your customers with a proforma invoice and state on it that a tax invoice will be issued as soon as your VAT number is received. Once you have been issued with your nine digit VAT number, you'll be able to provide your customers with VAT invoices.

To calculate the price to charge your customer, take your normal selling price and add the appropriate VAT rate for the item being sold. For example if you are selling a computer at £1,000, you will need to add 17.5% VAT, which equates to £175. Your total selling price to your customer, then, is £1,175.

Preparing VAT invoices

Specific rules apply to the content of these invoices to make sure that the right information is captured for you to be able to account for the output tax due on the sale. You customer will also be able to account for the input tax they will claim if they are VAT-registered. The main details required are:

- an identifying number
- your name, address and VAT registration number
- the date the invoice is issued – which must be within 30 days of the date of supply
- your customer's name and address
- a clear description of the goods or services supplied
- a quantity and unit price for these goods or services, plus the rate of VAT applicable
- details of any cash discount offered

- the total amount payable excluding VAT
- the amount of VAT charged

Retailers don't have to provide a VAT invoice for every transaction because they are primarily selling to consumers, rather than other businesses. If, however, a taxable person requires a tax invoice, the retailer must issue one.

Keeping account of VAT

All businesses are required to keep accounting records for tax purposes. Once you are VAT-registered, you'll need to ensure that your records show all your VAT transactions, and you will need to operate a separate VAT account in your accounting records. The normal monthly record keeping ledgers that you will need are:

- a **sales ledger** to record a summary of each VAT invoice issued to your customers and also to provide details of your sales turnover (excluding VAT) as well as the amount of VAT you have charged (your output tax)
- a **purchase ledger** to record a summary of each invoice the business has received from its suppliers, and to provide details of your purchase turnover (excluding VAT) as well as the amount of VAT that you have been charged (your input tax)
- a **cash ledger** to record other cash sales and purchases that have not been recorded in the sales or purchase ledgers, and any relevant VAT charged
- a **VAT account**. This records the amount of output tax you have charged your customers and the amount of input tax that your suppliers have charged you. This account will therefore show the net amount of VAT that needs to be paid to (or claimed back from) HMRC. Payments that you make to HMRC for VAT owed will also show in this account

Computerised accounting software packages greatly simplify the recording of VAT transactions and the interaction of the different ledgers, as well as producing reports for the regular VAT returns. If you do not use one of these packages prior to VAT registration, it is recommended that you look at doing so once you are VAT-registered as they can save you significant amounts of time in producing the information that is required for the VAT returns.

You could also talk to your accountant about services they can provide to help you conform with the VAT legislation and to complete your VAT returns. This can be done as part of a monthly service that includes producing your monthly accounts, or you may just ask them to complete the quarterly VAT return.

Investigating the various VAT accounting schemes

HMRC operates a number of different schemes to account for VAT, some of which have been created specifically for small businesses. The best one for you will, of course, depend on your particular trading circumstances, but the main ones are:

Standard accounting scheme

In this scheme your output VAT is levied as soon as you issue a sales invoice, while input VAT is reclaimable as soon as a purchase invoice is received. The date on which you actually receive payments from your customers or pay your suppliers is irrelevant. You make a quarterly return based on issued and received invoices in that period, and then payment of any VAT owed is made at the end of the next month.

Cash accounting scheme

This scheme is only available to businesses with a taxable turnover of less than £1,350,000 and is designed to reduce the cash-flow implications of VAT. Instead of accounting for VAT using issued and received tax invoices, you account for VAT based on when your customers actually pay you and when you pay your suppliers. You still need to complete quarterly returns and make payments at the end of the next month. The key benefit of the scheme is that you do not need to account for VAT and pay it to HMRC until you have received it from your customer.

Annual accounting scheme

If your business has a turnover of less than £1,350,000 you can join the annual accounting scheme, in which you make only one annual VAT return and pay regular interim payments of a fixed amount. This reduces the administrative burden and allows you to predict your cash flow. The annual return is submitted within two months of your accounting year-end and a balancing payment or refund is then made.

Flat-rate scheme

If your business has a taxable turnover of less than £150,000 you may be able to join the flat-rate scheme, which tries to simplify the administration of VAT for very small businesses. Under the scheme, businesses calculate their VAT payment by using a fixed percentage of their VAT-inclusive turnover. Different percentages have been assigned to different trade sectors. Newly VAT-registered businesses use the flat rate for their sector minus 1%. So, if the rate for your sector is 9%, you apply a flat rate of 8% in your first year of VAT registration.

Retail scheme

If you operate a retail business and make the majority of your sales to the general public, you may be able to join one of the retail schemes. These schemes simplify the accounting rules required for the issuing of VAT invoices (for example, you do not have to issue VAT invoices unless someone asks for one). You can be registered for a retail scheme as well as one of the other specialist schemes listed above.

VAT inspections

HMRC have the power to inspect individuals or companies to:

- examine business records
- inspect business premises
- assess underpaid tax and charge penalties for failing to register for VAT or to make returns or payments on time

Once your business registers, you will usually be visited by a HMRC officer within three years to ensure that you are accounting for VAT correctly, and then intermittently after that. If you don't send in tax returns, or send inconsistent or late returns, you will be visited more often. The officer will discuss your business, look at your records, give advice on how to correct any errors and discuss VAT problems. If your business does not produce the records asked for within a reasonable time, you run the risk of incurring a penalty.

COMMON MISTAKES

You don't factor VAT payments into your cash-flow projections

Do remember that you'll need to plan for your VAT payments when you're putting together your cash-flow records: you could be left with nothing in the bank otherwise. If you need extra help or advice, especially in the early years of trading, ask your accountant for his or her opinion.

You don't pay in full on time

If your business hasn't made its return or sent the full payment due on time, HMRC will regard you as being in default. If you default again within a 12-month 'surcharge period', you'll be hit with a penalty.

You don't keep your records for long enough

Make sure that you keep accounting records for six years, as HMRC may want to review them and you may need them to answer any queries.

USEFUL LINK

HM Revenue & Customs (HMRC): **www.hmrc.gov.uk**

Completing a VAT return and making payments

GETTING STARTED

Once you have registered for VAT, you must complete and send regular VAT returns to HM Revenue & Customs (HMRC) to account for VAT within your business. These returns identify the amount of VAT that needs to be paid or reclaimed from HMRC.

This fact sheet considers the information that you need when completing your VAT return, and how the form is used to calculate the amount of VAT payable. It also looks at what happens if your returns and payments are late, and the penalties that you may become liable for. It also includes useful tips and sources of further information.

FAQS

What is a VAT return?

All taxable persons (those individuals or legal entities registered or required to be registered for VAT) have a legal requirement to complete and submit regular VAT returns to HMRC. The return summarises all VAT transactions during the reporting period, and identifies the amount of VAT to be paid to or refunded by HMRC.

When are returns due?

VAT returns are most commonly completed every quarter. When you register for VAT, you will be allocated four accounting period end dates from one of the three options below:

- 31 January, 30 April, 31 July, and 31 October or
- 28 February, 31 May, 31 August, and 30 November or
- 31 March, 30 June, 30 September and 31 December

For example, if your first VAT return is for the period ending 31 March, then the actual period covered will be the 3 months from 1 January to 31 March. At the end of the accounting period you'll have a further month in which to complete your VAT return. This means that the return for the period ending 31 March is due to be submitted to HMRC by 30 April.

HMRC automatically sends you a return form to complete prior to the end of each quarter, which acts as a reminder that the return is due. If you are registered for the online service, an e-mail reminder will be sent to the main contact.

It is quite common for businesses to change their VAT return periods so that they coincide with their business's accounting year end, as this simplifies the reconciliation of your annual accounts with your VAT returns. You can also request to complete your VAT returns on a monthly basis, which may be done for a business that regularly receives a repayment of VAT.

The main exception to providing quarterly returns is for small businesses that qualify and register for the annual accounting scheme. They only need to complete one VAT return each year, which needs to be submitted within two months from the end of the annual accounting period.

MAKING IT HAPPEN

Completing the VAT return

The VAT return provides a summary of all of the relevant VAT transactions in an accounting period. You therefore need to have accurate accounting records for each period covering your business' sales and purchases and be able to produce detailed reports that support the return.

There are many accounting software packages that allow you to print these detailed reports as well as a summary of the data in the format of the VAT return. Alternatively, you may use the services of your accountant or a specialist bookkeeper to collate and prepare this information and then complete the return on your behalf.

The VAT return contains nine boxes. If you do not make any sales or purchases in the European Union (EU), then you do not need to enter any figures within Boxes 2, 8 or 9.

Box 1—VAT due in this period on sales and other outputs

This records the total VAT due on sales made by your business for the VAT return period. This figure should also include the VAT due for the following adjustments:

- scale charges—a payment made for the private use of cars when the business has recovered all of the VAT on the fuel purchase receipts
- supplies to staff—sales to staff or goods taken for your own personal use. If nothing is charged for the goods then the VAT should be accounted for on the cost price

Box 2—VAT due in this period on acquisitions from other EU member states

This records the VAT due on the acquisition of goods from another EU country. If you purchase goods from an EU country and you are not charged VAT on the purchase (when you have provided the supplier with your VAT registration number), then you must account for VAT on the goods at the rate that you would have been charged if you had bought the same goods in the UK.

Box 3—Total output VAT due

This is the total of boxes 1 and 2 added together, to get the total output tax due.

Box 4—VAT reclaimed during this period on purchases and other inputs (including acquisitions from the EU).

This records the total output tax reclaimable on your purchases for the VAT return period. You must hold the invoices and receipts for all your purchases that you are claiming VAT on. The calculated VAT for purchases from an EU supplier is also recorded in this total.

However, there are some purchases

where the VAT cannot be recovered, such as

- **business entertainment**—business expenses that have been incurred when entertaining clients or customers
- **personal expenditure**—purchases that have been paid for by the business but are not for the furtherance of the business—for example, home telephone bills
- **purchase of a car**—if the business buys a car then the VAT on the purchase is not recoverable

Box 5—Net VAT to be paid to or reclaimed from HMRC

This records the amount of VAT either to be paid or reclaimed from HMRC and is calculated by deducting Box 4 from Box 3. For most businesses this is the most important number because it represents the amount of cash that has to be paid to HMRC.

Box 6—Total value of sales and all other outputs excluding any VAT

This records the net amount of all sales (excluding VAT) used to produce the figure shown in Box 1 of the return. In addition, any zero rated or exempt sales will be included in this box.

Box 7—Total value of all purchases and all other inputs excluding any VAT

This records the net amount of all the purchases (excluding VAT) used to produce the figure shown in Box 4 of the return. In addition, any zero rated or exempt purchases will be included in this box.

Box 8—Total value of all supplies of goods and related costs, excluding VAT, to EU countries

This records the net amount of goods sold to customers located in the EU. The amount in Box 8 should also have been included in Box 6 of the return.

Box 9—Total value of the acquisition of goods and related costs, excluding VAT, from EU countries

This records the net amount of goods purchased from any suppliers located in the

EU. The amount in Box 9 should also have been included in Box 7 of the return.

Exclusions

There are a number of regular business transactions that should not be included in your figures on the VAT return. The most common are:

- VAT payments or reclaims from HMRC
- wages or salaries paid to employees
- PAYE, National Insurance (NI), student loan and pension contributions
- loans, dividends or drawings
- business rates

Check the return is accurate

Before you complete the return form, double-check all your figures.

- If you are completing a quarterly return, it's quite common to produce consolidated quarterly reports. By also producing reports for each month in the VAT period, you should check that the quarterly totals are correct and also identify any significant variations between the months.
- Check for consistency between *this* return and previous ones. If there is a considerable difference in the net VAT to be paid, try to identify what has caused this: for example, a one-off large sale or purchase may have gone through in one period and distorted the return.
- Calculate the percentage VAT on your *outputs* by dividing the total in box 3 by the total in box 6. If all of your sales are liable to the standard rate of VAT and there are no other adjustments, then this will be 17.5%. It is also useful to compare this figure against your other returns to check for consistency.
- Calculate the percentage VAT on your *inputs* by dividing the total in box 4 by the total in box 7. The maximum this should be, if all of your purchases are liable to the standard rate of VAT, is 17.5%. In most businesses, however, this percentage figure will be lower due to some purchases being exempt or zero rated. It is also useful to compare this figure against your other returns to check for consistency.

HMRC will also run automatic checks on your returns, which will flag up if any obvious blips, although they don't automatically report these to you. They'll also compare your returns to see if they are consistent and whether they are in line with other similar businesses. They'll also use the checks to work out how often they will inspect your business.

Submit the return

Once your business is registered for VAT, you'll automatically be sent a paper return form before your first accounting period end date, and you'll need to complete this and send it back by post by the due date.

HMRC is, however, encouraging all businesses to register to use their online service as it's a much more efficient method of collecting the data. The advantages to you of completing the return form online are that you get instant confirmation that your return has been received and you also benefit from an extended payment period. Once you opt for the online services, though, you'll no longer receive or be able to make postal returns.

Understand how payments are made

The traditional method of payment has been to send a cheque for the full amount identified in box 5, with the paper return in the post. This is done because payments by cheque are due by the same date as the return. However the move to electronic forms of payment—such as BACS and CHAPS—and the efficiency and cost advantages that this provides for HMRC, has resulted in extended payment terms being offered to encourage businesses to pay this way. Businesses sending paper returns can elect to pay by BACS, but they need to make sure that the money is paid to HMRC by the 7th of the month following the due date for their return.

If you register for online filing of VAT returns, you must pay via one of the electronic methods. HMRC are now further encouraging businesses to register for direct debit payment so that the due amount is automatically collected by HMRC. There is a further small incentive in that payment is not collected until the 10th of the month following the due date for their return.

For a return period ending 31 March, for example, the following dates would be relevant:

- return due to be submitted by 30 April
- payment by cheque due by 30 April
- payment by BACS due by 7 May
- payment collected by direct debit on 10 May

If you are using the annual accounting scheme, regular monthly or quarterly payments are made on account. The amount of the payment is either based on the VAT paid in the previous 12 months or the expected VAT to be paid within the next 12 months.

For many businesses, the value of the VAT payment due is one of the largest cash outflows in a quarter, and if this is not planned for it may present major difficulties. The main problem arises when a business has to pay VAT to HMRC that has not yet been collected from their customers. One way to reduce this risk is by registering for the cash accounting scheme, which allows VAT to be accounted for only when payments have been received or made.

Be aware of the penalties

HMRC has a wide range of powers to penalise businesses that do not submit returns or make payments, or incorrectly apply the VAT regulations. The penalties most likely to be encountered are:

- fines for late VAT returns or payments (default surcharge)
- fines for errors on VAT returns (mis-declaration penalty)

- interest on late payment of tax (default interest)

HMRC can also raise an assessment for VAT when returns have not been made, or if they believe that the returns submitted are incomplete or incorrect. The assessment will demand payment of VAT and will be based on past returns for your business or similar businesses.

Although the majority of violations are covered by civil penalties, HMRC can pursue criminal sanctions for the worst cases of fraud, which can result in imprisonment if the prosecution is successful.

If you discover you have made an error on your VAT return, you can make the adjustment on the next return without incurring any penalties—as long as the VAT adjustment for the error is less than £2,000. If the error is for more than this amount, however, you'll need to submit a voluntary disclosure of error to HMRC. If this is made before a VAT control visit, a mis-declaration penalty will not normally be imposed.

COMMON MISTAKE
You hope that problems will go away on their own

If you think you won't be able to make a VAT payment on time, don't bury your head in the sand. Act as quickly as you can and let HMRC know what the problem is and when you *will* be able to pay.

USEFUL LINK
HM Revenue & Customs (HMRC):
www.hmrc.gov.uk

An introduction to Pay as You Earn (PAYE)

GETTING STARTED

When your business starts to employ people, you'll need to operate Pay As You Earn (PAYE) wage deductions. This requires you to make the correct deductions from your employees' pay, make the necessary payments to HM Revenue & Customs (HMRC), and maintain an orderly system of pay-related records.

This actionlist explains the deduction of income tax, National Insurance (NI) contributions and student loans, as well as the paying of statutory payments, such as Statutory Sick Pay (SSP). It also describes the information that you have to include on pay statements, and contains useful hints and tips as well as sources of further information.

FAQS

When do you become an employer?

An employer can be defined as someone who employs an individual under a contract of employment, which may be a signed contract or an implied contract. In most cases, the employment status of a worker is obvious. However, sometimes it's not obvious whether someone who undertakes work for you is your employee or a self-employed contractor. HMRC provides guidance on how they determine employment versus self-employment (see **www.hmrc.gov.uk/pdfs/ir56.htm**).

If you operate your business as a sole trader or partnership, you and your partners will be registered as self-employed and you only become an employer when you employ your first member of staff. But if you set up your business as a company, the company becomes an employer when it begins trading, because directors are employees of the company.

You need to register as a new employer as soon as you know that you'll be employing someone, and you can do this by calling the HMRC helpline on 0845 60 70 143. You need to provide details about your business such as the names and addresses of any partners or company directors, the nature of the business and its contact details. HMRC will also need to know who your employees are, when they were employed, and details like how you'll operate your payroll system. See **www.hmrc.gov.uk/employers/first_step-s.htm** for more guidance.

What are your statutory obligations?

As an employer you have obligations to your employees and to HMRC. The main ones are that you must:

- pay your employees at least the national minimum wage (NMW)
- provide equal pay to female and male employees doing the same work
- deduct income tax and NI contributions from your employees' pay
- deduct student loan contributions from your employees' pay when so advised
- allow your employees to take paid annual leave
- provide an itemised pay statement to your employees when they are paid
- pay your employees any statutory pay-ments that they are due (e.g. for SSP or redundancy)

Failure to comply with these requirements can result in financial penalties being imposed and legal action being taken against you.

What's the PAYE scheme?

Under the PAYE system, income tax due for each employee is deducted from the employee's monthly salary or weekly wages. If PAYE is correctly operated, the employee should have no additional tax to pay at the end of the year.

Income Tax

Tax is payable if an individual's income in a tax year exceeds their personal allowance. The basic personal allowance used for the majority of employees is £5,225 for the tax year 2007/8. When their income exceeds this amount, tax is then paid at the following rates:

- starting rate of 10% on the first £2,230 of income above the personal allowance
- standard rate of 22% on the next £32,370
- higher rate of 40% on the remainder of the income, for which there's no upper limit

Explaining how to calculate an employee's tax is probably best done by using an example. If an employee earns £18,000 a year (gross) the calculation is as follows:

Gross income	£18,000
Tax-free allowance	£5,225
Taxable pay	£12,775
Tax payable on first £2,230 (@ 10%)	£223
Tax payable on next £32,370 (@22%)	£2,320
Total tax	£2,543
Net pay	£15,457

Under the PAYE scheme, tax deductions are usually averaged out over the year so that the net pay received by the employee is the same each month. Using the example given, the income tax for the month is calculated assuming that the monthly salary paid is a twelfth of the employee's annual salary. This means that the employee would therefore have about £212 per month deducted for income tax.

How is the PAYE system supervised?

HMRC undertakes regular inspection visits to businesses to ensure that they're keeping the correct records and that they're complying with their legal obligations. They'll review your business's pay records, as well as information relating to the payment of expenses and their correct disclosure on the annual return forms. The frequency of such visits will depend on:

- how long you've been trading—you'll usually have an inspection within the first two years of operating as an employer

- whether your record of making payments and returns is timely and accurate
- the type of business you run—businesses dealing in cash, employing casual labour or contractors are perceived as higher risk and warrant more frequent visits

If HMRC discovers any discrepancies during an inspection, they can calculate lost tax and National Insurance (NI) contributions for a period of up to six years. This period can also be extended if they suspect deliberate evasion, and they can also seek to charge additional financial penalties.

MAKING IT HAPPEN
Get to grips with tax codes

Every employee is allocated a tax code by HMRC, which takes account of their known personal circumstances relating to tax. It is used by the employer to calculate the correct amount of tax to deduct from the employee's salary.

If a new employee has worked before, they'll have been issued with a P45 form by their previous employer, and they should give this to you to provide their current tax code. If the employee doesn't have a P45, then you'll need to complete a P46 form and send this to HMRC, who will then issue you with the appropriate tax code for the employee.

A tax code is made up of one letter and several numbers. The number in the tax code can be multiplied by 10 to show the actual personal allowance for that employee. The letter in the code corresponds to the individual's personal circumstances and the types of allowances they're entitled to.

For example, the letter L is used for all employees entitled to the basic personal allowance, and this is expressed as a tax code 522L. If the employee has underpaid tax in previous years, and this is now being recovered through the PAYE system, they'll have a lower personal allowance, which could be £3,000 for example. This would be expressed as a tax code 300L and result in more tax being deducted each time the employee is paid.

In some situations an employee has a

negative personal allowance and the tax code K is used. This situation might occur where the employee is receiving a range of taxable benefits such as a company car and private medical insurance. If the employee is assessed to receive taxable benefits of £6,225 (£1,000 greater than the basic personal allowance), then they would have a tax code K100.

National Insurance (NI)

Both employers and employees pay Class 1 NI contributions. An employee must be aged between 16 and the state retirement age to pay NI contributions. The amount of an employee's contributions depends on the level of their salary:

- 11% of pay between the lower and upper earnings limits (£433 to £2,903 per month for the tax year 2007/8)
- 1% for all pay above the upper earnings limit

Employers' NI contributions are charged at a rate of 12.8% of the employee's salary above the lower earnings limit. This is a considerable additional cost for the business (for example, it equates to £1,638 per year for an employee being paid an annual salary of £18,000). Unlike the employee contributions there is no reduction in rate once the upper earnings limit is passed.

In addition to Class 1 NI contributions, an employer is also responsible for paying class 1A NI contributions on employee benefits. All benefits provided to employees need to be reported to HMRC annually on forms P9D and P11D and the total value of taxable benefits provided to all employees is liable to an additional charge of 12.8%.

Understand statutory payments

There are a number of payments that employees are legally entitled to, and which are paid through the PAYE system. These payments are subject to tax and NI contributions for both employee and employer.

Statutory Sick Pay (SSP)

Employers have to pay SSP to employees who satisfy certain conditions and who've been sick for at least four consecutive days, including weekends and bank holidays. SSP is funded by the government; however, it's paid by your business which then reclaims this money by deducting it from the regular NI contributions paid to HMRC. As far as the employee is concerned, SSP is treated as earnings.

SSP may only be recovered under the Percentage Threshold Scheme (PTS). Under this scheme an employer must:

(a) in the month SSP has been paid, establish the total (employee's and employer's) gross Class 1 NI contributions liability for the tax month across all PAYE records

(b) multiply by a set percentage (currently 13%), rounding down fractions of a penny

(c) establish the total SSP payments in that month

Where the amount at (c) is more than the amount at (b), the difference may be recovered.

Statutory Maternity Pay (SMP), Statutory Paternity Pay (SPP) and Statutory Adoption Pay (SAP)

SMP works in much the same way as SSP. The employer pays it to eligible employees and can claim most of it back from the Government by way of deductions from NI contributions. Employers can (but are not obliged to) add to this amount, although only the statutory element is recoverable.

New fathers are now entitled to take one or two consecutive weeks of paternity leave after their child is born. During their paternity leave, most employees are entitled to Statutory Paternity Pay (SPP) from their employers. The rate of SPP is the same as the standard rate of SMP.

Adoptive parents are entitled to up to 26 weeks ordinary adoption leave and up to a further 26 weeks additional adoption leave. During their adoption leave, most adopters are entitled to Statutory Adoption Pay (SAP) from their employers. SAP is paid for up to 39 weeks at the same rate as SMP.

Student loan deductions

The majority of graduates borrow money through the Government's student loan scheme and only start to repay the loan once they're earning more than £15,000 per year. When notified by HMRC or via a P45, employers are required to make student loan deductions from an employee's pay.

The rate of deduction is 9% and deductions are made on a non-cumulative basis. For more information, together with deduction tables and further advice, see **www.hmrc.gov.uk/helpsheets/e17.pdf**

Issue pay statements

All employees are entitled to receive a written pay statement or payslip, either on or before their pay day. The minimum requirements of a payslip are that they should show:
- the gross amount of pay
- the amounts and reasons for variable and fixed deductions
- the net amount to be paid
- if part payments are made, a breakdown of each payment

The payslip should clearly show deductions for tax, NI and student loan (if applicable) and details of any statutory payments received.

Understand what happens to the employee's deductions

The employer has responsibility for making the right deductions from an employee's pay and then for paying those deductions, plus the employer's NI contributions, to HMRC by the 19th of the month following the month in which the employee was paid. If payment is made by BACS, the money must be received by HMRC by the 22nd of the month.

If your combined bill for PAYE and NI contributions is less than £1,500 per month, you qualify as a 'small employer', and are entitled to make payments quarterly.

Annual returns

You're required to submit annual reports to HMRC by sending them P14 forms (end of year summary of records for each employee) and P35 forms (employer's

annual return). These forms summarise the total pay and deductions relating to each of your employees. They also allow a check to be made between the deductions that have been recorded and the amount actually paid to HMRC.

At the end of each year, you'll also need to give every employee a summary of their pay and deductions for the year (form P60), which they need to keep as evidence of tax and NI paid.

Keep on top of the system

Paying your employees via PAYE is very well regulated, and has so many rules and guidelines that it can become a minefield. You may well need to consider allocating this aspect of your business to someone who can dedicate time and concentration to what's required.

Do ensure that any deductions you make from an employee's pay are either legally required (PAYE & NI), are part of the employee's contract, or have been agreed in writing.

The standard recovery rate for SMP/SAP/SPP/SAP is 92% of these payments. However, if you're classed as a small employer, you'll be able to recover 104.5%. To qualify, your total gross Class1a contributions for the previous tax year must be less than the threshold (which at present is £45,000).

COMMON MISTAKE
You don't keep proper records

HMRC can make inspections at any time, and demand to see evidence of your PAYE payments and so on. It's vital, then, that you maintain accurate and up-to-date pay records and keep them for six years.

USEFUL LINKS

Department for Work and Pensions (DWP): **www.dwp.gov.uk**
HM Revenue & Customs (HMRC): **www.hmrc.gov.uk**
HM Revenue & Customs (HMRC) Business Support Team: **www.hmrc.gov.uk/bst/index.htm**

Understanding corporation tax

GETTING STARTED

If you're running a small business, you need to know about corporation tax. This is levied on the taxable profits of companies, as well as many clubs, societies, associations and co-operatives.

This actionlist looks at the scope, rates and payment methods of corporation tax. It explains who needs to pay the tax, and summarises some of the relief and allowances that may apply. It also gives you useful links to sources of further information.

FAQS

Who pays corporation tax?

If your business is a limited company, you'll have to pay corporation tax on its taxable income and profits made during a specific accounting period.

Different types of taxable profit can be divided up as follows:

- trading profits—this refers to income from your company's trading activities, after allowable expenses have been deducted
- capital gains—this refers to the profit you make when you sell a company asset such as land or buildings
- any other income—for example, money you make from leasing land or buildings, or interest on company savings

What are the different rates of corporation tax?

Different rates of corporation tax apply to different levels of profit, and these rates are explained below.

If your company's taxable profits in a year go over the thresholds even marginally, the company will be liable to pay more corporation tax on the excess. If you can see that profits are likely to exceed the thresholds, it may make sense to bring forward some planned expenditure. This could be achieved by awarding bonuses to directors (although this will push up the company's National Insurance contributions), or by bringing forward the timing of the purchase of tax-allowable items of expenditure, such as equipment.

Main rate

The main rate of corporation tax is 30% for the financial year ending 31 March 2007. However, there is a lower rate of 19% for small companies with taxable profits of less than £300,000 (see below).

Small companies' rate

For the purposes of corporation tax, 'small' is defined by a company's profits. For companies with profits below £300,000, the small companies' rate of 19% applies. In addition, there's marginal relief for companies with profits between £300,000 and £1.5 million.

The rates are summarised in the table below.

Taxable profit	% tax rate
£0–£300,000 (small companies' tax rate)	19
£300,001–£1.5m (marginal rate)	23.75
£1.5m+	30

MAKING IT HAPPEN

Understand how corporation tax is calculated

Your company must calculate the corporation tax due to HM Revenue and Customs (HMRC) under a self-assessment scheme. The amount of tax due will be based on:

- income from trading

- income derived under the Income Tax Schedules, such as interest from cash investments
- capital gains

Trading losses from previous years can be offset against your taxable profits and capital gains made in the current accounting period, in order to reduce your company's corporation tax bill. Capital losses can also be offset against capital gains.

Your company's annual accounts are the starting point for being able to calculate corporation tax, but the net profit that's declared on your company's profit and loss statement isn't the same as the chargeable profit that's used to calculate its corporation tax liability. There'll be a number of adjustments required to the accounts, based on the relief and allowances that are approved by HMRC.

Investigate the relief and allowances that apply to corporation tax

You must claim any relief and allowances on your company's tax return.

- Business expenditure can be offset against chargeable profit when it's incurred wholly and exclusively for the purposes of trade; for example, wages, salaries, power, rent, rates, stationery, telephone, cleaning and advertising expenditure. Note that despite what some people think, business entertainment is not an allowable expense.
- Depreciation and amortisation (charges for the write-down of tangible and intangible assets) aren't allowable expenses for tax. Instead, capital allowances are given for qualifying purchases made by the company for assets such as commercial property, fixtures, plant, office equipment and motor vehicles. These capital allowances are then used to reduce the company's tax liability.
- Charges on income, such as patent royalties or covenants to charities.
- Relief for trading losses—these can be set against income or gains of the current or previous accounting period. If the loss isn't claimed for some other relief, it'll automatically be carried over to be set against future profits of the same trade. If the company ceases to trade, the previous 12

months' losses can be set against trading profits of the previous three years.

Understand how corporation tax is collected

Under Corporation Tax Self-Assessment (CTSA), companies are expected to work out their own tax liability and to pay their tax without prior assessment by HM Revenue and Customs (HMRC).

Companies are under obligation to:

- inform HMRC that the company exists and is liable to pay corporation tax (this can be done by contacting your local HMRC office—see **www.hmrc.gov.uk/menus/ contactus.shtml** for details)
- calculate and pay their corporation tax without a prior HMRC assessment
- file a self-assessment corporation tax return when required by notice to do so
- keep adequate records of income and expenditure so that tax liability can be calculated accurately

You're liable to penalties if you don't submit your company's corporation tax return by the 'statutory filing date'—this is the date when your company tax return must be received by HMRC. You'll also have to pay a penalty if you fail to pay your corporation tax by the due date.

You may additionally face penalties if you complete your corporation tax return incorrectly or fail to notify HMRC that you're liable to pay corporation tax.

Pay on time

Corporation tax must be paid within nine months and one day from the end of the accounting period (the due date). HMRC will send a payslip and pre-paid envelope three months after the end of the accounting period, and then a further two reminders just before and just after the due date. The company's payment should go to HMRC's Accounts Office.

Interest (linked to commercial rates) is payable on under/over payments from the due date. In a case where your company underpaid corporation tax, the additional tax should be paid as soon as it's discovered. If the company has paid too much, it won't be reimbursed until after the company corporation tax return has been filed.

If the figures aren't finalised by the time corporation tax is due, and an exact assessment can't be made, corporation tax should be estimated and that amount paid by the due date. If it isn't paid, HMRC will demand any outstanding tax (together with any interest that has accrued) once it's received your company's corporation tax return.

File your return

Your company's completed corporation tax return will be due 12 months from the company's accounting date or three months from the HMRC notice, whichever is later. It must be on an official form or an accepted substitute. Incorrect or fraudulent returns incur interest and penalties.

Three months after the end of the accounting period, HMRC will send you a notice to send in a return form plus the form itself. If your company is liable for corporation tax but doesn't receive this notice, you need to contact HMRC before the due date to avoid penalties.

It's your company's responsibility to fill in and send the return to the Inspector by the filing date. The return should be submitted to the Inspector, including a copy of the company's full accounts and figures explaining how the accountant got from the account figures to the return figures.

In practice, it's usual for your company's accountants to prepare the tax return in association with preparing the company's annual accounts. The company's directors are then responsible for signing off the return, but it's usually submitted by the accountants, before the tax payment is due.

HMRC may carry out an inquiry into the tax return; it'll let you know when this is to take place. At the end of the enquiry, HMRC will tell you of any necessary adjustments and your company will have 30 days to amend the self-assessment.

Keep the right records

You'll need to record the following information in order to complete your company tax return:

- information about all expenses and receipts incurred during the course of operating your company
- details of all sales and purchases your company has made in the course of trade
- any supporting documents

Ask for help if you need it

If you're not sure what you're meant to be doing about corporation tax, remember that your financial adviser or accountant will be able to point you in the right direction. Also, HMRC has set up local Business Support Teams. They'll give advice and information free, both on a one-to-one basis and through workshops. Contact details can be found on the HMRC website. Also, HMRC now allows you to manage and monitor your corporation tax online, which can make paying the amount due a much easier process.

Don't forget that UK tax legislation is complex, so you should always check regularly with your company accountant to make sure your business is making accurate returns. If you don't, you're asking for trouble. Your accountant should also provide you with tax planning advice to enable you to minimise your company's future tax liabilities.

COMMON MISTAKE
You forget to allow for corporation tax in your cash-flow projections

When you're looking at your cash flow, do remember to allow for any tax liabilities; this will mean that you can pay any due tax on time. You're just throwing money away unnecessarily if you incur penalties for late payments.

USEFUL LINK
HMRC Corporation Tax web pages:
www.hmrc.gov.uk/ctsa/index.htm

An introduction to tax allowances for capital expenditure

GETTING STARTED

Capital expenditure on assets such as computers and other equipment is a major cost to most businesses and yet it is not directly allowable as a tax deductible expense. However, tax relief is available on this type of expenditure through the use of capital allowances.

By understanding how capital allowances are calculated and when they are available to your business, it is possible to achieve considerable tax savings, which can offset the high cost of purchasing business assets.

This fact sheet provides guidance on the tax relief that is available when buying assets, and how the tax relief is calculated. It includes hints and tips and sources of further information. Tax legislation is a complex area and this information is intended only as a starting point to understanding the issues involved. Professional advice should be sought before any decisions are made.

FAQS

What are capital allowances?

Capital allowances provide a tax deduction against a business's taxable profits. The value of the allowance is derived from the cost incurred when assets are purchased and used in your business. The most common examples of capital expenditure are where purchases are made of physical assets such as office equipment, manufacturing plant, and motor vehicles. Intangible assets that your business acquires—such as patent and licence rights and goodwill—are also eligible for capital allowances.

Your business is not entitled to full relief immediately on the whole cost of the asset, unless the asset is eligible for 100% first year allowances. Capital allowances typically give a percentage allowance each year to reflect the way in which the asset gradually depreciates in value.

To make sure that you comply with tax legislation, you need to clarify whether a purchase made by your business qualifies as capital or revenue expenditure. Revenue expenditure covers the purchase of items required for the day-to-day running of the business. These items do not qualify for capital allowances, but they are wholly tax deductible. Capital expenditure covers the purchase of assets that:

- are not consumed or resold by your business
- have a useful life of more than one year
- are expected to have a value after one year

The main legislation covering capital allowances is detailed in the Capital Allowances Act 2001 (CAA01), but it is an area of law that is regularly amended. As a result, it's wise to review the rules regularly, particularly if you are relying on the tax relief from capital allowances to help finance the purchase of an asset. Your accountant or HM Revenue & Customs (HMRC) will be able to advise you about which purchases qualify.

How do capital allowances differ from depreciation?

Depreciation is an accounting term that provides for the wear and tear to fixed assets, and is shown as a cost in your business's profit and loss account. The purpose of depreciation is to calculate a fair charge for the use of the assets, to ensure you cost your products or services accurately, and provide a realistic profit figure in each trading year.

Depreciation isn't, however, an allowable expense for tax purposes. Each business can employ slightly different depreciation policies to reflect their particular business's circumstances, providing they conform to general accounting standards. Capital allowances therefore replace the charge for depreciation in the business accounts, while still allowing the cost of assets to be written off against taxable profits.

When you calculate your business's taxable profit, you need to add the cost of depreciation for that year back into the profit figure in the accounts. You then deduct the capital allowances you are claiming for that tax year to calculate your adjusted taxable profit. The calculation is shown in the example below:

Profit in the accounts	£10,000
Add—Depreciation charge	£5,000
Deduct—Capital allowances	(£3,000)
Adjusted taxable profit	£12,000

You should note that the final taxable profit that determines the tax liability for a business may then have other expense adjustments made, depending on the circumstances of each business.

How are capital allowances given?

The capital allowances for a particular year are calculated by adding all of your assets of similar types together into a pool of expenditure. Certain assets may qualify for special allowances and these should be kept in separate pools.

If the asset is used solely for your business, the whole allowance is available for tax relief, but if any private use has been made of that asset a proportion is disallowed. The amount is reduced by a private use percentage. You need to keep accurate records of business and private use for each asset for each year, as this is an area that is closely looked at by HMRC when reviewing business and tax records.

Capital allowances can be calculated in various different ways. Examples of a reducing balance calculation, private use calculation and straight-line basis calculation are shown below.

The different types of calculation are used

for classes of asset that, in HMRC's opinion, need to be written off over various time scales. This means that the more usual calculation is the reducing balance calculation for assets that depreciate fairly quickly, such as vehicles, plant and machinery. For longer-life assets such as industrial buildings, tax relief is spread over a longer period as these are likely to be slowly depreciating assets.

Reducing balance calculation

The following example is a simple calculation for a reducing balance.

Business asset purchased for	£10,000
Year one writing down allowance at 50%	(£5,000)
Written down value carried forward	£5,000
Year two writing down allowance on balance at 25%	(£1,250)
Written down value carried forward	£3,750

In this example the writing down allowance is the value that is used to determine your capital allowance for that year. If the asset has been partly used for private purposes, then a second calculation needs to be made to deduct the proportion of allowances relating to that private use.

Private use calculation

Capital allowances given in the tax computation are then reduced for any private use:

Writing down allowance	£5,000
Less private use 20%	(£1,000)
Capital allowance	£4,000

The written down value carried forward remains the same, and the private proportions are reviewed according to the use made of the asset each year.

Straight-line basis calculation

For capital allowances on a straight-line balance basis, calculations are made on the writing down allowance in year one and the amount allowed remains the same in subsequent years.

Business asset purchased for	£100,000
Year one writing down allowance at 6%	(£6,000)
Written down value	£94,000
Year two written down allowance straight-line basis	(£6,000)
Written down value carried forward	£88,000

What are the main rates of capital allowance?

Different types of asset can qualify for different capital allowances—HMRC sets out the writing down rates for each class of capital expenditure. The rates have varied over the years and are frequently updated in annual Budget statements. In order for an asset to qualify for capital allowances it must comply with HMRC's definition of that type of asset. The rules are complex and backed up by a body of case law, so it is not always easy to say which category your asset falls into.

The table below gives some of the main current categories and rates of capital allowance relevant for small businesses—that is, a business with any two of the following: a turnover of £5.6 million or less; assets of £2.8 million or less; not more than 50 employees.

The figures given in this table are relevant for the tax year 2007/2008. There are a number of important changes that will become effective from April 2008. The most significant of these are:

- the standard allowance for plant and machinery decreases from 25% to 20%
- the allowance for long-life assets will increase from 6% to 10%
- there will be the introduction of an annual 100% investment allowance of £50,000, which will replace the current first year allowances

What if your profits are low in the first year?

A business does not have to take all the allowance in any year if the profits are

Class of asset	Criteria	Rate
Plant and machinery	Year 1 Write down on reducing balance	50% 25%
Energy saving technology	Year 1	100%
Motor cars	Write down on reducing balance If value greater than £12,000 Emitting less than 120g/km CO2	25% £3,000 max 100%
Know-how and intellectual property rights (IPR)	Write down on reducing balance	25%
Long-life assets	Year 1 Write down on reducing balance	6% 6%
Flat conversions	Year 1	100%

low, or if the business has made a loss for tax purposes after taking capital allowances which would reduce the profit further or increase the loss. For individuals and partners this could mean wasting the tax-free personal allowance in the tax year. It is acceptable to just claim enough capital allowances to reduce your profit to the level of personal allowances in the year.

For limited companies, each company needs to review its corporation tax calculation to see whether it is advantageous to carry the capital value forward or to claim an increased loss if there is other income to set this against. The remaining capital value after deducting anything claimed in the current year is carried forward to the next year.

How and when can you claim capital allowances?

You need to keep track of fixed assets by maintaining a register so that you know the cost and date of the purchase of business assets. When you are considering purchasing high-value assets, look at the timing in relation to your accounting year-end and the income tax year. Whether you are self-employed or running a limited company, capital allowances are given as a deduction from taxable profits.

The business accounting year may not coincide with the financial year, so you need to check the rates that are in force. In some cases rates can come into force at other times such as the date of a government Budget. The Corporation Tax accounting period ends on 31 March and the tax year ends on 5 April.

Any purchase made up to the last day of your accounting year counts for an entitlement to a full year's capital allowance, at the rate in force then. Therefore it makes sense to purchase assets before the year-end if there is a sound commercial reason at that time. If an asset is bought by hire purchase, it must be in actual use by the business by the last day of the accounting period.

The claim is made in your self-assessment tax return or corporation tax return as part of the tax calculations. You need to keep track of the written down values and the allowances claimed for the next year. If you have accounts that include a balance sheet the depreciated values will be shown there—but because the tax calculations are made in a different way, a separate record must be maintained.

What happens when you sell or dispose of assets?

When you sell or transfer an asset you need to compare the written down value in your books with the actual value at the time of disposal. The difference will be shown in your profit and loss account as a profit or loss on disposal. Like depreciation, this is not allowable for tax purposes and will be included in the adjustments when arriving at your taxable profits.

The sale proceeds are deducted from the tax written down value in the capital allowance calculations, which may give rise to a balancing allowance (tax deduction) or balancing charge (tax profit). These are then deducted or added to your profit for tax purposes. If you don't sell the item for money, but (for example) you give it to an employee or dispose of it, you need to use an estimate of the market value as the amount shown for proceeds of sale.

As you reduce the balance left in the asset register by deducting capital allowances each year, the remaining value is only an estimate of what it is worth. On a sale, a final adjustment is made to your capital allowances to reflect the actual proceeds received.

■ Example of loss on a sale

Written down value brought forward	£2,500
Sold for	(£2,000)
Balancing allowance deducted from taxable profit	£500

- Example of profit on a sale

Written down value brought forward	£2,500
Sold for	(£3,000)
Balancing charge added to taxable profit	£500

The accounts for the year in which the disposal takes place will include the adjustment.

Hints and tips

- Assets purchased on hire purchase or lease with an option to purchase can be included.
- If your accounting period is not 12 months, the capital allowances are reduced or increased proportionately.
- Capital allowances are also available for research and development costs at a rate of up to 175% of qualifying expenditure for small businesses.
- HMRC will review accounts that have high repairs and renewals in the profit and loss account. This is to see if any high value items have been incorrectly claimed as an expense instead of as a capital asset addition. This can lead to an enquiry into the accounts because anything disallowed would increase the tax payable in that year.

USEFUL LINKS

Capital Allowances Investment Scheme:
**www.hmrc.gov.uk/capital_allowances/
  investmentschemes.htm**
Capital Allowances Manual:
**www.hmrc.gov.uk/manuals/camanual/
  index.htm**
Enhanced Capital Allowances
www.eca.gov.uk

Providing cars and vans for employees

GETTING STARTED
A business provides vehicles for its employees to help them work more effectively, and as an employee benefit. If used in the right way, these vehicles offer many benefits to the business; if they're managed poorly, though, they can be a massive drain on resources.

The Government has targeted the value of this benefit and has greatly increased the amount of tax payable by both businesses and employees in the last few years, so there is a lot to think about as you weigh up the pros and cons of this issue.

FAQS
Why do businesses provide vehicles?
A business normally invests in cars or vans because there is an obvious commercial need for them: for example, sales staff may need to travel regularly to meet with customers and deliver goods to them. In these situations, the vehicle is seen as an essential tool for performing the job and the costs of operating the vehicles can easily be identified against the benefit that the business derives from them.

Many businesses, however, also provide cars to their employees because they are regarded as an attractive employee benefit, rather than an essential tool for doing their job. This allows the business to attract and retain high-quality staff who value not being responsible for the main running costs of the vehicle and often enjoy the status symbol it represents.

An alternative to providing individual employees with their own vehicle is to operate a pool system, whereby the business will have a number of vehicles, which are available to employees only when they have a specific reason to travel somewhere.

In general the main benefits to a business of providing vehicles are:
- staff have a flexible and convenient way to perform their duties
- the business has control over the quality and reliability of the vehicles being used
- it is relatively easy to budget for the costs of operating these vehicles
- it can be cost-effective if staff travel frequently (compared with alternative forms of transport)
- the business can promote its name and services on these vehicles
- it is a valued staff benefit

What is the best way to pay for a vehicle?
Despite the benefits of providing employees with cars and vans, vehicles incur high costs to a small business—so the decision to provide them needs to be carefully thought through. There are many funding options available.
- **Cash purchase.** You use the business's available cash reserves to purchase the vehicle outright, and its value is shown in your balance sheet as an asset. There are no ongoing monthly finance payments, you have the benefit of capital allowances to reduce your tax liability, and you have great flexibility as to when you dispose of the vehicle. However, this also ties up valuable cash, which could be used in other ways to grow your business—and you need to account for vehicle depreciation charges in your accounts (see pp. 178–182).
- **Hire purchase.** You take out a secured loan to buy the vehicle. The business is effectively the owner of the vehicle, but title does not pass until the loan is repaid in full. You make regular monthly payments, but if you default, the finance company will be able to repossess the vehicle. Balance sheet and depreciation treatments are similar to outright cash purchase, but you get tax relief on the interest charged and through capital allowances (see pp. 106–107).

- **Contract purchase.** This allows you to have the use of a vehicle for a fixed period of time, with a preset total mileage allowance at a fixed monthly cost. You have an option to arrange maintenance cover at an additional monthly charge. The vehicle can be returned to the finance company at the end of the contract, or it can be purchased for a predetermined amount at the end of the agreement. Balance sheet and depreciation treatments are similar to outright cash purchase, but you get tax relief on the interest charged and through capital allowances.

- **Contract hire leasing.** The key agreement terms are similar to contract purchase agreements. However, the vehicle remains the property of the finance company at all times, who take it back at the end of the contract period. The value of the vehicle does not show on your business's balance sheet, and rental payments are treated as a business expense.

Choosing the right finance option means thinking carefully about the following questions:

1 What can the business afford to pay (either as a lump sum or as a regular monthly commitment)?

2 How long do you expect to keep the vehicle (typically a period of 2–4 years)?

3 What are the accounting and tax implications to your business of the different finance options?

4 Does your business have an established trading record, and if not are you prepared to provide personal guarantees to the finance company?

This is a complex area, so you should discuss these issues with your accountant or other financial adviser before making any decisions.

What other costs are there?

Calculating the true cost of a vehicle to a business is much more complicated than simply considering its initial price or the ongoing finance cost. Motoring magazines and online price guides often supply data in the form of cost per mile. The main costs that you should budget for are:

- depreciation in the value of the vehicle
- vehicle road tax (which may be included in contract purchase and hire agreements)
- insurance premiums
- fuel costs
- service and maintenance costs
- parking, tolls and other incidental costs

Business insurance premiums can be significantly more expensive than private motor vehicle policies. Initially your business is likely to be treated as a new driver and so will have a limited no claims discount. In addition, few insurance companies offer competitive policies to businesses with only a small number of vehicles, so it is sensible to discuss your needs with a specialist insurance broker. Once you have five or more vehicles, you will become eligible for fleet vehicle policies which can help to reduce your insurance costs.

Fuel is one of the largest ongoing costs, so it's important to consider the fuel efficiency of the vehicles that you buy. Diesel cars are typically more fuel efficient than petrol ones—and converting petrol cars to run on liquid petroleum gas (LPG) can offer major cost per litre savings, although this needs to be offset by the costs of making the conversion and the fewer miles per gallon achieved.

You should also be aware that contract purchase and hire agreements will make additional charges if you exceed the agreed mileage over the hire period—and if the vehicle is returned in poor condition at the end of the contract term.

MAKING IT HAPPEN
Consider the tax implications

There has been a sustained increase in the level of tax charged against business vehicles over the last few years. The taxation of cars is now based on each vehicle's carbon dioxide (CO_2) emissions, with the aim of penalising cars which emit higher levels of CO_2.

Employee tax

The tax paid by an employee for using a car provided by the business is affected by four factors:

CO₂ emission	List price	Taxable % on list price	Value of car benefit	Employee's income tax rate	Income tax due
165 g / km	£15,000	23%	£3,450	22%	£759
195 g / km	£25,000	29%	£7,250	40%	£2,900

1 the list price of the car
2 the CO₂ emission figure for the car
3 the type of fuel used by the car (petrol cars incur lower tax than diesels)
4 the highest rate of income tax paid by the employee

The table above provides a comparison of the tax liability for two employees who have diesel cars, to show the potential difference in income tax payable for their car benefit.

Employees are also liable to tax on car fuel benefit if the business pays for any fuel used for private journeys, which is not then reimbursed by the employee. Private travel includes commuting journeys between home and work. The taxable car fuel benefit for 2007/8 is calculated by multiplying £14,400 by the same taxable percentage as would apply for the car benefit. (these figures are fixed by HMRC). In the examples above, this would equate to an additional tax charge of £728 and £1,670 for each employee respectively.

You will need to decide if your business will pay for private fuel and then discuss this with your employees, because the value of the benefit may be less than the additional tax they will pay.

An alternative approach is for the employee to pay for all fuel and then claim back as business expenses the cost of fuel used for business journeys. HMRC has agreed mileage rates for business travel, which are dependent on the engine size of the car and the fuel used.

For example, the agreed rates for cars from August 2007 are shown in the table opposite.

See the full table of rates published by HMRC at **www.hmrc.gov.uk/cars/advisory_fuel_current.htm**.

These rates are subject to review and usually change annually.

Engine size	Petrol	Diesel	LPG
1400cc or less	**10p**	**10p**	**6p**
1401cc to 2000cc	**13p**	**10p**	**8p**
Over 2000cc	**18p**	**13p**	**10p**

Vans have traditionally been more lightly taxed than cars, but from April 2007 the taxable benefit to the employee for the unrestricted use of a business van was increased to £3,000 (previously £500), and in addition there is a further benefit charge of £500 if private fuel is provided. There is no taxable benefit applicable for vans if restricted private use conditions are met.

As an employer, you are required to complete a P11D form for each employee who has the use of a business vehicle. This details the value of the benefit, and allows HM Revenue & Customs (HMRC) to determine the correct tax code for each employee in order to collect the additional tax through the Pay As You Earn (PAYE) system.

Business tax

Your business is required to pay employer's national insurance contributions (NICs) on the value of the total taxable benefit (vehicle and fuel) provided to employees each year. For the two employees detailed above, this would incur an additional cost to your business of £2,328, (£1,370 due for the car benefit, + £958 due for the private fuel benefit).

The business is also required to complete and submit an annual return to HMRC by 6 July each year (form P11D(b)), which details all benefits provided to employees, including the benefit derived from business vehicles. The additional NICs are also due to be paid at this time.

Your business can claim some business tax relief by way of capital allowances, which are based on the value of a vehicle. These are set at a rate of 25% per annum on the value of the car on a reducing balance basis, with a maximum tax deduction of £3,000 for a car costing over £12,000. Cars with CO_2 emissions of less than 120gm/km are entitled to 100% capital allowances. It is likely that the capital allowance regime will soon change so that the allowance for all cars is based on their CO_2 emissions, which is likely to penalise those vehicles with higher emissions.

There are also several areas where vehicles receive special treatment under the VAT legislation, which have an impact on VAT registered businesses.

- It is not normally possible to reclaim VAT charged on cars provided to employees. However, VAT charged on commercial vehicles such as a van may be reclaimed.
- If your business pays for the private fuel used by an employee then it must account for fuel scale charges in its VAT returns. This allows the business to reclaim the VAT on all fuel purchased, but the scale charge then claws back some of this VAT to account for the private usage. From May 2007 fuel scale charges have been based on the CO_2 emission of each vehicle.
- If a leased vehicle is also available for private use, then only 50% of the VAT charged for the finance fees can be reclaimed. VAT charged for service and maintenance fees is fully recoverable.

Think about employee policies
Employers will usually cover the basic provision of a vehicle in an individual's contract of employment. This will detail what type or value of vehicle the employee is entitled to, whether it is available for private use, whether there are restrictions on its use and when it will be replaced.

You will also need to draw up a general employee policy providing clear guidelines on what is expected of employees when they use business vehicles. Some of the key issues that need to be covered are:

- **payment for fuel.** Who is responsible for paying for fuel and what happens with private mileage? Employees should keep a log record of all business mileage undertaken. This is particularly important where not all the private mileage is paid for by the business
- **maintenance of the vehicle.** Explain the car user's responsibilities in respect of the ongoing maintenance of the vehicle
- **insurance.** Who is covered to drive the vehicle and what happens in the event of an accident?
- a process for **reviewing drivers' licences** at least annually to ensure that insurance policies remain valid, and to ensure employees notify you of all road traffic offences committed
- **responsibility for fines and other offences** such as speeding tickets
- **guidance on the use of mobile phones in vehicles** and what hands-free kit will be provided. Employees should also be made aware that smoking is not permitted in business vehicles
- what happens to the vehicle when an **employee leaves the business**?

Investigate the alternatives to providing business vehicles
You do not have to provide your employees with business vehicles, and you may be able to avoid some of the significant costs and administrative burdens by not doing so. Listed below are some of the alternative approaches that can be adopted.

Employees use their own vehicles
Employees can use their own vehicles and then receive expenses against the journeys made. The employee is required to insure their vehicle for business purposes and then submit expenses to account for when they have used their vehicle. HMRC have approved mileage rates to cover the costs of using private vehicles, which are exempt from tax and NICs and which allow for the

cost of fuel as well as maintenance and depreciation of the vehicle:

Up to 10,000 miles   40p per mile
Each additional mile   25p per mile

Pay the employee a car allowance

As a result of the increased tax rates for business vehicles, some employees find it financially attractive to receive money instead of a vehicle. They can then use their own vehicle for business travel when it is necessary. The employee pays income tax and NICs on this allowance and the employer pays employer's NICs. However, the employer does not have the administrative and cost burden of providing the vehicle.

Use hire vehicles and public transport

If your employees only need to travel infrequently, it can be cost-effective to hire cars or vans as and when required and use public transport at other times. Although each journey or hire period may seem more expensive, the total cost over the year may offer considerable savings.

Use specialist delivery services

Many businesses use the services of specialist delivery firms to deliver their goods, rather than using their own staff and vehicles. This is particularly effective when you are delivering goods nationally and each individual delivery may be relatively low value.

Short-term contract hire periods of three to six months may be available through some businesses. This is an attractive option if you are starting a new venture or taking on new employees and you do not want to be tied into a long-term hire agreement.

USEFUL LINKS

The Automobile Association (AA):
www.theaa.com
The Department for Transport (for details on the laws surrounding the use of mobile phones while driving):
www.dft.gov.uk/stellent/groups/ dft_rdsafety/documents/page/dft_ rdsafety_025216.hcsp
HM Revenue & Customs (HMRC) (for information on the taxation of business vehicles):
www.hmrc.gov.uk/cars/index.htm
LPG Gas Association (for information about using LPG in vehicles):
www.lpga.co.uk
www.boostlpg.co.uk
Society of Motor Manufacturers and Traders:
www.smmt.co.uk
The Royal Automobile Association (RAC):
www.rac.co.uk
Vehicle Certification Agency:
www.vca.gov.uk

Understanding the tax implications of corporate entertainment

GETTING STARTED

Corporate entertaining is an increasingly popular, and often effective, way to build good relationships with potential and existing customers in relaxed surroundings. Many businesses can see the benefits of entertaining clients, but the tax implications of providing corporate hospitality are often overlooked.

This actionlist outlines the different types of corporate entertainment and explains the tax implications of each for your business. It also provides links to sources of further information.

FAQS

What constitutes corporate entertainment?

Corporate or 'business' entertainment includes hospitality that's provided free of charge to the recipient. It also includes hospitality that's subsidised or in other words where any charge made to the recipient doesn't cover the cost to the business of providing the entertainment.

Any entertainment (including hospitality of any kind) provided by a business in connection with the work it undertakes is considered to be corporate entertainment. However, corporate entertainment doesn't include the provision of entertainment solely for employees of the business (or in the case of a company, its directors or people engaged in the management of the organisation).

The following are regarded by HM Revenue and Customs (HMRC) to be types of third-party entertainment (when not provided to an employee or directors):

- provision of food and drink
- provision of accommodation (for example, in a hotel)
- provision of theatre and concert tickets
- entry to sporting events and facilities
- entry to clubs and nightclubs
- use of capital goods such as yachts and aircraft for the purpose of entertaining

What are the tax implications for your business?

Expenses relating to corporate entertainment can't be offset against business profits. So any corporate entertaining costs must be added back onto profits when calculating the business's tax liability. Many years ago you used to be able to claim tax relief when entertaining overseas business people, but now the disallowance applies to all entertainment, whether or not the people entertained are from the UK or overseas.

MAKING IT HAPPEN

Understand the tax implications

Where corporate entertainment is provided for third parties but employees are incidentally involved, there may be a tax implication for your employees. As with the clients attending the corporate event, the cost of the employees' participation can't be deducted. However, depending on why the employees are at the event, their attendance may be regarded as a benefit in kind and therefore taxable.

For example:

- a business puts on a social event for its distributors and employees are required to serve the guests and wait on tables. Due to the length of the function, the employees are provided with refreshments that are part of the food and drink served to the guests. The employees' attendance is primarily to work, and their consumption of the food and drink is incidental to their duties. As a result, there's unlikely to be any benefit arising for the employees.
- a business puts on a golf day. Some employees who play golf are asked to help partner the guests. It's debatable whether

introduction to tax-allowable business
penditure

TING STARTED

u're running a business, you need to be able to account for all expenditure and to
erstand what can and can't be claimed as an allowance against tax. The taxable profit you
ke is calculated after business expenses are deducted. So to get your net profit right, you
d to know which type of expenses are allowable in the eyes of HM Revenue and Customs
RC).

While running a business, you may pay for things that are not strictly business expenses. It's
portant to be able to identify these and eliminate them from your accounts. Also, specific
xpenses and allowances for tax purposes may differ from the expenses in your accounts. For
is reason it's helpful to understand the different expenses and their treatment for tax
urposes.

This actionlist gives guidance on what to look out for when claiming expenses and how
hey're allowed when working out your tax bills.

FAQS

What are tax-allowable business expenses?

The exact expenses allowable for tax aren't defined in legislation. The rules recognise that the expenses you have to pay out in order to run your business will vary according to the work you do. HMRC rules allow you to deduct expenditure from business income only where it is 'wholly and exclusively' incurred for the purposes of that business.

When deciding if an expense is allowable, you need to look at the specific expense and show that it was purchased solely for the benefit of the business. The justification for expense must be primarily a business reason, and the items must be used in your business. If you've got more than one business, a separate account will help to show which business the expenses are for. Expenses can only be set against the business that the items were purchased for.

Does the legal status of a business affect the allowances made?

Limited companies, sole traders and partnerships all prepare accounts under similar accounting rules. The accepted methods of calculating allowable expenses are contained in detailed practice guides

used by accountants and accepted by HMRC. These statements are updated regularly and can be referred to by businesses.

MAKING IT HAPPEN
Understand which types of expense are allowable . . .

Your accounts tell you how your business has performed over a defined period and where the money was spent. Not all the expenses included in your accounts are allowable for tax purposes. It's important, however, to show everything you've spent in the business, to justify the purchases commercially. Your accounts will show main categories of business expense as follows:

- costs of purchases subsequently sold or consumed by the business, with adjustments for stock
- direct costs of doing the work, commissions, carriage, contract costs and tools
- employees and subcontractors, employer's National Insurance Contributions (NICs), recruitment, training and benefits provided
- premises, rates, energy, property insurance, security, rents and use of home
- repairs and renewals, maintenance of business premises and equipment
- general administration, telecoms, office

their playing a round of golf is 'work' or 'play'. Guidance may be required from the local tax office as to whether there's a taxable benefit for employees attending. If employees take advantage of the facilities of the day in order to play a round of golf, there's a taxable benefit, unless the employee meets the full costs of their share of the facilities.

- a manager takes a client out for lunch and another employee attends whose function is directly concerned with the particular business project. There's no taxable benefit for either employee, as they are involved in the performance of their duties.

In order to protect your employees from tax liability and yourself, as the employer, from Class 1A National Insurance (NI) contributions on any taxable benefits in kind, you need to:

- specifically instruct employees attending corporate events about the nature of their duties and the reason for their attendance. To avoid a beneficial provision, employees must attend as part of the necessary performance of their duties, and any 'enjoyment' by them of the facilities is merely incidental to the occasion.
- agree in writing any 'grey' areas with the local tax office, or agree a general policy as to what should happen on these occasions
- arrange to have any taxable liabilities covered under Pay As You Earn (PAYE) settlement agreements (PSAs) if you don't want employees to be taxed.

VAT

Providing corporate entertainment also has an additional cost, as you can't recover the VAT. This means that if your business ever provides corporate entertainment to anyone who isn't an employee, the VAT should be disallowed in full. VAT that relates to any employee attending a corporate event should also be disallowed in full.

There are, howev... where corporate ... apparently being p... associated VAT may ... example:

- providing entertainment ... as long as it's without s... is available to all subscrib...
- offering free drinks to cu... taurants where the amou... tomers for their meals is c... inclusive of the 'freely given'...
- airlines providing catering ... modation expenses for passe... been delayed
- organising free wine- or ... events for trade customers o... for sampling purposes
- local authorities providing entert... civic functions

COMMON MISTAKE
You don't think things through

Remember that when employees en... facilities of corporate entertainment, ... are likely to be taxable benefits a... Although there's no substitute for a ... corporate entertaining event, y... allowed to provide small gifts up to a va... of £50 per person in each accounting ye... You'll be able to receive a tax deduction ... this, and recover any VAT incurred whe... you bought the gifts. However, for tax pur... poses, the items can't be food, drink or tobacco and must contain an advert for your business. For example, branded items such as mouse mats, mugs, sports bags, pens and so on should be allowable for corporation tax purposes.

USEFUL LINKS
Chartered Institute of Taxation:
www.tax.org.uk
HMRC:
www.hmrc.gov.uk

expenses, professional subscriptions, insurance and consumable office supplies
- motor expenses, hire and lease, parking and mileage allowances
- travel, subsistence, taxis, accommodation, rail and air fares
- advertising and promotion, and free samples
- professional fees, accountancy, solicitors and professional indemnity insurance
- bad debts, amounts written off as unrecoverable and previously included in the turnover
- interest, and alternative finance payments on loans and overdrafts
- finance charges, bank charges, credit charges, hire-purchase interest and leasing costs
- depreciation and loss or profit on disposal of fixed assets

. . . and which aren't

Expenses that aren't allowable are things paid for by your business that have had some other use. These need to be disallowed, and include:
- non-business use of assets
- non-business work paid for by the business
- depreciation (capital allowances are given instead)
- costs of running non-business areas of the premises
- alteration, replacement or improvements to capital assets (these are added to acquisition costs)
- political or charitable donations
- non-business motoring costs
- fines and penalties
- business entertaining and hospitality
- tax investigation costs unless no tax is added to your liability
- professional costs for purchase of fixed assets (these are capital acquisition costs)
- repayments of capital in a finance agreement
- ordinary, everyday clothing

Know when and how to claim the allowances

Your annual accounts will reflect the income and expenditure for your accounting year. The accounts should be prepared along accepted accountancy practice lines and include the relevant costs of running your business for that year. An accounting year end may not be the same as the tax year end for historic or commercial reasons.

The tax due on your net profit after deduction of all these allowances is calculated by reference to the tax year rather than the accounting year. The accounts for which the year-end falls between 6 April 2007 and 5 April 2008 form the basis of your tax return for a tax year ending 5 April 2008, so there may be a delay before the expenses affect your tax calculation. This can have an impact on your January and July tax account when self-employed. If you think the current year's accounts show higher expenses and lower profit than the year before, you can ask to reduce your payments on account to HMRC.

Understand what you can claim if you run a business from home

If you run your business from home, the extra costs incurred are tax allowable. HMRC will accept a reasonable calculation of these expenses, provided you can show how you arrived at the figure in your accounts.

Based on the area, usage or time your home is actually available to your business, you can work out a proportion of the general and establishment costs. If you've got a separate office, workshop or studio, this may form, say, one in five of your rooms and so one-fifth of the following expenses would be allowable:
- energy
- council tax, insurance and mortgage interest
- water bills, cleaning and decorating

Allowable employee expenses

Paying for employees can be a major expense in your accounts, so it's essential that you collate all the following relevant costs under this heading:
- salaries and wages

- bonuses
- benefits in kind such as cars, fuel, medical insurance and so on
- pension provisions
- key man insurance—premiums paid on key man policies may be allowable, but if any claims are made this will be treated as taxable income. Where they aren't allowable, any claims are usually tax-free. However, this isn't guaranteed so it's best to get professional advice. A common use of key man policies is to provide cover for a director who's a major shareholder, but not for other employees, and in this case the premiums would be likely to be disallowed
- temporary and casual staff
- employer's NICs
- canteen and working lunches
- recruitment and training
- annual parties, incentives and awards (up to certain limits)
- locum fees
- travel and subsistence expenses

Investigate retrospective claims

If you've spent money researching and preparing your business *before* actually starting to trade, some of these expenses can be claimed in your first accounts. This pre-trading expenditure must have been wholly and exclusively for the business you subsequently set up.

If you find expenses have been missed out of one year's accounts, you can amend your tax return to include them in the correct year's accounts.

Keep tabs as you go along

It makes sense to keep a close eye on your expenses so you know you're claiming what you can against tax due. Always keep a record of business and private use as you go along, so you can support any private proportions used in your tax computations. This will make life much easier for your accountant.

Don't forget that if you work from home and you use one room exclusively for business purposes, you may incur a liability for capital gains tax when you sell your property.

COMMON MISTAKES
You don't keep records

Do make sure that you keep all receipts for expenses and annotate them or make a note at the time describing what the purpose of the expenditure was. Otherwise you'll be in a real mess when it comes to preparing your accounts.

You don't distinguish between business and personal expenses

When you're planning expenditure, remember to focus on the benefits that the purchase will bring to your business, so you avoid unnecessary spending and possible queries from HMRC. You need to be able to show that purchases are purely for business use, if you plan to claim them as tax-allowable expenses.

You claim expenses that aren't allowable

It's important that you check your receipts while bookkeeping during the year so you don't inadvertently include things that aren't business expenses. When it comes to self-assessment or corporation tax calculations, ensure private expenses are added back for any usage made by you, family or employees. Other accounting adjustments include making sure depreciation is replaced by capital allowances.

If there's an enquiry about your tax return, HMRC may start an investigation into your accounts. At this point you need to be able to back up any claims made with documentation and explanations.

If you claim expenses that are subsequently disallowed by HMRC, you'll have to pay the increased tax due plus backdated interest and penalties.

USEFUL LINKS

HM Revenue & Customs (HMRC):
www.hmrc.gov.uk
TaxAid:
www.taxaid.org.uk

Setting up and running a payroll system

GETTING STARTED

Once you employ your first members of staff, you will need to set up and operate a payroll system so that you can pay them according to the arrangements laid out in their contracts of employment. It also allows you to comply with your statutory obligations to make and record income tax and national insurance deductions.

FAQS

What are the key issues I need to think about as I set up a payroll system?

When you recruit staff, you take on a contractual obligation to pay them according to their terms of employment. One of the easiest ways of losing staff—as well as leaving your business exposed to an employment tribunal claim—is to fail to pay them what they are due and on the date that they expect to be paid. Your employees have a legal entitlement to their pay, but they also need the money to pay their mortgages, rent and other essential living costs.

You also have a statutory obligation to register with HM Revenue & Customs (HMRC) as an employer, operate Pay As You Earn (PAYE) and National Insurance (NI) deductions, pay these deductions to HMRC, and maintain and keep accurate payroll records. In addition you need to comply with the national minimum wage (NMW) legislation.

A payroll system is used when you pay your employees, which may be weekly, fortnightly, every four weeks or monthly— and there may be serious consequences for your business if it is run incorrectly or is fundamentally flawed. Annual changes to PAYE and NI rates and thresholds also need to be implemented. Therefore you need to plan how to set up and operate the payroll process very carefully as it is a vital business system.

Why are the terms of employment important?

As an employer you must provide each employee with terms of employment within two months of starting work. This document is known as the 'statement of main terms of employment', and it is good practice to get the employee to sign a copy before starting to work. If an employee is not given—or does not sign—a statement of Terms of Employment or a Contract of Employment, they automatically have implied rights under general employment legislation. The main issues relating to paying your employees that are covered under the Statement or Contract of Employment are:

- the hours of work, per day and per week
- the basic pay and how it is calculated (per hour or per month, say)
- when payment will be made and how—for example, weekly or monthly, and by BACS or cheque
- entitlement to additional benefits—overtime, commission or bonus, or a car
- annual holiday entitlement

Other areas that may also be covered include:

- pension scheme arrangements
- any entitlement to enhanced sick or maternity pay
- policies applicable to unpaid absences
- the treatment and payment of expenses
- what happens when employees leave

By having the correct formal documentation in place when you employ someone, you will avoid a number of potentially contentious issues that may arise when you pay your staff.

How does a payroll system operate?

The main processes that your payroll system will need to comply with are:

- collecting and recording employee details
- calculating gross and net pay
- providing employees with pay statements
- paying deductions to HMRC and pension providers

- producing other standard forms when required
- making annual employers' returns
- maintaining and keeping accurate records

Initially, a payroll system can be operated using the manual paper records and tables that HMRC supplies with their employer starter kits. However, most businesses quickly progress to using computerised systems to manage their payroll, as these packages are relatively cheap and can reduce administration time and costs. Computer programmes can make automatic calculations of deductions, produce payslips and prepare end-of-year returns.

HMRC Payroll Standard Accreditation is awarded to payroll software products that meet certain quality standards. For more details about which products are currently approved, see **www.hmrc.gov.uk/ebu/acclist.htm**

What information do you need to collect and record for each employee?

An accurate payroll system relies on some basic employee information. The key information includes:

- employee's full name
- home address
- employment start date
- date of birth
- National Insurance number
- amount and basis of pay—split by hourly or monthly rates
- bank details if you are paying by BACS

If your new members of staff have worked elsewhere before joining your business, they should be able to provide you with a P45 form from their former employer, and this will provide some of the required information. Some of these details—such as home address and rates of pay—may change during a person's employment with you so make sure that your records are updated as necessary.

You'll also need to record details of expenses and benefits provided to each employee: this information must be provided to HMRC annually, and can affect the amount of tax payable by your employee as well as the amount of your NI contributions as an employer.

MAKING IT HAPPEN
Calculate gross pay

You may employ someone on an hourly rate and pay them weekly or monthly, or on an annual salary basis and pay them monthly. The pay rate that you quote in your terms of employment will be the gross rate, which will then be subject to PAYE, NI and any other deductions.

For employees paid by the hour, you'll need to have a system of recording the actual hours worked on each day, particularly if they are entitled to overtime rates for any hours worked over their basic hours. For example, if employees are paid £8 per hour and work their contracted 40 hours in a week, their gross pay for that week is £320. If they are entitled to overtime, say at 1.5 times the hourly rate, and work 44 hours the next week, their gross pay will then be £368 for that week.

For employees paid an annual salary, it is usual to spread the payments equally throughout the year. Therefore an employee on £18,000 per year will receive a gross monthly salary of £1,500. Adjustments may need to be made if an employee takes unpaid leave or starts or leaves part way through a month. In these situations you can make adjustments to the monthly salary by calculating a day rate and deducting this as appropriate. For example, if the employee has one day's unpaid leave in a month, the amount to be deducted can be calculated as follows: £18,000 divided by 52 weeks, divided by 5 working days = a day rate of £69.23. You can also calculate an hourly rate by dividing the day rate by the normal number of working hours in a day, which—if it is 7.5 hours—would be £9.23.

Calculate net pay

The net pay that an employee receives is gross pay *less* statutory tax, NI deductions and any other agreed deductions. The basic steps that you need to follow are:

1. Calculate the gross pay due.

2. Determine if any statutory payments such as sick or maternity pay are due.
3. Calculate the tax and NI contributions due and deduct from the gross salary.
4. Make any other deductions such as pension contributions or student loan payments.
5. Pay the net pay due.

You need to keep a record of all payments made to employees, with details of the gross pay and the deductions made. The standard form used to record this information manually is a P11 deductions working sheet (provided by HMRC) although computerised payroll packages maintain and provide similar reports.

Provide written pay statements

You must give a written pay statement or payslip to all employees on or before the day that they are paid, which sets out how their net pay has been calculated. The table below shows an example of a pay statement.

If you produce your own payslips, you can choose the layout that you use. If you are using a standard payroll package that prints the payslips, then you may be restricted to using your supplier's standard layout, although some packages allow modification, It is customary to provide payslips in a sealed envelope, with the employee's name on it, so that the information contained on the payslip remains confidential.

Remember the deductions

The employee deductions for tax, NI and student loan payments that are made in one month need to be paid by the employer to HMRC by the 19th day of the following month. For example, any deductions made in January need to be paid to HMRC by 19 February. If payment is made by BACS then the money must be in HMRC's bank account by 22 February. Computerised payroll packages produce a standard monthly report (form P32), which details the breakdown of deductions that are due to be paid to HMRC and any statutory payments that are being reclaimed.

Pension contributions are another standard deduction made to employees' pay and they must also be paid to the pension provider by the 19th of the following month.

Other standard forms

There are a number of other forms that you must provide to your employees and HMRC when operating your payroll system. The main ones are:

Employee	Number	Employer
Jane Smith	***	Smith and Sons

Payments		Deductions		To Date	
Gross:	£1,500.00	PAYE: NI: Pension:	£212.57 £117.04 £100.00	TAXABLE: TAX: NI: PAY DATE: TAX PERIOD: 2 TAX CODE: NI No:	£3,000.00 £425.14 £234.08 25/05/07 522L NZ-12 34 56 A
Total:	£1,500.00	Total:	£429.61	**NET PAY:**	**£1,070.39**

For employees starting or leaving your employment

- **P46.** This is a notice of new employees starting work, which is completed and sent to HMRC when the employee does not provide you with a P45 from their previous employer.
- **P45.** This form contains employee details when they leave your business. Three copies of this document are given to the employee, two of which are passed on to the new employer.

Annual forms

- **P60.** An end of tax year (6 April to 5 April) summary given to each employee providing details of pay and statutory payments received, plus the deductions for tax, NI and student loans.
- **P14.** A copy of the P60 that is provided to HMRC.
- **P35.** The employer's annual return, providing a breakdown of tax, NI and student loan deductions made, as well as statutory payments recovered.
- **P38A.** The employer's supplementary return, which is used for reporting details of payments made to workers for whom you have not completed a P14 form.
- **P11D/P9D.** An annual return of expenses and benefits paid to each employee whose earnings exceed £8,500. If earnings are less than this, form P9D should be used.

Make annual returns to HMRC

You are required to submit an annual employer's return to HMRC by sending them P14 forms for each employee and a P35 employer's summary form. This provides the information for HMRC to reconcile the deductions you have made with the amount that has been paid during the last tax year. There are automatic late filing penalties if your returns are not received by 19 May, and interest may be charged on deductions that have not been paid to HMRC by this date.

Online filing of annual returns is mandatory for medium and large employers and will be compulsory for small employers (fewer than 50 employees) from 2010, but in the interim period there are tax incentives for small businesses to file online. To file your annual return online, you need to be registered with HMRC PAYE Online for Employers, which is accessed through the HMRC website. See **www.hmrc.gov.uk** for more information and select the 'PAYE for Employers' option to follow the instructions online.

An annual return is also required for expenses and benefits paid to employees (form P11D or P9D) and should be sent to HMRC by 6 July. Employer's class 1A National Insurance contributions are chargeable against any employee benefits and must be paid to HMRC by 19 July to avoid interest charges.

Operate your own payroll service

One of the main decisions that you will have to make is whether to operate the payroll system yourself (in-house) or to use a bureau that provides a payroll service. There are a number of issues that you need to consider:

- operating a system in-house gives you control, but also requires you or your staff to have the appropriate knowledge and time to run it.
- it may be cheaper to buy a payroll package than to use an outsourced service, but you need to cost your own or your staff's time and consider what happens during holidays. Who will take on the responsibility for keeping records up to date when you're away, for example?
- because there are changes every year to the PAYE system, you will need to take out an annual licence for the software that you use to ensure that the package is kept up to date.
- you need to consider how you will pay employees. BACS is the preferred method of payment for most employers and employees, but you must have the necessary electronic banking facility to do this.
- are you confident about managing the year-end forms and returns to HMRC?

Consider using a payroll bureau service

Most accountants and book-keepers offer payroll services to their small business clients. They are usually eager to offer a full package of services and can offer some very competitive prices, but it may also be worth comparing the service available from a payroll firm that specialises in this type of service. You can usually specify the type of service that you require, which may range from just receiving payslips and monthly deduction calculations, to receiving a complete payroll service—which will include all standard payments and returns, as well as the calculation of expenses and benefits.

Obviously the cost of the service will be a major consideration when comparing providers. However, you should ensure that you take account of what is included as standard within a monthly charge and which parts of their service are chargeable as extra costs.

One particular advantage of using a bureau is that many of the problems associated with sorting issues out with HMRC are removed and you have the confidence that the job is being done properly. Even if you out-source the payroll service, you'll still need someone to liaise with the service provider, as they will need to receive details of new employees and changes to pay rates, as well as the details of those leaving your employment.

COMMON MISTAKES
You don't safeguard personal information

The employee information that you hold for your payroll records *must* comply with the Data Protection Act (even though you don't need to notify the Information Commissioner and become a registered data controller to hold this type of information). Also make sure that any employees who operate your payroll system are aware that records must be regarded as strictly confidential information.

You don't give employees an itemised payslip

Don't see this as a tiresome piece of extra paperwork: your staff have the right to take you to an employment tribunal if you don't provide them with a detailed payslip.

USEFUL LINK
HM Revenue & Customs:
www.hmrc.gov.uk

Setting up a stakeholder pension scheme

GETTING STARTED

It's increasingly apparent that people aren't saving enough for their retirement, and state pensions on their own are unlikely to be adequate to maintain a reasonable lifestyle. In response to this, the Government passed the Welfare Reform and Pensions Act 1999, which introduced stakeholder pensions. The intention has been to make the process for finding and choosing a private pension easier, as well as providing a low-cost way for individuals to build a second pension for retirement.

This actionlist explains what stakeholder pensions are and when you, as an employer, must make one of these schemes available to your employees. It also considers what you need to do to operate a stakeholder scheme for your employees, what your obligations are and where you can go to get advice. The legislation for this topic is very detailed and the information below is only a guide. For detailed advice, seek help from an IFA or consult the sources below.

FAQS

What's a stakeholder pension?

Stakeholder pensions have been available since April 2001, and have to meet stringent standards as defined in the Welfare Reform and Pensions Act 1999 and the Stakeholder Pension Schemes Regulations 2000 (as amended).

They are 'money purchase' private pensions where contributions are invested for long-term growth, usually in stocks and shares. The size of the fund at retirement depends on the amount of contributions, how well the investments have performed and the level of charges that have been deducted. On retirement, the pension owner can choose to take up to 25% of the pension fund as a tax-free lump sum, and can use the rest (or all) of it to buy an 'annuity' which will pay a regular income during their retirement (but which may be taxable).

These pensions are intended for people who:

- don't have access to an occupational pension or group personal pension scheme
- are likely to move frequently between jobs
- are put off by the restrictions and costs of traditional personal pensions
- are generally unaware of the benefits of private pensions

Who provides stakeholder pensions?

Stakeholder pension schemes are provided by the major banks, insurance and other financial services businesses. You can find a list of registered schemes at: **www. thepensionsregulator.gov.uk/ stakeholderPensions/theRegister/ RegisterSearch**

They're tightly regulated and have to meet a number of minimum conditions, which include:

- allowing regular or irregular contributions to be paid
- allowing a minimum contribution level of £20
- having maximum management charges of 1.5% of the value of the fund each year, which are taken from the fund
- not making additional charges if a member stops and then starts payments, or transfers their fund to another scheme
- making any extra charges for the provision of advice to scheme members entirely optional
- providing all members with annual information detailing how much has been paid in and how the individual's fund is performing. Individuals can sign up for a stakeholder pension directly with one of the approved scheme providers, or they may register through an employer-chosen scheme.

Which regulatory bodies are involved with stakeholder pensions?

This is an extremely well-policed area with several Government departments and bodies having responsibility, at least in part, for regulating the industry.

All organisations offering stakeholder pension schemes must register those schemes with HM Revenue and Customs (HMRC) and the Pensions Regulator. The latter organisation has primary responsibility for ensuring that the rules and regulations are complied with and enforced. The Pensions Regulator also has the power to impose fines on employers of up to £50,000 for a company, and up to £5,000 for an individual, for failure to comply with the legislation.

The FSA (**www.fsa.gov.uk**) examines, regulates and approves individual IFAs, and provides strict operating guidelines for the provision of advice in the pensions sector.

MAKING IT HAPPEN

If your business employs five or more people and doesn't already provide a qualifying alternative pension scheme, you must select and provide access to a stakeholder pension scheme for your employees—even if fewer than five of them are eligible to join. And you must do this within three months of your fifth employee starting work for you, or you may be liable for a fine.

Your employees can then decide whether they want to sign up to the stakeholder pension scheme, although there's no obligation for them to do so. As the employer, you don't have to contribute to your employees' pension schemes, although you can if you want to.

You don't need to provide your employees with access to a stakeholder pension if you meet one of the following conditions:

- you employ fewer than five people counting all employees, including part-time workers and company directors
- you already offer employees access to a qualifying 'group personal pension scheme'
- you already offer an 'occupational pension scheme' that all staff can join within a year of starting work for the business

- you offer an occupational scheme for some staff and a personal scheme for the rest

Even if you're exempt from offering a stakeholder pension scheme, you can still offer access to one if you feel it might be beneficial for your employees.

Think over the key issues ahead of choosing a stakeholder pension scheme

You can approach some of the scheme providers directly, but as there are over 40 registered schemes, it's worth consulting an independent financial adviser (IFA) who can explain the processes you need to go through, and help you to choose the most suitable one for your business. To find an approved adviser or to check that an adviser you're thinking about using is accredited, go to **www.fsa.gov.uk/Pages/register** where you can search against their name or location.

Some of the key issues you'll need to consider when deciding which scheme to choose are:

- What's the performance record of the fund?
- Are the management charges less than 1.5%?
- Is full advice provided for members under the standard management charges and if not, what are the additional charges for providing such advice?
- What information will be provided to employees before and after joining the scheme?
- What's the administrative process for making contributions?
- If you're using an IFA, will they receive a commission from the scheme provider or will you be expected to pay a fee for their advice?

Before formally choosing your scheme, you're obliged to consult your employees. Your IFA or preferred scheme provider should be able to provide you with relevant information to share with your staff, or you can download an example consultation letter from **www.thepensionsregulator. gov.uk/stakeholderPensions/ informationPack/exampleConsultationLetter2007.pdf.**

Even though you're not obliged to act on them, it's wise to consider the views of your staff as you gear up for this big decision.

You can then formalise your choice of stakeholder pension scheme by having an agreement with the provider stating that employees can join the scheme and that payroll deductions will be made for contributions if required.

Inform your employees

Once you've chosen a scheme, you'll need to provide your employees with details of how they can obtain more information and join it. As a minimum, you need to give them the scheme provider's contact details. However, many IFAs or scheme providers will provide information packs that can be given to all employees. Some will also visit your premises to talk to employees about the scheme and the benefits of joining.

You're not expected to provide your employees with advice about your chosen scheme, as this area is regulated by the Financial Services Authority (FSA). Your obligations are simply to choose a suitable scheme, ensure your employees have access to it, and undertake payroll deductions and the payment of contributions as necessary.

If any of your employees don't want to join the scheme initially, you've a duty to ensure information about the scheme is available to them on an ongoing basis, as their circumstances may change and they may want to join at a later date. In addition, you'll need to provide new employees with details of the scheme. Ideally this should be included as part of their induction to your business.

Administer the scheme

When your employees decide to join the pension scheme, they'll need to complete an application form, which is sent to the scheme provider. At this stage, they should let you know if they want to make contributions through payroll deductions or whether they'll make the payments themselves.

If payroll deductions are requested, you'll need to:

- deduct the requested contribution amount (which should be net of basic rate income tax). This could be a fixed amount or a percentage of salary, from the employee's net pay
- clearly show details of this deduction on their payslip
- record these deductions in your payroll records
- supply the scheme provider with a list of contributions for each pay period so they can allocate your payment correctly
- pay these deductions to your scheme provider within 19 days of the end of a month. For example, deductions made in January need to be paid to the scheme provider by 19 February

You should also make employees aware of how:

- they can confirm a change in their contributions
- they can make changes to their contributions, which they should be able to do at least every six months
- they can ask for their contributions to stop at any time

If your employees decide to make their own contributions, you don't have any responsibility in relation to those contributions.

Your scheme provider will supply your employees with annual statements detailing the contributions received and updating them on the performance of their funds. If your employees have any issues with this documentation, they should contact the scheme provider directly, rather than discuss these points with you.

It's good practice regularly to review the performance of your stakeholder pension scheme provider to ensure they continue to offer a good service.

COMMON MISTAKE
You don't provide a stakeholder scheme

If you employ more than five people, you're *legally obliged* to offer them the chance to invest in a recognised stakeholder pension.

There's no legal requirement for employers to pay into stakeholder pensions but it is good practice to do so and could be a possible aid to recruitment.

USEFUL LINKS

Financial Services Authority (FSA):
www.fsa.gov.uk

HM Revenue & Customs (HMRC):
www.hmrc.gov.uk/stakepension
The Pensions Advisory Service (TPAS):
www.pensionsadvisoryservice.org.uk
The Pensions Regulator:
www.thepensionsregulator.gov.uk
The Pension Service:
www.thepensionservice.gov.uk

Tax self-assessment for the self-employed

GETTING STARTED

If you're running your own business as a sole trader or as part of a partnership, you'll be treated as self-employed for tax purposes. You need to register your business with HM Revenue and Customs (HMRC) within three months of beginning to trade to avoid an automatic penalty being imposed. HMRC will then send you a self-assessment tax return or a notice requiring you to complete a return each 6 April.

This actionlist gives guidance on preparing for and completing your tax self-assessment return. It also offers hints and tips, and lists sources of useful information.

FAQS

Who can complete a self-assessment tax return?

Self-assessment applies to sole traders, subcontractors, partnerships and limited liability partnerships (LLPs). You are required by law to notify HMRC if you've any income which makes you liable for tax. Once you become self-employed, you'll need to complete a self-assessment tax return annually. If you run a business at a loss, you still have to complete a self-assessment to claim loss relief. It's also useful to claim exemption from National Insurance Contributions (NICs) if you have low profits.

The limited company tax rules require companies to make a corporation tax self-assessment. If you're a director of a limited company and only receive a salary which is taxed under Pay As You Earn (PAYE), you may not need to complete a self-assessment unless you've other sources of income to declare.

What is self-assessment?

Self-assessment is your declaration of all the income and capital gains you received in an income tax year ending on 5 April. If you're asked by HMRC to make a self-assessment, you're required by law to do so and must include all your sources of income for that year. For a business, this means the tax results for the accounting year which ends in that tax year. So if your accounts are made up for the year ending 31 July 2006, those figures (for the whole of that year) would be entered on your self-assessment for the year ending 5 April 2007.

The self-assessment tax return asks for all your income, including the following main classes:

- UK savings and investments
- UK pensions and other social security benefits
- gains on life products
- employments and directorships
- share schemes
- self-employment
- partnerships
- land and property
- foreign income and investments
- trusts
- capital gains
- non-residence

You'll need to complete not only the core tax return, but also the self-employed supplementary pages and any other relevant supplementary pages according to your circumstances. A step-by-step guide to completing the tax return will be included with your self-assessment pack.

What relief can you claim in the self-assessment?

You can claim for any relief that's being deducted for income tax purposes for that year. This includes:

- pension contributions
- interest paid on qualifying loans
- community investment, venture and enterprise trust subscriptions
- charitable gifts
- blind person's allowance
- married couple's allowance if born before 6 April 1935
- income-contingent student loans

You should include expenses connected with running your business in the self-employment pages of the return.

What about business partnerships?

If you're in a partnership, your personal self-assessment tax return will have a partnership page. This just requires you to show your net share of the partnership income for that year. The partnership itself will also receive a full or short tax return to declare all the income and expenses for the year.

The type of return you need to make depends on the type of income received by the partnership. If the partnership receives investments, income from property, foreign income or capital gains, a full tax return is required. If the partnership only receives income from a business, a short return usually provides all the information needed. One partner is designated to sign and submit the return on behalf of all the partners.

If the partnership tax return isn't submitted on time, all the partners will be fined £100 each. These fines can't be reduced even if there's no tax due, as fines are enforced under different legislation from the individual return.

What if your accounts don't end on 5 April?

Your annual accounts are usually made up to the same date every year. That year-end may not be the same as the tax year for historic or commercial reasons. The tax due on your net profit is calculated by reference to the tax year rather than the accounting year. The accounts year ending in the period 6 April 2006 to 5 April 2007 form the basis of your tax return for a tax year ending 5 April 2007.

When you start your business, the profit to 5 April is used as the taxable figure, so this may mean apportioning your first year's results. For example:

Year ended 31 July 2007 gives a profit of £12,000 and is assessed as follows:

- 2006/07 tax year August to March is 8 months out of 12—£8,000.

- 2007/08 tax year the first 12 months is used—£12,000.

The first eight months' results have been used twice to work out the tax due for two tax years. This produces an overlap relief which is carried forward until you cease the business or change the accounting date. At that point, the initial overlap relief is deducted from your final year's profit.

What trading year end should you choose?

The choice of accounting date can produce planning opportunities. An early accounting year-end gives you more time to prepare accounts and financial statements. With an accounting date early in the tax year, you could not be taxed on those particular profits for up to 21 months after you have earned the money. This may benefit your cash-flow if your profits are rising. You'll still have to pay tax on account and make a balancing payment on 31 January, if your profit is higher than it was the year before.

There may be other factors that you can benefit from, such as choosing a year-end date that is during a quiet time of year so your stock-take is easier. Having a year-end that coincides with your VAT quarters is also likely to save you paperwork.

If your business is seasonal, choosing a date after the end of the busy period will more accurately reflect the activity for that season's trade.

MAKING IT HAPPEN
Send your return back on time

If you can't complete your tax return online and you want HMRC to do the calculation for you, manual self-assessment forms need to be submitted before 30 September.

The final deadline is usually 31 January following the 5 April year end. So for a tax return issued on 6 April 2007 asking for details of your income for the year ending 5 April 2007, the last day HMRC can receive it is 31 January 2008. If the tax return gets to HMRC after the deadline you'll suffer an automatic penalty of £100 (or the tax due if less than this).

204 Company admin, tax and payroll

HMRC has indicated its intentions to bring forward some of these deadlines, so that from 2008 the deadline for electronic filing of personal tax returns will be brought forward from 31 January to 30 November, and to 30 September for those filing paper returns.

Currently, if HMRC issues you with a tax return for a particular year later than 31 October, you have three months from the date of issue to send it back.

Make sure you meet payment dates without fail

If you file your tax return online (see over for website details), the calculation is completed for you. This tells you how much tax is payable for that particular tax year. You'll usually have paid some tax already in the previous year.

If you've a tax liability of more than £500, you may also be required to pay one half of that liability as a payment on account of the following year by 31 January, and a second payment on account by 31 July. Balancing payments will also be calculated to account for any previous over- or under-payments.

The payment dates are:
- Tax year ended 5 April 2007
- 31 January 2008: Balancing payment + payment on account

The balance is due if the total tax and NI payable is *more than* the amount you paid on account in January and July of the previous year.
- 31 July 2008: Payment on account

The payments on account in January and July are based on the total tax and NI due for the year ended 5 April 2007. Half of that sum is payable in January and the other half in July.

If your profits are rising, a balancing payment is usually due in addition to the payments on account. If your profits are falling, you may need to reduce your payments on account to make sure you don't pay too much. If you do pay too much on account, you can claim a refund. However, it's better to get your self-assessment completed early and not pay too much in the first place.

National Insurance (NI) payments

If you're self-employed, part of your NI is paid at a fixed rate as you go along. You pay Class 2 NICs (currently £2.20 per week, although this changes annually) from the date you register as self-employed. This is paid directly to HMRC; the easiest way to deal with this is to pay it by direct debit quarterly.

The second part of your NI bill (Class 4 NICs) is based on a percentage of your profits, and is worked out and paid with your tax in January and July. There's no need to make a separate payment as the self-assessment calculates the Class 4 NICs due on your profits at the same time as the tax.

Fill in the form

Not everything you prepare for accounts has to go on the return:
- if your accounts include a balance sheet, this does not have to be entered on the return
- management accounts and forecasts aren't used in preparing the return
- you need to include only the final agreed figures
- if any figures are doubtful by the time the return goes to HMRC, you must indicate this on the return by marking them 'provisional'—and then notify HMRC of the confirmed figures as soon as possible to avoid an enquiry and penalties
- if your turnover for a year is below £15,000, you can submit an abbreviated return showing only your total turnover and total expenses. You still have to keep accurate records to support the figures

COMMON MISTAKE
Your records are untidy

If you keep everything to do with the tax year together (such as subcontractor vouchers, and bank and building society interest certificates), it'll make it much easier for you or your accountant to refer to them as you complete the return. You can make the self-assessment process simpler by getting your accounts prepared as soon as possible after your accounting year end.

And always check your payments on account to see whether they need to be reduced especially if your profits or other income has gone down.

You don't plan for tax payments

If you keep up to date, you can predict and plan for the tax liabilities in advance. Try to have everything worked out before the due dates for tax in January and July, so you've got the funds set aside to pay the bills and don't have to find the cash at the last minute.

USEFUL LINKS

HM Revenue & Customs (HMRC):
www.hmrc.gov.uk/sa
TaxAid:
www.taxaid.org.uk

A guide to business rates

GETTING STARTED

Almost all businesses have to pay rates to their local authority as a contribution to the cost of operating local services. The national non-domestic rate has been in force since 1990, but the system of taxation is more commonly-known as business rates.

Shops, offices, warehouses, factories, and any other kind of property not classed as a domestic dwelling will usually be liable for business rates. In some cases, people running a business from home can also incur a business rate charge for the part of the property they use for their work, depending on the extent of business use of the room and modifications made to the property.

This actionlist explains how business rates are calculated, the businesses that are exempt from the charges and the penalties for failing to pay. It contains useful tips and a list of the relevant organisations you may need to contact. The business rates system varies according to region, so the information below focuses initially on England and Wales, and then provides details about procedures in Scotland and Northern Ireland.

FAQS

What are business rates?

Business rates are a contribution to the costs of services provided by local authorities. In principle, they're the equivalent of council tax, but are calculated in a different way and paid by businesses in respect of non-domestic properties.

Local authorities still collect business rates, but have to hand over all the money to the Government, which reallocates the total pool back to local authorities according to their population size and the type of authority.

MAKING IT HAPPEN
England and Wales

Understand how bills are calculated

In order to calculate business rate bills, a separate rateable value is determined for each individual business property, and this value is multiplied by a rate per pound known as the Uniform Business Rate (UBR). This is set by the Government annually on 1 April.

In England, there are two UBRs set each year—the standard multiplier and the small-business multiplier (the rate applicable to businesses that qualify for small-business rate relief, as explained below). The standard multiplier for 2007/8 is 44.4p and

the small-business multiplier is 44.1p. There is a separate UBR for all businesses in Wales, which is set at 44.8p.

You can access the latest UBR figures for England and Wales by visiting the official government website at **www.mybusinessrates.gov.uk/rates/ ubr/index.html**

Business rating and council tax valuation lists for England and Wales are compiled by the Valuation Office Agency (VOA), and it's their officers who decide the rateable valuations for their local areas. How much a business actually pays depends on various factors that are taken into account when deciding the rateable value. These include the size and location of the property, how it is to be used and the nature of the business.

Calculate the rateable value of your premises

The rateable value is based on an estimate of the property's rental value, if it were for rent on the open market on a specific date. This figure may differ from the actual rent paid for a number of reasons; for example, the business has negotiated particularly favourable rental terms.

Each VOA gathers as much evidence as possible about actual rents paid for properties in the particular area they cover to determine an appropriate rental value in each case. The rent calculation assumes that the theoretical tenant would be paying all the expenses (such as rates, taxes, insurance and repairs) that would be required to maintain the property in a fit state to justify the rent.

The VOA then prepares a summary valuation that explains how the rateable value of the business property has been calculated. These summary valuations provide a full breakdown of how the rateable value has been calculated, based on the characteristics of the business property. New valuations came into effect on 1 April 2005 and are valid for five years.

Exemptions for non-domestic properties

The following types of non-domestic property, assuming they are occupied, are exempt from business rates:
- all agricultural land and buildings
- fish farms
- certified places of religious worship, including church halls
- property used for people with disabilities

There are several other exemptions for occupied properties, but most of these are unlikely to apply to small-business owners. They include lighthouses, sewers (but not sewage disposal works), parks, bridges, viaducts and tunnels that provide access across water, and the property of drainage authorities.

Empty factories and warehouses are exempt from business rates. Other unoccupied properties are generally liable to pay an empty-property rate of 50% of the full rate after they have been empty for more than three months. Newly built unoccupied properties are also wholly exempt for three months after completion, as are properties that have just undergone major structural alterations or renovations. Other exempt unoccupied properties include listed buildings, ancient monuments and certain classes of property that have been acquired through inheritance.

Homeowners offering bed and breakfast (B&B) accommodation only have to pay council tax on the property if it's their sole residence, if they intend to accommodate no more than six people at any one time during the coming year, and if B&B is a subsidiary use of the property. Once the business becomes a significant enterprise that uses more than half the property for B&B, accommodates more than six people at any one time, or if adaptations have been made for the benefit of guests, a liability for business rates will arise.

Grounds for appeal

Other than incorrect details on the summary valuation, you may be able to appeal if the following circumstances apply:
- removal of properties from the rating list
- a change between domestic and non-domestic use
- the splitting-up or merging of properties

The first point of reference for any queries in relation to business rates in England and Wales is the VOA, and you can appeal if you think your rateable value is wrong in relation to the circumstances listed above. If an appeal is not resolved satisfactorily, the matter can be taken to an independent valuation tribunal. For more information, go to **www.valuation-tribunals.gov.uk**

Applying for rate relief

There are certain circumstances where businesses can apply for rate relief:

Small Business Rate Relief (SBRR). This is a scheme to assist small businesses that was introduced on 1 April 2005. The amount of mandatory rate relief is 50% for business properties up to a rateable value of £5,000. The relief available then decreases on a sliding scale for business properties with a rateable value of up to £9,999.

In addition to this relief on liability, eligible businesses whose properties have rateable values of between £10,000 and £14,999 (or between £10,000 and £21,499 in London) will have their liability calculated using the small-business multiplier.

You must apply for the relief each year and must be eligible on 1 April of each year. The application for the relief should be submitted to your local authority within six months of the end of the financial year to which it relates. You can only claim relief on one property.

See **www.mybusinessrates.gov.uk/rates/other_reliefs/index.html** for more details and **www.mybusinessrates.gov.uk/wales** for information about the SBRR available in Wales.

Charitable and Discretionary Rate Relief. Charities qualify for 80% rate relief. Local authorities may actually cancel all or part of the rate bill for properties occupied by not-for-profit organisations, although this is decided on a case-by-case basis. Consult your local authority (**www.direct.gov.uk**) for more information.

Rural village of population under 3000. General stores, food shops and Post Offices that appear on the rural settlement list qualify for 50% relief provided they are the only such service in the area and their rateable value is £7,000 or less. Similarly, village pubs and petrol stations with a rateable value of less than £10,500 qualify if they are the only local service.

If your local authority feels your business is of great benefit to the rural or village community, and it has a rateable value of less than £14,000, it may grant 100% rate relief. Again, your local authority should be able to give you more information.

Scotland

The business rates system in Scotland is very similar to that in England and Wales, but Scottish Assessors rather than the VOA decide on the categorisation of properties as either domestic or non-domestic. They also set rateable values for properties based on their rental value, which is reassessed every five years. The standard rate is 44.9p for 2006/7, but for 2007/8 (subject to parliamentary approval) the rates will be brought in line with those set for England—where the standard rate for 2007/8 is 44.4p and the small business multiplier is 44.1p. See **www.saa.gov.uk** for more details.

Local authorities issue bills based on a national poundage rate, which is set annually by the Scottish Parliament, and which is multiplied by the rateable value of the property.

Scotland has operated a SBRR scheme since April 2003, and properties with a rateable value of £11,500 or less are eligible for relief at a rate of between 5% and 50% on the rate poundage. Go to **www.scotland.gov.uk/Publications/2006/02/17092654/0** for more information.

Other charitable and discretional relief is available for similar categories to those in England and Wales—for more detailed information see **www.scotland.gov.uk/Resource/Doc/30859/0024812.pdf**

Northern Ireland

In Northern Ireland, rates for non-domestic properties are based on the rental value of the property, known as the net annual value (NAV). This is determined by the Valuation and Lands Agency (VLA)—see **www.vla.nics.gov.uk**

Rates bills comprise a district rate, which is decided by each local authority, and a regional rate, which is fixed by the Department of Finance and Personnel (DFP—**www.dfpni.gov.uk**). The regional rate is set at 29.1p for 2007/8.

In order to calculate bills, the NAV is multiplied by a non-domestic rate poundage figure, which varies in each local authority area. Rates are collected by the Rate Collection Agency (RCA—**www.rca.nics.gov.uk**).

Hardship relief for non-domestic properties is available to help businesses recover from temporary crises as a result of exceptional circumstances.

Paying business rates

There are two basic ways of making payment:

1 in full, within 14 days of the annual rates bill on 1 April each year.
2 by monthly instalments. If you have not previously paid monthly, a 'catch-up' payment of six months' rates must be paid up-front, followed by monthly instalments. Normally payment is spread over ten monthly instalments.

Understand the action that will be taken if you don't pay your rates on time

The penalties for late or non-payment operate as follows.

- If you are paying by instalments, your local authority will send a reminder notice that gives you seven days to make up the arrears. If you fail to do this, the full amount outstanding becomes payable immediately. Even if you comply with the extended seven-day payment period on the first occasion, should you later miss another payment the authority may send a final notice, which could lead to court action if full payment is not made. However, provided you've maintained good communications with the authority throughout, it'll be more likely to allow you a second reminder notice.

- If your local authority has to proceed to court action, you'll be liable for all costs, including the issue of the original summons.

- If the court authorises your local authority to enforce payment and you still fail to pay, it'll send in bailiffs to seize your goods and equipment. These will then be sold at auction to recover all monies due, and you'll also have to pay for the additional costs incurred through the bailiffs' actions.

- Finally, should the bailiff be unable to recover the value of the total debt, your local authority may still pursue amounts owing—even if your business has closed. The penalty for non-payment after appearing at the magistrate's court could be additional costs and imprisonment for up to 90 days. If you're a sole trader or in a partnership, you'll be personally liable for this debt.

Paying your business rates is an inescapable part of running a business, But do remember that the UBR is assessed every year and fixed in line with inflation. So be aware that your rates may change, and check your business rates bill annually.

If you decide to appeal against the business rate that's been set, don't delay in lodging your appeal—you need to take action as soon as you can. Similarly, if you receive a form from the VOA requesting information about your business premises, you are legally required to complete and return it, so don't ignore it.

Don't forget that registered charities and non-profit organisations should contact their local authority to ascertain the applicable reduction in business rates.

COMMON MISTAKES
You ignore payment demands

If you foresee that you might have problems paying your business rates, contact your local authority as soon as possible to explain your circumstances. You're legally obliged to pay business rates, so it's no good pretending that the problem will go away.

You *assume* you're being charged the correct rate

Occasionally, local authorities do make mistakes and charge businesses an incorrect amount for their rates. So do make a point of checking that you're paying the correct amount—if you're paying too much, it could make a big difference to your cashflow.

If you think your premises have been valued incorrectly, the Royal Institution of Chartered Surveyors (RICS) has a rating helpline (0870 333 1600) that can put businesses in touch with a chartered surveyor who'll provide advice about the valuation of business premises.

USEFUL LINKS

Department for Communities and Local Government:
www.communities.gov.uk
Royal Institution of Chartered Surveyors (RICS):
www.rics.org.uk

COPING IN A CRISIS

Coping in a cash-flow crisis

GETTING STARTED

Many businesses face a cash-flow crisis at some point in their existence. Good financial management should generally prevent this, but there are some circumstances that are difficult to avoid—especially in a company's early days. Events such as a major customer refusing or becoming unable to pay their debts can often saddle small businesses with cash-flow problems.

Running out of cash is probably the biggest cause of small businesses failing. There can be many reasons behind a cash crisis, so it's essential that you understand them and know how to prevent or mitigate short-term problems which might otherwise lead to business failure. No matter how good your balance sheet may look in terms of physical assets and outstanding debtors, your ability to convert these to cash at critical times can make the difference between survival and failure.

FAQS

What are the main causes of cash-flow problems?

Typical causes of cash-flow problems include:

- slow payment by your customers
- a key customer becomes insolvent owing you a large sum of money
- insufficient working capital
- focusing on turnover instead of profit
- poor financial planning
- buying too much stock

How can you spot when you're heading for a crisis?

Sometimes a cash-flow crisis will suddenly jump up and hit you, such as when a major debtor announces out of the blue that they cannot pay what they owe. Clearly, you can't always predict that things like this are going to happen, but you can take some steps to soften the blow. Spotting the problem in advance and doing something about it early is still the best step you can take, though—so try to bear this in mind, especially if you have one or two very large customers that you rely on.

You can spot the warning signs by keeping a close eye on your balance sheet. Is the number of debtors rising when everything else is constant? Are your stock levels, especially of finished goods, rising? If the answer to either of these is yes, then you may need to take remedial action. You also need to keep a close eye on your profit and loss account, although it may take longer to spot problems. Is your profit falling? Worse, are you losing money? If the answer to either of these is yes, then your available working capital will be reducing, and this spells trouble.

MAKING IT HAPPEN

Make sure that you have procedures in place to safeguard, as far as possible, against cash-flow disasters. Even if these can't be prevented, the procedures you've worked out should at enable you to spot the warning signs and take emergency action.

Control your finances effectively

The best form of preparation is an effective and robust system of financial control. Preparing a cash-flow forecast and—crucially!—putting it to good use is the basis for avoiding many cash-flow problems. The forecast allows you to anticipate most cash-flow-related issues that could occur during the normal course of running your business. It allows you to do a 'sensitivity analysis' in which you can test the effect of lower sales or slower payment on your cash flow.

Make sure that you're costing your products or services accurately, and that what you charge for them will let you make a profit. Adopt tight credit control systems and establish procedures for managing the whole process of giving your customers credit. Start by giving credit only to approved customers; check when their accounts are due for payment and that they pay according to your agreed terms. If you have efficient procedures for raising invoices promptly and sending statements to your customers, you won't be adding to payment delays yourself.

Consider encouraging your clients to pay more quickly by offering a discount if they pay either on delivery or within a certain number of days (typically 7–14) from the invoice date. Generally the discount is between 2% and 5% of your sale price, but the exact level will depend on your profit margins and how important early payment is to you.

To speed up payments, you could use the services of an invoice discounter or factoring company (see pp. 130–131). These companies enter into an arrangement where they will provide your business with an advance (usually 80%) on the value of your invoices as soon as they're raised. Interest is then charged on the balance drawn and there is a service charge. Factoring companies can also take control of collecting payments from your customer directly, which save you the costs of using your own staff to manage the process. This type of service is particularly suitable for businesses that are growing rapidly because they reduce the likelihood that you'll run out of working capital. However, you may still suffer if a major customer goes down—the factor will usually recover the outstanding debt from you.

As your business grows, you may be able to negotiate better credit terms with your suppliers. Initially, this could be achieved by progressing from paying at the time of purchase, to having a 30-day credit account. If the majority of your customers expect to have 60-day credit accounts, you should aim to agree 60-day payment terms with your suppliers.

An agreed overdraft facility allows you to borrow money as and when required, up to an agreed limit. It's a relatively cheap way to finance working capital if you have large variations in cash flow during the course of

a month (or if your business is very seasonal), because you only pay interest on the amount actually borrowed. However, if you're continually relying on your overdraft it can be expensive; more importantly it may also highlight that your business needs a longer-term form of finance. With an overdraft, you're exposed to 'repayment on demand', which means that your lender can ask for full repayment at any time.

If your business needs to invest in new equipment but doesn't have the cash, you may be able to fund this with a term loan, a hire purchase loan, or a leasing deal. This avoids the large cash outflow on the full price of the equipment, and gives you a fixed level of repayment over a set period (usually two to five years). In situations where the asset is being used as security for the finance, it's likely that you will still need to provide a deposit.

It's also sensible to manage your business so that you aren't reliant on just one or two major customers, as you'll be dangerously exposed if one of them has a problem. Spread your customer base as widely as you can, aiming for at least five or six customers.

Build up your working-capital availability by retaining some of the profit in your business. This will provide a reserve when you need to buy equipment or have unexpected expenditure to deal with, but will also provide a cushion against possible cash-flow problems.

Take emergency action if necessary

If you're hit with a cash flow crisis you have to act very quickly if the business is to survive. The first thing to do is to make an accurate assessment of the scale of the problem. Prepare an updated cash-flow forecast and decide if you'll be able to trade out of your difficulty. If this seems unlikely, look carefully at how much support you need and whether you can provide this from your own personal resources.

If the answer is no, you'll have to go to the bank and explore the possibility of increasing your overdraft. Even if you think you can trade out of the problem, it may be sensible to inform your bank at an early stage in case you discover later that you do need additional working capital after all.

If the bank is unwilling to help, or can only provide partial support, the next step is to inform your creditors. It's sensible to talk to larger creditors directly, explain your position and ask them for longer to pay. They can be very understanding if they think that you're being straight with them and that a little leniency now will result in full payment later. If necessary, offer them reduced payments now with the outstanding balance in instalments as your business recovers. If they are crucial suppliers, you need to keep them on your side or else you won't be able to continue trading.

You should also consider developing a business disaster plan, which will help the business cope with any unexpected events that could damage cash flow. This enables you to prepare for the aftermath of incidents such as computer viruses, major power cuts, loss of key personnel, natural disasters, and terrorist attacks.

If all these options fail, you may have no alternative but to consider the future of your company. If your business runs into severe financial difficulties and becomes insolvent, you must cease trading. The options then are either to seek the appointment of a receiver or liquidate the business.

COMMON MISTAKES
You get taken by surprise

Keep a close eye on your balance sheet, your debtors, and your bank balance. Look ahead at your cash-flow requirements for the next few weeks and consider what receipts you expect and what payments you'll have to make. Cash-flow problems are best caught early and the more time you can give yourself to respond the better.

You procrastinate

These issues rarely resolve themselves— they require positive action. Talk to your bank and your creditors as soon as you suspect there may be a problem. This way, you assure them you're at least doing your homework, even if there are difficult times ahead. If you don't act you run the risk of affecting relationships with all your key stakeholders including the bank, suppliers, and customers. Your bank will be far more receptive to dealing with your difficulties if you approach them before the problem occurs. It is bound to be a worrying time for you, but burying your head in the sand won't help and you'll feel better for doing something about the problem.

USEFUL LINK
Business Link:
www.businesslink.gov.uk

Valuing a business

GETTING STARTED

This actionlist looks at valuing a business, outlining the major factors you need to take into account. There are many different reasons why a business might be valued—including to sell or to buy a business, to raise finance or to benchmark the business's development. If you've been ploughing through turbulent financial times, however, you probably want to value the business as part of your review of exit options.

FAQS

Isn't it pretty difficult to put an exact figure on a business?

Yes! Valuing a business is by no means an exact science, particularly in relation to small businesses. It is difficult to set the value of a business at a single figure, as there are many factors that need to be taken into account. Buyers and sellers will also inevitably have different objectives (usually minimising or maximising the price), but in the end the real value of a business can only be determined by the price that a buyer is prepared to pay and a seller is prepared to accept.

MAKING IT HAPPEN

Understand what makes up the value of a business

The value a business has is made up of a combination of elements:

■ the value of its assets (what it owns)
■ its historical profitability
■ its future profit and cash earning potential

The *theoretical* basis for this is that if you invest your money in a business, you will expect to achieve a return on your investment that is higher than the return you could achieve by investing your money in a bank. You (potentially) get a better return because you're taking a riskier route.

The *actual* financial return you achieve from investing in a business is determined by the profits the business generates. Therefore, for two similar businesses that require the same amount of capital to set up, the one that generates the greater profit is more valuable, because it gives you, the investor, a greater return on your invested money.

However, theory and practice don't always coincide. Sellers typically inflate the value of their business because they place more value on the time and effort they have put into their business than a buyer does. Buyers can also base their valuations on reasons that aren't purely linked to financial return. It's often the case that buyers of small businesses value the business against its ability to provide them with a living and a certain lifestyle, rather than a specific return on their investment.

Use financial criteria to value a business

The current financial state of a business is often the starting point for basing any valuation. There are two main methods used.

Net asset valuation

This is the simplest way of valuing a business, and is particularly appropriate for businesses with significant tangible assets that operate in relatively stable markets.

The net assets figure, equal to the net worth or 'net book value', is shown on a business' balance sheet. In theory, if everything was sold at the value recorded on the balance sheet, the amount of money raised (minus any liabilities) would be equal to the net assets.

The net assets figure may need to be adjusted to reflect the true value of the assets a business has. For instance, buildings may be worth more than shown on the balance sheet, while equipment, such as computers, may be worth less due to their low second-hand market value. Businesses may also have intangible assets like intellectual property rights (IPR) and goodwill valued on their balance sheets, which are far harder to attribute a real value to.

Goodwill usually appears on the balance sheet as a result of the purchase of another business. It equates to the purchase price paid less the net asset value of the business that was bought, and reflects the value of that business' reputation, brand names and customer base.

For businesses that are heavily dependent on their assets to generate income, such as property firms, this method often proves a good basis for valuation. However, net asset valuation can also be used to set a minimum valuation for all businesses. If you can determine the market values of a business' assets, you can identify what the business is worth if it ceases trading and its assets are sold off.

Multiple of net earnings (P/E ratios)

A business can also be valued using its average historical net earnings (net profits after tax). This valuation assumes the business will continue to generate these average profits into the future, and the valuation is based on a multiple of these earnings. A typical price to earnings (P/E) ratio range used for small businesses is two to seven times average earnings, with the actual multiple chosen being dependent on the perceived risk of the business and its growth potential. Hence if a business has generated an average net profit after tax of £20,000 over the last three years, and is assumed to have an average P/E ratio of five, it would be valued at £100,000.

The P/E ratio is one of the figures provided on the share price page for companies quoted on the Stock Exchange. The P/E ratio gives an indication of how much investors are prepared to pay to buy shares in a business. P/E ratios can vary widely for different industry sectors and even for different businesses within a sector. While you can look at the P/E ratios quoted on the Stock Exchange to get an indication of the market rate for a particular sector, you must be aware that privately-owned businesses typically have at least a 50% to

70% discount compared with publicly quoted companies, because of the greater risk involved and the difficulty for investors wishing to sell their stakes.

The share price quoted for a market-listed company is based on the net earnings of the company multiplied by the P/E ratio and divided by the number of shares. This approach can be used to attribute a value to the shares of a company, which can be a useful benchmark for monitoring the growing value of the company over time.

Although this form of valuation appears to be fairly straightforward, there are a number of issues you may want to consider when calculating average net earnings and the actual P/E ratio to use. When calculating the average net earnings for a business, you should look to exclude exceptional and non-recurring income and expenditure, as this may have distorted one year's trading results or the future earnings potential of the business. You should also always consider the financial forecasts for the business over the next two to three years. Are the business' current earnings likely to be stable, or is it exposed to changes in technology or other competitive pressures that may reduce demand for some of its products?

Industry-related valuations

In some industry sectors, business valuations can be derived from factors other than asset valuations or net earnings figures.

Industry standard formulae

Certain types of business (such as milk rounds, newsagents, estate agents and Post Offices) which are bought and sold on a regular basis, can be valued based on accepted critical factors to business success. For example, the value of a milk round is closely associated with its average daily delivery, and estate agents can be valued according to the number of branches they have.

Cost of entry

You can also value a business by working out the cost of setting up a similar venture from scratch. Consider costs such as hiring and training staff, buying equipment, developing the products, and marketing them to your existing or new customers. You also need to factor in the time it will take you to do this and what you perceive to be the risks to this approach. This can then be compared with the goodwill value of buying an existing business, which has an established reputation and customer base.

Market consolidation

In some mature markets, individual businesses may have little value based on their financial performance, but they can have considerable value to a competitor because of the pool of loyal customers that the business may have built up. In these circumstances, a buyer will look at the potential income stream from these customers—who they may be able to service through their existing business or with a considerably lower cost base than the current operation incurs. A valuation can then be calculated based on the business' turnover or expected gross profit contribution.

Other factors to consider

There is a wide range of additional factors that you will need to consider when you value a business. These may be difficult to quantify, but can add significant value to a business, or may highlight significant risk and hence depress the value of the business to a potential purchaser. These include:

Market and external factors

- What is happening in the market in which the business is operating? What are the trends—including size, growth, changes in technology, regulations, and any political and economic factors—affecting the sector?
- Does the business have a growing or declining market share?
- Who are the business' competitors, where are they located and what are their strengths and weaknesses?
- Are there similar businesses being advertised for sale and do they have a quoted sale price?

Customers and suppliers

- Is the business dependent on one or two major customers, which could result in a major loss of income if a contract is lost?
- Does the business generate recurring income from its customers, or does it rely on one-off sales from new customers?
- Does the business have good relations with its suppliers and is it dependent on one or two key firms?
- Are sound commercial contracts set up with key customers and suppliers?

Business organisation

- Is the business dependent on the owner or any other key members of staff? This can be a particular problem with sales or creative businesses where a large part of the value of the business resides with key individuals.
- Is there a stable workforce and are the employees well trained?
- Does the business have established processes and systems which reduce the dependency on one or two key individuals?
- Are the assets that the business owns modern and well maintained?
- Is there clear ownership over intangible assets such as intellectual property, or are there formal agreements in place for licensing and patent rights?

Businesses that develop effective management information and control systems, particularly those that have tight control of their finances, will lower their exposure to risk. This can add significantly to the perceived value of the business.

COMMON MISTAKE

You put all your eggs in one basket

The sale value of any business will increase if you can find more than one prospective buyer, so it is worth using several different channels to market your business once you have decided to sell it.

USEFUL LINK
BDO Stoy Hayward:
www.bdo.co.uk

Finding potential buyers for your business

GETTING STARTED

If you've decided to sell your business, potential buyers could come from a number of sources—including competitors, suppliers, customers and new market entrants. While you might want to reach as many potential buyers as possible, you will probably want to keep your dealings confidential until you decide to inform employees, suppliers and customers.

For many small businesses, networking is one of the most effective ways of communicating with parties who may be interested in buying you out. However, if you need to be more pro-active about the process, and do not have the time to pursue it yourself, you could employ the services of a business broker (see below for more information). A broker will actively seek out interested parties, either directly or through networking with other business brokers. Your broker could also advise and support you through the negotiation and sale of your business. To advertise your business yourself, the most effective media are newspapers, magazines (both in your sector and specialist publications advertising businesses for sale) and the Internet. The Internet is fast becoming one of the most popular ways to advertise a business for sale, its main advantage being that it can reach a wide and global audience quickly. Although not the best source of advertisements for all businesses (for example, those with a very defined, local appeal), it's highly recommended for small businesses with a wider appeal.

FAQS

What is a sales memorandum and why use one?

A sales memorandum is a detailed description of your business that you can provide to prospective purchasers. It outlines the history, products and services, assets, and market and financial performance of your business. It needs to include your reason for selling and your asking price. The memorandum should also include a detailed business plan for the next few years, and the likely outcomes of that plan. The aim of the memorandum is to inspire interest from prospective buyers, as well as to anticipate some of the questions that they may want answered.

What could a business broker do for me?

A business broker will research the market for prospective purchasers of your business. She or he will work with you to establish a list of businesses or individuals who might be interested in finding out more about your business. Your broker will arrange the signing of confidentiality agreements, and hold preliminary discussions with some or all of the interested parties. He or she will then process the responses and advise you

on which options are worth pursuing, leaving you with more time to get on with running the business.

How do I keep the process confidential?

When you advertise your business in a newspaper or magazine, or on the Internet, do not mention your business name. Simply describe the sector you are in, your turnover and your asking price, as well as your regional location (but do not give the exact town or city). Give the interested parties a PO Box or an e-mail address to reply to. Before you provide any information to an interested party, get a confidentiality letter or agreement signed by the interested party (this usually only relates to information that is not publicly available). You can then release a sales memorandum with a request for a response on a given date.

What is a qualifying buyer?

When you consider the replies to your adverts, you need to sort out those expressions of interest that are serious from those that will only waste your time. Draw up a list of qualifying buyers, and limit your distribution of sales memoranda to this group only.

MAKING IT HAPPEN
Spend time preparing the business for the sale

Spending some time preparing the business for sale can enhance the price. Issues to consider include: reducing discretionary expenditure (for example travel and entertainment); reducing business costs without cutting back on vital areas (buyers will look for consistent spending patterns and sales figures); making sure that any property and equipment is well maintained; and reducing excess stock levels to improve the level of working capital.

Decide what type of buyer you want

If you want cash from a deal, it may rule out buyers below a certain size. If you're looking for a friendly purchaser who will safeguard future employment of staff and management, there is little point talking to known 'asset strippers'—that is, those who set out to acquire a company and sell its assets for a profit without regard for the acquired company's future business success.

In conjunction with your professional advisers, you should put together a list of possible buyers. You may well hold market information about prospective trade buyers, but do not rule out prospective new entrants to the sector. Non-executive directors, or specialist professional advisers, should have the ability to identify 'non-trade' buyers who may be prepared to pay a premium to enter your market.

Keep your target list to manageable proportions. If you have to advertise, the time drags on and you end up sending out the wrong signals to the industry as well as receiving time-wasters.

Prepare a sales memorandum

It is advisable to prepare your sales memorandum with an adviser or accountant, or with the business broker who is helping you sell your business. You could consider preparing a summary of the main points of interest as well as a more comprehensive document. The former can be sent out to all parties that express an interest in your business. The latter should only be sent to those parties who then request more information.

Select qualifying buyers

Look for buyers who want to add to their own business profiles; these are generally the most likely to put in a serious offer. They will often be players already in your sector, so they will understand how your business would contribute to their own. They will also have a good idea of the financial benefits they could derive. It is important that you try to establish whether the interested party has the finance necessary to purchase your business. Otherwise, this might become a problem as your negotiations proceed.

Send out confidentiality letters

Once you have identified those parties that you believe to be serious about buying your business, you need to send confidentiality letters to them. Make sure that the letters are professionally drafted. They will need to be signed and returned before you send out the sales memoranda. It is a good idea to give a deadline of about a fortnight. This will also help you establish which parties are prepared to give priority to the matter.

Send out sales memoranda

This can be done in two phases. The first phase involves sending out a summary. Distribution of the full sales memoranda should then be limited to those parties who have read the summary and have requested a full document. This indicates that they are genuinely interested in finding out more.

COMMON MISTAKES
You release too much information to competitors

One of the dangers of putting your business up for sale is that it presents your competitors with an opportunity to gain access to sensitive financial information. In this respect, it is useful to have the input of a business broker. Your broker can advise you on whether your competitors' interest is genuine or not, and will also maintain your anonymity right up to the stage of narrowing down to a few genuinely interested parties. You will need carefully to balance the need for interested parties to see your financial history, with the possible commercial advantage that a competitor could gain from this information.

You spend too much time with time-wasters

There are bound to be a number of responses to your advertisements which simply do not warrant following up. It is important that you identify these as early as possible, as you will probably need to spend a considerable amount of time with each of the interested parties in the near future. You should only pursue expressions of interest from parties that look like serious businesses with enough finance to make a reasonable offer. Carrying out a credit check, or sourcing a company report, can provide useful insights into your potential buyers.

USEFUL LINKS

Companies for Sale:
www.companiesforsale.uk.com
UK Business Base:
www.ukbusinessbase.com

Understanding bankruptcy

GETTING STARTED

Bankruptcy is a formal procedure that affects individuals who can't pay their debts. This may happen because of a build-up of personal debt or as a result of business debts for which you have personal liability. It results in you losing control of your personal assets, which are shared with your creditors, but also frees you from the burden of overwhelming debt.

This actionlist explains what's meant by bankruptcy, the procedures involved and the effects of bankruptcy on you and your business. It provides useful hints and tips, and also lists sources of further information.

FAQS

What is bankruptcy?

An individual becomes insolvent when they're unable to meet a specific debt when it's due, or they have insufficient assets to meet all of their debts. Bankruptcy is the legal procedure that may follow this. It's managed by the courts, and provides a formal procedure for your debts to be paid in full or in part, by the distribution of your income and personal assets to your creditors.

Although this process only applies to individuals, many people face bankruptcy because their business runs into financial problems. If you set up in business as a sole trader or a partnership, you automatically assume personal liability for the debts of your business.

However, you may also face bankruptcy proceedings as a company director, if you've signed personal guarantees with your bank or other financier and your company is unable to pay those debts.

The advantages to you of bankruptcy are:

- it frees you from overwhelming debt, allowing you to make a fresh start once you're discharged (see below)
- it provides a formal framework for communicating with your creditors and for fairly sharing your assets with them

How do you become bankrupt?

Bankruptcy proceedings start when the High Court in London, or a county court in England and Wales, receives a bankruptcy petition and grants the petitioner a bankruptcy order (see below for the special rules operating in Scotland and Northern Ireland). A bankruptcy petition may be submitted by:

- one or more creditors who are owed over £750 (creditor's petition)
- the debtor him- or herself (debtor's petition)

Self-bankruptcy is usually the preferred option when you face overwhelming debts that you can never reasonably expect to repay.

It's in your interests to co-operate fully if a bankruptcy order is made, although the order will still be made even if you refuse. However, if you dispute the creditor's claim, you should try to reach a settlement before the bankruptcy petition is due to be heard in court.

A bankruptcy petition can be presented even if you're no longer resident in England or Wales. As long as you have either lived in or had residential or business connections in England or Wales in the last three years, a bankruptcy petition can be filed.

What is the role of the Official Receiver?

A bankruptcy order will be published in local newspapers and the London Gazette (the official publication for legal notices). The court will, in the first instance, appoint an Official Receiver (OR). The OR, though an officer of the court, is a civil servant employed by the Government's Insolvency Service. Their function is to manage and protect the bankrupt person's estate until such time as a 'trustee' is appointed. The OR will:

- investigate your financial affairs and report any criminal activities
- report on your business dealings to your creditors and the Insolvency Service
- give the required notice of your bankruptcy to local authorities, utility suppliers, courts, sheriffs, bailiffs, the Land Registry, National Savings and Investments (premium bonds) and any relevant professional bodies
- make enquiries regarding other persons or organisations that can provide details of any assets or liabilities you have (they're likely to contact banks, building societies, mortgage, pension and insurance companies, solicitors and landlords)

The OR may decide not to deal with your case once its investigations are carried out, and may appoint a 'trustee in bankruptcy' (trustee) to take over your assets. This will be a qualified insolvency practitioner. They will then be responsible for disposing of your assets and making payments to your creditors.

What are the effects of being made bankrupt?

A bankruptcy order transfers control of your business assets and income, and also (where authorised) your personal assets and income to the OR or your trustee.

Until all your debts are settled or the time limit for your bankruptcy expires, you're an undischarged bankrupt and as such you must:

- pass on any requests for payment to the OR
- provide any information and attend any interviews or meetings about your financial dealings as requested by the OR
- submit a full list of your assets and liabilities to the OR
- look after and hand over all your assets, together with all books, records, bank statements, insurance policies and other financial papers relating to money or property requested by the OR
- inform the OR about assets acquired and income obtained (such as legacies and redundancy payments) during your bankruptcy

- attend court to explain your situation as required
- refrain from using bank, building society, credit card and other accounts immediately

As an undischarged bankrupt you must not:

- obtain credit (for example, hire purchase agreements) worth more than £500 without first disclosing you are a bankrupt
- make direct payments to your creditors

Failure to co-operate or comply with the above could render you liable for arrest or delay your discharge.

Which of my assets can my trustee seize?

Your business's assets and all your personal property, including your house, car and personal possessions (with some exceptions, such as 'the tools of your trade' and essential domestic and personal items) may be seized by the trustee and sold to pay your debts.

If you own your home, even if it's jointly with a partner, your share will form part of your estate and must be passed to the trustee, who may have to sell it in order to pay your debts. If your family lives with you, it may be possible to put off the sale until after the end of your first year of bankruptcy, allowing you to make other living arrangements. The trustee can retain control of your house for three years, after which, if it hasn't been sold, it may be returned to you.

Your trustee also has certain powers regarding property that doesn't belong to you. For example, if you've sold property to a friend or relative for less than it's worth, the trustee can apply to the court for its seizure.

In addition to seizing property and assets, trustees can ask the court for an Income Payment Order (IPO) which will deduct a proportion of any income you earn to help pay off your debts.

The Enterprise Act 2002 also introduced Income Payment Agreements (IPAs). These are legally binding written agreements between the bankrupt person and the OR or trustee. An IPA requires you to make payments to the trustee for a specified period. This will be enforceable in the same way as an IPO. Both IPOs and IPAs can last for a maximum of three years.

Some assets are exempt from seizure (except in exceptional circumstances), including pensions.

What about my creditors?

The OR or trustee will inform the people to whom you owe money that you're bankrupt, and will organise meetings to discuss and arrange for their payment in full or in part. You may be required to attend these meetings.

Creditors have to make a formal claim for the amount they're owed. The trustee may place an advertisement in your local newspaper asking creditors to submit claims. There's a strict order of precedence for creditor payments:

1 court costs, fees and other expenses of the bankruptcy are always paid first
2 preferential creditors, for example employees, are next on the list
3 unsecured creditors, for example businesses that have supplied goods and services to the failed business, are next. This also includes HM Revenue and Customs (HMRC), which lost its status as a preferential creditor following the introduction of the Enterprise Act 2002
4 Secured creditors—for example, banks and other lending institutions that have a legal interest (called a charge) in a debtor's property—don't have to rely on the trustee for repayment of the debt. They can realise the asset that was provided as security for the debt in order to release the money they require. For example, if your business premises were provided as security, the secured creditor can sell them in order to get the amount of money they need. If there's not enough money from the sale, the secured creditor will have to claim the balance from the trustee as an unsecured creditor. If there's too much money, the balance goes to the trustee for distribution among the other creditors.

If there's any money left over after all the debts are paid, it'll be returned to you and you may apply for the bankruptcy to be annulled (cancelled).

What are the restrictions during bankruptcy?

You remain an undischarged bankrupt until all your debts are settled, or the time limit for your bankruptcy expires. During this time you must not:

- carry on a business (directly or indirectly) in a different name without informing all the people with whom you do business of the name in which you were made bankrupt
- act as a company director or promote, manage or form a limited company without the court's permission
- hold certain public offices
- act as a trustee of any charity or pension fund
- write cheques knowing they will be dishonoured
- obtain an overdraft, or open a new bank or building society account without declaring your bankruptcy
- obtain credit of £500 or more either alone or jointly with another person without disclosing your bankruptcy

You may, however, carry on a business as a sole trader without the express permission of the court—providing you comply with all the restrictions above.

When does a bankruptcy expire?

Anyone made bankrupt will generally be discharged one year after the date of the bankruptcy order. In some cases, the bankruptcy discharge period will be less than one year. This will only occur:

- if you've fully co-operated with the OR and/ or trustee
- if your creditors haven't raised any matters relating to your conduct and affairs which require further investigation
- if the OR has filed a notice at the court stating that the investigation of your affairs has been concluded or they think an investigation is unnecessary. However, the OR can apply to the court to have your discharge postponed if you haven't correctly co-operated or carried out your duties as a bankrupt

You won't be automatically discharged if this is your second bankruptcy in a 15-year period. In this case, you must apply to the court for discharge and you may only do so after five years. Even then, discharge is at the discretion of the court.

What's the effect of discharge?

Discharge will release you from most of your outstanding debts, except debts arising from:

- fraud
- personal injury claims (unless the court agrees)
- non-provable debts (for example, court fines, maintenance payments and student loans)

Once you're discharged, the restrictions listed above no longer apply. You can borrow money and carry on a business as before. You may become a company director unless you are disqualified from doing so by the Department of Business, Enterprise and Regulatory Reform (BERR; see **www.berr.gov.uk**).

What are the rules in Scotland?

The insolvency procedure for individuals in Scotland is very similar to that in England and Wales, although there are some key differences.

- The term for individual insolvency in Scotland is 'sequestration'. To be sequestrated you must owe at least £1,500 and one or more of your creditors must have taken you to court to enforce or demand you repay a debt.
- A creditor to whom you owe more than £1,500 can petition for your sequestration at either a local sheriff's court or the Court of Session in Edinburgh. You can also apply for your own sequestration.
- Initially the court will appoint the Accountant in Bankruptcy to be your trustee (they have a similar role to the OR), after which a private insolvency practitioner may be appointed to act as trustee.
- Sequestration usually lasts three years.

Contact the Accountant in Bankruptcy (**www.aib.gov.uk**) for further information about your own situation.

What are the rules in Northern Ireland?

Bankruptcy in Northern Ireland is largely covered by the Insolvency (Northern Ireland) Order 1989.

- Creditors can make a bankruptcy petition to the High Court if they're owed more than £750, or the debtor can petition themselves.
- In Northern Ireland, Government departments such as HMRC are still preferential debtors and can make a claim on any assets before unsecured creditors.
- Bankrupts will be discharged after two years.

Contact the Insolvency Service Northern Ireland (**www.detini.gov.uk/cgi-bin/ get_builder_page?page**=2182&site=8) for further information.

MAKING IT HAPPEN ✔

In any bankruptcy proceedings, resulting from either a creditor's or your own petition, you should consult a qualified insolvency practitioner. Your solicitor, accountant or business adviser may be able to recommend one. If you're considering declaring yourself bankrupt, you must be very careful about how you conduct your business activities prior to submitting your petition. Continuing to trade knowing that you're insolvent may constitute a criminal offence, so you must seek professional guidance and advice as soon as possible. You may be in a position to consider alternatives to bankruptcy, such as an Individual Voluntary Arrangement (IVA) which is a formal arrangement to repay money owed and is set up by a licensed insolvency practitioner. Seek professional advice to determine whether this might be an option for you. The Government is proposing to introduce a new 'debt relief order' for individuals who have smaller liabilities (the proposed level is £15,000) and also low-value assets. This order won't involve the courts and will discharge the debtor from paying their debts after one year. Legislation isn't currently going through Parliament, however, so this remedy won't be available in the near future.

USEFUL LINKS

Accountant in Bankruptcy:
www.aib.gov.uk
Business Debtline:
www.bdl.org.uk
Citizens Advice Bureau:
www.citizensadvice.org.uk
HM Courts Service:
www.hmcourts-service.gov.uk

Insolvency Service:
www.insolvency.gov.uk
Insolvency Service Northern Ireland:
**www.detini.gov.uk/cgi-bin/
get_builder_page?page=2182&site=8**
Lawyers For Your Business:
**www.lawsociety.org.uk/choosingand-
using/helpyourbusiness/
foryourbusiness.law**

Understanding company insolvency and liquidation

GETTING STARTED

Although the aim of most small businesses is to be profitable, it's a fact of life that many have to be wound up. This actionlist is designed to help you understand the process of insolvency and liquidation for private limited companies. It looks at the relevant legislation and describes the responsibilities and options available to the directors of companies that encounter severe financial difficulties.

It also explains how you can quickly spot that your company is insolvent and outlines the various liquidation procedures that you can use, as well as giving useful tips and sources of further information.

FAQS

What is insolvency?

Insolvency occurs when a business can't meet its debts when they fall due, or when the value of its assets falls below the level of its liabilities. This state of affairs may occur gradually over time due to poor trading, or can happen very suddenly when there's a major change in the company's trading position.

The main legislation covering insolvency is the Insolvency Act 1986 (as amended; most recently by the Enterprise Act 2002). The Insolvency Rules 1986 also apply, as do the Insolvency Regulations 1994. These Acts set a framework for dealing fairly with the assets of the insolvent company and the claims of its various creditors.

What are the common reasons for insolvency?

Companies can become insolvent for many reasons, some that maybe within the directors' control and some that may not, including:

- declining revenues while the costs of the company remain the same
- loss of a major contract
- rapid growth with insufficient working capital
- poor credit-control procedures leading to extended customer credit
- bad debts from customers becoming insolvent

- increased prices from suppliers for raw materials or other major costs such as rent

Poor financial management that results in no, or very poor, regular financial reporting is a frequent cause of insolvency because it prevents the directors from identifying when the problems listed above are becoming acute.

What can alert me to potential problems?

A company's balance sheet is a key indicator of whether the company is slipping towards a difficult financial state, so read it carefully. It shows the net asset value of the company which, if negative, indicates that the company may be insolvent. It also shows the amount of money owed to the company by its customers and owed by the company to its suppliers and other creditors.

What are the directors' responsibilities regarding insolvency?

All directors should be aware that trading while insolvent is illegal. If you discover that you're insolvent, or believe you're about to become insolvent, you must take immediate action. Once a company becomes insolvent, there's a shift in the directors' duty of care from acting for the shareholders to minimising the potential loss to the company's creditors.

MAKING IT HAPPEN
Take action if insolvency looks likely

In the event of serious financial difficulty, it's essential for directors to take immediate action and to retain evidence of this course of action. A director who allows a company to carry on trading in the knowledge (or when they should have known) that there's no reasonable likelihood of avoiding insolvency may be found guilty of wrongful trading. In these circumstances, the directors may become personally liable to make up any losses incurred by trading after that time. Resigning as a director at the time of the insolvency doesn't remove the potential liability for wrongful trading and isn't an answer.

Consider potential alternatives
Once insolvency seems likely, there are a number of routes to consider if you feel that the company could be viable if its current financial pressures were reduced.

Informal creditors' agreement
In this scenario, the company writes to all its creditors to see whether a mutually acceptable agreement can be reached to repay all or some of the existing debt. The directors retain control of the company, but any of the creditors can refuse the proposal or take action that could result in the company being liquidated.

Company voluntary agreement (CVA)
Here, the directors of the company apply to the courts, usually with the help of an insolvency practitioner (a licensed person who specialises in insolvency, authorised by a professional body or the Secretary of State), to set up a formal arrangement with their creditors to make payments under an agreed plan. A creditors' meeting must be held where at least 75% (by value) of the creditors agree to the arrangement. The directors retain control of the company and manage the payment schedule, and the creditors are bound by the terms of the agreement so long as the payment schedule is adhered to.

Administration
Here, an insolvency practitioner is appointed as an administrator and attempts to rescue the company while it's protected from its creditors. An administrator may be appointed by the directors filing the requisite notice at court, by the holder of a floating charge (normally the bank) or by court order. The administrator acts to achieve the best result for all the company's creditors, either by setting up a CVA, by the sale of the business as a going concern, or by the sale of the company's assets. The directors lose control of the company, but may be asked to continue to run it under the administrator's guidance.

Liquidation
Liquidation is a legal process that dismantles a company so that it ceases to exist. It involves realising the company's assets in order to pay off its debts. The company's assets are placed in the hands of an insolvency practitioner to carry out this process. The purpose of liquidation is to ensure that a company's affairs are resolved properly and in an orderly way. The liquidator will then apply to the Registrar of Companies for the firm to be formally dissolved. A company may be wound up either voluntarily or through the courts.

Voluntary liquidation
If a company is facing serious financial trouble, its shareholders or directors may decide that liquidation is the only option. However, a company can only be put into voluntary liquidation by its shareholders. In order to vote for a voluntary liquidation, shareholders must hold a general company meeting and pass a voluntary winding-up resolution, stating that they can't continue to trade due to their liabilities.

There are two types of voluntary liquidation.

1 A Members' Voluntary Liquidation (MVL) may be pursued by solvent companies. This can only be done when a company has sufficient assets to meet all its debts when the shareholders decide to put it into liquidation. The directors sign a

declaration of solvency, which must include a statement that they'll be able to pay off all debts within 12 months from the date of the liquidation. The declaration must also include an account of all the company's assets and liabilities, which must be as up-to-date as possible and be made by the majority of directors within the company. Members must hold a meeting to pass a resolution to wind up the company voluntarily, and to appoint an authorised insolvency, practitioner as liquidator to handle the affairs of the company and distribute assets in order to pay off creditors. If the liquidator discovers that the company is in fact insolvent, they'll immediately have to call a creditors' meeting and the liquidation becomes a Creditors' Voluntary Liquidation.

2 A Creditors' Voluntary Liquidation (CVL) is chosen when the company becomes insolvent or if the majority of directors don't make a solvency declaration. A creditors' meeting must be held to inform them of the company's financial position. Creditors are given the opportunity to nominate an authorised insolvency practitioner as liquidator, and their decision will generally take priority over any nomination made by the company.

Both of these processes require a liquidator to be appointed to take over the control of the company's affairs. The directors are obliged to work with the liquidator and provide all necessary and relevant information and papers requested. The liquidator then oversees the disposal of the company's assets, and distributes any surplus money (after costs) to the creditors. The liquidation process ends when the company is dissolved after its affairs have been fully wound up and a final meeting has been held.

Compulsory liquidation

Compulsory liquidation occurs when a court orders a company into liquidation. This normally happens following a winding-up petition from a creditor, or group of creditors, who must be owed an undisputed debt of at least £750. Occasionally, a company itself may file a winding-up petition, as may its directors or shareholders. Following a court order, an Official Receiver (OR) will be appointed by the court to handle the winding-up of the company and investigate the possible causes of the liquidation.

While it's uncommon, the Government can also petition for a company to be liquidated if it believes it's contravening legislation such as Trading Standards.

Penalties of insolvency

Following the failure of a company, those responsible for overseeing the insolvency procedure (the liquidator, administrator or receiver) have a duty to send a report to the Secretary of State detailing the conduct of all directors in office over the last three years.

After assessing the director's conduct, the Secretary of State then has to make a decision about whether it's in the public's interest to seek a disqualification order against them. Criminal convictions can be made under the Company Directors Disqualification Act 1986, which may lead to disqualification from acting as director for any company for between 2 and 15 years. Directors can also be made personally liable for the company's debts.

How will insolvency affect employees?

When a company becomes insolvent, it may not be able to pay its employees' salaries. Employees have a special status in that they're regarded as preferential creditors and are therefore given priority treatment over other creditors.

Employees can claim some of the specific monies owed to them through the Department for Business, Enterprise and Regulatory Reformy (BERR), including up to eight weeks' pay in arrears, notice period pay, up to six weeks' holiday pay and basic compensation for unfair dismissal. Employees may also be able to claim statutory redundancy pay from the BERR. The payment from the BERR is restricted either to the amount the employee is owed or the maximum weekly limit payment (£310 as at February 2007).

How can insolvency be prevented?

There are ways of preventing insolvency occurring. Many businesses run into financial trouble because of unrealistic assumptions about their cash-flow. It's important to use realistic forecasts and 'what if' scenarios to see what would happen if there was a sudden drop in sales. It's also vital to keep control over credit management, not to offer extended terms if you can't afford to, and not to offer credit to customers who may not be financially sound.

Directors should meet regularly to keep track of current events and ensure that things are running smoothly. Regular monthly management accounts should be used to assess the company's current financial position and to compare its performance against the forecasts.

If financial problems seem likely, the most important thing is to act quickly. For short-term problems it may be possible to improve cash flow by obtaining support from the bank, selling any non-essential assets and recovering debts. You should speak to suppliers and other creditors to informally arrange new payment terms, and be rigorous in chasing customers for outstanding payments. If the company can't meet its debts, it's essential that you get help straight away. Initially you should speak to your accountant, who'll be able to advise on the best way to handle the situation. This could significantly improve the company's chances of survival.

COMMON MISTAKE
You take your eye off the ball

Financial difficulties aren't always a sign of bad management, but it's important to monitor company performance and be aware of the implications should your business face insolvency. The best sources of advice on insolvency are financial advisers, solicitors, accountants, licensed insolvency practitioners or your local Citizens' Advice Bureau.

The Insolvency Service also has an excellent website (address below) which provides a wealth of information about insolvency and what happens to a company that becomes insolvent. Initial consultations are generally free of charge, but be aware that insolvency practitioners' fees can vary greatly, so you'll need to consider all options to make sure you get the best deal. If you're required to sign a personal guarantee to support a bank loan or other form of finance, remember that you'll be personally liable for any debts that aren't fully repaid during the liquidation process.

USEFUL LINKS

Association of Business Recovery
  Professionals:
www.r3.org.uk
Companies House:
www.companies-house.gov.uk
Insolvency Service:
www.insolvency.gov.uk

ESSENTIAL
INFORMATION
DIRECTORY

Business Angels

A14 Angels
Capital & Commercial Finance Ltd,
Whitecroft House 8 Cloister Croft, Royal
Leamington Spa, Warwickshire, CV32 6QQ

Advantage Business Angels
Edgbaston House, 3 Duchess Place,
Edgbaston, Birmingham, B16 8NH
T: +44 (0) 121 456 7940
F: +44 (0) 121 455 8547
www.advantagebusinessangels.com

Alan Bristow Partners
49 Devonshire Close, London, W1N 1LH
T: +44 (0) 207 580 7100
F: +44 (0) 207 580 9609

American Habitats LLC
23 Cornwall Gardens, Flat 4, London,
SW7 4AW
www.americanhabitats.com

Angels for Growth
Harbour Court, Compass Road, North
Harbour, Portsmouth, Hampshire, PO6 4ST
T: +44 (0) 239 265 8268
www.angelsforgrowth.org.uk

Archangel Informal Investments Limited
20 Rutland Square, Edinburgh, EH1 2BB
T: +44 (0) 131 221 9876
F: +44 (0) 131 229 1956
www.archangelsonline.com

Aspen Dene
5 Lower Addiscombe Road, Croydon,
Surrey, CR0 6PQ
T: +44 (0) 208 688 5506
F: +44 (0) 208 688 5507

Auker Rhodes
Royd House, 286 Manningham Lane,
Bradford, West Yorkshire, BD8 7BP
T: +44 (0) 1274 548 000
F: +44 (0) 1274 548 888

Aurora Private Equity Limited
Riverview Business Centre, Centurion
Court, North Esplanade West, Aberdeen,
AB11 5QH
T: +44 (0) 1224 212 900
www.auroraequity.co.uk

Avonmore Developments Ltd
60 Chandos Place, Covent Garden, London,
WC2N 4HG
T: +44 (0) 7752 332 802
F: +44 (0) 207 836 8363
www.avonmoredevelopments.com

Beer & Partners
Head Office, Masters Yard, South Street,
Dorking, Surrey, RH4 2ES
T: +44 (0) 8701 633033
F: +44 (0) 8701 633044
www.beerandpartners.com

Braveheart Ventures Ltd
Algo Business Centure, Glenearn Road,
Perth, PH2 0NJ
T: +44 (0) 1738 587555
F: +44 (0) 1738 587666
www.braveheart-ventures.co.uk

Business Link Northamptonshire
Northamptonshire Chamber, Royal Pavilion,
Summerhouse Road, Northampton,
NN3 6BJ
T: +44 (0) 1604 643 777
F: +44 (0) 1604 670 362

c2Ventures - Home Counties
Ashridge House, 121 High Street,
Berkhamsted, Hertfordshire, HP4 2DJ
T: +44 (0) 7050 263 500

c2Ventures - London
1 St Andrews Hill, London, EC4V 5BY
T: +44 (0) 7050 263 500
F: +44 (0) 870 706 2199
www.c2ventures.com

Cambridge Angels
Library House, Kett House, Station Road,
Cambridge, CB1 2JY
www.cambridgeangels.net

Cambridge Business Services Limited
Centenary House, St. Mary's Street,
Huntingdon, Cambridgeshire, PE29 3PE
T: +44 (0) 1480 846 414
F: +44 (0) 1480 846 478

Capital and General Services
The Belfry Flat, Scotney Castle,
Lamberhurst, Kent, TN3 8JN
T: +44 (0) 1892 890 627
F: +44 (0) 1892 890 995

Cavendish Management Resources
31 Harley Street, London, W1G 9QS
T: +44 (0) 207 636 1744
F: +44 (0) 207 636 5639
www.cmruk.com

Chamber of Commerce Herefordshire & Worcestershire
Enterprise House, Castle Street, Worcester,
Worcestershire, WR1 3EN
T: +44 (0)1299 861 284
F: +44 (0) 8700 568 800

Credo Corporate Finance
33 Margaret Street, London, W1G 0JD
T: +44 (0) 207 291 3200
F: +44 (0) 207 291 3290
www.credogroup.com

D & L Finance
12 Station Road, Kenilworth, Warwickshire,
CV8 1JJ
T: +44 (0) 1926 853 390
F: +44 (0) 1926 863 323
www.dandlgroup.com

DCX Developement Capital Exchange
4 Moggie Lane, Adlington, Macclesfield,
Sk10 4NY
T: +44 (0) 8707 420 998
F: +44 (0) 1625 859 142
www.dcxworld.com

Denbarb Limited
21 Besbury Close, Dorridge, West Midlands,
B93 8NT
T: +44 (0) 1564 772 657

Dunbar Bank Plc
9-15 Sackville Street, London, W1A 2JP
T: +44 (0) 207 437 7844

Dunstable Management Group
PO Box 18, Dereham, Norfolk, NR20 4UL
T: +44 (0) 1362 637 948
F: +44 (0) 1362 637 581
www.dunstablemanagement.co.uk

East Midlands Business Angels Ltd
PO Box 333, Newark, Nottinghamshire,
NG23 6FQ
T: +44 (0) 1636 708 717
F: +44 (0) 1636 708 717
www.embaltd.co.uk

Entrust
Portman House, Portland Road, Newcastle
upon Tyne, NE2 1AQ
T: +44 (0) 191 244 4000
F: +44 (0) 191 244 4001
www.entrust.co.uk

Envestors LLP
1 Lancaster Place, London, WC2E 7ED
T: +44 (0) 207 240 0202
F: +44 (0) 207 168 8017
www.envestors.co.uk

Equity Link Bedfordshire and Luton
2 Railton Road, Woburn Road Industrial
Estate, Kempston, Bedfordshire, MK42 7PN

Equity Link Cambridge
The Business Centre, Station Road, Histon,
Cambridge, CB4 9LO
T: +44 (0) 345 882 255
F: +44 (0) 1223 235 383

Equity Link Essex
Alexandra House, 36a Church Street, Great
Baddow, Chelmsford, Essex, CM2 7HY
T: +44 (0) 7799 881 577
F: +44 (0) 1245 241 400
www.bl4e.co.uk

Equity Link Hertfordshire
Business Link Hertfordshire, 45 Grosvenor
Road, St. Albans, Hertfordshire, AL1 3AW
T: +44 (0) 1727 813 495
F: +44 (0) 1727 813 403
www.exemplas.com

Equity Link Kent
26 Kings Hill Avenue, Kingshill, West
Malling, Kent, ME19 4AE
T: +44 (0) 1732 878 000
F: +44 (0) 1732 874 818
www.equitylink.exemplas.com

Equity Link London North West
Kirkfield House, 118-120 Station Road,
Harrow, Middlesex, HA1 2RL
T: +44 (0) 208 901 5000
F: +44 (0) 208 901 5007

Equity Link Norfolk and Waveney
St Andrews House, St Andrews Street,
Norwich, Norfolk, NR2 4TP
T: +44 (0) 1603 218 218
F: +44 (0) 1603 218 201

Equus Capital
St Johns Innovation Centre, Cowley Road,
Cambridge, Cambs, CB4 0WS
T: +44 (0) 1223 421 228
www.equuscapital.co.uk

FirstCapital
Elsinore House, 77 Fulham Palace Road,
London, W6 8JA
T: +44 (0) 208 563 1563
F: +44 (0) 208 563 2767
www.firstcap.co.uk

Great Eastern Investment Forum
Richmond House, 16-20 Regent Street,
Cambridge, CB2 1DB
T: +44 (0) 1223 357 131
F: +44 (0) 1223 720 258
www.geif.co.uk

Halo
5th Floor, 40 Linenhall Street, Belfast,
BT2 8 BA
T: +44 (0) 2890 331 136
F: +44 (0) 2890 331 137
www.haloni.com

Hotbed Limited
Shirwell Crescent, Lakeside, Furzton, Milton
Keynes, Buckinghamshire, MK4 1GA
T: +44 (0) 1908 523 440
F: +44 (0) 1908 523 459
www.hotbed.uk.com

IDJ Ltd
81 Piccadilly, London, W1J 8HY
T: +44 (0) 207 355 1200
F: +44 (0) 207 495 1149
www.idj.co.uk

Intellect
20 Red Lion Street, London, WC1R 4QN
T: +44 (0)7887 520 146 mobile
F: +44 (0)207 404 4119

Isis Angels Network
Ewert House, Ewert Place, Summertown,
Oxford, OX2 7DD
T: +44 (0) 1865 272 411
F: +44 (0) 1865 272 412
www.isis-innovation.com

Ivo Associates
Chestnut House, 1c Sheepfold, St. Ives,
Cambridgeshire, PE27 5FY
T: +44 (0) 1480 390 648
F: +44 (0) 1480 390 648
www.ivo-associates.co.uk

Kingston Business Angels
3 Kingsmill Business Park, Chapel Mill
Road, Kingston upon Thames, KT1 3GZ
T: +44 (0) 208 545 2875
F: +44 (0) 208 543 8748
www.kingstoninnovation.com

Kurt Nybroe-Nielsen
171 Berkeley Tower, 48 Westferry Circus,
London, London, GB-E14 8RP

Latitude LLP
68 Charlotte Street, London, W1T 4QF
T: +44 (0) 207 637 3330
F: +44 (0) 207 636 3104
www.latitude.co.uk

LINC Scotland
19 St. Vincent Place, Glasgow, G1 2DT
T: +44 (0) 141 221 3321
F: +44 (0) 141 221 2909
www.lincscot.co.uk

London Business Angels
New City Court, 20 St Thomas Street,
London, SE1 9RS
T: +44 (0) 207 089 2327
F: +44 (0) 207 089 2301
www.lbangels.co.uk

London Partnership
4 Creed Court, 5 Ludgate Hill, London,
EC4M 7AA
T: +44 (0) 207 248 0656
F: +44 (0) 207 213 0591

MBAngels
18 Convent Close, Hitchin, Hertfordshire,
SG5 1QN

MBI MBO Limited
20 Garrick Street, London, WC2E 9AX
T: +44 (0) 207 664 7801
F: +44 (0) 207 664 6396

Mercantile 100
Kidsons Impey Chartered Accontants,
Beckenridge House, 274 Sauchiehall Street,
Glasgow, G2 3EH
T: +44 (0) 141 307 5000
F: +44 (0) 141 307 5005
www.kidsons.co.uk

Minerva Business Angel Network
The Venture Centre, Sir Willliam Lyons
Road, Coventry, CV4 7EZ
T: +44 (0) 2476 323 123
F: +44 (0) 2476 323 001
www.minerva.uk.net

MMC Ventures Ltd
Braywick House, Gregory Place,
Kensington, London, W8 4NG
T: +44 (0) 207 361 0211
F: +44 (0) 207 938 2259
www.mmcventures.com

Morpheus Consulting
1 Hadham, Mill Cottages, Hertford,
Hertfordshire, SG10 6EY
T: +44 (0) 1279 843 302
F: +44 (0) 1279 843 302
www.morpheusgroup.com

New Sarum Enterprises
8 Centre One, Lysander Way, Salisbury,
Wiltshire, SP4 6B
T: +44 (0) 1722 415 026
F: +44 (0) 1722 415 028

Northwest Business Angels
Northwest Development Agency, PO Box 37
Centre Park, Warrington, Cheshire,
WA1 1XB
T: +44 (0) 1925 400 301/2
F: +44 (0) 1925 400 400
www.techinvest.org.uk

Oxford Early Investments
Oxford Centre for Innovation, Mill Street,
Oxford, OX2 0JX
T: +44 (0) 1865 811 120
F: +44 (0) 1865 209 044
www.oxin.co.uk

Oxford Innovation
Oxford Centre for Innovation, Mill Street,
Oxford, Oxon, OX2 0JA
www.oxin.co.uk

Oxfordshire Investment Opportunity Network
Oxford Centre For Innovation, Mill Street,
Oxford, OX2 0JX
T: +44 (0) 1865 811 143
F: +44 (0) 1865 209 044
www.oion.co.uk

P3 Capital
Hume House, Burleigh, GL5 2PW
T: +44 (0) 8453 455 288
www.p3capital.com

Propeller Capital Limited
Milford Suite 1, Millpool House, Mill Lane,
Godalming, Surrey, GU7 1EY
T: +44 (0) 1483 869 898
F: +44 (0) 1483 869 898

SE Private Equity
Greenacre Court, Station Road, Burgess Hill,
West Sussex, RH15 9DS
T: +44 (0) 1444 259 259
F: +44 (0) 1444 259 188

Silverstone Investment Network
Silverstone Circuit, Silverstone,
Northamtonshire, NN12 8GX
T: +44 (0) 1327 856 156
F: +44 (0) 1327 856 001
www.silverstoneinvest.co.uk

Solent Business Angels
Deepsprings, Emsworth, Hampshire,
PO10 8RL
T: +44 (0) 1243 373 959
F: +44 (0) 1243 373 959

South East Capital Alliance
Devonshire Place, New Road, Crowthorne,
Berkshire, RG45 6NA
T: +44 (0) 1344 758 548
F: +44 (0) 1344 762 002
www.financesoutheast.co.uk

St. Pauls Corporate Finance Ltd
8 Creed Lane, London, EC4V 5BR
T: +44 (0) 207 329 3639
F: +44 (0) 207 248 0809

SWAIN
Argentum, 510 Bristol Business House,
Coldharbour Lane, Bristol, BS16 1EJ
T: +44 (0) 8700 606 560
F: +44 (0) 1179 063 635
www.swain.org.uk

Tetheringstones Ltd
18 Convent Close, Hitchin, Hertfordshire,
SG5 1QN
T: +44 (0) 1462 458 634
F: +44 (0) 1462 458 634

Thames Valley Investment Network
T Wing, Crowthorne Business Estate, Old
Wokingham Road, Crowthorne, Berkshire,
RG456AW
T: +44 (0) 1344 753 365
F: +44 (0) 1344 751 601
www.tvin.co.uk

The Enterprise Consortium Ltd.
253 High Street, Henley-in-Arden,
Warwickshire, B95 5BG
T: +44 (0) 1564 794 898
F: +44 (0) 870 708 580

The Enterprise Forum
45 The Close, Norwich, NR1 4EG

The Henley Business Partnership Ltd
31 Valley Road, Henley on Thames,
Oxfordshire, RG9 1RL
T: +44 (0) 1491 575 616
F: +44 (0) 1491 411 076

The Tinsley Lockhart Group
66-68 Thistle Street, Edinburgh, EH2 1EN
T: +44 (0) 131 225 5000
F: +44 (0) 131 225 2000
www.inform.org.uk

The Venture Site Limited
5 The Maltings, Walkern, Hertfordshire,
SG2 7NP
T: +44 (0) 7092 161 866
F: +44 (0) 7092 396 143
www.venturesite.co.uk

Tyne & Wear Enterprise Trust Ltd (Entrust)
Portman House, Portland Road,
Newcastle-upon-tyne, NE2 1AQ
T: +44 (0) 191 244 4000
F: +44 (0) 191 244 4001
www.entrust.co.uk

Winsec Corporate Exchange
1 The Centre, Church Road, Tiptree,
Colchester, Essex, CO5 0HF
T: +44 (0) 1621 810 263/815 047
F: +44 (0) 1621 817 965
www.winsec.co.uk

Xenos - The Wales Business Angels Network
Oakleigh House, Park Place, Cardiff,
CF10 3DQ
T: +44 (0) 2920 338 144
F: +44 (0) 2920 338 101
www.xenos.co.uk

Xenva Ltd
79 George Street, Ryde, Isle of Wight,
PO33 2JF
T: 44 (0) 1983 817 017
F: 44 (0) 1983 817 001
www.xenva.com

Yorkshire Association of Business Angels

1 Hornbeam House, Hornbeam Park, Hookstone Road, Harrogate, North Yorkshire, HG2 8QT
T: +44 (0) 1423 810 149
F: +44 (0) 1423 810 086
www.yaba.org.uk

Corporate Venturers

BAE Systems

Warwick House, Farnborough Aerospace Centre, Farnbrough, Hampshire, GU14 6YU
T: +44 (0) 1252 384 089
www.baesystems.com

BT Group

HWH 598, PO Box 400, London, N18 1XU
T: +44 (0) 207 777 6018
F: +44 (0) 207 777 6019

BTG PLC

10 Fleet Place, Limeburner Lane, London, EC4M 7SB
T: +44 (0) 207 575 0000
F: +44 (0) 207 575 0010
www.btgplc.com

Cable & Wireless plc

124 Theobalds Rd, London, WC1X 8RX
T: +44 (0) 207 315 5142
www.cw.com

Cisco Systems

9-11 New Square, Bedfont Lakes, Feltham, Middlesex, TW14 8HA
T: +44 (0) 208 824 1000
F: +44 (0) 208 824 1001
www.cisco.com

IBM Global Financing

PO Box 41, North Harbour, Portsmouth, Hampshire, PO6 3AU
T: +44 (0) 23 92 561 525
F: +44 (0) 870 870 8760
www-03.ibm.com/financing/uk

Imperial College Innovations

11-12 Electical & Electronic Engineering Building, Imperial College London, South Kensington Campus Exhibition Road, London, SW7 2AZ
T: +44 (0) 207 581 4949

Intel Capital c/o Intel Semiconductor

33 St. James' Square, London, SW1Y 4JS
T: +44 (0) 207 661 8043
www.intel.com/capital

Invensys plc

Portland House, Stag Place, London, SW1E 5BF
T: +44 (0) 207 8343 848
www.invensys.com

LF Europe Ltd

85 Wimpole Street, London, W1G 9RJ
T: +44 (0) 207 224 3883
F: +44 (0) 207 224 0110
www.lfvc.com

Lloyds TSB Strategic Ventures

48 Chiswell Street, London, EC1Y 4XX
T: +44 (0) 207 522 5018
F: +44 (0) 207 522 5925
www.lloydstsb.co.uk

Logica plc

Strephenson House, 75 Hamstead, London, NW1 2PL
T: +44 (0) 207 637 9111
F: +44 (0) 207 468 7006
www.logicacmg.com

Microsoft Limited

Microsoft Campus, Thames Valley Park, Reading, RG6 1WG
T: +44 (0) 1189 093 632
www.microsoft.com

Reuters Group PLC

85 Fleet Street, London, EC4P 4AJ
T: +44 (0) 207 250 1122
F: +44 (0) 207 353 3002

RM plc

Unit 140 Milton Park, Abingdon, Oxon, OX14 4SE
T: +44 (0) 870 9200 200
www.rm.com

Rolls-Royce plc

PO Box 31, Derby, DE24 8BJ
T: +44 (0) 1332 248 101
F: +44 (0) 1332 245 315
www.rolls-royce.com

UK Steel Enterprise Limited
The Innovation Centre, 217 Portobello,
Sheffield, South Yorkshire, S1 4DP
T: +44 (0) 1142 731 612
F: +44 (0) 1142 701 390
www.uksteelenterprise.co.uk

UK Steel Enterprise Ltd
The Innovation Centre, 217 Portbello,
Sheffield, S1 4DP
T: +44 (0) 114 224 2424
F: +44 (0) 114 270 1390
www.uksteelenterprise.co.uk

UK Steel Enterprise Ltd Scotland
Grovewood Business Centre, Strathclyde
Business Park, Bellshill, Lanarkshire,
ML4 3NQ
T: +44 (0) 1698 845 045
F: +44 (0) 1698 845 123
www.uksteelenterprise.co.uk

UK Steel Enterprise Ltd Wales
Titan House, Cardiff Bay Business Centre,
Ocean Park Lewis Road, Cardiff, CF24 5BS
T: +44 (0) 2920 471 122
F: +44 (0) 2920 492 622
www.uksteelenterprise.co.uk

UK Steel Enterprise North of England
The Innovation Centre, Vienna Court,
Kirkleatham Business Park, Redcar,
TS10 5SH
T: +44 (0) 1642 777 888
F: +44 (0) 1642 777 999
www.uksteelenterprise.co.uk

Private Equity Investors
Accel Partners
16 St James's Street, London, SW1A 1ER
T: +44 (0) 207 170 1000
F: +44 (0) 207 170 1099
www.accel.com

Alliance Trusts
Meadow House, 64 Reform Street, Dundee,
DD1 9YP
T: +44 (0) 1382 201 700
F: +44 (0) 1382 225 133
www.alliancetrusts.com

Charterhouse Capital Partners LLP
Warwick Court, Paternoster Square, St
Paul's, London, EC4M 7DX
T: +44 (0) 207 334 5300
www.charterhouse.co.uk

Cinven Limited
Warwick Court, Paternoster Square, London,
EC4M 7AG
T: +44 (0) 207 661 3333
F: +44 (0) 207 661 3888
www.cinven.com

Dunedin Capital Partners Ltd
10 George Street, Edinburgh, EH2 2DW
T: +44 (0) 131 225 6699
F: +44 (0) 131 718 2300
www.dunedin.com

Equity Partnership Investment Company
EPIC Private Equity, 22 Billiter Street,
London, EC3M 2RY
T: +44 (0) 207 553 2341
www.epicip.com

Exponent Private Equity LLP
12 Henrietta Street, London, WC2E 8LH
T: +44 (0) 207 845 8520
F: +44 (0) 207 845 8521
www.exponentpe.com

Goldman Sachs International
Peterborough Court, 133 Fleet Street,
London, EC4A 2BB
T: +44 (0) 207 774 1000
F: +44 (0) 207 774 4477
www.gs.com/pia

Granville Baird Capital Partners Ltd.
Mint House, 77 Mansell Street, London,
E1 8AF
T: +44 (0) 207 667 8400
F: +44 (0) 207 667 8481
www.bcpe.co.uk

HgCapital
Third Floor, Minerva House, 3-5 Montague
Close, London, SE1 9BB
T: +44 (0) 207 089 7888
F: +44 (0) 207 089 7999
www.hgcapital.net

Indigo Capital Limited
25 Watling Street, London, EC4M 9BR
T: +44 (0) 207 710 7800
F: +44 (0) 207 710 7777
www.indigo-capital.com

Intermediate Capital Group PLC
20 Old Broad Street, London, EC2N 1DP
T: +44 (0) 207 628 9898
F: +44 (0) 207 628 2268
www.icgplc.com

Langholm Capital LLP
16 Charles II Street, 5th Floor, London,
SW1Y 4QU
T: +44 (0) 207 747 7747
F: +44 (0) 207 747 7748
www.langholm.com

Legal and General Ventures Ltd
Bucklersbury House, 3 Queen Victoria
Street, London, EC4N 8NH
T: +44 (0) 207 528 6456
F: +44 (0) 207 528 6444
www.legalandgeneralventures.com

Lehman Brothers
25 Bank St, 30th Floor, London, E14 5LE
T: +44 (0) 207 102 1000
www.lehman.com

Lyceum Capital LLP
Burleigh House, 357 The Strand, London,
WC2R 0HS
T: +44 (0) 207 632 2480
F: +44 (0) 207 836 3138
www.lyceumcapital.co.uk

Matrix Private Equity Partners Limited
1 Jermyn Street, London, SW1Y 4UH
T: +44 (0) 207 925 3300
F: +44 (0) 207 925 3285
www.matrixgroup.co.uk

Merrill Lynch Global Private Equity
Ropemaker Place, 25 Ropemaker Street,
London, EC2Y 9LY
T: +44 (0) 20 7628 1000
F: +44 (0)20 7867 2867
http://gmi.ml.com/private/index.asp

Momentum Capital
42 Brook Street, London, W1K 5DB
T: +44 (20) 7958 9006
F: +44 (20) 7958 9090
www.momentum-capital.com

Montagu Private Equity LLP
2 More London Riverside, London, SE1 2AP
T: +44 (0) 207 336 9955
F: +44 (0) 207 336 9961
www.montagu.com

Montagu Private Equity LLP
15th Floor, St James's House, Charlotte
Street, Manchester, M1 4DZ
T: +44 (0) 161 233 6660
F: +44 (0) 161 233 6666
www.montagu.com

Platina Finance Limited
40 George Street, London, W1U 7DW
T: +44 (0) 207 467 3190
F: +44 (0) 207 467 3195
www.platinafinance.com

Pricoa Capital Group Ltd
47 King William Street, 6th Floor, London,
EC4R 9JD
T: +44 (0) 207 621 8421
F: +44 (0) 207 621 8448
www.pricoacapital.com

Rhone Capital LLC
5 Princes Gate, 3rd Floor, London, SW7 1QJ
T: +44 (0) 207 761 1100
F: +44 (0) 207 761 1111
www.rhonegroup.com

Risk Capital Partners
28-30 Litchfield Street, London, WC2H 9NJ
T: +44 (0) 207 379 8580
F: +44 (0) 207 379 8581
www.riskcapitalpartners.co.uk

Royal London Private Equity
55 Gracechurch Street, London, EC3V 0UF
T: +44 (0) 207 506 6717
F: +44 (0) 207 506 6528
www.rlam.co.uk

Stirling Square Capital Partners
Liscarton House (4th Floor), 127-131 Sloane Street, London, SW1X 9AX
T: +44 (0) 207 808 4130
F: +44 (0) 207 808 4131
www.stirlingsquare.com

TDR Capital LLP
One Stanhope Gate, London, W1K 1AF
T: +44 (0) 207 399 4200
F: +44 (0) 207 399 4242
www.tdrcapital.com

Secondary Fund Managers
Coller Capital
33 Cavendish Square, London, W1G 0TT
T: +44 20 7631 8566
F: +44 20 7631 8555
www.collercapital.com

Pomona Capital
16 Hanover Square, London, W1S 1HT
T: +44 (0) 207 408 9433
F: +44 (0) 207 408 9434
www.pomonacapital.com

Venture Capitalists
3i Aberdeen
70 Queens Road, Aberdeen, AB15 4YE
T: +44 (0) 1224 638 666
F: +44 (0) 1224 641 460
www.3i.com

3i Birmingham
Trinity Park, Birmingham, B37 7ES
T: +44 (0) 1217 823 131
F: +44 (0) 1217 826 161
www.3i.com

3i Bristol
1 The Square, Temple Quay, Bristol, BS1 6DG
T: +44 (0) 8702 433 131
F: +44 (0) 1179 279 433
www.3i.com

3i Cambridge
121 Cambridge Science Park, Milton Road, Cambridge, CB4 0FZ
T: +44 (0) 1223 420 031
F: +44 (0) 1223 420 459
www.3i.com

3i Group PLC
16 Palace Street, London, SW1E 5JD
T: +44 (0) 207 928 3131
F: +44 (0) 207 928 0058
www.3i.com

3i Manchester
The Observatory, Chapel Walks, Manchester, M2 1HL
T: +44 (0) 1618 393 131
F: +44 (0) 1618 339 182
www.3i.com

Aberdeen Murray Johnstone Private Equity
10 Queens Terrace, Aberdeen, AB10 1YG
T: +44 (0) 1224 631 999
F: +44 (0) 1224 425 916
www.aberdeen-asset.com/privateequity

Aberdeen Murray Johnstone Private Equity - Birmingham
1 Cornwall Street, Birmingham, B3 2JN
T: +44 (0) 121 236 1222
F: +44 (0) 121 233 4628
www.aberdeen-asset.com/privateequity

Aberdeen Murray Johnstone Private Equity - Glasgow
Sutherland House, 149 St Vincent Street, Glasgow, G2 5NW
T: +44 (0) 141 306 7400
F: +44 (0) 141 306 7401
www.aberdeen-asset.com/privateequity

Aberdeen Murray Johnstone Private Equity - Inverness
Ballantyne House, 4th Floor, 84 Academy Street, Inverness, IV1 1LU
T: +44 (0) 1463 717 214
F: +44 (0) 1463 717 211
www.aberdeen-asset.com/privateequity

Aberdeen Murray Johnstone Private Equity - Leeds
3 The Embankment, Sovereign Street, Leeds, LS1 4BJ
T: +44 (0) 113 242 2644
F: +44 (0) 113 242 2640
www.aberdeen-asset.com/privateequity

Aberdeen Murray Johnstone Private Equity - London
One Bow Churchyard, London, EC4M 9HH
T: +44 (0) 207 463 6452
F: +44 (0) 207 463 6595
www.aberdeen-asset.com/privateequity

Aberdeen Murray Johnstone Private Equity - Manchester
St James's House, 7 Charlotte Street,
Manchester, M1 4DZ
T: +44 (0) 161 233 3500
F: +44 (0) 161 233 3550
www.aberdeen-asset.com/privateequity

Abingworth Management Ltd
Princes House, 38 Jermyn St, London,
SW1Y 6DN
T: +44 (0) 207 534 1500
F: +44 (0) 207 287 0480
www.abingworth.com

Abingworth Management Ltd
Wellington House, East Road, Cambridge,
CB1 1BH
T: +44 (0) 1223 451 032
F: +44 (0) 1223 451 100
www.abingworth.com

Acacia Capital Partners
7 Cavendish Square, London, W1G 0PE
T: +44 (0) 207 299 7399
F: +44 (0) 207 299 7390
www.acaciacp.com

Acorn Capital Partners
Bollin House, Riverside Park, Wilmslow,
Cheshire, SK9 1DP
T: +44 (0) 870 122 5420
F: +44 (0) 870 122 5421
www.acorncapital.co.uk

Adams Street Partners
20 Grosvenor Place, London, SW1X 7HN
T: +44 (0) 207 823 0640
F: +44 (0) 207 823 0659
www.adamsstreetpartners.com

Add Partners Ltd
53 Davies Street, London, W1K 5JH
T: +44 (0) 20 7152 6902
F: +44 (0) 20 7152 6903
www.addpartners.com

Advantage Capital Ltd
37 Harley Street, London, UK, W1G 8QG
T: +44 (0) 207 436 6022
F: +44 (0) 207 636 7890
www.advantagecapital.co uk

Advantage Early Growth Fund
PO Box 11679, Tamworth, B78 2YD
T: +44 (0) 1530 222009
F: +44 (0) 1530 222669
www.aegf.co.uk

Advent International (Europe)
123 Buckingham Palace Road, London,
SW1W 9SL
T: +44 (0) 207 333 0800
F: +44 (0) 207 333 0801
www.adventinternational.com

Advent International plc
111 Buckingham Palace Road, London,
SW1W 0SR
T: +44 (0) 207 333 0800
F: +44 (0) 207 333 0801
www.adventinternational.com

Advent Venture Partners LLP
25 Buckingham Gate, London, SW1E 6LD
T: +44 (0) 207 932 2100
F: +44 (0) 207 828 1474
www.adventventures.com

Ahli United Bank (UK) Plc
35 Portman Square, London, W1H 6LR
T: +44 (0) 207 487 6500
F: +44 (0) 207 487 6808
www.ahliunited.com

Albany Venture Managers Ltd
Forth House, 28 Rutland Square, Edinburgh,
EH1 2BW
T: +44 (0) 1312 216 510
F: +44 (0) 1312 216 511
www.albanyventures.co.uk

Albemarle Private Equity Ltd
1 Albermarle St, London, W1X 3HF
T: +44 (0) 207 491 9555
F: +44 (0) 207 491 7245

Alchemy Partners LLP
20 Bedfordbury, London, WC2N 4BL
T: +44 (0) 207 240 9596
F: +44 (0) 207 240 9594
www.alchemypartners.co.uk

Alliance Fund Managers Ltd
Merseyside Special Investment Fund, 5th
Floor, Cunard Building Pier Head,
Liverpool, L3 1DS
T: +44 (0) 151 236 4040
F: +44 (0) 151 236 3060
www.msif.co.uk

Alta Berkeley Venture Partners
9-10 Savile Row, London, W1S 3PF
T: +44 (0) 207 440 0229
F: +44 (0) 207 734 6711
www.alta-berkeley.com

Amadeus Capital Partners Limited
Mount Pleasant House, 2 Mount Pleasant,
Huntingdon Road, Cambridge, CB3 0RN
T: +44 (0)1223 707 000
F: +44 (0)1223 707 070
www.amadeuscapital.com

Amadeus Capital Partners Ltd
16 St James's Street, London, SW1A 1ER
T: +44 (0) 207 024 6900
F: +44 (0) 207 024 6999
www.amadeuscapital.com

Angle Technology Ltd
Surrey Technology Centre, The Surrey
Research Park, Guildford, GU2 7YG
T: +44 (0) 1483 295 830
F: +44 (0) 1483 295 836
www.angletechnology.com

Apax Partners Worldwide LLP
15 Portland Place, London, W1B 1PT
T: +44 (0) 207 872 6300
F: +44 (0) 207 666 6441
www.apax.com

Argus Capital Group
Academy House, 36 Poland Street, London,
W1F 7LU
T: +44 (0) 207 439 0088
F: +44 (0) 207 439 0092
www.arguscapitalgroup.com

**Arts Alliance Advisors part of Hegh
Capital Partners**
60 Sloane Avenue, London, SW3 3DD
T: +44 (0) 207 361 7700
F: +44 (0) 207 594 4004
www.artsalliance.com

Atlas Venture Ltd
55 Grosvenor street, London, W1K 3BW
T: +44 (0) 20 7529 4444
F: +44 (0) 20 7529 4455
www.atlasventure.com

August Equity Ltd
10 Bedford Street, Covent Garden, London,
WC2E 9HE
T: +44 (0) 207 632 8200
F: +44 (0) 207 632 8201
www.augustcapital.co.uk

Avlar BioVentures Ltd
Highfield Court, Church Lane, Madingley,
Cambridge, CB23 8AG
T: +44 (0) 1954 211515
F: +44 (0) 1954 211516
www.avlar.com

AXA Venture Capital Ltd
Dilke House, 1 Malet St, London, WC1E 7JN
T: +44 (0) 870 909 6333
F: +44 (0) 870 133 6872
www.ccfund.co.uk

axiomlab plc
Yorkshire Technology Park, Armitage
Bridge, Leeds, Yorkshire, HD4 7NR
T: +44 (0) 8452 008 340
F: +44 (0) 8452 008 341
www.axiomlab.com

Bain Capital Ltd
Devonshire House, Mayfair Place, London,
W1J 8AJ
T: +44 (0) 207 514 5252
F: +44 (0) 207 514 5250
www.baincapital.co.uk

Bank of Scotland (Structured Acquisition and Int. Finance)
Level 7, 155 Bishopsgate, London, EC2M 3YB
T: +44 (0) 207 012 9418
F: +44 (0) 207 012 9433
www.bankofscotland.co.uk

Bank of Scotland Equity Investments
Corporate Banking, New Uberior House, 11 Earl Grey Street, Edinburgh, EH3 9BN
T: +44 (0) 131 659 0565
F: +44 (0) 131 659 0596
www.bankofscotland.co.uk

Barclays Private Equity Ltd
5 The North Colonnade 3rd Floor, Canary Wharf, London, E14 4BB
T: +44 (0) 207 512 9900
F: +44 (0) 207 653 5350
www.barclays-private-equity.com

Barclays Private Equity Ltd Birmingham
4th Floor, Bank House, 8 Cherry Street, Birmingham, B2 5AD
T: +44 (0) 121 631 4220
F: +44 (0) 121 631 1071
www.barclays-private-equity.com

Barclays Private Equity Ltd Manchester
55 King Street, Manchester, M2 4LQ
T: +44 (0) 161 214 0800
F: +44 (0) 161 214 0805
www.barclays-private-equity.com

Barclays Private Equity Ltd Reading
4th Floor, Apex Plaza, Forbury Road, Reading, RG1 1AX
T: +44 (0) 1189 394 796
F: +44 (0) 1189 394 695
www.barclays-private-equity.com

Barclays Ventures
Third Floor, 50 Pall Mall, London, SW1Y 5AX
T: +44 (0) 207 441 4213
F: +44 (0) 207 441 4212
www.barclaysventures.com

Baring Communications Equity (Emerging Europe) Channel Islan
P.O. Box 255 Trafalgar Court, Les Banquest, St. Peter Port, Guernesey, GY1 3QL
www.bcee.net

Baring Private Equity Partners Limited
33 Cavendish Square, London, W1G 0BQ
T: +44 (0) 207 290 5000
F: +44 (0) 207 290 5020
www.bpep.com

BC Partners Ltd
43-45 Portman Square, London, W1H 6DA
T: +44 (0) 207 009 4800
F: +44 (0) 207 009 4899
www.bcpartners.com

Beck Group Ventures
2nd Floor, Berkeley Square House, London, W1J 6BD
T: +44 (0) 207 887 1591
F: +44 (0) 207 887 1571
www.the-beck-group.com

Benchmark Capital
20 Balderton Street, London, W1K 6TL
T: +44 (0) 207 016 6800
F: +44 (0) 207 016 6810
www.benchmark.com

Berengia Ltd
39 Earlham Street, London, WC2H 9LT
T: +44 (0) 207 845 7820
F: +44 (0) 207 845 7821
www.berengia.co.uk

Bestport Ventures LLP
29 Gloucester Place, London, W1U 8HX
T: +44 (0) 207 487 2555
F: +44 (0) 207 487 5535
www.bestport.co.uk

Birmingham Technology (Venture Capital) Ltd
Aston Science Park, Faraday Wharf, Holt Street, Birmingham, B7 4BB
T: +44 (0) 121 260 6000
F: +44 (0) 121 250 3567
www.astonsciencepark.co.uk

Blackstone Group International Limited
40 Berkeley Square, London, W1J 5AL
T: +44 (0) 207 451 4000
F: +44 (0) 207 451 4120
www.blackstone.com

Bloomsbury Bioseed Fund
3rd Floor, Queens House, 180 Tottenham
Court Road, London, W1T 7PD
T: +44 (0) 207 907 1448
www.bbsf.org

BNP Private Equity
10 Harewood Avenue, London, NW1 6AA
T: +44 (0) 207 595 2000
F: +44 (0)20 7595 2555
www.bnpparibas.com

Botts & Company Ltd
41-44 Great Queen Street, London,
WC2B 5AA
T: +44 (0) 207 841 1550
F: +44 (0) 207 242 5160
www.bottscompany.com

Bowmark Capital
3 St James's Square, London, SW1Y 4JU
T: +44 (0) 207 189 9000
F: +44 (0) 207 189 9044
http://www.bowmark.com/

BP Marsh & Partners PLC
Granville House, 132 Sloane St, London,
SW1X 9AX
T: +44 (0)20 7730 2626
F: +44 (0)20 7823 5225
www.bpmarsh.co.uk

Brainspark plc
The Lightwell 12/16 Laystall Street,
Clerkenwell, London, EC1R 4PA
T: +44 (0) 207 843 6600
F: +44 (0) 207 843 6601
www.brainspark.com

Bridgepoint Capital
30 Warwick Street, London, W1B 5AL
T: +44 (0) 207 432 3500
F: +44 (0) 207 432 3600
www.bridgepoint.eu

Bridges Community Ventures Ltd
1 Craven Hill, London, W2 3EN
T: +44 (0) 20 7262 5566
F: +44 (0) 20 7262 6389
www.bridgesventures.com

BTG plc
101 Newington Causeway, London, SE1 6BU
T: +44 (0) 207 575 0000
F: +44 (0) 207 575 0010
www.btgplc.com

BWD Rensburg - Capital For Companies
Quayside House, Canal Wharf, Leeds,
LS11 5PU
T: +44 (0) 113 243 8043
F: +44 (0) 113 245 1777
www.cfc-vct.co.uk

Cabot Square Capital
Byron House, 7 St Jamess Street, London,
SW1A 1EE
T: +44 (0) 207 579 9320
F: +44 (0) 207 579 9330
www.cabotsquare.com

Cairnsford Associates Ltd
32 Hampstead High Street, London,
NW3 1JQ
T: +44 (0) 207 435 9100
F: +44 (0) 207 435 7377
www.globalfinanceonline.com

Cambridge Quantum Fund
36 Maids Causeway, Cambridge, CB5 8DD
T: +44 (0) 1223 366 655
F: +44 (0) 1223 303 506

Cambridge Research BioVentures
St Michael's House, St Michael's,
Longstanton, Cambridge, CB4 5BZ
T: +44 (0) 1954 204 002
F: +44 (0) 1954 204 003
www.crbioventures.com

Carbon Trust
3 Clement's Inn, London, WC2A 2AZ
T: +44 (0) 207 170 7000
F: +44 (0) 207 170 7020
www.thecarbontrust.co.uk

Carlyle Europe Venture Partners
Lansdowne House, 57 Berkeley Square,
London, W1J 6ER
T: +44 (0) 207 894 1200
F: +44 (0) 207 894 1600
www.thecarlylegroup.com

Catalyst Fund Management and Research Ltd.
15 Whitcomb Street, London, WC2H 7HA
T: +44 (0) 207 747 8600
F: +44 (0) 207 930 2688
www.catfund.com

Catalyst Investment Group
10-13 Lovat Lane, London, EC3R 8DN
T: +44 (0) 207 929 5090
F: +44 (0)207 929 5086
www.catalystinvestment.co.uk

Catapult Venture Managers
Malt House, Narborough Wood Business
park, Desford Road Enderby, Leicester,
Leicestershire, LE19 4XT
T: +44 (0) 8701 161 600
F: +44 (0) 8701 161 601
www.catapult-vm.co.uk

Cavendish Asset Management
Chelsea House, West Gate, London, W5 1DR
T: +44 (0) 208 810 8041
www.cavendishassetmanagement.co.uk

Cazenove Private Equity
20 Moorgate, London, EC2R 6DA
T: +44 (0) 207 155 5000
F: +44 (0) 207 155 9800
www.cazenove.com

Celtic House
53 Davies Street, London, W1K 5JH
T: +44 (0) 1453 836 370
F: +44 (0) 207 838 6909
www.celtic-house.com

CET London
55 Bryanston Street, 17th Floor, Marble Arch
Tower, London, W1H 7LZ
T: +44 (0) 207 258 7100
F: +44 (0) 207 258 7101
www.cet.co.uk

Clarendon Fund Managers Ltd
12 Cromac Place, Belfast, BT7 2JB
T: +44 (0) 2890 326 465
F: +44 (0) 2890 326 473
www.clarendon-fm.co.uk

Classic Fund Management
3rd Floor, Marble Arch Tower, 55 Bryanston
Street, London, W1H 7AJ
T: +44 (0) 207 868 8883
F: +44 (0) 207 868 8719
www.classicfunds.co.uk

Clayton Dubilier & Rice Limited
Cleveland House, 33 King Street, London,
SW1Y 6RJ
T: +44 (0) 207 747 3800
F: +44 (0) 207 747 3801
www.cdr-inc.com

Close Brothers Private Equity LLP
10 Throgmorton Avenue, London,
EC2N 2DL
T: +44 (0) 207 065 1100
F: +44 (0) 207 588 6815
www.cbpel.com

Close Venture Management Limited
4 Crown Place, London, EC2A 4BT
T: +44 (0) 207 422 7830
F: +44 (0) 207 422 7849
www.closeventures.co.uk

Clydesdale Bank Equity Ltd
150 Buchanan Street, Glasgow, G1 2HL
T: +44 (0) 141 223 3727
F: +44 (0)141 223 3724

Company Guides Venture Partners Limited
13 Christopher Street, London, EC2A 2BS
T: +44 (0) 207 247 6300
www.companyguides.com

Compass Venture Management Limited
33 Cork Street, London, SW1S 3NQ
T: +44 (0) 207 434 4484
F: +44 (0) 207 434 3374
www.compass.uk.com

Complyport Ltd
58 Grosvenor Street, London, W1K 3JB
T: +44 (0) 207 399 4980
F: +44 (0) 207 629 8002
www.complyport.co.uk

Conduit Ventures Limited
Unit B 2nd Floor Colonial Buildings, 59-61
Hatton Garden, London, EC1N 8LS
T: +44 (0) 207 831 3131
www.conduit-ventures.com

Create Partners Limited
Victory House, Vision Park, Histon,
Cambridge, Cambs, CB4 9ZR
T: +44 (0) 1223 202 876
F: +44 (0) 1223 484 511
www.createpartners.com

**Credit Agricole Indosuez
Private Equity**
122 Leadenhall Street, London, EC3V 4QH
T: +44 (0) 207 971 4303
F: +44 (0) 207 971 4362

Credit Suisse First Boston Private Equity
One Cabot Square, London, E14 4QJ
T: +44 (0) 207 888 8888
F: +44 (0) 207 888 4450
www.csfb.com

Crescent Capital NI Limited
5 Crescent Gardens, Belfast, BT7 1NS
T: +44 (0) 2890 233 633
F: +44 (0) 2890 329 525
www.crescentcapital.co.uk

Cross Atlantic Partners
Conference House, 152 Morrison Street,
Edinburgh, EH3 8EB
T: +44 (0) 131 343 1361
F: +44 (0) 1312 006 200
www.xacp.com

CVC Capital Partners Limited
111 Strand, London, WC2R 0AG
T: +44 (0) 207 420 4200
F: +44 (0) 207 420 4231
www.cvceurope.com

Dam Advisors Ltd
1 Great Cumberland Place, London,
W1H 7AL
T: +44 (0) 207 535 3900
F: +44 (0) 207 533 3901
www.damgroup.com

Dawnay Day Lander Ltd
9-11 Grosvenor Gardens, London,
SW1W 0BD
T: +44 (0) 207 979 7575
F: +44 (0) 207 979 7585
www.D2L.com

DB eVentures
Austin Friars House, 2-6 Austin Friars,
London, EC2N 2HE
T: +44 (0) 207545 7800
F: +44 (0) 207 545 4314
www.dbeventures.com

**DBG Development Capital Eastern
Europe Ltd**
P.O. Box 727, St. Pauls Gate, New Street, St.
Helier - Jersey, Channel Islands, JE4 8ZB
T: +42 02 24 09 84 00
F: +42 02 24 09 84 44

**Derbyshire First Investments
Limited**
Bridge House, Riverside Village, Hady Hill,
Chesterfield, Derbyshire, S41 0DT
T: +44 (0) 1246 207 390
F: +44 (0) 1246 221 080
www.dfil.co.uk

**Derbyshire First Investments
Limited**
95 Sheffield Road, Chesterfield, Derbyshire,
S41 7JH
T: +44 (0) 1246 207 390
F: +44 (0) 1246 221 080
www.dfil.co.uk

Derwent London plc
25 Saville Row, London, W1S 2ER
T: +44 (0) 207 659 3000
F: +44 (0) 207 659 3100
www.derwentlondon.com

Dilmun Investments Ltd
27 Berkeley Square, London, W1J 6EL
T: +44 (0) 207 495 8974
F: +44 (0) 207 499 6768
www.dilmun.com

DN Capital Limited
28 St James's Square, London, SW1Y 4JH
T: +44 (0) 207 451 2804
www.dncapital.com

Doughty Hanson & Co
45 Pall Mall, London, SW1Y 5JG
T: +44 (0) 207 663 9300
F: +44 (0) 207 663 9350
www.doughtyhanson.com

Duke Street Capital Ltd
Almack House, 28 King Street, London,
SW1Y 6XA
T: +44 (0) 207 451 6600
F: +44 (0) 207 451 6601
www.dukestreetcapital.com

Dunedin
28 Savile Row, London, W1S 2EU
T: +44 (0) 207 292 2110
F: +44 (0) 207 292 2111
www.dunedin.com

EBT Venture Fund Limited
46 Hill Street, Belfast, BT1 2LB
T: +44 (0) 2890 311 770
F: +44 (0) 2890 311 880
www.emergingbusinesstrust.com

ECI Partners LLP - London
Brettenham House, Lancaster Place,
London, WC2E 7EN
T: +44 (0) 207 606 1000
F: +44 (0) 207 240 5050
www.ecipartners.com

ECI Partners LLP - Manchester
40 Peter Street, Manchester, M2 5GP
T: +44 (0) 161 819 3160
F: +44 (0) 161 819 3161
www.ecipartners.com

Eden Ventures (UK) Ltd
1 Widcombe Crescent, Bath, BA2 6AH
T: +44 (0) 1225 472950
F: +44 (0) 1225 481767
www.edenventures.co.uk

Elderstreet Investments Ltd
32 Bedford Row, London, WC1R 4HE
T: +44 (0) 207 831 5088
F: +44 (0) 207 831 5077
www.elderstreet.com

Electra Partners Europe Ltd
65 Kingsway, London, WC2B 6QT
T: +44 (0) 207 831 6464
F: +44 (0) 207 404 5388
www.electraeurope.com

Elwin Capital Partners Ltd.
95 Chancery Lane, 4th floor, London,
WC2A 1DW
T: +44 (0) 207 025 3653
F: +44 (0) 207 025 3660
www.elwincapital.com

Englefield Capital LLP
Michelin House, 81 Fulham Road,
LONDON, SW3 6RD
T: +44 (0) 207 591 4200
F: +44 (0) 207 591 4222
www.engcap.com

Enterprise Equity (NI) Ltd
78a Dublin Road, Belfast, Antrim, BT2 7HP
T: +44 (0) 2890 242 500
F: +44 (0) 2890 242 487
www.eeni.com

Enterprise Ireland
2nd Floor Shaftesbury House , 151
Shaftesbury Avenue, London, WC2H 8AL
T: +44 (0) 20 7438 8700
F: +44 (0) 20 7438 8749
www.enterprise-ireland.com

Enterprise Ventures Ltd
Preston Technology Management Centre,
Marsh Lane, Preston, Lancashire, PR1 8UQ
T: +44 (0) 1772 270 570
F: +44 (0) 1772 881 195
www.enterprise-ventures.co.uk

Enterprise Ventures Ltd Manchester
Preston Technology Management Centre,
Marsh Lane, Preston, Lancashire, PR1 8UQ
T: +44 (0) 1772 270 570
F: +44 (0) 1772 881 195
www.enterprise-ventures.co.uk

Enterprise Ventures Ltd. Leeds
1 Whitehall, Whitehall Road, Leeds,
LS1 4HR
T: +44 (0) 870 766 8237
F: +44 (0) 870 766 8238
www.enterprise-venture.co.uk

ePlanet Ventures
2 Kensington Square, London, W8 5EP
T: +44 (0) 207 361 0140
F: +44 (0) 207 361 0149
www.eplanetventures.com

Equity Source
32 College Close, Flamstead, Hertfordshire,
AL3 8DJ
T: +44 (0) 1582 843 896
F: +44 (0) 1582 843 896
www.equitysource.co.uk

Equity Ventures Ltd
23 Berkeley Square, London, W1J 6HE
T: +44 (0) 207 665 6611
F: +44 (0) 207 665 6650
www.equityventures.co.uk

E-Synergy Ltd
6-7 New Bridge Street, London, EC4V 6AB
T: +44 (0) 207 583 3503
F: +44 (0) 207 583 3474
www.e-synergy.com

ET Capital Ltd
St Johns Innovation Centre, Cowley Road,
Cambridge, Cambridgeshire, CB4 0WS
T: +44 (0) 1223 422 010
F: +44 (0) 1223 422 011
www.etcapital.com

ETV Capital
First Floor, 1 Tenterden Street, London,
W1S 1TA
T: +44 (0) 207 907 2370
F: +44 (0) 207 907 2399
www.etvcapital.com

European Acquisition Capital Ltd
26 Finsbury Square, London, EC2A 1DS
T: +44 (0) 207 382 1700
F: +44 (0) 207 588 3401
www.eacgroup.com

European Equity Partners
76 Brook Street, London, W1K 5EE
T: +44 (0) 207 629 9992
F: +44 (0) 207 629 2072
www.eeplp.com

Eurovestech plc
29 Curzon Street, London, W1J 7TL
T: +44 (0) 207 491 0770
F: +44 (0) 207 491 9595
www.eurovestech.co.uk

Favonius Ventures
20 Balderton Street, London, W1K 6TL
T: +44 (0) 207 629 8035
F: +44 (0) 207 491 2645
www.favoniusventures.com

Ferranti Ltd
43 Rosary Gardens, London, SW7 4NG
T: +44 (0) 207 835 1325
F: +44 (0) 207 244 8387
www.ferranti.com

Fidelity Ventures
25 Cannon Street, London, EC4M 5TA
T: +44 (0) 207 664 2304
F: +44 (0) 207 664 2309
www.fidelityventures.com

Fife Enterprise
Kingdom House, Saltire Centre, Glenrothes,
Fife, KY6 2AQ
T: +44 (0) 1592 623 000
F: +44 (0) 1592 623 149
www.scottish-enterprise.com/fife

Finance Cornwall Ltd
14 High Cross, Truro, Cornwall, TR1 2AJ
T: +44 (0) 1872 272 288
F: +44 (0) 1872 272 298
www.financecornwall.co.uk

Finance Wales Investments Limited
3rd Floor Oakleigh House, Park Place,
Cardiff, Wales, CF10 3DQ
T: +44 (0) 800 587 4140
F: +44 (0) 2920 338 101
www.financewales.co.uk

Fleming Family Partners Ltd
Ely House, 37 Dover Street, London,
W1S 4NJ
T: +44 (0) 207 409 5600
F: +44 (0) 207 409 5601
www.ffandp.co.uk

Foresight Venture Partners
ECA Court, South Park, Sevenoaks, Kent,
TN13 1DU
T: +44 (0) 1732 471 800
F: +44 (0) 1732 471 810
www.foresightventurepartners.com

Foursome Investments Ltd
The Mews, 1a Birkenhead Street, London,
WC1H 8BA
T: +44 (0) 207 833 0555
F: +44 (0) 207 833 8322
www.fousome.co.uk

**Framlington Investment Management
Ltd**
155 Bishopsgate, London, EC2M 3FT
T: +44 (0) 845 777 5511
www.axaframlington.com

Fresh Capital Group Ltd
14-16 Hans Road, London, SW3 1RS
T: +44 (0) 207 581 1477
F: +44 (0) 207 589 3542
www.freshcapital.com

**Friedman Billings Ramsey International
Ltd.**
Eighth Floor, Berkeley Square House,
Berkeley Square, London, W1J 6DB
T: +44 (0) 207 409 5300
F: +44 (0) 207 409 5301
www.fbr.com

Frontiers Capital Ltd
Castle House, Second Floor, 75 Wells Street,
London, W1T 3QH
T: +44 (0) 207 182 7700
F: +44 (0) 207 182 7701
www.frontierscapital.com

**Gartmore Investment Management
Limited (Gartmore Private Equity)**
Gartmore House, 8 Fenchurch Place,
London, EC3M 4PB
T: +44 (0) 207 782 2191
F: +44 (0) 207 782 2034
www.gartmoreprivateequity.com

GE Commercial Finance
30 Berkeley Square, London, W1J 6EW
T: +44 (0) 207 302 6000
F: +44 (0) 207 302 6893
www.ge.com

Genacys
298 Regents Park Rd, Finchley, London,
N3 2UA
T: +44 (0) 208 371 3902
F: +44 (0) 208 371 3958
www.genacys.co.uk

General Atlantic LLP
83 Pall Mall, London, SW1Y 5ES
T: +44 (0) 207 484 3200
F: +44 (0) 207 484 3290
www.generalatlantic.com

Generics Asset Management Ltd
Harston Mill, Harston, Cambridge, CB2 5NH
T: +44 (0) 1223 875 200
F: +44 (0) 1223 875 201
www.genericsgroup.com

GI Partners
64 5th Floor, 35 Portman Square, London,
W1H 6LR
T: +44 (0) 207 034 1120
F: +44 (0) 207 034 1156
www.gipartners.com

GLE Invoice Finance
New City Court, 20 St Thomas Street,
London, SE1 9RS
T: +44 (0) 20 7403 0300
F: +44 (0) 20 7403 1742
www.gle.co.uk

GMT Communications Partners Ltd
Sackville House, 40 Piccadilly, London,
W1J 0DR
T: +44 (0) 207 292 9333
F: +44 (0) 207 292 9390
www.gmtpartners.com

GoEast Ventures Ltd
Universal House, 88-94 Wentworth Street,
London, E1 7SA
T: +44 (0) 207 377 8821
F: +44 (0) 207 375 1415
www.goeastventures.co.uk

Graphite Capital
Berkeley Square House, Berkeley Square,
London, W1J 6BQ
T: +44 (0) 207 825 5300
F: +44 (0) 207 825 5399
www.graphitecapital.com

Greenpark Capital Ltd
2-5 Old Bond Street, London, W1S 4PD
T: +44 (0) 207 647 1400
F: +44 (0) 207 647 1440
www.greenparkcapital.com

Gresham LLP
One South Place, London, EC2M 2GT
T: +44 (0) 207 309 5000
F: +44 (0) 207 374 0707
www.gresham.vc

Guernsey International Fund Managers
PO Box 255, Trafalgar Court, Les Banques, St
Peter Port, Guernsey, GY1 3QL
T: +44 (0) 1481 745 001
F: +44 (0) 1481 745 051
www.gifm.com

HarbourVest Partners (U.K.) Ltd.
8th Floor, Suite 7, Berkeley Square House,
London, W1J 6DB
T: +44 (0) 207 399 9820
F: +44 (0) 207 399 9840
www.harbourvest.com

Henderson Equity Partners Limited
4 Broadgate, London, EC2M 2DA
T: +44 (0) 207 818 2963
F: +44 (0) 207 818 7310
www.hendersonprivatecapital.com

Herald Investment Management Ltd
10-11 Charterhouse Square, London,
EC1M 6EH
T: +44 (0) 207 553 6300
F: +44 (0) 207 490 8026
www.heralduk.com

Hermes Private Equity
Lloyds Chambers, 1 Portsoken Street,
London, E1 8HZ
T: +44 (0) 207 680 2848
F: +44 (0) 207 680 2508
www.hermesprivateequity.co.uk

IFG Mezzanine Limited
69-71 Warnford Court, Throgmorton Street,
London, EC2N 2AT
T: +44 (0) 207 628 9911
F: +44 (0) 207 628 9933
www.ifg-ltd.co.uk

Impax Asset Management Ltd
Broughton House, 6-8 Sackville Street,
London, W1S 3DG
T: +44 (0) 207 434 1122
F: +44 (0) 207 437 1245
www.impax.co.uk

Index Ventures
52 53 Conduit Street, London, W1S 2YX
T: +44 (0) 207 154 2020
F: +44 (0) 207 154 2021
www.indexventures.com

Industri Kapital Ltd
Brettenham House, 5 Lancaster Place,
London, EC2E 7EN
T: +44 (0) 207 304 4300
F: +44 (0) 207 304 4320
www.industrikapital.com

Industrial Mezzanine Fund
Linen Hall, 162-168 Regent Street, London,
W1B 5TE
T: +44 (0) 207 038 3983
F: +44 (0) 207 038 3984
www.ifg-ltd.co.uk

Inflexion Private Equity
40 George Street, London, W1U 7DW
T: +44 (0) 207 487 9888
F: +44 (0) 207 487 2774
www.inflexion.com

Innvotec Ltd London
Painters' Hall Chambers, 8 Trinity Lane,
London, EC4V 2AN
T: +44 (0) 207 630 6990

Innvotec Ltd. Birmingham
Wellington House, 31-34 Waterloo Street,
Birmingham, B2 5TJ
T: +44 (0) 121 262 5145
F: +44 (0) 121 262 5149
www.advantage-vc.com

International Biotechnology Trust plc
Louise Richard, 31 Gresham Street, London,
EC2V 7QA
T: +44 (0) 207 658 3206
F: +44 (0) 207 658 3538
www.internationalbiotrust.com

Interregnum plc
22-23 Old Burlington Street, London,
W1S 2JJ
T: +44 (0) 207 494 3080
F: +44 (0) 207 494 3090
www.interregnum.com

Invest Northern Ireland
Corporate Finance Appraisal & Advisory
Division, Bedford Square, Bedford Street,
Belfast, BT2 7EH
T: +44 (0) 2890239090
F: +44 (0) 2890436536
www.investni.com

Invest Northern Ireland (InvestNI)
Corporate Finance Appraisal & Advisory
Division, Bedford Square, Bedford Street,
Belfast, Antrim, BT2 7EH
T: +44 (0) 289 069 8687
F: +44 (0) 289 049 0490

Investcorp International
48 Grosvenor St, London, W1K 3HW
T: +44 (0) 207 629 6600
F: +44 (0) 207 499 0371
www.investcorp.com

Investindustrial
53-54 Grosvenor Street, London, W1K 3HU
T: +44 (0) 207 659 4444
F: +44 (0) 207 659 4455
www.investindustrial.com

Investindustrial Holdings Ltd
1 Duchess Street, London, W1W 6AN
T: +44 (0) 207 631 2777
F: +44 (0) 207 631 2778
www.investindustrial.com

IP2IPO Group Plc
24 Cornhill, London, EC3V 3ND
T: +44 (0) 207 444 0050
F: +44 (0) 845 074 2928
www.ip2ipo.com

ISIS EP LLP Birmingham
Bank House, 8 Cherry Street, Birmingham,
B2 5AN
T: +44 (0) 1212 531 600
F: +44 (0) 1212 531 616
www.isisep.com

ISIS EP LLP London
2nd Floor, 100 Wood Street, London,
EC2V 7AN
T: +44 (0) 207 506 5600
F: +44 (0) 207 726 8857
www.isisep.com

ISIS EP LLP Manchester
First Floor, Colwyn Chambers, 19 York
Street, Manchester, M2 3BA
T: +44 (0) 121 912 6500
F: +44 (0) 1619 126 501
www.isisep.com

Isis Innovation Ltd
Ewert House, Ewert Place, Summertown,
Oxford, OX2 7SG
T: +44 (0) 1865 280 830
F: +44 (0) 1865 280 831
www.isis-innovation.com

J O Hambro Capital Management Limited
Ryder Court, 14 Ryder Street, London,
SW1Y 6QB
T: +44 (0) 845 450 1970
F: +44 (0) 845 450 1974
www.johcm.co.uk

J. P. Morgan Partners LLP
125 London Wall, London, EC2Y 5AJ
T: +44 (0) 207 777 3365
F: +44 (0) 207 777 4731
www.jpmorgan.com

Javelin Ventures Ltd
Suite 4, 46 Dorset Street, London, W1U 7NB
T: +44 (0) 207 486 7456
F: +44 (0) 207 486 7463
www.javelin-ventures.com

Jerusalem Venture Partners
2C Drax Ave, London, SW20 OEH
T: +44 (0) 800 051 7018
F: +44 (0) 207 758 8208
www.jvpvc.com

Jupiter Asset Management Ltd
PO BOX 300, West Malling, London,
ME19 4YY
T: +44 (0) 207 314 7600
F: +44 (0) 207 412 0705
www.jupiteronline.co.uk

JZ International
17A Curzon Street, London, W1J 5HS
T: +44 (0) 207 491 3633
F: +44 (0) 207 493 6650
www.jzieurope.com

Katalyst Ventures Limited
10 Fenchurch Avenue, London, EC3m 5BN
T: +44 (0) 207 665 5454
F: +44 (0) 871 990 6338
www.katalystventures.com

Kaupthing Singer & Friedlander
Head Office, One Hanover Street, London,
W1S 1AX
T: +44 (0) 203 205 5000
F: +44 (0) 203 205 5001
www.kaupthingsingers.co.uk

KBC Bank NV
5th Floor, 111 Old Broad Street, London,
EC2N 1BR
T: +44 (0) 207 638 5812
F: +44 (0) 207 256 4846
www.kbc.be

Kennet Venture Partners Ltd
St Jamess House, 23 King Street, London,
SW1Y 6QY
T: +44 (0) 207 839 8020
F: +44 (0) 207 839 8485
www.kennetventures.com

Kingstree Group
68 Chandos Place, London, WC2N 4HG
T: +44 (0) 207 836 5575
F: +44 (0) 207 240 0688
www.kingstreegroup.com

Kohlberg Kravis Roberts & Co Ltd (KKR)
Stirling Square, 7 Carlton Gardens, London,
SW1Y 5AD
T: +44 (0) 207 839 9800
F: +44 (0) 207 839 9801
www.kkr.com

Korda Associates
The Outer Temple, 222 The Strand, London,
WC2 1DE
T: +44 (0) 207 583 3377
F: +44 (0) 20 7251 487

Kreos Capital
4th Floor, Cardinal House, 39-40 Albermarle
Street, London, W1S 4TE
T: +44 (0) 207 518 8890
F: +44 (0) 207 409 1034
www.kreoscapitalcom

Lambert Fenchurch Corporate Ventures
133 Houndsditch Street, London, EC3A 7AH
T: +44 (0) 207 560 3000
F: +44 (0) 207 560 3540
www.heathlambert.com

Landmark Partners Europe LLC
29-30 St. James's Street, London, SW1A 1HB
T: +44 (0) 207 343 4450
F: +44 (0) 207 343 4488
www.landmarkpartners.com

Lazard & Co Services Ltd
50 Stratton Street, London, W1J 8LL
T: +44 (0) 207 187 2000
F: +44 (0) 207 187 6581
www.lazard.com

LDC - West Midlands
6th Floor, Interchange Place, Edmund
Street, Birmingham, B3 2TA
T: +44 (0) 121 237 6500
F: +44 (0) 121 236 5269
www.ldc.co.uk

LDC East Midlands
Butt Dyke House, 33 Park Row, Nottingham,
NG1 6GZ
T: +44 (0) 115 947 1280
F: +44 (0) 115 947 1290
www.ldc.co.uk

LDC London
Stanbrook House, 2-5 Old Bond Street,
London, W1S 4PD
T: +44 (0) 207 518 6810
F: +44 (0) 207 518 6820
www.ldc.co.uk

LDC Manchester
8th Floor, 1 Marsden Street, Manchester,
M2 1HW
T: +44 (0) 161 831 1720
F: +44 (0) 161 831 1730
www.ldc.co.uk

LDC Thames Valley
1st Floor, One Forbury Square, Reading,
Berkshire, RG1 3BB
T: +44 (0) 118 958 0274
F: +44 (0) 118 956 8991
www.ldc.co.uk

Lexington Partners UK Ltd.
42 Berkeley Square, London, W1J 5AW
T: +44 (0) 207 318 0888
F: +44 (0) 207 318 0889
www.lexingtonpartners.com

London Seed Capital
52/54 Southwark Street, London, SE1 1UN
T: +44 (0) 207 089 2309
F: +44 (0) 207 089 2301
www.londonseedcapital.com

London Ventures (Fund Managers) Ltd
103 Eastbourne Mews, London, W2 6LQ
T: +44 (0) 207 706 8878
F: +44 (0) 207 434 2426

LTG Development Capital Ltd
Chelsea House, West Gate, London, W5 1DR
T: +44 (0) 208 991 4606
www.ltgdevcap.com

Ludgate Investments Limited
46 Cannon Street, London, EC4N 6JJ
T: +44 (0) 207 236 0973
F: +44 (0) 207 329 2100
www.ludgate.com

Lynx Capital Ventures
4th Floor, 45 Old Bond Street, London,
W1S 4QT
T: +44 (0) 207 659 5100
F: +44 (0) 207 659 5111
www.lynxcapitalventures.com

Merchant Capital Ltd
Aldermary House , 10-15 Queen Street,
London, EC4N 1TX
T: +44 (0) 207 332 2200
F: +44 (0) 207 379 4477
www.merchant-capital.com

Merlin Biosciences Cambridge
329 Cambridge Science Park, Milton Road,
Cambridge, CB4 0WG
T: +44 (0) 1223 437 000
F: +44 (0) 1233 226 166

Merlin Biosciences Ltd
33 King Street, St James's Square, London,
SW1Y 6RJ
T: +44 (0) 207 811 4000
F: +44 (0) 207 811 4001
www.merlin-biosciences.com

Merseyside Special Investment Fund
5th Floor Cunard Building, Pier Head,
Liverpool, L3 1DS
T: +44 (0) 151 236 4040
F: +44 (0) 151 236 3060
www.msif.co.uk

Mezzanine Management UK Ltd.
Manfield House, 1 Southampton Street,
London, WC2R 0LR
T: +44 (0) 207 655 5000
F: +44 (0) 207 655 5001
www.mezzanine-management.com

Middlefield Group
199 Bishopsgate, London, EC2M 3TY
T: +44 (0) 20 7814 6644
F: +44 (0) 20 7600 5127
www.middlefield.com

Midven Ltd
37 Bennetts Hill, Birmingham, B2 5SN
T: +44 (0) 1217 101 990
F: +44 (0) 1217 101 999
www.midven.com

Milestone Capital Partners Ltd
14 Floral Street, London, WC2E 9DH
T: +44 (0) 207 420 8800
F: +44 (0) 207 420 8827
www.milstone-capital.com

Monitor Clipper Partners
Michelin House, 81 Fulham Road, London, SW3 6RD
T: +44 (0) 207 838 6600
F: +44 (0) 207 838 6875
www.monitorclipper.com

Montagu Newhall
52 Upper Brook Street, London, W1K 2BU
T: +44 (0) 207 468 7405
F: +44 (0) 207 468 7411
www.montagunewhall.com

Moorfield Investment Management Ltd
Premier House, 44-48 Dover Street, London, W1S 4NX
T: +44 (0) 207 399 1900
F: +44 (0) 207 499 2114
www.moorfield.com

Morgan Stanley Private Equity
25 Cabot Square, Canary Wharf, London, E14 4QA
T: +44 (0) 207 425 8000
F: +44 (0) 207 425 8990
www.morganstanley.co.uk

MTI Partners Limited
Langley Place, 99 Langley Rd, Watford, Hertfordshire, WD17 4BE
T: +44 (0) 1923 250 244
F: +44 (0) 1923 247 783
www.mtifirms.com

MVM Ltd
6 Henrietta Street, London, WC2E 8PU
T: +44 (0) 207 557 7500
F: +44 (0) 207 557 7501
www.mvfund.com

NBGI Private Equity
Old Change House, 128 Queen Victoria Street, London, EC4V 4BJ
T: +44 (0) 207 661 5678
F: +44 (0) 207 661 5667
www.nbgipe.co.uk

NEL Fund Managers Ltd
3 Earls Court, 5th Avenue, Team Valley, Gateshead, NE11 0HF
T: +44 (0) 845 111 1850
F: +44 (0) 845 111 1853
www.nel.co.uk

NESTA
1 Plough Place, London, EC4A 1DE
T: +44 (0) 207 438 2500
F: +44 (0) 207 438 2501
www.nesta.org.uk

NewMedia SPARK plc
33 Glasshouse Street, 4th floor, London, W1B 5DG
T: +44 (0) 207 851 7777
F: +44 (0) 207 851 7770
www.newmediaspark.com

Nichimen Europe plc
3 Shortlands, London, W6 8DA
T: +44 (0) 207 886 7000
F: +44 (0) 207 886 7090
www.nichimen.co.uk

Noble Fund Managers Limited
76 George Street, Edinburgh, EH2 3BU
T: +44 (0) 1312 259 677
F: +44 (0) 1312 255 479
www.noblegp.com

Nomura Private Equity
6th Floor, Normura House, 1 St Martin's-le-Grand, London, EC1A 4NP
T: +44 (0) 207 521 2000
F: +44 (0) 207 521 2235
www.nomura.com

Nordic Mezzanine
100 Pall Mall, St James's, London, SW1Y 5HP
T: +44 (0) 207 663 9890
F: +44 (0) 207 663 9891
www.nordicmezzanine.com

North West Equity Fund
Antler House, Crouchley Lane, Lymm,
Cheshire, WA13 0AN
T: +44 (0) 1925 759 246
F: +44 (0) 1925 759 792
www.nwef.co.uk

North West Seed Fund
6th Floor, City Wharf, New Bailey Street,
Manchester, M3 5ER
T: +44 (0) 161 828 5221
F: +44 (0) 161 834 6357
www.nwseedfund.com

Nova Capital Management Limited
11 Strand, London, WC2N 5HR
T: +44 (0) 207 389 1540
F: +44 (0) 207 389 1541
www.nova-cap.com

NVM Private Equity Limited
Northumberland House, Princess Square,
Newcastle upon Tyne, NE1 8ER
T: +44 (0) 191 244 6000
F: +44 (0) 191 244 6001
www.nvm.co.uk

NVM Private Equity Limited
Forbury Court, 12 Forbury Road, Reading,
Berkshire, RG1 1SB
T: +44 (0) 181 951 7000
F: +44 (0) 1189 517 001
www.nvm.co.uk

NVM Private Equity Limited
50 Moray Place, Edinburgh, EH3 6BQ
T: +44 (0) 131 260 1000
F: +44 (0) 131 260 1001
www.nvm.co.uk

NVPBrightstar
Columba House NG10, Adastral Park,
Martlesham Heath, Ipswich, IP5 3RE
T: +44 (0) 1473 636 703
F: +44 (0) 1473 636 718
www.nvpllc.com

NW Brown Group & Company Limited
Richmond House, 16-20 Regent Street,
Cambridge, Cambridgeshire, CB2 1DB
T: +44 (0) 1223 357 131
F: +44 (0) 1223 720 258
www.nwbrown.co.uk

NW Brown Ventures Ltd
Richmond House, 16-20 Regent Street,
Cambridge, CB2 1DB
T: +44 (0) 1223 357 131
F: +44 (0) 1223 720 258
www.nwbrown.co.uk;
www.geifventures.co.uk

Octopus Asset Management Ltd
8 Angel Court, London, EC2R 7HP
T: +44 (0) 207 710 2800
F: +44 (0) 207 710 2801
www.octopusam.com

Odyssey Ventures Ltd
36 Maids Causeway, Cambridge,
Cambridgeshire, CB5 8DD
T: +44 (0) 1223 366 655
F: +44 (0) 1223 303 506

OM Technology Investments
Dresdner Kleinwort Wasserstein, PO Box
52715, 30 Gresham Street, London,
EC2P 2XY
T: +44 (0) 207 623 8000
F: +44 (0) 207 623 4069
www.drkw.com

Oxford Capital Partners
201 Cumnor Hill, Oxford, OX2 9PJ
T: +44 (0) 1865 860 760
F: +44 (0) 1865 860 761
www.oxcp.com

Pacific Investments
124 Sloane Street, London, SW1X 9BW
T: +44 (0) 207 225 2250
F: +44 (0) 207 591 1650

Palamon Capital Partners LP
Cleveland House, 33 King Street, London,
SW1Y 6RJ
T: +44 (0) 207 766 2000
F: +44 (0) 207 766 2002
www.palamon.com

Pantheon Ventures Ltd
Norfolk House, 31 St Jamess Square,
London, SW1Y 4JR
T: +44 (0) 207 484 6200
F: +44 (0) 207 484 6201
www.pantheonventures.com

Parallel Private Equity Limited
49 St James's Street, London, SW1A 1JT
T: +44 (0) 207 600 9105
F: +44 (0) 207 491 3372
www.parallelprivateequity.com

Partnerships UK plc
10 Great George Street, London, SW1P 3AE
F: +44 (0) 207 273 8368
www.partnerships.org.uk

Pennine Fund Managers Ltd
Rathbone Nelson Cobbold, Port of Liverpool
Building, Pier Head, Liverpool, L3 1NW
T: +44 (0) 151 236 6666
F: +44 (0) 151 243 7001

Penta Capital Partners Ltd
150 Vincent Street, Glasgow, G2 5NE
T: +44 (0) 141 572 7300
F: +44 (0) 141 572 7310
www.pentacapital.com

Pentech Ventures (Divison of Penta Capital
150 VIncent Street, Glasgow, G2 5NE
T: +44 (0) 141 572 7303
F: +44 (0) 141 572 7310
www.pentechvc.com

Permira Advisers Ltd.
20 Southampton Street, London, WC2E 7QH
T: +44 (0) 207 632 1000
F: +44 (0) 207 497 2174
www.permira.com

Phoenix Equity Partners
33 Glasshouse Street, London, W1B 5DG
T: +44 (0) 207 434 6999
F: +44 (0) 207 434 6998
www.phoenix-equity.com

Pi Capital Ltd
49 St James's Street, London, SW1A 1JT
T: +44 (0) 207 529 5656
F: +44 (0) 207 529 5657
www.picapital.co.uk

Piper Private Equity
Eardley House, 182-184 Campden Hill Road,
London, W8 7AS
T: +44 (0) 207 727 3842
F: +44 (0) 207 727 8969
www.piperprivateequity.com

Pond Venture Partners Ltd
Bridge House, Heron Square, Richmond,
Surrey, TW9 1EN
T: +44 (0) 208 940 1001
F: +44 (0) 208 940 6792
www.pondventures.com

Porton Capital
12 St James's Square, London, SW1Y 4RB
T: +44 (0) 207 849 5547
F: +44 (0) 207 849 5548
www.portoncapital.com

Postern Fund Management Ltd
Adam House, 7-10 Adam Street, London,
WC2N 6AA
T: +44 (0) 207 520 9362
F: +44 (0) 207 520 9363
www.postern.com

PPM Ventures Ltd
1 New Fetter Lane, London, EC4A 1HH
T: +44 (0) 207 822 1000
F: +44 (0) 207 822 1001
www.ppmventures.com

Prelude Ventures Limited
Sycamore Studios, New Road, Over,
Cambridge, CB4 5PJ
T: +44 (0) 1954 288 090
F: +44 (0) 1954 288 099
www.prelude-ventures.com

Primary Capital Ltd.
Augustine House, Austin Friars, London,
EC2N 2HA
T: +44 (0) 207 920 4800
F: +44 (0) 207 920 4801
www.primaryeurope.com

Prime Technology Ventures

Suite 217, Wellington House, East Road,
Cambridge, CB1 1BH
T: +44 (0) 1223 451 294
F: +44 (0) 1223 451 100
www.ptv.com

Principal Global Investors (Europe) Limited

6th Floor, 16 St. Martin's Le Grand, London,
EC1A 4EN
T: +44 (0) 207 710 0220
F: +44 (0) 207 710 0221
www.principalglobalfunds.com

Providence Equity LLP

78 Brook Street, First Floor, London,
W1K 5EF
T: +44 (0) 207 514 8800
F: +44 (0) 207 629 2778
www.provequity.com

Qubis Ltd

Lanyon North, The Queens University of
Belfast, University Road, Belfast, BT7 1NN
T: +44 (0) 289 068 2321
F: +44 (0) 289 066 3015
www.qubis.co.uk

Rathbone Investment Management

159 New Bond Street, London, W1S 2UD
T: +44 (0) 20 7399 0000
F: +44 (0) 20 7399 0011
www.rathbones.com

Root Capital LLP

2 Wardrobe Place, London, EC4V 5AH
T: +44 (0) 207 243 2693
F: +44 (0) 207 248 2694
www.rootcapital.co.uk

Rothschild

1 King Williams Street, London, EC4N 7AR
T: +44 (0) 207 280 5000
F: +44 (0) 207 929 1643
www.rothschild.com

Russell Investment Group

Rex House, 10 Lower Regent Street, London,
SW1Y 4PE
T: +44 (0) 207 024 6000
www.russell.com

Rutland Partners LLP

Rutland House, Rutland Gardens,
Knightsbridge, London, SW7 1BX
T: +44 (0) 207 556 2600
F: +44 (0) 207 581 8766
www.rutlandpartners.com

RVC Europe Limited

11 Upper Grosvenor Street, Mayfair,
London, W1K 2NB
T: +44 (0) 207 355 5700
F: +44 (0) 207 355 5722
www.rvc.com

Saffron Hill Ventures

52 Upper Brook Street, London, W1K 2BU
T: +44 (0) 207 693 8300
F: +44 (0) 207 693 8346
www.saffronhill.com

Sand Aire Private Equity

101 Wigmore Street, London, W1U 1QU
T: +44 (0) 207 290 5200
F: +44 (0) 207 495 0240
www.sandaire.co.uk

Schroder Ventures Life Sciences

71 Kingsway, London, WC2B 6ST
T: +44 (0) 207 421 7070
F: +44 (0) 207 421 7077
www.svlifesciences.com

Scottish Enterprise

5 Atlantic Quay, 150 Broomielaw, Glasgow,
G2 8LU
T: +44 (0) 141 228 2828
F: +44 (0) 141 228 2089
www.scottish-enterprise.com

Scottish Equity Partners

17 Blythswood Square, Glasgow, G2 4AD
T: +44 (0) 1412 734 000
F: +44 (0) 1412 734 001
www.sep.co.uk

Scottish Equity Partners

84 Brook Street, London, W1K 5EH
T: +44 (0) 141 273 4000
F: +44 (0) 141 273 4001
www.sep.co.uk

Seed Capital Ltd
The Magdalen Centre, Oxford Science Park, Oxford, OX4 4GA
T: +44 (0) 1865 784 466
F: +44 (0) 1865 784 430
www.oxfordtechnology.com

SG Capital Europe Ltd
Exchange House, Primrose Street, London, EC2A 2EF
T: +44 (0) 207 762 5134
www.sgce.com

Shore Capital Group plc
Mellier House, 26a Albemarle Street, London, WS1 4HY
T: +44 (0) 207 408 4080
F: +44 (0) 207 408 4081
www.shorecap.co.uk

Sigma Technology Management Ltd
6th Floor Bucklersbury House, 83 Cannon Street, London, EC4N 8ST
T: +44 (0) 207 653 3200
F: +44 (0) 207 653 3201
www.sigmacapital.co.uk

Sitka Ltd
23 Buckingham Gate, London, SW1E 6LB
T: +44 (0) 207 592 0499
F: +44 (0) 207 592 9861
www.sitkapartners.com

Smedvig Capital Ltd.
Twenty Saint James's Street, London, SW1A 1ES
T: +44 (0) 207 451 2100
F: +44 (0) 207 451 2101
www.smedvigcapital.com

South West Ventures Fund
Argentum, 510 Bristol Business Park, Coldharbour Lane, Bristol, BS16 1EJ
T: +44 (0) 117 906 3410
F: +44 (0) 117 906 3646
www.southwestventuresfund.co.uk

Sovereign Capital Partners LLP
25 Buckingham Gate, London, SW1E 6LD
T: +44 (0) 207 821 2503
F: +44 (0) 207 828 9958
www.sovereigncapital.co.uk

SPP
Trinity Tower, 9 Thomas More Street, London, E1W 1GE
T: +44 (0) 207 578 8290
F: +44 (0) 207 578 8499
www.spp.se

Standard Life Investments (Private Equity) Ltd
1 George Street, Edinburgh, EH2 2LL
T: +44 (0) 131 225 2345
F: +44 (0) 131 245 6105
www.standardlifeinvestments.com

STAR Capital Partners Ltd.
39 St Jamess Street, London, SW1A 1JD
T: +44 (0) 207 016 8500
F: +44 (0) 207 016 8501
www.star-capital.com

Strathdon Investments Limited
Jewry House, Jewry Street, Winchester, Hampshire, SO23 8RZ
T: +44 (0) 1962 870 492
F: +44 (0) 1962 844 064
www.strathdon.com

Stratos Ventures
41 Dover Street, London, W1X 3RB
T: +44 (0) 207 510 8961
F: +44 (0) 207 491 2855
www.stratosventures.com

Sulis Innovation Ltd
1 Widcombe Crescent, Bath, BA2 6AH
T: +44 (0) 1225 472953
F: +44 (0) 1225 481767
www.bath.ac.uk/sulis-innovation

Summit Partners Ltd.
Berkeley Square House, 8th Floor, Berkeley Square, London, W1J 6DB
T: +44 (0) 207 659 7500
F: +44 (0) 207 659 7550
www.summitpartners.com

Sussex Place Ventures
18-20 Huntsworth Mews, London,
NW1 6DD
T: +44 (0) 207 535 8868
F: +44 (0) 207 535 8804
www.spventures.co.uk

Tay Euro Fund
Enterprise House, 45 North Lindsay Street,
Dundee, DD1 1HT
T: +44 (0) 1382 223 100
F: +44 (0) 1382 201 319
www.scotent.co.uk

Teather & Greenwood
Beaufort House, 15 St Botolph Street,
London, EC3A 7QR
T: +44 (0) 207 426 9000
F: +44 (0) 207 426 9595
www.teathers.com

Technomark Medical Ventures
King House, 11 Westbourne Grove, London,
W2 4UA
T: +44 (0) 207 229 9239
F: +44 (0) 207 792 2587
www.tmv.eu.com

Terra Firma Capital Partners Limited
2 More London Riverside, London, SE12 AP
T: +44 (0) 207 015 9500
F: +44 (0) 207 015 9501
www.terrafirma.com

Texas Pacific Group (Europe) Ltd
2nd Floor, Stirling Square, 5-7 Carlton
Gardens, London, SW1Y 5AD
T: +44 (0) 207 544 6500
F: +44 (0) 207 544 6565
www.texaspacificgroup.com

TH Lee Putnam Ventures
1 Livonia Street, London, W1V 3PG
T: +44 (0) 207 758 3501
www.thlpv.com

The Cambridge Gateway Fund
Manager to the Cambridge Gateway Fund,
Highfield Court, Church Lane, Madingley,
Cambridgeshire, CB3 8AG
T: +44 (0) 1954 211 515
F: +44 (0) 1954 211 516
www.cambridgegateway.com

The Carlyle Group - UK
Lansdowne House, 57 Berkeley Square,
London, W1J 6ER
T: +44 (0) 207 894 1630
F: +44 (0) 207 894 1600
www.carlyle.com

The Manchester Technology Fund Ltd
Kilburn House, Manchester Science Park,
Lloyd Street North, Manchester, M15 6SE
T: +44 (0) 161 232 6064
F: +44 (0) 161 226 1001
www.mantechfund.com

The Summit Group Ltd
The Pavilion, 3 Broadgate, London,
EC2M 2QS
T: +44 (0) 207 614 0000
F: +44 (0) 207 614 0066
www.summit-group.co.uk

The University of Cambridge Challenge Fund
William Gates Building, JJ Thomson
Avenue, Cambridge, CB3 0FD
T: +44 (0) 1223 763 723
F: +44 (0) 1223 763 753
www.challengefund.cam.ac

Think Ventures
Suite 385, 456-458 The Strand, London,
WC2R 0DZ
T: +44 (0) 207 653 0230
F: +44 (0) 207 653 0286
www.thinkventures.co.uk

Thompson Clive & Partners Ltd
24 Old Bond Street, London, W1X 4AW
T: +44 (0) 207 491 4809
F: +44 (0) 207 493 9172
www.TCVC.com

Threadneedle Investments
60 St Mary Axe, London, EC3A 8JQ
T: +44 (0) 207 464 5000
F: +44 (0) 207 464 5050
www.threadneedle.com

Tianguis Ltd.
5 Edwardes Place, London, W8 6LR
T: +44 (0) 207 603 7788
F: +44 (0) 207 603 7667
www.tianguis-ltd.com

TLcom Capital Partners Limited
Carrington House, 126-130 Regent Street,
London, W1B 5SE
T: +44 (0) 207 851 6930
F: +44 (0) 207 851 6931
www.tlcom.co.uk

Top Technology Ventures Ltd
20-21 Tooks Court, Cursitor Street, London,
EC4A 1LB
T: +44 (0) 207 242 9900
F: +44 (0) 207 405 2863
www.toptechnology.co.uk

Tower Gate Ltd
International House, 1 St Katharine's Way,
London, E1W 1UN
T: +44 (0) 207 481 8002
F: +44 (0) 207 481 8003
www.tower-gate.com

Transatlantic Capital Fund
The Shrubberies, George Lane, South
Woodford, London, E18 1BD
T: +44 (0) 208 532 2342
F: +44 (0) 208 532 2343
www.transatlantic-capital.com

TTP Venture Managers Ltd
Melbourn Science Park, Cambridge Road,
Melbourn, Royston, Herts., SG8 6EE
T: +44 (0) 1763 262 626
F: +44 (0) 1763 262 265
www.ttpventures.com

Tufton Capital Ltd
Albemarle House, 1 Albemarle Street,
London, W1X 3HF
T: +44 (0) 207 529 7800
F: +44 (0) 207 529 7801

Unicorn Asset Management Ltd
First Floor Office, Preacher's Court, The
Charterhouse Charterhouse Square,
London, EC1M 6AU
T: +44 (0) 207 253 0889
F: +44 (0) 207 251 4028
www.unicornam.com

Unilever Ventures
6th Floor, 16 Charles II Street, London,
SW1Y 4QU
T: +44 (0) 207 321 6199
F: +44 (0) 207 321 6198
www.unileverventures.com

Unison Capital
Berkeley Square House Second Floor,
Berkeley Square, London, W1X 6EA
T: +44 (0) 207 887 6135
F: +44 (0) 207 887 6100
www.unisoncap.com

University of Central Lancashire
Adelphi Building, Preston, Lancashire,
PR1 2HE
T: +44 (0) 1772 894 476
F: +44 (0) 1772 894 497
www.uclan.ac.uk/hkp

VenCap International plc
King Charles House, Park End Street,
Oxford, OX1 1JD
T: +44 (0) 1865 799 300
F: +44 (0) 1865 799 301
www.vencap.com

Venture Finance
Sussex House, Perrymount Road, Haywards
Heath, RH16 1DN
T: +44 (0) 144 444 1717
F: +44 (0) 144 445 3026
www.venture-finance.co.uk

Venture Technologies Ltd
High Holborn House 6th Floor, 52-54 High
Holborn, London, WC1V 6SE
T: +44 (0) 207 404 9729
F: +44 (0) 207 404 9730

Vertex Management UK Ltd.
20 Berkeley Square, London, W1J 6EQ
T: +44 (0) 207 629 8838
F: +44 (0) 207 629 3338
www.vertexmgt.com

Viking Fund
Metic House, Ripley Drive, Normanton,
West Yorkshire, WF6 1QT
T: +44 (0) 1924 227 237
F: +44 (0) 1924 892 207
www.vikingfund.co.uk

Vodafone Ventures
Vodaphone House, The Connection,
Newbury, RG14 2FN
T: +44 (0) 1635 33251

Wales Fund Managers Ltd
Cedar House, Greenwood Close, Cardiff
Gate Business Park, Cardiff, CF23 8RD
T: +44 (0) 2920 546 250
F: +44 (0) 2920 546 251
www.wfml.co.uk

Warburg Pincus & Co. International Ltd.
Almack House, 28 King Street, St Jamess,
London, SW1Y 6QW
T: +44 (0) 207 306 0306
F: +44 (0) 207 321 0881
www.warburgpincus.com

West Coast Capital
The Hunter Foundation, Glasgow,
www.westcoastcapital.co.uk

West Lothian Venture Fund & WL Ventures
Geddes House, Kirkton North, Livingston,
EH54 6GU
T: +44 (0) 1721 730 749
www.wlventures.co.uk

WestLB Asset Management
Woolgate Exchange 25, Basinghall Street,
London, EC2V 5HA
T: +44 (0) 207 020 7444
F: +44 (0) 207 020 7430
www.westam.com

What If Ventures
The Glassworks, 3-4 Ashland Place, London,
W1U 4AH
T: +44 (0) 207 535 7500
F: +44 (0) 207 224 0433
www.whatifinnovation.com/ventures

WL Ventures Ltd
Geddes House, Kirkton North, Livingstone,
West Lothian, EH54 6GU
T: +44 (0) 1506 415 144
F: +44 (0) 1506 415 145
www.wlventures.co.uk

WM Enterprise
Wellington House, 31-34 Waterloo Street,
Birmingham, B2 5TJ
T: +44 (0) 1212 368 855
F: +44 (0) 1212 333 942
www.wm-enterprise.co.uk

YFM Private Equity
Saint Martins House, 210-212 Chapeltown
Road, Leeds, West Yorkshire, LS7 4HZ
T: +44 (0) 1132 945 000
F: +44 (0) 1132 945 003
www.yfmgroup.co.uk

YFM Venture Finance
Saint Martins House, 210-212 Chapeltown
Road, Leeds, West Yorkshire, LS7 4HZ
T: +44 (0) 1132 945 000
F: +44 (0) 1132 945 003
www.yfmgroup.co.uk

Young Associates
Harcourt House, 19 Cavendish Square,
London, W1G 0PL
T: +44 (0) 207 447 8800
F: +44 (0) 207 447 8849

Zouk Ventures
140 Brompton Road, London, SW3 1HY
T: +44 (0) 207 947 3400
F: +44 (0) 207 947 3449
www.zouk.com

INDEX